MY SECRET IS MINE

STUDIES ON RELIGION AND EROS
IN THE GERMAN MIDDLE AGES

STUDIES IN SPIRITUALITY SUPPLEMENTS
Edited by Titus Brandsma Instituut – Nijmegen – The Netherlands

1. **Steggink, O.**, *"Juan de la Cruz, Espiritu de Llama"*. *Estudios con ocasión del cuarto centenario de su muerte (1591-1991)*, 1991, VIII-945 p., ISBN: 90-242-2454-3.
2. **Imoda, F.**, *Human Development. Psychology and Mystery*, 1998, 397 p., ISBN: 90-429-0028-8.
3. **van Baest, M.**, *Poetry of Hadewijch*, 1998, VIII-330 p., ISBN: 90-429-0667-7.
4. **Keller, H.E.**, *My Secret Is Mine. Studies on Religion and Eros in the German Middle Ages*, 2000, X-297 p., ISBN: 90-429-0871-8.

STUDIES IN SPIRITUALITY
Supplement 4

MY SECRET IS MINE
STUDIES ON RELIGION AND EROS
IN THE GERMAN MIDDLE AGES

HILDEGARD ELISABETH KELLER

PEETERS

2000

Library of Congress Cataloging-in-Publication Data

Keller, Hildegard Elisabeth, 1960-
  My secret is mine: studies on religion and Eros in the German Middle Ages / Hildegard
Elisabeth Keller.
    p. cm. -- (Studies in spirituality. Supplements; 4)
  Includes bibliographical references.
  ISBN 9042908718 (alk. paper)
    1. Erotica--Religious aspects--Christianity--History of doctrines--Middle Ages,
600-1500. 2. Marriage--Religious aspects--Christianity--History of doctrines--Middle
Ages, 600-1500. 3. Monastic and religious life of women--Germany--History--Middle
Ages, 600-1500. 4. Christianity in literature. I. Title. II. Series.

BT708.4.K45 2000
274.3'05'082--dc21

                                                                        00-055743

Published with support of the Swiss National Science Foundation,
of the STEO-Stiftung Zürich, and of the UBS Kulturstiftung

© Peeters, Bondgenotenlaan 153, B-3000 Leuven 2000

ISBN 90-429-0871-8
D. 2000/0602/76

Contents

FOREWORD   1

INTRODUCTION   3

ONE METAPHOR, SEVERAL REALITIES   3
ONE BOOK, SEVERAL READINGS   5

CHAPTER 1
   EROTIC RELIGIOSITY AS A MOTIF IN CULTURAL HISTORY   11

A BELLOWS IN HER EARS: EROTIC LOVE AND A PERSONAL RELATIONSHIP
   WITH GOD   11

   Non-Christian Views   13
   Jewish and Christian Views   14
   Prophets, an Oriental Couple, and Christian Textual Practices   14
   The Longevity of the Ecclesiastical Bride   19

BRIDES, BRIDEGROOMS AND THEIR GENDER   21

   Relationship Roles   21
   A Significant Terminology   23
   Casting the Roles   27
   Irreversible Narrowing of Focus   30
   Men in the Supporting Role?   36
   And the Consequences   37
   A Chance to Contradict   41

REPRESENTATION OF THE BRIDE IN LITERATURE   44

   Inside Views   45
   Bridal and Textual Practices   47
   Outside Views   51
   Offices and Their Authority   53
   Brides Plural and Their Singular Bridegroom   58

CONCLUSION   60

CHAPTER 2
   INTERFACES: LOVE AND MARRIAGE, SPIRITUAL AND
   SECULAR   63

THE DISCOURSES OF LOVE AND MARRIAGE   67

   Chronology   68
   Hierarchy   73

SPIRITUAL AND SECULAR MARRIAGE   77

   Bridegrooms Compared   80
   Elevated and Degraded Brides   84
   Victima and *Sacrificium:* The Sacrificial Status of the Bride from a
   Theological Perspective   89
   The Sacrificial Status of the Bride in Epic Texts   94

CONCLUSION   100

CHAPTER 3
   BRIDES OF GOD: A SYNOPTIC VIEW   105

SIX BRIDES FOR SIX LITERARY WORKS   107

   Mechthild von Magdeburg: *Das fließende Licht der Gottheit*   107
   St. Trudperter Hohelied   110
   Lamprecht von Regensburg: *Tochter Syon*   112
   Die Hochzeit   115
   Priester Wernher: *Driu liet von der maget (Maria)*   117
   Hartmann von Aue: *Der arme Heinrich*   120

THE FIRST MOVE – MASCULINE   122

   The King's Bidding   122
   Being Human, Being a Bride   128
   Delivered Up   133

FEMALE RESPONSES   137

   The (Dis)Obedient Yes of the Bride   138
   The Silent Yes of the Bride   140
   The Vehement Yes of a Passionate Bride   148

BECOMING ONE   154

   Heavenly Inclinations   154
   Death as Homecoming and Wedding   158

Cohabitatio: Living With/In One Another as Man and Wife   166
The Silence of the Brides   172

TRIBULATIONS   175

Brides in Bliss   175
Brides as Refugees and Exiles   177
Hurt and Alienated Brides   179
Repudiated Brides and Concubines   181

CHAPTER 4
    PRIVATION UND PRIVACY: ONE LATE BRIDE OF GOD   185

GENDER DISCOURSE AS STRUCTURE   191
MARRIAGE AND PRIVATION   194

Secular Marriage as Shock Tactics   194
Secular Marriage as an Image of Alienation   200
Secular Marriage as an Allegory of Asceticism   202

EROTIC LOVE AND INTIMACY   211

The Woman and the Restoration of Balance   212
The Couple and the Others   221

CONCLUSION: MARRIAGE BETWEEN HEAVEN AND EARTH   227

CHAPTER 5
    SETTING ONE'S SIGHTS ON GOD: ATTACKS OF LOVE   231

VROUWE MINNE: LOVE AS AGGRESSIVE PERSONIFICATION   231
AN ARCHERESS   233

Her Sex   234
Her Power and Violence   240
The Main Points of Interest in Her Attacks   243

THE ATTACKS OF LADY LOVE   245

Case 1   245
Case 2   246

BRIDES WOUND TOO   248

Case 3   248
Case 4   252
Case 5   253

CONCLUSION: FEMALE METAMORPHOSIS   260

EPILOGUE   263

IMAGES OF A HERMENEUTIC TIGHTROPE ACT   263
IMAGES OF THE INEFFABLE   264
IMAGES OF PERPETUAL MOTION   266

BIBLIOGRAPHY AND ILLUSTRATIONS   269

PRIMARY SOURCES   269
SECONDARY SOURCES   272
LIST OF ILLUSTRATIONS   295

In the mystery of man and woman, there is God.

Foreword

This book comes before the reader with a title which does not promise talkativeness. As its author, I will disclose its secret.

The sentence "My secret is mine", or *Secretum meum mihi* is characteristic of many of the texts treated in this book. Brides of God have this sentence constantly at the tip of their tongue, and in the context relevant here it always holds a double message. It demarcates the border between what can and cannot be said, and yet this border area can only be addressed through speech. The prophet Isaiah, the originator of "My secret is mine", continues to speak even though his vision of God strikes him dumb. What he experiences is ineffable, and for that very reason it must be said again and again. Worlds apart from this Old Testament teller of mysteries, Bernard of Clairvaux puts the sentence into the mouth of the soul whom God has chosen for his bride. Since "the day only gives forth words to the day" (*dies tamen diei eructat verbum*), as Bernard says mysteriously, the sentence "My secret is mine" becomes the trade mark of all of those who speak of themselves as brides of God. In this way the sentence, with its inherent paradox, comes to stimulate literary production. If in the case of Bernard it is still voiced by a didactic mouthpiece (which is really an absurdity in terms of cultural anthropology, as without a centre of self and an awareness of something which is one's own and cannot be lost, there can be neither a 'my', nor a 'secret'), nevertheless this did initiate a substitution of voices which was important from a literary point of view. In the later Middle Ages, many people – women, for the most part, but also a few men – take on the role of the Bride themselves. Now from an internalized perspective, they weave the sentence "My secret is mine" into texts of their own, under specific historical conditions. One should read the text nine times, one Bride demands. She has made the secret her own, just as she has appropriated the literary means to tell it. The sentence "My secret is mine" and its echoes through the ages – through genders and through texts – form the leitmotiv for this book.

For constructive help, advice, admonitions, suggestions and discussion, I wish to thank Rüdiger Brandt, Donatella Bremer, Michael Clanchy, Barbara Duden, Ivan Illich, Alois M. Haas, Jeffrey Hamburger, Bernard McGinn, Ingrid Kasten, Urs Kram, Paul Michel, Nigel Palmer, Meinolf Schumacher, and Peter von Moos. – My heartfelt thanks go to Jeffrey Hamburger, Bernd Konrad, and Pater Odo Lang for their generous and willing help with photographs and with questions relating to manuscripts. – If Ineke Wackers had not encouraged me to write this book for the *Studies in Spirituality* series, then neither the idea for its present conception, nor its English form would ever have come about. Liesbeth Verloove at Peeters publishing house in Louvain showed amazing patience with my frequent 'Last Things', and for this she too deserves my sincere thanks. – The medievalist Maria Sherwood-Smith really brought the English version to light. As a competent midwife, she showed great staying power and remained at my side (long-distance) from Oxford and Leiden; the book owes much to her care and skill.

All those who have stood by me in friendship and love, I thank without ceasing: Margrith, Gabriella, Christian, and Christof.

Zurich, Easter 2000

Introduction

*Want ze glîcher wîse als ein ê ist ân entwesen
zwischen frouwen unde man, alsô sol ein ê sîn
zwischen iuwern sêlen unde got. – For just as a
marriage is without end between a woman and
a man, there should be a marriage between your
souls and God*[1].

One Metaphor, Several Realities

Every year, the Doges of Venice underwent a ceremony of marriage with the
sea. This ritual was intended to proclaim and seal a profitable alliance between
unequal partners. In the Venetian state galley, the *Bucintoro*, the Doge sailed
out to the harbor of San Niccoló, where the bishop of San Pietro awaited him.
The bishop then threw his golden ring into the water, saying: *Desponsamus te
mare, in signum veri perpetuique domini* (We betroth ourselves to you, O sea, in
the token of the true and perpetual lord). In this way, the bishop requested protection and success for all those at sea[2].

The same ritual, though celebrated by a different set of participants, gave force
to the legal installation of a bishop and demanded the same loyalty to the diocese.
Each time a new bishop was inducted into his office in the Italian town of Pis-
toia, he had to break his journey in the women's convent of San Pier Maggiore in
order to marry himself to his diocese. This took place on a symbolic level in a very
realistic marriage ritual with the abbess of the convent.

Even the late twentieth century still has recourse – at least metaphorically – to
nuptial rituals and their language. This age associates marriage with instability,
and its religious and social institutions have abandoned rules for sexual behavior.
In this secular age, the notion of marriage has been transferred from physical to
virtual bodies. Thus, economic marriages between leviathans of business ensure
the buoyancy of the economy. "Making the most of economic synergies" and
"assuring market shares" are then the new terms of affection between bride and
groom, and innovative "corporate identity" is their common vision for the future.

---

[1] *Meister Eckhart, Pf II, 100,15.*
[2] Réginald Grégoire, 795 ff.

Through the years, metaphorical marriages have not been limited to sealing maritime and economic alliances or symbolizing the initiation of dignitaries into office. The history of religion demonstrates the firm anchor-hold of the belief that all Creation results from an intimate gesture between a male and a female, inclining to one another as heaven and earth. These sorts of cosmogonies extend geographically from Oceania via Asia and Africa to North and South America; they are also found in other monotheistic religions besides Christianity. In all cases they conjure up a limitless bond between Creation and Creator. The bond is so all-powerful that it encompasses and permeates not only the Whole but also – as the above quotation from Meister Eckhart postulates – each individual soul.

Conversely, individual and cosmic life appear so closely intertwined with their Creator that they reveal the sacral dimension of human sexuality and love, their transcendent anchoring in a mysticism of eros and sexus[3]. Already in the 1960's Mircea Eliade pointed out that the sacral aspect of human sexuality was difficult to grasp for the non-religious individual of modern society[4]. In more recent scholarship, the historian of spirituality Bernard McGinn has held that its potential as a guideline for living has not yet been exhausted and is thus still valid. McGinn's value is that for an age entertaining hopes of finding spiritual orientation in medieval mysticism, he emphatically points out the unity of all realities of love[5].

Erotic, sexual and marital images constitute a sort of alphabet of cultural history. Semiotically, they belong to the fundamental stock of signs for commitment and union, but they also imply the perilous nature of such unions. Images of the sexes and of sexuality do not merely show that biological and hermeneutic gender-categories can combine and, in so doing, reinforce one another. More to the point, over and over again they demonstrate that a role defined as male or female can be played by either sex and thereby become transcendable. Images of the sexes also suggest a closeness and intimacy that one – as a human being, woman or man – feels one recognizes and feels one understands in an immediate way. However, they also evoke a strangeness, reminding us that these sorts of images are challenging; in a religious context they are also paradoxical, therefore standing in particular need of interpretation. For this reason – and this is probably the basis of their inexhaustible potential – they set people thinking; they "give rise to thought," as Paul Ricœur puts it[6]. There can scarcely

---

[3] Cf. Lettre sur la sainteté, ed. Charles Mopsik.

[4] Mircea Eliade 1965, 127 ff. – How closely marital and sexual relations between the sexes were subject to religious regulation is documented by Clifford Bishop 1996, who also provides a wealth of illustrative material.

[5] Cf. Bernard McGinn 1992a, 1992b, 1993, 1995, 1996 and 1997.

[6] Paul Ricœur, The Symbol Gives Rise to Thought, in: Ways of Understanding Religion, ed. Walter H. Capps, quoted in Saskia M. Murk-Jansen 1996, 52.

be another religion of which this statement is so universally true as it is of
Christianity.

The motif of the erotic relationship with God feeds on Old and New Testament sources and then goes on to mold early-Christian ecclesiastical institutions and rites as well as the gender-history archived in them. As Bernard
McGinn so aptly states with regard to the mystical tradition, the motif becomes
really and truly a "pattern of presentation of mystical consciousness"[7].

Concepts of erotic spirituality filtered into Western art and literature, where
they have maintained a firm hold for more than fifteen centuries. This union
has certainly inspired controversies, proving Ricœur's point that it gives rise to
critical thought. Since the Enlightenment or even earlier, the Christian perspective on the connection between religion and eros, or sexus, has been repeatedly
at the center of criticism of religion and the Church. In his *Philosophische Vorlesungen* (Philosophical Lectures), composed between 1771 and 1774, Jakob
Michael Reinhold Lenz completely commits himself to the Christian Creator.
Against "short-sighted pygmies" (clerics who condemn sexuality), he vehemently
defends sexuality as a divine "institution" that "encompasses all of nature to
make everything that lives happy". Indeed it was "imposed by him [God] as a
blessing on the whole of animate nature; that is, as an excellent proof of his
goodness towards all that lives"[8]. In the same vein, but even more sharply, Heinrich Heine criticizes the Christian connection between eros and religion when,
in his treatise "Elementargeister" (Elementary Spirits), he laments that Venus as
the embodiment of eros had been transformed in Christianity into the "Arch
she-devil"[9]. Friedrich Nietzsche, finally, assesses the matter with bitterness: "The
passions become evil and pernicious if they are considered evil and pernicious.
In this way Christianity succeeded in making Eros and Aphrodite – great powers with ideal potential – into hellish goblins and deceptive spirits"[10].

One Book, Several Readings

In Christianity alone, and particularly in medieval cultural history, the complex
of themes from the history of religion centering around religion and eros has

---

[7] Bernard McGinn expresses this view in the introduction of the third volume of his history
of mysticism (McGinn 1998a).

[8] Jakob Michael Reinhold Lenz, *Unverschämte Sachen*, in: Philosophische Vorlesungen für
empfindsame Seelen, 51-72, here 54 and 56. Cf. the concluding discussion by the editor
Christoph Weiss, particularly 93*ff.

[9] Heinrich Heine, Sämtliche Werke. Düsseldorfer Ausgabe, ed. by Manfred Windfuhr in
association with the Heinrich-Heine-Institut, Hamburg 1973 ff.; On the textual history, cf. IX,
301 ff. Cf. also Heine's philosophical writing *Religion in Deutschland*.

[10] *Morgenröte*, in: Sämtliche Werke, Kritische Studienausgabe in 15 Bänden, vol. 3, 73.

diversified into a multi-branched river delta. As a specialist in medieval literature, I will scoop out from a few branches of the river – a series of medieval and
early modern, mainly German, texts from different literary genres – whatever
contributes to our comprehension of this phenomenon of literary, spiritual, and
gender history. Of course, as much as I may draw from the river, a great deal
more will run past unheeded; so I will now try to identify what I have scooped
out by sketching various ways of reading it[11].

One could read this book as a sort of nuptial florilegium of Christian eroticism. It conjures up blossoms that flourished between the 12th and 18th century in the soil of a relationship between God and humanity, a relationship
imagined in sexual terms. The collection neither pretends to be exhaustive, nor
wishes to concentrate in an elitist way on exquisite texts of German mysticism.
Quite the contrary: we will come across the more familiar and famous exponents of the motif, but also little-known blossoms, some even with an overpowering scent; these rare blossoms from the margins of the bridal imagery also
mark its boundaries in terms of the discourses of women, men, and gender
(chapter 4). This florilegium is dependent on the linguistic devices, the
intended message and the intended audience of the individual texts. The different types of texts and their functions, therefore, also constitute the soil for the
blossoms presented here.

I would like first to introduce the interwoven traditions in which Christian
eroticism between God and humanity develops, viewing the development from
the perspective of the history of religion. Then I will give an account of the
specifically Christian variant and how it defines the gender-roles in the drama of
the relationship, and of the history of its hermeneutics – from the initially suprasexual definition to its gradual narrowing and specification to the female sex. I
aim, by investigating the representation of the bride, to show the implications of
these structural and gender-specific coordinates for medieval literature (chapter
1). Each individual bride of God develops within an inner dynamic that almost
always thrives not only on the interplay of the marital and the erotic speech registers but also on dimensions of secular and spiritual relationships (chapter 2).
The proportions of each add spice to the individual literary realizations of the
bride of God and her divine partner (chapter 3), but they can also allow them
to become distortions (chapter 4). Precisely the simultaneous overview of the
brides of God confirms the insight that there is not one who is constructed as a
stable entity in herself, independent of her author, recipients and media. Rather,
in the course of a few centuries and in quite specific social conditions, there

---

[11] In each case, the chapters in which a given aspect is handled particularly are noted in
parentheses. It goes without saying that there are many more ways in which this book should **not**
be read. To avoid confusion, I mention some of the possible readings.

flourishes a nuptial flora full of promise in terms of the history of literature and spirituality.

One could read this book – with appropriate attention to the hermeneutics of linguistic images – as a sort of divine love story and family history, to which each of the texts presented here contributes its own chronicle. The brides of God are bound in a very particular way into the love-fate of the Christian God, his becoming Man (and husband): *Christus Sponsus*. One text makes the woman who will be Christ's mother into the bride of God; another makes her the mistress and mother of brides of God in a southern German convent. A third tells us that without brides of God there would be neither Creation nor the human race, and several others agree that God's loveplay with those he has created is part of the most fundamental fulfillment of being human. In this way, the family of God extends via the brides of Christ and the medieval convent to humanity as a whole, so that eventually being "God's free daughter, his son's bride"[12] becomes the principal purpose of human existence.

By the expression "God's family history," I mean one aspect of the comprehensive system of metaphors writers and theologians have developed to speak of their God. The erotic, sexual, and amorous metaphors belong to this stock of images of God and self-representations of human beings[13]. In this book I hope to show that they represent an attempt, both obvious and bizarre, to translate human conditions into images of God while rendering the experience of God in interhuman dimensions (chapters 1, 2 and 5).

If one tries to disregard this hermeneutic stance, one falls prey to that typical, almost hackneyed, alienation that had its followers even in the high Middle Ages and obviously continues to reverberate in research in medieval studies right into the late 20th century. Vern L. Bullough's reflections in his academic biography[14], for example, and the provocative title of medievalist Nancy F. Partner's article "Did Mystics Have Sex?" are evidence of this. Partner herself comments: "Thus, the question in the title of my essay about mystics having sex is so basically foreign to the medievalist enterprise that it strikes even me as simply crude"[15]. The author puts this discomfort down to a research climate in which, for instance, the sexual encounters between the English visionary Margery Kempe and Christ are never analyzed and sexual intercourse continues to be referred to euphemistically as "marriage": "[...]there are no orgasms at all"[16].

---

[12] Holy maidenhood, 34,13, ed. Bella Millett / Jocelyn Wogan Browne.

[13] For a fundamental study, with a multitude of other metaphors for God, see Friedrich Ohly 1995.

[14] Vern L. Bullough, in: Jacqueline Murray / Konrad Eisenbichler (Eds.), 3-22.

[15] Nancy F. Partner, in: Jacqueline Murray / Konrad Eisenbichler (Eds.), 300.

[16] Nancy F. Partner, in: Jacqueline Murray / Konrad Eisenbichler (Eds.), 302.

For a first look at the gender issues immanent within the motif of the bride, one must start with the way in which the roles of bride and bridegroom become fixed with regard to gender, more particularly the gradual narrowing of the role of the bride to (primarily religious) women on the one hand, the successive masculinization of the divine bridegroom on the other hand (chapter 1). This sort of reading engages with the complicated gender-specific hermeneutic of religious eroticism. The bride of God herself can change form, shimmering between an abstract artificial figure and a woman. This becomes apparent in all the residues of the earthly dynamic between the sexes, but nowhere more clearly than in the motif of the attack of love (chapter 5). Within her being, the love-aggressor combines those two hermeneutic levels of the category "gender" that constitute religious eroticism in general: the levels of mythological and biblical-exegetical allegory (the personification of love and the bride in the Song of Songs) and of the biologically female human being. The gradual transition from symbolical, allegorical female to human woman will change the figure of the aggressive bride of God and the scope of activity permitted her with regard to her male partner.

Another gender-historical reading of this book could focus on the history of female stylizations (both idealizing and denigrating) and of marital and erotic identity building. Both embody high values and serve as powerful instruments for converting the hearers and readers to God. The expression "bride of God," with its associated status, represents first and foremost a way of life and a Christian honorary title for a woman. Being the beloved of a God who is imagined as masculine is the ideal way, especially for a medieval woman, to acquire a dignified identity or to have it prescribed for one by others. This dignity – and this is significant – rises in direct proportion to the dignity of the erotically-charged transcendental partner (chapters 2 and 3).

It will emerge that the history of female identity building proceeds first along marital paths. In a certain way, worldly and spiritual marriage options are closely related in terms of structure. Marriage with a divine partner will always trail its worldly counterpart behind it like a shadow and may even be determined by it if spiritual marriage turns out to be a structure of dominion whereby the divine bridegroom – like human bridegrooms – persistently asserts his right to discipline and tame his bride (chapter 2 and, above all, chapter 5).

Secondly, the literary paths of the Song of Songs will be essential in order to analyze gender-specific stylizations. Its erotic verses do not only serve to introduce a monastic woman to her role (a professional one, to a certain extent) of bride (chapters 1, 3 and 5). They also function as a model to praise and explain the mysterious charisma of a woman. In the case of Hildegard of Bingen, the authors of her *Vita*, Gottfried and Theoderich, are not the only ones to put her visionary gifts down to the "touch" of the heavenly bridegroom on her body. In his letters, liberally sprinkled with quotations from the Song of Songs, her assiduous partner in correspondence, Wibert of Gembloux, also addresses her effusively as the bride of the Song of Songs, whose *ubera* (breasts) – interpreted as "the flow of your speech" – really do taste better than wine. For him, too, her revelations are no less than the reflection of a mysterious eroticism[17].

This sort of gender-historical reading will open our eyes to the unpredictable aspects of erotic metaphor. Female (self-)stylization by means of a transcendental eroticism is Janus-headed, since the bride of God and the concubine of the Devil, the witch, are sisters with an invisible connection in the underworld. For many years, this is where one of the most uncanny projection-areas in the history of gender and sexuality developed: the motif of the erotic relationship with a non-human partner acquires a new, perfidiously sexualized meaning with the power to degrade[18]. The history of Christian eroticism with transcendental partners not only creates literary "mirrors" for the female sex, in which women are intended to recognize the beauty of the divine bride (at least one of the texts investigated, the *St. Trudperter Hohelied*, falls into this category). Much more, it is precisely the incomplete outlines of these bridal models – or model brides – that can be used for the projection of almost unlimited sexual images (chapter 1). A reflection of these sometimes forces its way into the texts of bridal mysticism. In this way, the "master, taken from Lucifer's school" comes to the bride of God in Mechthild von Magdeburg's *Das fließende Licht der Gottheit* as a sort of bride-tester. He is a particularly skillful devil who puts on a pyrotechnical display of temptations. One of these is an unambiguous offering of the devil, who conjures up for the soul promises of the same unheard-of social ascent that is granted the bride of God: *"In dem trone uf dem stůle solt du alleine die hôhste juncfrôwe sin und ich der schôneste jungeling bi dir."* ("In the throne room, upon this seat you alone shall be the most exalted virgin, and I, the fairest youth, beside you"). The bride blithely recognizes the conjuring trick and holds on to her real, if limited, dignity[19]. So the recognition that there are both "wise" and "foolish" brides is just as much a part of the history of gender-stylization as the sudden transformation of a sacred erotic secret with God into a sinister erotic encounter with the Devil.

This brings us to our protagonists and our interpretation of literary structures. This is a symposium with greatly differing literary brides – and their beloveds –

---

[17] *Vita S. Hildegardis*, II,I-II, ed. Monika Klaes, 20 ff.; *Epistolarium*, letter 102 and ff.

[18] On the gender-specific semanticization of motifs, see Ina Schabert in: Hadumod Bußmann / Renate Hof (Eds.). Cf. Gerhild Scholz Williams.

[19] Mechthild von Magdeburg, *Das fließende Licht der Gottheit*, IV, 2,50-52; Tobin 1998, p. 141.

found in not only spiritual and monastic but also secular texts from the Middle
High German literature of the Middle Ages. This assembly of the protagonists
will reveal both the functions and the literary intentions the motif of the bride
can serve and the genres it inspires (chapter 3). The brides themselves will help in
this, some of them telling of their initiation into the divine mysteries and
reflecting poetically on this apparently authentic experience of God. Others are
presented by priests who cite them as exemplary models for the individual and
collective education of women. A bride of God can also be exciting from a narrative point of view if her biography is sacrosanct and unique, as seems to be
the case for one particular bride of God, Mary. But even an allegorical, and
therefore abstract, protagonist in a mystical love-epic or an unspectacular
farmer's daughter can move the narrative forward in the role of bride of Christ,
for example, by opting radically for a non-earthly husband.

All these variants, drawn together in a synoptic view, will show that the
motif operates differently in each case, though the nuptial backdrop remains
the same; the blank space for the bride is filled differently each time within the
framework of each literary genre. This presentation of the erotic relationship
with God from a multitude of viewpoints reveals – in the mirror of texts from
different genres and periods, but also in the relations between textual and pictorial sources (chapter 5) – both the literary potential of this relationship and
the changing faces, depending on the genre, of those filling the roles. It will be
shown that when they speak of God, the mainly (if not exclusively) clerical or
monastic authors, whether men or women, become the engineers of gender,
marriage and love – thus of a sizeable bit of "world".

Finally, a practical word about the texts. The quotations from primary sources
are given in the original and in English translation. Unless otherwise noted,
these translations were made by Maria Sherwood-Smith or the author. All the
primary and secondary sources, the manner in which they are cited, and, where
applicable, the translations used[20], can be identified in the bibliography.

---

[20] Of the primary sources quoted frequently, only the text by Mechthild von Magdeburg,
some of the letters of Hildegard von Bingen, and the letters of Abelard and Heloise have been
translated into English; unless otherwise stated, I use the translations listed in the bibliography.
The texts of *Tochter Syon*, *Christus und die minnende Seele*, and the *Driu liet* of Priester Wernher
are not even available in modern German translation; in these cases the English version is based
on a translation by the present author. On the subject of the existing English translations of
Mechthild von Magdeburg's *Das fließende Licht der Gottheit*, see Frank Tobin 1994, 14-15.

Chapter 1
Erotic Religiosity as a Motif in Cultural History

> *Jetzt ein anderes Sein: göttliche, zuckende*
> *Lippen bückten sich über ihm nieder und sogen sich*
> *an seine Lippen; er ging auf sein einsames Zimmer.*
> *Er war allein, allein! – Now a different being: divine,*
> *trembling lips leant down to him and pressed*
> *themselves to his lips; he went to his solitary room.*
> *He was alone, alone![1]*

A Bellows in Her Ears: Erotic Love and a Personal Relationship with God

In the thirty-sixth chapter of her book, Margery Kempe tells of wondrous noises in her ears (*divers tokenys in hir bodily heryng*). One of these noises sounds like the blowing of a pair of bellows. This is the sound of the Holy Ghost, it is explained to her. Christ then turns the blowing into the voice of a dove and later into the singing of a robin, which often cheers her along by singing in her ear: *"(…) and sithyn he turnyd it into the voys of a lityl bryd whech is callyd a reedbrest, that song ful merily oftyntymes in hir ryght ere"* ("and afterwards he turned it into the voice of a little bird which is called a redbreast, that often sang very merily in her right ear"). Her bridegroom Christ later reveals the secret of this acoustical joking. He explains that these signs are proof of his love for Margery; since he loves her for being like a mother to himself and the whole world, in her there is a great love, of which he himself is the cause[2]. Shortly before this, Christ, as a husband, wishes to lie with her in bed, since *"it is convenyent the wyf to be homly wyth hir husbond"* ("it is appropriate for the wife to be intimate with her husband"). He reaffirms his desire and incites his bride to bold maternal-marital eroticism:

> *"(…) thu mayst boldly, whan thu art in thi bed, take me to the as for thi wed-*
> *dyd husbond, as thy derworthy derlyng, and as for thy swete sone, for I wyl be*

---

[1] Georg Büchner, *Lenz*, in: *Werke und Briefe*, München, 1979, 70.
[2] *The Book of Margery Kempe*, chapter 36, ed. Barry Windeatt, 196-197; trans. Barry Windeatt 1994, 127.

lovyd as a sone schuld be lovyd wyth the modyr, and wil that thu love me, dow-
tyr, as a good <wife> owyth to love hir husbonde. And therfor thu mayst boldly
take me in the armys of thi sowle and kyssen my mowth, myn hed and my fete as
swetly as thow wylt. And, as oftyn-tymes as thu thynkyst on me er woldyst don
any good dede to me, thu schalt have the same mede in hevyn als yyf thu dedist
it to myn owyn precyows body whech is in hevyn(...)"
"[...] you may boldly, when you are in bed, take me to you as your wedded
husband, as your dear darling, and as your sweet son, for I want to be loved
as a son should be loved by the mother, and I want you to love me, daughter, as a good wife ought to love her husband. Therefore, you can boldly take
me in the arms of your soul and kiss my mouth, my head, and my feet as
sweetly as you want. And as often as you think of me or would do any good
deed to me, you shall have the same reward in heaven as if you did it to my
own precious body which is in heaven [...]"[3]

Margery Kempe, the bride of Christ, experiences a divine beloved with two
sides to him: Christ develops an unconventional, sensual sign-language for her,
but can also behave like a conventional husband and demand conjugal intimacy. Thus he communicates with her using as much provocative imagination
as awareness of conventions. This broad spectrum of communication is typical
for human individuals and is a characteristic element of personal relationships
between human beings – and obviously also between human beings and God,
as Margery shows. She is addressed by Christ as daughter, as wife and beloved,
and as mother; the heart of her late-medieval visionary testimony is, however,
her erotic relationship with Christ. In the same way, medieval bridal mysticism
centers around the encounter between God and human being that is called "a
kiss between heaven and earth". This chapter will first introduce the motif of
the erotic relationship with God, its roots in the history of ideas and of religion,
and its specifically Christian form. Then we will focus on the inner structure of
this personal spirituality: here it is a question of how the two roles are defined
(what constitutes the bride /beloved/wife and bridegroom/beloved/husband?),
how the roles are allocated to God and a human being (who takes on the male
role, who the female?) and how they are filled in the course of Christian cultural history (do both male and female Christians become "brides of Christ"?).
This last aspect will lead to certain findings closely related to the rich phenomenology of the concept of the bride of Christ in medieval literature in the German language. Particular patterns of literary representation influence the perspectives from which the texts present the brides to us. This chapter concludes
with an attempt to categorize these literary perspectives on brides of Christ.

---

[3] *The Book of Margery Kempe*, chapter 36, ed. Barry Windeatt, 196; trans. Barry Windeatt
1994, 126-127.

Non-Christian Views

Religions which embrace a personal concept of God develop various ways for human beings – whether as a collective group or as individuals – to enter into a relationship with this personal God. In monotheistic religions this occurs within the bounds of family, friendship, or erotic relationships: as relatives (father or mother and child, brother and sister), friends, or lovers. The latter relationship can be traced directly to archaic religious structures. It goes without saying that these personal images of God are closely related to human beings' understanding of themselves. An erotic image of God is constituted by, and emerges from, the historical living – and loving – conditions of human beings[4]. All the forms of personal relationships listed above are possible with regard to the Christian, tri-une God. Of them all, the erotic is one of the most mysterious and productive in terms of cultural history. Medieval testimonies abound of brides or lovers who maintain a deep and intimate relationship with a transcendent partner. Using selected testimonies, predominantly from the German-speaking area, this study highlights the figure which made the erotic relationship to the Christian God so prominent: Christian bridal mysticism in medieval literary history. This prominence is due not least to the fact that the figure's cultural creative power towers above all other personal relationships with God.

Erotic religiosity is certainly not an exclusively Christian privilege. Throughout the history of civilization, religion and human sexuality have been linked in many and various ways, including erotic relationships to God. One can follow these traces in the development of the history of religions from the earliest farming societies through Egyptian, Babylonian and Assyrian cultures to Hellenistic, Jewish and Christian circles. If one looks further afield than Europe and the Near East, then the *Upanishads* are also part of this[5]. There can be no doubt that erotic forms of religiosity – these can be grouped under the term 'Sacred Marriage' (*hieros gamos*) – belong among the fundamental stock of religious phenomena. This fact shows that an awareness that religion and relations between the sexes are interwoven is inherent in human culture, and this awareness influences the way in which human sexuality is viewed and experienced. At the same time, it becomes clear that sexuality and the relations between the sexes were probably always regulated by religion. Here it makes no difference, in principle, whether this resulted in the profanation or the sanctification of human sexuality[6].

---

[4] Cf. Kari Elisabeth Børresen, 205.

[5] Cf. Mircea Éliade, Sur l'érotique mystique indienne, in: M. Éliade 1997, 7-24.

[6] Cf. Gerhard J. Bellinger and – a classic – Walter Schubart 1941; for a short orientation, see John Bugge, 59-60. Cf. also Ulrich Müller 1983.

Jewish and Christian Views

Jewish and Christian conceptions are also linked within this cultural network: "Christian writers appropriated numerous ideas and practices from pagan and Jewish sources. Among their borrowings was the perception that sex is closely related to the sacred, that sexual ecstasy is in some way linked to the sublime"[7]. The model of erotic relationship with God found in the Judaeo-Christian area has a history[8].

Prophets, an Oriental Couple, and Christian Textual Practices

Its origins are linked to certain books of the Old Testament which allocate roles to God and the human being in the following way: the people of Israel is the allegorical *sponsa*, whose counterpart is a Jahweh allegorized as the *sponsus*. For Jewish theology it is, moreover, unthinkable to understand the bridegroom as the Messiah, and this holds true for Jewish allegorical interpretation of the Song of Songs right up until the Middle Ages[9]. The Jewish collective marriage follows an extremely dramatic course, culminating in passionate acts of divine repudiation, revenge, and reconciliation. The story is recounted by the Old Testament prophets Hosea, Jeremiah, Ezechiel and Isaiah in language which can at times be drastic. Again and again the bride commits 'adultery' and 'betrays' her divine partner in turning to other gods, though Jahweh's jealousy is formidable. And then… reconciliations, again and again. This allegory of the crisis-ridden marriage between Jahweh and Israel tells the story of the Chosen People[10].

That the Old Testament also resounds with more sensuous and gentle tones, is shown by the Song of Songs, the Song of Love, and its two protagonists. For the Jewish – but particularly for the Christian – cultural history of the Middle Ages, it becomes a system of signs, tirelessly deciphered. The process of interpretation aims at laying bare deeper dimensions of meaning than that expressed literally: what happens to the two lovers is to be decoded in a so-called allegorical

---

[7] James A. Brundage 1987, 2 (referring to Mircea Éliade, Chasteté, sexualité et vie mystique chez les primitifs, in: Mystique et continence: Travaux scientifiques du VIIe Congrès international d'Avon, Bruges, 1952, 34-35, 49-50).

[8] Cf. Hans Windisch, 322; Vittorio Dellagiacoma; C. Chavasse; the articles 'Brautsymbolik', in: Lexikon für Theologie und Kirche, II, 660-661, 'Brautschaft, heilige', in: Reallexikon für Antike und Christentum, II, 541-543, and 'Mariage spirituel', in: Dictionnaire de spiritualité, Vol. 10, 389-390. For further conceptions of marriage, some of which are gnostic, cf. John Bugge, 5-29.

[9] For Cabbalist use of the motif of the bride, cf. 'Brautsymbolik', in: Lexikon des Mittelalters, II, 589-591; Gershom Sholem 1960, 77 ff. and also Gershom Sholem 1957, and David Biale, chapter 5.

[10] Cf. Hos 1-3; Jer 3:1; Ez 16:8, 16:38, 23:25; Jes 50:1, 54:4 ff., 62:5.

interpretation[11]. The history of Judaeo-Christian allegorical interpretation of the Song of Songs[12] is all one elaborate attempt to decipher the *sponsa* and the *sponsus* and their bodies, interaction and gestures hermeneutically. "In the exegesis of the Song of Songs, amorous and physical experiences became valid symbols for religious mysteries"[13].

What does this tireless curiosity about the hermeneutics of a single text imply? In the first place, it is a clear indication of an awareness that one is dealing with an inexhaustible text, one that requires a particular apparatus if it is to be understood. This open-ended quality starts with the interpretation of the female protagonist. The one bride of the Song of Songs may encompass the Christian church, Mary, consecrated virgins, the human soul of women and men, medieval nuns, an anonymous woman with a spiritual advisor, or a blessed mystic whose name is known to posterity through literary records. Theological writers, practicing an exclusively male occupation, envelop the *sponsa Canticis* in interpretation. The bride multiplies in this interpretative house of mirrors and comes to resemble a Russian doll, screwed open again and again throughout the centuries to reveal, each time, a new little allegorical figure inside. The most important factor for the literature of bridal mysticism, however, is the emergence of individualizing interpretations which become prevalent – due to favorable developments in cultural history – from the twelfth century[14]. First in the

[11] Allegory is the expressive, finished form (of a thought which is dressed up in a way which is appropriate for its meaning) – allegorical interpretation, on the other hand, is its interpretative application, i.e. the hermeneutic process of decoding a text or object which is assumed to have deeper dimensions of meaning. Cf. Christel Meier 1976, 8; Paul Michel 1987, 460; for the history of the concept of allegory, see Hartmut Freytag 1982.

[12] Friedrich Ohly 1958 and George L. Scheper 197 and 1974 are still fundamental for the history of the allegorical interpretation of the Song of Songs from patristic times until the Middle Ages. Denys Turner furnishes an anthology with translated extracts from patristic and medieval exegesis of the Song of Songs and an essay on the subject. For an overview of medieval hermeneutics and the allegorical interpretation of the Song of Songs, with further bibliography, see Hildegard E. Keller 1993, 175-210 and 452 ff.; Ann W. Astell and Ann E. Matter 1990; on the latter, cf. Bernard McGinn 1992; detailed textual comparison between the interpretations of the Song of Songs by Origen, Gregory the Great and William of St. Thierry is undertaken by Frederic Raurell, 23-53 and – with great care – by Karl Suso Frank. Bernhard Teuber 1993 very astutely traces the continuing effect of the allegorical tradition (of the Song of Songs) in Cuban literature of very recent times.

[13] Klaus Schreiner 1996, 101: "In der Auslegung des Hohenliedes wurden Liebes- und Körpererfahrungen symbolfähig für religiöse Geheimnisse".

[14] From the work of M.-D. Chenu (1969) and Colin Morris (1972) right up until Aaron Gurjewitsch (1994) there has been talk of the discovery of medieval individuality in the twelfth century, thus also of the discovery of love as the passionate force at the basis of the whole cosmos (cf. the works by Johan Chydenius 1970 and 1977, Hans Eggers, Peter Dinzelbacher 1981 and 1990). This is accompanied by the emotionalization and feminization of spirituality and the language associated with it – particularly in the context of commentary on the Song of Songs

monastic framework of the 12th century and then in the circles of the beguines in the later Middle Ages, the bride of the Song of Songs comes to have a some-what wider impact by virtue of this mystical allegorical exegesis[15].

This forms the background against which the idea of the human being as a receptive inner space is discovered and is explored in language. For the Jewish – but particularly for the Christian – cultural history of the Middle Ages, it becomes a system of signs which is deciphered tirelessly. The process of inter-pretation aims at laying bare deeper dimensions of meaning in that which was expressed literally: what happens to the two lovers is to be decoded in the so-called allegorical interpretation[16]. The history of Judaeo-Christian allegorical interpretation of the Song of Songs[17] is all one elaborate attempt to decipher the *sponsa* and the *sponsus* and their bodies, interaction and gestures hermeneu-tically. "In the exegesis of the Song of Songs, amorous and physical experiences became valid symbols for religious mysteries"[18].

The Song of Songs serves to promote and articulate receptivity towards God; thus, in the twelfth century, it becomes the basis for sermons and an Ariadne's thread for the *homo spiritualis*. The number of those addressed by the bride of the Song of Songs multiplies. This is particularly true with regard to medieval pastoral care of women, where the numerous female religious were encouraged to see themselves as Christ's bride in an institutional way and/or on the basis of personal experience.

(cf. Hildegard E. Keller 1993, 25 ff. and 425 ff.). Informative overviews can be found in Peter Dinzelbacher 1981, 243 ff. and idem, (ed.) 1993, 18-38 and 120-137.

[15] Cf. Barbara Newman 1995; Urban Küsters 1985; oriented on the exegesis of St. Bernard, Ulrich Köpf 1987.

[16] Allegory is the expressive, finished form (of a thought which is dressed up in a way which is appropriate for its meaning) – allegorical interpretation, on the other hand, is its interpretative application, thus the hermeneutic process of decoding a text or object which is assumed to have deeper dimensions of meaning. Cf. Christel Meier 1976, 8; Paul Michel 1987, 460; for the his-tory of the concept of allegory, see Hartmut Freytag 1982 and Christel Meier 1996.

[17] Friedrich Ohly 1958 and George L. Scheper 197 and 1974 are still fundamental for the history of the allegorical interpretation of the Song of Songs from patristic times right up until the Middle Ages. Denys Turner furnishes an anthology with translated extracts from patristic and medieval exegesis of the Song of Songs and an essay on the subject. For an overview of medieval hermeneutics and the allegorical interpretation of the Song of Songs, with further bibliography, see Hildegard E. Keller 1993, 175-210 and 452 ff.; Ann W. Astell and Ann E. Matter 1990; on the latter, cf. Bernard McGinn 1992; detailed textual comparison between the interpretation of the Song of Songs by Origen, Gregory the Great and William of St. Thierry is undertaken by Frederic Raurell, 23-53 and – with great care – by Karl Suso Frank. Bernhard Teuber 1993 very astutely traces the continuing effect of the allegorical tradition (of the Song of Songs) in Cuban literature of very recent times.

[18] Klaus Schreiner 1996, 101: "In der Auslegung des Hohenliedes wurden Liebes- und Kör-pererfahrungen symbolfähig für religiöse Geheimnisse".

The hermeneutic discussion of the Song of Songs is very closely linked with its eroticism and with the dynamic of passion between the lovers. In this attraction, monastic theologians recognize a fundamental strength for the spiritual life. For the Song of Songs kindles a longing which can reach beyond the Earthly and into the Spiritual[19]. Its stock of erotic images can, however, also provide support for the strong pull of the Carnal – a danger which was countered very consciously, above all in the monastic context. From the perspective of nuns and monks, who are required to renounce the world, the physical and erotic nature of the Song of Songs poses a fundamental hermeneutical question which seems to preoccupy male exegetes of the Song of Songs: how are the images to be used in this erotic sense[20], which is, after all, the original one? "(…) for the Song is a very special case, in which the mediaeval predilection for allegorical and typological readings is reinforced by the very particular difficulty the mediaeval commentator had in accepting any literal interpretation of a blatantly erotic and apparently secular poem"[21].

The twelfth-century interpreters of the Song of Songs[22] updated the most ancient instrument of Christian thought developed in patristic times, that had proven its efficacy in just this delicate issue: allegorical interpretation, i.e., exegesis according to the spiritual sense of the Scripture. Gregory of Nyssa[23], and also, about two hundred years later, Gregory the Great, see this as a hermeneutic *machina*, to a certain extent a powerful lifting-apparatus, which gradually winches the unwieldy literal sense into allegorical dimensions[24]. The numerous

---

[19] On this, see Jacques Leclerq 1963.

[20] Gregory of Nyssa's view is informative (see Franz Dünzl, 353 ff.). Denys Turner seeks to understand the attractiveness of the Song of Songs in terms of the eschatological orientation of the monastic life. He views this as the reason that the Song of Songs was interesting not despite, but because of, the eroticism and the inherent longing for future fulfillment (Denys Turner, 37 and 42). A central argument in this issue is constituted by the corporeality which is introduced into spiritual discourse extensively by the Song of Songs, with possible advantages which are explored in Hildegard E. Keller 1993, chapters 3 and 4. – Ann Astell judges the question against the background of psychoanalysis. She is of the opinion that the theory of the emotions and Jungian concepts of individuation play a role in the gender exchange of the Song of Songs (Ann W. Astell, 38, 178 f.).

[21] Denys Turner, 37.

[22] On Bernard of Clairvaux's sermons on the Song of Songs, the most influential exegetical work on this topic in the 12th century, see the helpful introduction by Ulrich Köpf (Bernhard von Clairvaux, vol. 5, 27-47 on sermons 1-38) and the continuation by Gerhard B. Winkler (vol. 6, 31-43 on sermons 39-86).

[23] See Gregory of Nyssa's introduction to the Canticum homilies and homilies 1 and 2, which continually revolve around the question of the correct way to understand the erotic texts (cf. Franz Dünzl, 56 ff.). A good account of the hermeneutic problem of the eroticism is given by Franz Dünzl, 360 ff.

[24] Gregor der Grosse, Einleitung zu seiner Hoheliedauslegung, ed. Frank, 93.

commentaries on the Song of Songs from the high medieval period testify to this sort of reading of the deeper, spiritual dimensions. Wedding and marriage imagery "played a part in the effort of preachers to diffuse Christian ideas and images more widely, which marked a new stage in the Christianisation of Europe"[25]. A different hermeneutic approach to the Song of Songs, its eroticism and corporeality – its literal sense, in other words – is attested by various literary endeavors by female authors. I will return to this in the context of the literary representation of the bride of Christ.

Although Martin Luther is partly responsible for the alteration in people's understanding of the concept of the bride (and thus also for the "mutation du lecteur" in Ricœur's sense), he still endorses the spiritualization of the images in the Song of Songs. He too wishes to tame its shrewish sensuality[26]. With an awareness of danger which virtually exceeds that of the patristic and monastic theologians of the Middle Ages, he gives the reader guidelines about how to understand the awkward images of the Song of Songs. It should be possible not to look at their 'flesh and blood', and this can be done with the help of Christ. Like a bird-catcher, Christ lays down fleshly bait; but no sooner has someone become hooked on the flesh, than he drags him back to spiritual understanding with a tug:

> (…) auch welche die Bibel lesen wollen, die müssen nicht ansehen Blut und Fleisch, und Braut und Bräutigam, wie in Canticis der Mann und Frau beschrieben wird von der Scheitel biss auf die Versen, sondern der heil. Geist, der führet den Menschen durch das Fleisch in den Geist. Gleichwie der Vogler, der Aatz unter die Seile leget, also auch Christus, so bald er den Menschen bringt in das Fleisch, so bald ruckt er ihn daraus in den Geist, ut in Canticis: quam speciosa ubera, sicut hinnuli &c. So bald nun der Mensch gedenckt an die Brust und fleischliche Lust, rückt ihn Christus daraus und führet ihn in den Geist und spricht: Dass die Brust sey die heil. Geschrifft.
>
> […] and those who want to read the Bible should not look at flesh and blood, or bride and bridegroom, when in the Song of Songs the man and the woman are described from head to toe; for the Holy Spirit leads human beings through the flesh to the spirit. Like a bird-catcher who puts carrion on his lines, as soon as he leads a human being to the flesh, Christ tugs him out again into the spirit, as in the Song of Songs: quam speciosa ubera, sicut hinnuli etc. As soon as a human being thinks of breasts and the will of the flesh, Christ pulls him out and leads him into the spirit and says: let the breasts be the Holy Scriptures[27].

---

[25] Nicole Bériou / David L. D'Avray, 111.

[26] Paul Ricœur 1998, 444 (where he develops his view of the "altered reader"). For exegesis of the Song of Songs in the Reformation, see the highly informative work of George L. Scheper 1974, here 555 ff.

[27] Martin Luther, *Fragmentum Sermonis in Die Divi Martini habiti*, Weimar edition 1,52, 52.

Thus throughout many centuries the tool of allegorical interpretation was applied to the textbook example of the Song of Songs – a fact affecting all the medieval primary sources presented here. The history of the allegorical interpretation of the Song of Songs is, nonetheless, also accompanied by criticism of this hermeneutic neutralizing of the sensual literal wording. And this is the sense in which Johann Gottfried Herder observes: *Kein Buch des alten Testaments ist gemisshandelter als das sogenannte Hohelied Salomons* (no book in the Old Testament has been mishandled more than the so-called Song of Solomon). Herder makes an indignant plea for the original meaning of the words and against the undermining of the direct amorous message. He points to a gulf between the wording and the established spiritual dimensions of meaning which had been opened and confirmed by centuries of interpretation of the Song of Songs: *Ich dächte wir nähmen also sicher den Satz an, dass hier Liebe gesungen werde, nicht blutige Erobrung, nicht Policeiwesen, noch Busse und Bekehrung. Es ist weder ein Dialog der Todten im Grabe, noch ein compendium der Ketzergeschichte; sondern, was es ist und in jedem Wort sagt, ein Lied der Liebe* (I would think that we should certainly accept the proposition that it is love which is being sung here, not bloody conquest, not policing, and not atonement and conversion either. It is neither a dialogue of the dead in the grave, nor a compendium of the history of heresy; but rather, what it is and what it says in every word, a song of love)[28].

The Longevity of the Ecclesiastical Bride

Nor was the Christian exegesis of the Song of Songs alone in eroticizing the connection between God and Man. Following the Jewish tradition of an erotic relationship between Jahweh and the people of Israel, an ecclesiastical idea of the bride crystallizes in the New Testament[29]. It amounts to a love relationship between the Christian church and Christ. The allocation of the roles becomes established: the male part is fitting for God, the female one for the human being. Thus Christ refers indirectly to himself as bridegroom when he talks of the wedding and the Messianic bride[30]. Ecclesiology develops from these and further New Testament images of a collective marriage in the Pauline writings or the Apocalypse of St John[31]. For Greek, and above all

---

[28] Johann Gottfried Herder, Werke, ed. by Suphan, VIII, 529 and 532 resp.; quoted by Martina Eicheldinger, 1.

[29] For further bibliographical references, cf. Wilhelm Imkamp, 204-205.

[30] Mk 2:19-20; Mt 9:15, 22:1ff., 25:1 ff.; Joh 3:29.

[31] E.g. 2 Cor 11:2; Eph 5:22,32 and Apoc 19:7-9.

Latin, patristic writers, erotic and marital motifs continue to have a decisive influence in the context of ecclesiology and asceticism. Bishop Ambrose of Milan goes so far as to interpret the etymology of *religio* in a nuptial sense. He takes up Lactantius' etymological derivation of *religare*: that the concrete form of the bond expressed by the word *religio* is furnished in the virginity of the woman dedicated to God. This means that the most prominent 'ligature' to the Christian God is that of the bride[32]. Additionally, in a Christian context the link between the incarnation and the erotic relationship with God suggests itself if this relationship is understood in an individualized way. Here the early Mariological interpretation of the Song of Songs exerts its influence. God lets himself be born of his first individual bride as a human child. Thus the concept of Mary as a bride of God leads directly to ideas of the birth of God, to the motif that becomes fundamental in the Christian mysticism of the high and late Middle Ages. Many mystical texts of the German-speaking Middle Ages attempt to guide the brides of Christ they address to the idea of being the mother of God[33].

On the basis of these theological traditions[34], the erotic relationship with God fertilizes medieval art and literary history in a process which is sustained over many years. The erotic model of spirituality influences many high and late medieval religious didactic texts, texts for pastoral care of women, but also texts by women themselves and fictional literature[35]. Brides of Christ and God as erotic lover become almost omnipresent figures, particularly in the literary nunneries in Southern Germany and Switzerland. Even in the early modern period the tradition of the erotic relationship with God does not break off. In prominent figures of Spanish mysticism it experiences a revived and reviving blossoming and also retains its importance in the Reformation[36]. With almost bizarre lyrical tones it reverberates again in the Pietist movement until about the middle of the 18th century. The peculiar blossoms of Zinzendorff's bridal mysticism will be discussed briefly below because of their original interpretation of the male and female roles in the relationship[37]. The rich and extensive evidence of this material in the medieval visual arts also deserves mention. Sculptors and illuminators develop the complex relationship between Judaism and

---

[32] Ambrose, *De virginibus*, Vol. 14/1, 151 and note 172.

[33] Cf. Peter Dinzelbacher 1994, but above all Dinzelbacher 1995, 101 ff.

[34] For a summarizing overview, see Wilhelm Imkamp, 208-212.

[35] Cf. E. Ann Matter 1994.

[36] For the Reformation, cf. George L. Scheper 1974; on the subject of Spanish mysticism, Denys Turner observes that San Juan de la Cruz's treatment of the Song of Songs is "bereft of its roots" and has become a formalistic game (Turner 1995, 175 ff.). With a different opinion cf. Alois M. Haas 1996, 446 ff (on San Juan de la Cruz) and Alois M. Haas 1998 (on Teresa de Avila)

[37] For Pietistic bridal mysticism, see the study by Paul Alverdes, which is still helpful.

Christianity in the form of erotic allegories by presenting it as the story of a betrayed love and a new one. On the South portals of Strasbourg cathedral, we see a man (Christ) repudiating his earlier bride (the Jewish Synagoga) and turning towards the triumphant new bride (the Christian Ecclesia) – the stone sculpture of a symbolic love triangle indistinguishable from a human one[38].

Although bridal mysticism peaks for the last time in the first half of the eighteenth century, it is not difficult to prove that the erotic model of a love-relationship between God and humanity continues to be passed on right into the modern period[39]. This is visible in the religious ritual of the consecration of the bride of Christ (see below) as well as in other guises. Interestingly, it was precisely the settlement of the "New World" that tempted people to see the erotic relationship with God as the basis for a new society. Thus, ideas of virginity and brideship played a certain role in the Shaker movement under Ann Lee. The motif of brideship also turns up again and again in the circles of European sects in the modern period, e.g., in a Swiss sect led by Dorothea Boller, going by the name of the "Sect of the Resurrection". She herself took the roles of "bride of Christ" and "Mother of Zion"[40].

Brides, Bridegrooms and their Gender

Relationship Roles

According to a legend illustrating the sin of spiritual sloth, Mary, mother of God, is involved in a spiritual love relationship with a young man. Mary is the heavenly bride whom he encounters in prayer. Entreaties and conjurations on the part of his relatives, however, lead him to a breach of faith. He allows a young woman to be brought to him as a bride. But immediately before the wedding, he withdraws once again to the chapel of his heavenly bride. There she appears to him, rebukes him angrily, and accuses him of unchastity. The bridegroom steals away from the wedding company and secretly enters a

---

[38] Further iconographical references in the articles 'Brautsymbolik', in: Lexikon des Mittelalters, II, 591-592, 'Bräutigam und Braut', in: Lexikon der christlichen Ikonographie, I, 318 ff. For the high and late medieval iconography of the Song of Songs, see the *Rothschild Canticles* (which, among other works, is presented masterfully in Jeffrey F. Hamburger 1990, particularly 84 ff.), for the Southern Netherlands from the 13th century, the exhibition catalogue *Le jardin clos de l'âme*, 1994.

[39] For the further development of the image of God in Pietism, see Paul Alverdes, 25 ff; for the persistence of motifs drawn from bridal mysticism in Annette von Droste-Hülshoff's *Geistliches Jahr*, see Meinolf Schumacher 1998.

[40] On Ann Lee, see John Bugge, 139; on Dorothea Boller, see H. Messikommer 1908, 31 ff.

monastery to consecrate his chastity to Mary, his lady[41]. Another erotic constellation – just as unusual, albeit in a different way – is that found in a statement
given by Jörg Bäntziger in the 17th century. Bäntziger, from Eastern Switzerland, reports in his "witch-confession" of early June 1674, that the devil *in einer*
weibsgestallt in einem schwartzen klaidt mit einem wyssen brüchli widerumb zue
ihme komen, mit wellcher er sich gleich verliebet unnd fleischlich vermischet, unnd
habe ihme versprochen, er müeße sein buoll sin, sige ohngefahr 6 jahr seit (had
come to him once again in the form of a woman in a black dress with a white
bodice, and he had immediately fallen in love with her and had carnal union
with her, and she had promised that he would be her lover; this had been about
6 years ago)[42].

Bäntziger, the devil's lover, and the anonymous Knight of Mary, are the
exceptions that prove the rule of erotic relationships with transcendent beings.
First, that the human partner in a relationship with a transcendent partner
habitually takes the *female* role while the male role is reserved for God or the
Devil. Secondly, the literary sources generally attest *women* as human brides of
Christ, but also brides of Satan whereas, apart from examples which are as
prominent as they are uncommon, men (or their souls) seldom fill this role of
the female lover. Réginald Grégoire, too, acknowledges this as the balanced
conclusion of his account of bridal mysticism[43], despite noting a small number
of counter-examples from the high medieval period. John Bugge terms this state
of affairs a "side-product" of the feminization of the soul[44] – this issue will be
thematized in the following section.

Referring to brides of Christ and of the Devil in one breath probably seems
disconcerting at first. However, precisely the ambivalent erotic terminology
("bride of Christ" and "bride of the Devil") marks the tip of a cultural-historical
iceberg – misogyny; it also represents the choice between Christ and Anti-Christ
that determined the fate of women in the late Middle Ages and the early modern

---

[41] This legend from the *Altes Passional* originated in the context of the German Order and
ends with an exhortation to the addressees (knights of Mary). A similar story is told by Anselm
of Canterbury, but there it is Mary's beauty rather than chastity which is the issue (in *Marienlegenden*, 39-40; quoted by Beatrice Kälin 1993, 90 ff.). Caesarius of Heisterbach records another
story, in which Mary converts a young knight who is unhappy in love to spiritual love for herself,
promises him marriage and escorts him to the bridal chamber of Heaven (cf. Bea Lundt, 167f).

[42] Quoted from Emil Schiess 1920, 159 f.; Cf. the similar constellation in a Danish woodcut
in Christoph Daxelmüller, 25.

[43] Réginald Grégoire, 782 ff. and passim. The fact that men appear in the role of the *sponsus*
is generally connected with the motif of the *sponsus marianus*, of which Grégoire gives several
examples; the most spectacular is the antenatal marriage of Robert of Molesmes (died 1110), but
there are also the cases of Edmond Rich, Archbishop of Canterbury (died 1240), and Francis of
Assisi (died 1226) and his marriage to "Mistress Poverty". See Grégoire, 744 ff. and 771 ff.

[44] John Bugge, 108 f.

period: two different possibilities for an erotic relationship with a transcendent being, one holy and the other an unholy disaster[45]. For each and every bride, one had to ascertain whether the signs pointed to divine grace and prophetic calling, or the diabolical insinuations and intrigues of a concubine of Satan[46]. Accordingly, the more recent concept of the bride of Satan seems to intrude itself upon consciousness whenever people reflect on the bride of Christ, more or less as a negative counterpart to the positive image. This is confirmed not only by medieval sources but also by the tenor of current discussion centered on Réginald Grégoire[47]. This is certainly no coincidence. Even the terminology, which stands out in a non-Christian context, indicates an interconnection between the phenomena that deserves to be taken seriously[48]. In any case, reflection about the sexually-defined roles in a spiritual relationship and whether they are filled by men or women inevitably leads one into the terrain of gender history.

A Significant Terminology

This starts with terminology for relationships with a divine love-partner or for this figure's counterpart. Those involved in a religious partnership are referred to as "lover", "betrothed", "bride" or "bridegroom", "woman" or "man", "wife" or "husband". The terms are polar, and define both heterosexual roles. Therefore, the sex indicated is basically a symbolical one: when the roles are being filled, both sexes – in principle – come into consideration. Nonetheless, it seems logical that the symbolical woman's role is primarily allotted to women. This is noticeable even in early non-Christian expressions of the pattern of religious brideship. The role of the bride or lover is especially associated with the female sex, a tendency in which biological reasons – particularly in the context of fertility magic – may be an important factor. For women, as those who give birth, have a biological connection to cosmic rituals of fertility and fertilization[49].

[45] Several titles of books, or chapters of books, point to this highly ambivalent view of the female sex. For this, and the theme in general, see R. Howard Bloch and Peter Dinzelbacher 1995b. In French sermons of the thirteenth century there are three kinds of possible partners for the human soul: the World, the Devil, and God. Cf. the elucidating study by Nicole Bériou and David L. D'Avray.

[46] The ambivalent proximity between the motifs of the bride of God and the bride of the Devil is reflected in Dominican writings of the Observance movement in the 15th century, which warned of *falschen gesihten* (visions as the work of the Devil). Cf. Hans-Jochen Schiewer 1996, 303-305. – On the eroticism of the Devil, see Luther Link 1997.

[47] See Réginald Grégoire, 795 ff.; for more on the medieval sources (*Holy Maidenhood*, Mechthild von Magdeburg: *Das fließende Licht der Gottheit, St Trudperter Hohelied*), see below.

[48] The discussion also tends in this direction (cf. Réginald Grégoire, 795 ff.).

[49] Cf. Mircea Eliade 1985, 122-129; 'Brautschaft, heilige', in: Reallexikon für Antike und Christentum, II, 529-566.

If one takes a closer look at the terminology of erotic religiosity one cannot but be amazed at the fact that women whose ways of life are scarcely comparable at all are designated in the same way. The temple prostitutes of the Near East are called "Brides of God" in the same way as religious women in medieval convents[50]. Women in the classical and Hellenistic world lived differently as well: yet in addition to love relationships among the gods, there was also the notion of nuptial relations between gods and humans. A woman in that world might also be given the title "God's bride" or "God's wife"[51]. Here one has, for example, prophetesses such as the virgin Pythia of the Delphic oracle[52], who positions herself on a tripod over the crevice in the earth so that her lower abdomen may soak up the "prophetic" or "enthusiastic spirit" which rises from it. This receiving of the spirit signifies becoming *deo plena* and thus rendered capable of prophecy. "In scornful depth", as Leisegang puts it, Origen and John Chrysostome write their accounts of this prophetess of Apollo, who could also receive the *pneuma* through sexual intercourse with a male prophet. Certainly such invectives should be treated with caution. But they do demonstrate an interesting overlap between physical and pneumatological reception, a phenomenon also important in Christian terms. Translated literally, male and female prophets are referred to as "those who tell with their lower abdomen", which is evidence for the fact that the lower abdomen, or the womb, was the area which was considered to be taken over by the divinity[53].

It is not insignificant that these two Christian theologians express polemical views about pagan erotic religiosity. For it is Origen, the exegete of the Song of Songs, who – with his spiritualized concept of the bride – lays the foundations of Christian bridal mysticism, in which a suprasexual soul (i.e., the soul of either a man or a woman) could take the position of the bride. Certainly, both Origen and John Chrysostome are at pains to distance themselves firmly from the pagan understanding of a sexualized concept of the bride of God and to

---

[50] They are also referred to as "dedicated" and "sisters of God". For the temple prostitutes, who in Canaan were also called "Betrothed of Baal", see the article 'Brautschaft, heilige', in: Reallexikon für Antike und Christentum, II, 530.

[51] An overview of Greco-Roman use of the motif of the *hieros gamos* is given by the article 'Brautschaft, heilige', in: Reallexikon für Antike und Christentum, II, 530-535.

[52] In this context, Hans Leisegang (35) also mentions sybils, gnostic prophetesses, and women who participate in mystery cults.

[53] Origin, *c. Celsum* 3, 25; 7,3; John Chrysostom, *Homil. 29, ad 1 Kor. 12* (both quoted by Hans Leisegang, 32, and the article 'Brautschaft, heilige', in: Reallexikon für Antike und Christentum, II, 535) and apologist writings by Christians (cf. Leisegang, 33 f.). Leisegang, 35 and the article 'Brautschaft, heilige', in: Reallexikon für Antike und Christentum, II, 535-537. Christopher Forbes, 1995, undertakes a comparison between Hellenistic and early Christian prophecy and the concept of inspired speaking. Further bibliography on the subject of the possessed Pythia, spoken through by Apollo because she is éntheos, i.e., plena deo, can be found in E.R. Dodds, chapter III.

defame it – but without relinquishing erotic terminology for the relationship with God[54].

Female terms for the role of the human being in erotic relationships with a transcendent partner are customary, then, right across cultural and religious boundaries. One would have to examine them in each case in their specific context. As for the motif itself, it would be clear even from the terms themselves what meaning was intended – regardless of whether one is dealing with the expression "bride of God", or "bride of the Devil"[55]. What is undisputed is that the terminology of erotic relationships with God reserves the female part (the bride) for the human being. But this certainly need not forcibly imply that the female role should indeed only by filled by female human beings. As the history of the motif demonstrates, however, the female character of the role obviously did favor the fact that, in the Christian context at least, it increasingly came to be filled by women[56]. It makes no difference in this whether one is dealing with positive concepts ("bride of God") or negative ones (*prostituta, adulterae Christi*[57] or "bride of the Devil"). These two concepts are an early Christian definition of the female ideal and anti-ideal, which are closely connected and live on, for example, in typologies of brides in the high Middle Ages. This Janus-faced quality of bridal mysticism is characteristic and may be employed by the texts very deliberately. A vivid example of this is furnished by *Holy Maidenhood*, a Middle English treatise for pastoral guidance, which seeks to induct its addressee as a bride of Christ but warns in the same breath that the institution "prostitutes" itself with the Devil and conceives spiritual children (sins of all descriptions) with him[58]. It is not until the late Middle Ages that the concept of the bride of the Devil breaks free from the context of erotic religiosity, becomes a separate entity, and develops truly uncanny and disturbing overtones[59]. The

[54] For the Origenist worldview, see John Bugge, chapters 1 and 2; Peter Brown 1988, chapter 8 and 282 ff.

[55] Cf. Lyndal Roper's introduction and Gerhild Scholz Williams in Rüdiger Schnell 1997, 280-302.

[56] For the contribution of the Middle High German term *sêle*, which is grammatically feminine, cf. Dinzelbacher 1995, 95-96.

[57] Even Cyprian and Ambrose use the term "adulteresses of their marriage with Christ" to refer to dedicated virgins who have broken their vow to an ascetic life (quoted by Consolino 1984, 409). For the term *adultera* in Ambrose, see the discussion of *adulterio*, in Vol. 14 / II, 317; for the term *prostituta*, see Ambrose: *De virginibus*, I,52, Vol 14 / I, 151.

[58] *Holy Maidenhood*, ed. by Millett and Wogan-Browne, 36,20ff. Not only does the Devil creep into the texts (see next page), but also into the illuminations in the manuscripts. For instance, he lies in wait for the cross-bearing female figure beside Christ in Cod. 710 (322) fol. 1r (containing *Christus und die minnende Seele*).

[59] For the typology of brides in the *St. Trudperter Hohenlied*, see chapter 3 and Hildegard Elisabeth Keller 1993, 150 ff., 500.

concept of the bride of the Devil is not only reduced to one biological sex, but also, fatefully, to one sexual practice. It encompasses sexual images only made possible by the linking of the female role to the female sex and thereby closely connected with the biological polarity of the sexes. These sorts of fabrications are well-known from Jakob Sprenger and Heinrich Institoris' handbook for witch-hunters, the *Malleus maleficarum*, but they also occur in literature in the vernaculars, as one can see from such expressions as *wie die Teuffelsbraut mit jrem Kalt-samigen Stinckbräutgam* (like the bride of the Devil with her cold-spermed stink-bridegroom)[60]. One of the texts considered in more detail in chapter 3 depicts the union between the Devil and his "bride", the *verdampnete sele* (damned soul) infrequently but vividly, on one occasion as an eschatological event and on another as the situation of the earthly temptation of the bride of God[61]. The Prince of Darkness himself takes care of his "chosen one" and caresses her in his own way: *Die valschen heligen setzet er* [i. e. Lucifer] *in sine schos und kússet si vil grúwelich (…) Die hie zesamen sint unkúsche gewesen, die müssent vor Lutzifer in solicher ahte gebunden ligen; kumt er aber alleine dar, so ist der túfel sin gumpan.* (The false saints he [Lucifer] puts upon his lap, kisses them hideously, […]). Those who were unchaste together on earth have to lie bound in like manner before Lucifer; but if such a one comes there alone, the devil is his partner)[62].

On another occasion, during mass, the first-person narrator has a vision of herself before the Devil, who tries to seduce her with erotic allures, promising the potential bride of the Devil an exquisite place at his side: *"In dem trone uf dem stúle solt du alleine die hóhste juncfrówe sin und ich der schóneste jungeling bi dir."* ("In the throne room upon this seat you alone shall be the most exalted virgin, with me the fairest youth next to you")[63].

The historical development of erotic relationships with God or with the Devil fundamentally demonstrates the constraints imposed on the motif if the role

---

[60] Johann Fischart, *Geschichtklitterung*, ed. by Schnabel, 107, 723-4; quoted in Pia Holenstein, 218. The Devil performs his sexual task in two stages: as a *succubus* (lying underneath) he collects sperm from a man, then, as an *incubus* (lying on top) he impregnates a woman with it; this transport of sperm had to take place quickly, since cold sperm was a hallmark of the Devil. Illustrations from the period can be found in Christoph Daxelmüller, figs 12, 14 and 16, and, very plentifully, in the catalogue of the exhibition *Hexen und Hexenverfolgung im deutschen Süd-westen*. Cf. Gerhild Scholz Williams, chapters 4 and 6, who shows clearly the extent to which such a relationship is combined with a discourse of power and dominian; see also Gerhild Scholz Williams in Rüdiger Schnell 1997 (with special interest on the mutual dependence between different types of texts and their gender discourse).

[61] Mechthild von Magdeburg, *Das fließende Licht der Gottheit*, III,11,2-5.

[62] Mechthild von Magdeburg, *Das fließende Licht der Gottheit*, III,21,39-40 and 46-48; trans. Tobin, 129.

[63] Mechthild von Magdeburg, *Das fließende Licht der Gottheit*, IV,2,50-51; trans. Tobin, 141.

defined as female is confined to biologically female human beings. What then emerge are monstrous shrunken shells of the original concept, caricatures of brides (of the Devil) and (Satanic) bridegrooms, culminating in distorted forms of copulation between human females and devils acting as "men", which fantasies are worked out right down to the physiological details[64]. A gender-specific obsession develops on the basis of a sexually-defined role which gradually comes to be reserved for one sex. The gradual narrowing of the female role, which means, in concrete terms, that of the bride of God, is the subject of the following section.

Casting the Roles

This section too begins with a situation which I would like to term atypical, insofar as the role of the bride of God is filled by a man, or rather his soul. In vernacular literature between the twelfth and fifteenth centuries, brides of God tend to be female[65]. But in some ways the anecdote is also very typical because the marriage between the Soul and Christ is depicted as a legal occasion. The legal exactitude contrasts with the strikingly childlike portrayal of the lovers, and precisely this is very significant for the filling of the roles. Shortly after Christmas, the chaplain Friedrich Sunder is celebrating mass in the Dominican nunnery of Engelthal. Many angels and saints are present; together with the mother of God, they are witness to a wondrous occurrence. After communion, *Ihesuslin*, the childlike divine bridegroom, begs his mother: *"Liebes mueterlin, mach mir vnd miner vil lieben gemaheln ain vil wunnekliches bettlin, da ich vnd min vil liebe gemahel mit ain ander vnser kurczwil hahind"*. (Dearest little mother, make a blissful little bed for me and my most beloved bride, where I and my most beloved bride may amuse ourselves and pass the time together)[66].

---

[64] For sexual imagination at work in the witch-hunts, see Charles Zika and the introductory account of Regina Bartholome, who stated officially that she was the wife and lover of the Devil, in Lyndal Roper's chapter "Oedipus and the Devil"; for the connection between saints and witches in general, cf. Peter Dinzelbacher 1995.

[65] I hope to make clear that men (and, with regard to the monastic theology of the twelfth century, especially men) make use of female and therefore bridal roles. But there are important differences in the way they use them. When, for instance, Bernard of Clairvaux represents the role of the abbot as a maternal one, Bynum concludes: "Medieval women, like men, chose to speak of themselves as brides, mothers and sisters of Christ. But to women this was an accepting and continuing of what they were; to men, it was reversal"(Bynum 1982, 110-169 and Bynum 1991, 48). If a monk views his soul as a bride of God, or his office as female, then he is consciously renouncing the prestigious masculine position – this applies particularly, if not exclusively, to the role of the abbot and St. Bernard's presentation of it.

[66] *Gnadenleben des Friedrich Sunder*, quoted in Siegfried Ringler, 415, 880 ff.

Then the little lover gets into bed, Mary lays the bridal soul of Friedrich Sunder beside him and unites them with one another. The newly-weds enjoy such great erotic pleasure that the guests from the next world who are present ask how it is possible that a human being who experiences such grace on earth can really still be alive[67].

What here perhaps seems "strange, even deviant" (Ringler), is a legally viable marriage ceremony, a *concubitus*, in concrete terms, with the assistance of the bridegroom's mother[68]. The chaplain's soul, viewed as a female figure, is married to the child Jesus, who also vehemently begs to be accepted as a "little brother" to the chaplain[69]. The third-person account gives the impression that the male "I" is following the children's marriage within him as a distanced, perhaps even somewhat alienated observer – a distancing reminiscent of the illustration of a similar marriage between Christ and the childlike soul of Heinrich Seuse. In this depiction, reproduced in a woodcut and a later illumination (cf. figs 1 and 2), the two lovers are placed on the Dominican's knee as homunculi.

Setting aside the question of whether artistic conventions or actual subjective impressions are the determining factor here, the present witness is, in any case, unusual and highly significant in its composition: a man tells of the marriage of his female soul with Christ. The main actors in this marriage ceremony do not give the impression of being a man and a woman, but rather are depicted in a remarkably childlike way – a feature which is radicalized in Robert of Molesmes' antenatal marriage to Mary, at whose wish the ceremony is carried out by Robert's pregnant mother Ermegardis[70].

The pronounced devotion to the baby Jesus in the circles of Dominican nuns, in which both Friedrich Sunder and Heinrich Seuse were active, may have contributed to the childlike representation of the divine bridegroom. Christ does not show any signs of masculinity, neither is the bride emphatically female. In Friedrich Sunder's case, a mother marries two children. This remarkable fact confirms a development which had already been characteristic for the motif of the bride of God for a long time. In early Christianity, Origen developed an understanding of brideship embracing the souls of all Christians, male and female. Additionally, there are less esoteric ways by which every human being becomes a bride of God – first, a martyr's death (anyone who dies for Christ "marries" the divine bridegroom); and second, the sacrament of baptism, which makes every person baptized the bride of Christ (the white Christening

---

[67] For Friedrich Sunder (1254-1328) and his work (which was completed by about 1330 at the latest), see Siegfried Ringler, ²VL 9 (1994) 532-536.

[68] See Siegfried Ringler's commentary on the passage (261 ff.)

[69] *Gnadenleben des Friedrich Sunder*, quoted by Siegfried Ringler, 414, 830 ff.

[70] Robert, who died in 1110, is a spectacular case of a *sponsus marianus*, which is recounted in the *Vita Roberti Molismensis*, 2; Acta Sanctorum, April III (1866), 677; quoted in Grégoire, 747.

robe was interpreted as a wedding gown)[71]. This baptismal soul was tradition-
ally represented as a (generally naked) child, i.e., with almost no sexual marking, as with Friedrich Sunder. Later I will show through textual examples that
the suprasexual, non-sexualized concept of the bride is indeed still known to
Middle High German texts but that it fades into the background behind sexualized modes of understanding. This development, moreover, will shape the
depiction of the mystical loving couple in both text and image[72].

---

[71] Cf. Alfred C. Rush, 86 ff. and chapter 3 (*Die Hochzeit*).

[72] The following figure is an illumination from a manuscript of *Christus and die minnende
Seele* destined for a female audience.

If the role of the bride is primarily taken by women and very seldom by men, i.e., if the sex of the brides of God gradually becomes less ambiguous, then this fixing of the gender of the role is also true for that of the divine bridegroom. Both partners are then no longer childlike little soul-figures for whom marriage seems to be a game; instead they become sexualized and polarized into man and woman[73]. The *sponsa* becomes increasingly feminine, beautiful and faithful, obedient and nobilitated by her husband – and the *sponsus* increasingly masculine and lordly, rich and generous, powerful and immortal. The comparisons between secular and spiritual marriage in chapter 2, and particularly the gender-allegories in chapter 4, will demonstrate the impact of this on medieval literature.

Irreversible Narrowing of Focus

With regard to the literary – especially the vernacular – texts of the High and Late Middle Ages, one thing seems clear, if not absolute imagining: oneself as

---

[73] See the study by Nicole Bériou and David L. d'Avray; the audience for the sermons they investigate is not clearly defined – probably they were intented both for male clerics at the university as well as male and female lay-people. The concept of the bride of God is there related (in a non-sexualized form) to the "human soul".

an adult bride of God was obviously more readily thinkable for women than for men. This explains why there are scarcely any male, but very many female, brides of God in literary and historical sources of the Middle Ages. Réginald Grégoire investigates many early and high medieval sources, concluding: "in the tradition of bridal mysticism, women are the most frequently attested protagonists in the female role"[74]. Barbara Newman's results also demonstrate the same narrowing down of the role to women. She cites model sermons from the late twelfth-century *Summa de arte praedicandi* of Alan of Lille, which recommend gender-specific subjects for sermons. For *claustrales* (monks and canons), Psalm 132,1, with its leitmotif of brotherhood, is a suitable introductory text; this is incidentally also reminiscent of Friedrich Sunder, for whom Christ is indeed both bridegroom and brother. Sermons for nuns ("virgins"), on the other hand – Alan believes –, can best be introduced with the Pauline self-representation of

---

[74] "(...) nel matrimonio mistico, il protagonista più spesso attestato nella tradizione è la donna": Réginald Grégoire, 782-783.

the leader giving the "chaste virgin" to her bridegroom (2 Cor 11,2)[75]. This statement, which I will discuss further in the context of the literary views of the bride from the outside, points to the fact that the nuns were socialized nuptially in the pastoral context. It is consistent – and not, for example, the result of the random selection of texts – that it is primarily women who appear as brides of Christ in the texts investigated in this study. This situation is representative far and beyond the German literature of the Middle Ages and continues to operate in our own spontaneous identification of the bride of Christ with a religious woman – or does anyone involuntarily think of a monk when he or she hears the expression "bride of Christ"?

However, the association of the female role with females filling the role is not a given from the beginning. Above, I pointed to the brides developed in exegesis, in whom an individual or a collective entity enters into an erotic or marital relationship with Christ. In those interpretations, the role of the bride is essentially tailored to both men and women, e.g., as a community of male and female Christians (*ecclesia*) or the genderless soul of a male or female individual (*anima*). There was thus no lack of attempts to transcend the gender of the role, and these attempts have left their traces in the Latin exegesis of the Canticles as well as in vernacular literature. The very pioneers of the mysticism of the Song of Songs fashioned bridal roles to fit the bodies – or perhaps rather the souls – of a male monastic audience.

But the force pulling in the opposite direction, towards sexualization, was obviously stronger. In the following discussion, I use the term "sexualization" to refer to both the process and the result of the increasing tendency to fill the female role of the bride exclusively with people who are biologically female. Although the term "feminization" would be more precise with relation to the female part, the more general term "sexualization" seems to me more suitable. For it makes clear that the narrowing process affects both roles, that is to say, charges them with sexual connotations. Gender-stereotypes register in both the role of the bride and that of the bridegroom. The feminized bride goes hand in hand with an increasingly masculinized bridegroom.

The history of the sexualization of the role of the bride of Christ has an institutional basis. This should be understood literally since the first Christian definition of the bride of God arises in an early Christian ecclesiastical institution.

---

[75] Quoted from Barbara Newman (1995, 35), who accentuates a different aspect of this contrast: motifs of brotherhood for men, themes of virginity for women. Other examples of sermons (by Robert de Sabon, Adam Picardus and others) are edited and discussed in this context by Nicole Bériou / David L. D'Avray. In her *Strofische Gedichten* (Stanzaic Poems), Hadewijch works with sex-changes; God, really (courtly) Love, becomes the courtly lady, the human being or the (female) speaking 'I' of the poem takes on the courtly role of a knight. Cf. the analysis by Saskia M. Murk-Jansen 1996.

That this so-called consecration of virgins was tailored for women from the out-
set strengthens the link between the symbolical femininity of the bride and the
biological sex of the actual brides of Christ. What should we understand by an
early Christian "bride of God"? From the second half of the 4th century,
unmarried virgins and – more rarely – widowed women who wanted to lead a
religious life of abstinence could have themselves consecrated in an official,
marriage-like ritual. Male theologians of their time respectfully refer to them as
"brides of God"[76]. A flood of theoretical discussions by Tertullian, Cyprian,
Clement of Rome, Methodius of Olympos, Basil of Ancyra, Gregory of Nyssa,
John Chrysostome, Ambrose of Milan, Jerome and Augustine[77], thematize –
very often in idealistic terms – the *virgines consecratae*, their status, or the ritual
of consecration itself. Consecration ritually initiates the virgin's marriage with
Christ and thus reveals that the woman has chosen a matrimonial alternative to
worldly marriage.

The ritual is modeled on the secular marriage ceremony: with the bridal veil
(as Ambrose relates), the bride of Christ is symbolically subordinated to a bridegroom – not to an earthly one as is the secular woman, but Christ[78]. A bishop
celebrates the "heavenly wedding" with the bride, standing in for the divine
bridegroom[79]. In the beginning, the consecrated virgins mainly continued to
live in their parents' households as hermits or in communities of women; from
the early Middle Ages onwards they lived increasingly in mixed monasteries or
in women's convents. Religious life presented itself to them originally as an
emancipatory alternative to the life of a wife and mother[80] – an aspect which is
also used by high medieval didactic texts to motivate women to choose the *vita
religiosa*. Thus, in the Middle English *Holy Maidenhood*, dating from the first
half of the 13th century, patristic arguments against marriage make a reappear-
ance, now in favor of the woman who is supposed to be liberated from the yoke
of marriage[81].

---

[76] For the terminology, see René Metz, 50 ff. and 92, Réginald Grégoire, 720 ff. (778 ff. on
the subject of widows as brides of Christ).

[77] This list follows the account by Monique Alexandre in Georges Duby / Michelle Perrot 1.
Cf. Peter Brown, esp. chapters 7 and 13; Susannah Elm and John Bugge, 66.

[78] Ambrose, *De virginibus*, ed. Gori, Vol. 14 / I,, 47 f. and 163, note 210. For the origins and
ritual of the dedication of virgins, see René Metz 1954, esp. 95 ff. and 185 ff.; for the connection between secular and spiritual marriage, see 121 ff. and 357 ff. – That the idea of being a
bride of Christ and the wedding-like dedication ritual can still form part of the self-understanding of nuns in the present day, is documented photographically in Giorgio von Arb, 128 ff.

[79] According to Pope Siricius, quoted in René Metz, 121.

[80] This statement must be viewed against the background of late Roman social history, which
is shown by Peter Brown (in Peter Brown and Philippe Ariès / Georges Duby 1).

[81] Cf. John Bugge, 88 and the comparison of secular and spiritual marriage in chapter 2
below. I could not compare this treatise with another Middle English text (*The Wooing of our*

Ambrose has an important part in this gender-specific definition of the bride of Christ as a virginal woman when he identifies the bride of Christ with those young women whom he spurs on to a life dedicated to God. As one would expect, his reflections on virginity and dedicated virgins concentrate the various interpretations of the bride in the Song of Songs on the hymnically eulogized *virgines consecratae*. If the *sponsa Canticis* had been interpreted by Origen as the *Ecclesia* and the *anima*[82] – and by Athanasius, Methodius and Jerome as the *virgo consecrata* –, Ambrose synthesizes all these interpretations, alternating subtly and playfully between one interpretation of the bride and another – "un sottile gioco di passaggi dall' anima alla virgo" (Franca Ela Consolino). With waltzing elegance – "come in un giro di valzer"[83] –, he combines the forces of the Church, the male and female soul, the mother of God, and consecrated virgins[84]. The latter group steps clearly into the foreground: the term *sponsa Christi* establishes itself early as the title of honor exclusively for these institutional ascetic women. These are the first group to be celebrated – i.e., defined – ritually as "brides of Christ" in accordance with the theological (male) consensus of opinion, and they are women.

There is a second force helping to sexualize the motif of the bride of Christ. It is the idea of virginity in its changing forms from patristic times to the high Middle Ages, though here I will mention only the aspects contributing to the narrowing of the valency of the motif[85]. It is connected with the ecclesiastical institution of consecrated virgins. In Origen's understanding, the Christian idea of the bride of Christ signifies a universal relationship between God and Man, which applies to both men and women since their souls are all potential brides of Christ because they can receive the seed of the divine Logos. This archetype of Christian bridal mysticism originated in the early Christian ascetic movement, which was influenced by gnosis. For this movement, virginity was the mode of being closest to the paradisiacal state of human nature and

---

Lord, ed. N. F. Blake, Middle English Religious Prose) possibly destined to women; this text works also with an idealized notion of the divine husband.

[82] For Origen's interpretation of the Song of Songs, see Marcel Borret 1989, 477 ff.

[83] Franca E. Consolino 1984, 410 and 413.

[84] Cf. Franca E. Consolino 1984 and René Metz. For early Christian women's education and patristic allegorical interpretation of the Song of Songs, which prepared the way for the amalgamation of the brides, cf. Hildegard E. Keller 1993, 94-102.

[85] Apart from John Bugge's history of ideas (Leclercq's criticism is directly mainly towards his abbreviating depiction of the *vita angelica*; Medium Aevum, 46 (1977), 129-131), my main sources in this area were Barbara Newman 1995, 28 ff., and Franco Gori's excellent introduction in his Italian-Latin edition of Ambrose's treatises on virginity (Vol. 14 / I 12 ff.); for virginity as an ideal of womanhood in the high and late Middle Ages, see Clarissa Atkinson 1991, Jocelyn Wogan-Browne, in: Sarah Kay / Miri Rubin (eds), 24 ff.; Amy Hollywood 1995 and (for the German-language epic), Maria E. Müller 1995.

was therefore also central to the economy of Salvation and the concept of the monastic life. Bugge reconstructs the framework in theological history for a series of shifts in the concept of virginity which continue into the high Middle Ages. Augustinian teachings on sexuality, Anselm of Canterbury's teachings on satisfaction, and the high-medieval requirement of celibacy for the priesthood all play important roles. Bugge also assesses the Cistercian attempt to revitalize the original pneumatological understanding of spiritual marriage[86]. This could have prevented or at least retarded the narrowing of the concept of the bride of Christ to women. But Bernard of Clairvaux's efforts to re-establish the bridal metaphor in the monastic life of both sexes mark precisely the beginning of the definitive exclusion of monks from the concept. Thus the impulses emanating from Bernard's bridal mysticism and Hugh of St Victor's conception of marriage were remarkably counterproductive: "Though well acquainted with the identification of the *sponsa* with the nun, Bernard nevertheless thought to transcend that interpretation by adopting the doctrine sacred to Christian gnosis. He did not anticipate interference from this more westernized view of nuptial metaphor because he evidently considered the Origenist definition to include it. But the popularization of his reading actually resulted in an apotheosis of the woman's marriage to Christ, such that, eventually, the Christian-gnostic soul marriage became almost the exclusive province of female virgins" – this, for Bugge, is the momentous "second expropriation of the bridal idea by the female sex"[87].

Consequently, the male promotion of bridal mysticism in the twelfth century helps – *nolens volens* – to turn the bride into a figure of identification for female religious: "The sexualization of virginity unwittingly spawned by Bernardine mysticism first occurred in England, where – in the context of monastic Christianity strongly tied to Rome and the Augustinian tradition – the *sponsa Christi* motif had applied almost exclusively to female virgins"[88]. Bernard McGinn sees the Middle High German *St. Trudperter Hohelied*, written probably only a few years after the death of St. Bernard, as a milestone in this restriction of the sex of the bride: "One of the earliest signs of an important shift to female identification with the Bride, and one found, significantly, in a vernacular text, is the misnamed *St. Trudpert Song of Songs*"[89].

Meanwhile, for medieval monks there is a concept of identity – also with early Christian roots – that continues to be valid. The male religious is a

---

[86] For Cistercian exegesis of the Song of Songs in this connection, cf. John Bugge, 90 ff., Ann W. Astell and Ann E. Matter 1990.

[87] John Bugge, 92.

[88] John Bugge, 135. On this subject, see also Ulrich Köpf 1985 und 1987.

[89] Bernard McGinn 1994b, 347. Cf. chapter 3.

brother of Christ, but above all a *miles Christi*, whose aim is assist the Redeemer
to victory in an ascetic battle. This identity comes to bear when a man must
stand by his vocation to the religious life in the face of social pressure – a frequent motif in male hagiography. The ascetic struggle and/or pure devotion are
sufficient legitimization of a man's choice of lifestyle; thus, he does not argue
along matrimonial lines, as do most women, who have to profess a life as a virgin and a bride of Christ and who must continue to fight for it[90].

Men in the Supporting Role?

What is interesting, then, is that the sexualization of the bride of Christ does
not simply catapult men out of the context of the erotic relationship with God.
It is true that men seldom see themselves personally in the role of the bride. But
in the pastoral care of women they are linked into the motif. Very often, they
take over the pastoral role of the person who gives away the bride, woos the
bride of Christ, prepares her for the wedding, and watches over her until her
definitive union with the bridegroom[91]. Texts which serve for the spiritual
instruction of women in the convent often attest to the author's having this sort
of understanding of the roles. He may portray an ideal bride of Christ from an
outside perspective and present her as a model for the women addressed by the
text but, simultaneously, he may also portray Christ as the ideal husband. I will
return to this aspect in the context of literary perspectives on the bride of
Christ.

In addition, men are linked to the motif of the bride because of the clerical
role of the bridegroom, which every priest fulfils in relation to the Church and
its members. Like the bishop in the consecration of virgins and the secular
bridegroom in the account of Count Zinzendorff (in the following section), the
priest, by virtue of his office, represents Christ, the bridegroom, with regard to
the Church, his bride. A (human) man represents the (divine) husband. Moreover, this line of argument, where the gender of the role necessarily dictates the
sex of the person filling the role, is still used today by Pope John Paul II in
rejecting the ordination of women, as one can read in his encyclical *Mulieris
dignitatem* (1988). *Sponsi figura est masculini sexus*, he states – from the masculinity of the bridegroom figure comes the conclusion that women cannot be

---

[90] One example from the 7th century is cited by Réginald Grégoire, 719 ff.: Cirano has to
resist an arranged marriage and declares that he wishes to remain a *devotus in Domino*.

[91] One special – because autobiographical – case of a male mystical writer is constituted by
Heinrich Seuse and his *Exemplar*. For this question, especially in light of the Einsiedeln cod. 710
(322) (see chapter 4), see Jeffrey F. Hamburger 1998, who considers both medias – text and illumination.

priestly representatives of the bridegroom with regard to the Church as bride[92]. There remains the contradiction that male lay people are very much able – and required – to slip into the role of the bride (in the collective, ecclesial sense), as Elisabeth Gössmann remarks[93].

And the Consequences

As far as his soul is concerned, a married man – like every Christian woman – is a female Christian: a female soul, a bride of Christ, and "a candidate to rest in his arms"[94]; however, as far as his body and his sexual role in marriage are concerned, he is indubitably a male representative of Christ, a "procurator", Christ's "steward" or "vice-Christ". Standing in for Christ, the human husband performs marital sexual intercourse with his wife, who is, of course, really the wife of another. Thanks to the sanctity of sexual anatomy (sanctified by Christ and Mary), this sort of sexual practice is free from shame, *da die ehelichen Glieder heilig und wichtig [seien], (...) weil wir im Ernst glauben, dass der Schöpfer aller Creatur ein männliches Glied an sich getragen und in der Person seiner heiligen Mutter alle weiblichen Glieder auf ewig geheiligt und das Wort Scham in Ansehung der theuren Glieder unter Christen abolieret hat* (since the marital organs [are] holy and important, [...] because we earnestly believe that the Creator of all creatures bore a male organ and hallowed all female organs eternally in the person of his blessed mother and abolished the word shame amongst Christians with regard to these valuable organs)[95].

Thus speaks a late example of Pietistic bridal mysticism – the highly unconventional amalgamation of marital instruction and bridal mysticism by Nikolaus Ludwig Count Zinzendorff (1700-1760). He and his Herrenhuter circle could certainly not be accounted leading exponents of classical bridal mysticism[96]. However, Zinzendorff here lays bare two hermeneutical difficulties also fundamental for the medieval motif of the bride of Christ: first, he attempts to solve the problem of how a sexually-defined role can be attractive to both sexes. The history of the motif outlined above makes clear that the idea of being a bride of Christ was increasingly confined to women. For the last time in the

---

[92] Acta Apostolica Series 80, 1988, 1714 and 1716.

[93] Elisabeth Gössmann in her newspaper article "Die 'Braut Kirche' und der Priester als Bräutigam", *Frankfurter Rundschau*, 5th February 1996, 12 (this, like the item mentioned in the last note, was kindly pointed out by Meinolf Schumacher, Dortmund).

[94] Quoted without provenance in Johannes Wallmann, 373-374.

[95] *Brüdergesangbuch von 1741*, preface, 3rd part, quoted in Paul Alverdes, 120.

[96] Fundamental evaluation and a few objections in Johannes Wallmann; more comprehensive coverage in Paul Alverdes, 116 ff.

history of bridal mysticism to date, Zinzendorff attempts to universalize the motif. Against the background of his teachings on marriage, he arrives at this strangely polygamous solution no longer generally accepted. Secondly, the Pietistic understanding of the bride draws attention to the particular difficulties for men of how to fulfill the female role of the bride and how to assess the androgyny which seems to result. Zinzendorff comes up with a sort of split formula: a bride of Christ who is female in soul, though biologically male. The latter is probably as consistent as the Christian in Martin Luther's treatise *Von der Freiheit eines Christenmenschen*, internally absolutely free but externally enslaved.[97]

Essentially, Zinzendorff thematizes fundamental paradoxes of erotic religiosity. His bizarre solution shows that specific historical gender roles and timeless relationship roles, biological and spiritual ways of seeing oneself all overlap in bridal mysticism and put both men and women in irresolvable situations. This results not only from the fact – common to all bridal mysticism – that religion is couched in sexual, thus earthly, terms. The situation is intensified above all by the increasingly exclusive allocation of the role of the bride to women since this forces the erotic relationship with God into the sphere of historical relations between the sexes. The relationship with the heavenly bridegroom sinks noticeably down to earth. Three aspects reveal the extent to which the historical conditions of the sexes and their relations also shape the erotic relationship with God.

First, Zinzendorff's model of bridal mysticism reveals the extent to which – even merely in terms of structure – the secular and the spiritual discourses of marriage overlap, a characteristic radicalizing his attempt to combine secular and spiritual marriage. That the borders between heaven and earth as well as between relationships with a God and earthly relations of the sexes can become blurred to this extent is connected with the sexualization of the bride of Christ. For this makes it possible for men and women in secular marriages – almost without comment – to become figures one can compare and contrast with the bride of God and her divine Beloved. The wife in a secular marriage is the counterpart of the bride of Christ in the convent; the human husband has his analogue in the divine bridegroom. In all the subsequent chapters of this book, we will observe this drawing together of the two discourses of love and marriage (even up to the point of apparent congruence).

Second, as a direct consequence of the aspect mentioned above, gender stereotypes overlay the religious discourse. Gender-specific behavioral patterns of a man begin to be reflected in the reactions of the divine figure – *Christus*

---

[97] These, of course, are not new solutions. Already Bernard of Clairvaux (and Origen) had to deal with them. Cf. Ann Astell and her psychoanalytical explanation.

sponsus is the perfect (human) husband; the bride of Christ wants or tries to fit in with a specifically female code. The very expectations normally fulfilled by a secular wife but from which a religious is removed by renouncing the biological role, find their way into the religious life of women. The sexualized under-standing of the bride of Christ intensifies the fact that the nun continues to be referred to female self-images far more than the monk to male ones. In the case of the comparisons between secular and spiritual marriage problematized in chapter 2, it becomes clear that it is precisely on the basis of erotic and matri-monial concepts that the female virgin is exhorted to be a desired bride, obedi-ent wife and fruitful mother. Barbara Newman pinpoints the contradiction clearly: "Recruited as virgins, defined as virgins, guarded as virgins, and ideally canonized as virgins, consecrated women were nevertheless seen as fulfilling to perfection their feminine roles of wife and mother[98].

Third, the overlap between historical views of the sexes and the spiritual sphere manifests itself in the dynamic between the sexes – for example, in the way in which activity and passivity are allocated among the lovers and the hier-archical order the allocation creates. The all-important "first move" in a love relationship, therefore, also becomes a central theme in religious love literature. John Bugge mentions an interesting shift: "Under the classic theory of atone-ment (…), the role of the virgin had been essentially an active one, conjoined to the continuing redemptive struggle in which both male and female virgins took part. With the feminization of virginity, however, the new role of the vir-gin was made to conform to the passive role of the female in the normal sexual relationship"[99]. It makes sense to include a few fundamental reflections about how the sexualization of a motif can form the basis for the linking of activity, masculinity and transcendence, on the one hand, and passivity, femininity and immanence, on the other[100].

Medical and theological traditional thinking paves the way for the medieval perspective that the man should occupy an active position, the woman a passive one. Views of conception, based on sources from Antiquity, attribute the active and formative function to the man, or rather his sperm[101]. Because the woman is naturally bashful, medieval authorities advise men to initiate sexual inter-course with cautious and gentle moves[102]. The most influential theological legitimation of the "principality of the man" is presented by the exegesis of

---

[98] Barbara Newman 1995, 31-32.

[99] John Bugge, 106.

[100] Cornelia Klinger 1995, 43 ff. refers to them as "universals of the Western history of thought".

[101] Various medieval images of the "active man" and the "passive woman" being the norm in the medical context are investigated comprehensively by Joan Cadden 1993.

[102] Britta-Juliane Kruse, 149; cf. Vern L. Bullough / James A. Brundage, 1-152.

Genesis. From the very beginning, it condemns the one sex to act and the other to react while raising one to the level of the norm and making the other a *variation* on the norm: "Principality means: forming the beginning and being called to dominance. This precondition is not called into question by either the majority of the Church Fathers or the majority of medieval Scholastics. The construct 'woman' is explained essentially as a negation or a diminution of the construct 'man'. Although there are counter-traditions diverging from this andronormative view of humanity, the main tradition of official theology continues to assert its influence (in both traditions) into modern times with the help of constantly renewed ecclesiastical affirmation, whereas the counter-traditions – whether they are grounded in the plurality of theological schools or carried by women referred to as mystics or poets – retreat into the shadows"[103]. Thus the one who stands at the beginning of Creation should make the first move. Adam has initiative in the true sense of the word. Eve's secondary being – like her name[104] – derives solely from the primary being of the First-created.

Female initiative is not a requirement either in hagiographical writings or in the medieval warrior-ethic. Women are not even permitted to act in a communicative way. In social rituals such as the contracting of marriages, there can be no talk at all of freedom of action[105]. Her domain seems to be that of keeping silent. Where the "first move" is concerned, this means that a woman may not woo a man. If she wishes nonetheless to communicate her desire, she should do this indirectly and non-verbally, either through a third party or by disobedience. Self-mutilation or pining to death are messages containing an ultimatum. There are a few exceptions who prove this rule – such as Laudine in the courtly epic *Iwein* by Hartmann von Aue. In passing, Hartmann mentions that it is not customary for women (*der wîbe site*) to woo a husband. Skillfully, he puts the reflections about what is seemly for women into the protagonist Laudine's own mouth. She breaks with tradition and proposes to Iwein, which forces her to explain why she has given up the reserve demanded. As a widow, she says, she has nobody to defend her possessions, and Iwein (her husband's murderer) seems to her a convincing fighter: she cannot afford to do without him[106]. She tells Iwein of her affection and – successfully – proposes marriage to him: *ich*

---

[103] Elisabeth Gössmann 1991, 483. The term "andronormative", which was coined by Katharina Fietze (Fietze, 20-21), goes beyond the term "androcentric" and refers to the exclusion of women from thought, which normatively relates only to men.

[104] Gen 2:23.

[105] Cf. Philippe Ariès / Georges Duby 2, 124 ff.; for the roles of each sex in the contracting of a marriage, see Michael Schröter passim (see the index under "Männlichkeit" and "Weiblichkeit").

[106] Hartmann von Aue, *Iwein*, 2295-2326.

wil iuch gerne: welt ir mich?[107] Another work by Hartmann von Aue shows the same limited scope for action by the woman in her love for a divine partner. For as the beloved, God, too, is in the position of the man; therefore, the woman may not woo him. In the legend in verse known as *Gregorius*, Gregorius's mother chooses God as her beloved in order to expiate her sin of incest. The text interprets her intense prayer as a wooing gesture and promptly points out the affront to conventions:

> *swie vastez sî wider dem site*
> *daz dehein wîp mannes bite,*
> *sô lac si im doch allez an,*
> *sô si des state gewan,*
> *mit dem herzen zaller stunde,*
> *swie joch mit dem munde:*
> *ich meine den gnædigen got.*

No matter how completely it goes against good custom for any woman to woo a man, she still placed all before him with increasing constancy, both silently in her heart, and with her mouth: before the merciful God, that is[108].

A Chance to Contradict

Previously, I have sought to outline the consequences arising from the sexualization of the bride of Christ ("feminization" of the bride, "masculinization" of the bridegroom). The most decisive factor is shown to be the possibility that earthly gender relations impose themselves upon religious dimensions, constituting a scdimcnt of strong historical and emotional influence on the idea of marriage with a divine beloved, which is conceived as timeless. If, in the sexualized motif of the bride of Christ, secular gender relations become deposited on religious texts, this provides an opportunity precisely for those seeking insights into the history of gender: the many allegorical figures in texts associated with bridal mysticism are also men or women and interesting as such. Every discourse on gender has its starting-point in images of femininity and masculinity, which are based both on actual conditions and on fictions and imagination. Literary gender-depictions, whether they are embodied by the protagonists of fictional texts or by allegorical figures, can directly or indirectly either confirm an actual (gender-)reality or undermine it. The latter case might

---

[107] Hartmann von Aue, *Iwein*, 2333. Thomas Cramer sees this turn of speech as a "customary German betrothal formula" as found in the *Nibelungenlied* or *Meier Helmbrecht* (ed. by F. Panzer, 1514, 1527-1528). For Laudine's success, see *Iwein*, 2344-2355.

[108] Hartmann von Aue, *Gregorius*, 879-885.

include subversive texts which could be read as a "palimpsest"[109]. As artificially constructed representatives of their sex, allegorical figures, e.g., the pair of lovers from the Song of Songs or the love-archeress in chapter 5, belong either to the world of men or the world of women. These sorts of myths of femininity or masculinity in the texts of bridal mysticism can equally be investigated "as an emblem of cultural history"[110].

I would like to illustrate what this means, using two contrasting examples from two texts which will be examined in chapter 3. The first text is a psychogram (devised by a male author) of the male and female Blessed; in the second text, a female author portrays the allegory of a female bride of Christ.

In *Tochter Syon*, the Franciscan theologian Lamprecht von Regensburg develops a typology of gender. It is based around the different way in which men and women attain experience of God and react to it[111]. Women – in Lamprecht's view – are distinguished by excessive vehemence when they penetrate divine mysteries. They overshoot the mark, so to speak, since women's mildness of disposition would naturally favor the experience of grace anyway[112]. Shortly afterwards, Lamprecht relativizes this high level of receptivity. The fact that the Blessed scream and thrash around does not in itself guarantee intense experience: to someone who has never had anything hot in his mouth, even something lukewarm would seem fiery[113]. The nature of men is given a very different showing by Lamprecht: they are harder and more immovable spiritually, which means that they give themselves up to mystical experience less easily but are also more self-controlled and discreet in public. Men make up for their slow start in mystical experience by their insight, which is all the deeper for it[114]. Lamprecht's comparison shows that he detects a lack of *mâze* (the golden mean), or in other words *zuht* (self-discipline), in the female nature[115]. One would hardly expect a female mystic portrayed in this way to be able to preserve her *occulta cordis* – the secrets of her heart, which must certainly include her erotic experiences – in her "inner person". She will be much more likely to communicate them – through the *exterior homo* – in excessively extravagant body language[116].

---

[109] Elisabeth Gössmann uses the term "palimpsest", borrowing the terminology of American feminist literary criticism (Elisabeth Gössmann 1994, 19-41, here 20). It refers to a sort of multiple message which emerges from the babble of conventional and countering voices in a discourse.

[110] Sigrid Weigel 1994a, 23. Further literature in Sigrid Weigel 1994a, 24-25 and Sigrid Weigel 1994b.

[111] For Lamprecht's personal position, see *Tochter Syon*, 2815-2825 and 3024-3040.

[112] Lamprecht von Regensburg, *Tochter Syon*, 2841-2864.

[113] Lamprecht von Regensburg, *Tochter Syon*, 2979-2994.

[114] Lamprecht von Regensburg: *Tochter Syon*, 2851-2863.

[115] Cf. Lamprecht von Regensburg: *Tochter Syon*, 2855 ff. and 2979 ff.

[116] Peter Moos 1992, 4. For the possibility of reading physical signs, see Horst Wenzel 1994, esp. 215 ff. and Wenzel 1995, passim.

It is not known whether Mechthild von Magdeburg was aware of the topos of the woman as Lamprecht presents it, or whether her work was in any way a reaction to this sort of defamation. What is certain is that she gave a contrasting form to allegorical women figures in delicate passages like the following. She has the bride of Christ show such awareness of her situation that she foils the construct of femininity proposed by such as Lamprecht von Regensburg. In so doing, Mechthild proves that at least literary brides of Christ can have a distinctive and unconventional face, which only becomes visible among the many faces of the many brides represented in literature. Mechthild's figure of the bride is aware of her exclusive love for her divine beloved. For this reason she recognizes the intention of a devilish attempt to coax her love-secret from her[117]. A devil pretends to be Christ, showing his stigmata to convince her. He tells the female "I" to proclaim this apparition publicly as an experience of grace and promises her much gain[118]. The bride of Christ sees through the devil and unmasks his intentions with great composure:

> *"Ich weis dine meinunge wol; solte ich allen lúten min herzeheimelicheit sagen, es solte mir ein kurze wile wol behagen, so woltest du mit flisse da nach stan, das sich das spil mûste verschlan. (…)".*

"I well know your intentions; if I were to tell everyone the secrets of my heart, things would be quite nice for me in the short term. But then you would intently strive to make the fun end badly"[119].

This bold defense of the secrets of her heart puts the devil to flight. But the bride of Christ can also put less subtle opponents in their place, e.g., when Lady Knowledge nosily enquires into the relationship between the soul and God:

> *"Eya, vro brut, went ir mir noch ein wortzeichen sagen der unsprechlicher heim-licheit, die zwúschent gotte und úch lit?"*

"Mistress Bride, would you say a word to me about the ineffable intimacy that exists between God and you?"[120]

Calmly and quick-wittedly the bridal soul sets clear limits on third-party knowledge of her secret. In so doing, she reserves a place of absolute privacy for herself and her beloved – to a certain extent a *locus intactus*:

---

[117] Similarly to this incident in Mechthild, in the *Speculum naturale* of Vincent of Beauvais, the devil is denied the sight of a person's most intimate secrets, the *interiora animae* or *occulta cordis*. See Lionel L. Friedman, 104 f.

[118] Mechthild von Magdeburg, *Das fließende Licht der Gottheit*, IV,2,55-58; trans. Tobin, 141.

[119] Mechthild von Magdeburg, *Das fließende Licht der Gottheit*, IV,2,62-65; trans. Tobin, 141.

[120] Mechthild von Magdeburg, *Das fließende Licht der Gottheit*, II,19,31-2; trans. Tobin, 82.

"Vrŏwe bekantnisse, das tŭn ich nit. Die brúte môssent alles nit sagen, was in beschiht. Dú helig beschŏwunge und dú vilwerde gebruchunge sont ir han von mir, die userwelte bevindunge von gotte sol úch und allen creaturen iemer me verborgen sin sunder alleine mir."

"Lady Knowledge, that I shall not do. Brides may not tell everything they experience. Holy contemplation and precious enjoyment you shall learn about from me. My privileged experience of God must always be hidden from you and from all creatures except for myself"[121].

Representation of the Bride in Literature

The bride of Christ and her bridegroom appear in many forms, as many as there are genres and literary perspectives from which to represent the pair of lovers. The texts show the protagonists in accordance with the particular effects intended; these aims, in turn, are determined by the literary genre chosen. Consequently the phenomenology of the erotic relationship with God cannot be separated from the possibilities of literary representation – the roles presented lead to specific points of view, and vice versa. In the following sections I would like to investigate these reciprocal effects by attempting to classify the literary viewpoints of the representation of the bride.

Fundamentally, I distinguish literary views from the inside (the views of brides themselves) from literary views from the outside (views on brides and bridegrooms). Both types of representation of the bride come to bear in the texts – which will be analyzed in depth from chapter 3 – though it is seldom a case of just one type. More often they are accumulated and combined, which is undoubtedly more fascinating from a literary point of view. This sort of collage of perspectives is characteristic for many mystical texts, in which didactic aims and witness of experience are inherently interwoven.

Even a cursory glance over the palette of medieval bridal mysticism in German, French, English, Spanish, and Italian demonstrates that views of the bride from the inside can mostly be traced back to female authors who give a really or apparently authentic account of their own brideship, whereas the views from the outside often originate with male priests who write exegetical commentaries on the model of the bride, often in texts for pastoral guidance whose aim is to guide a female audience to mystical spirituality: sermons, treatises or letters. If we take into account the history of the motif and its sexualization outlined above, then there is one assertion which is by no means too bold: the existence of literary first-person perspectives depends more or less directly on propagated

---

[121] Mechthild von Magdeburg, *Das fließende Licht der Gottheit*, II,19,33-36; trans. Tobin, 82.

images of the exemplary bride. First, the views of the bride of Christ from the inside and the outside are mutually dependent; secondly, the sexualization of the motif suggests that the internal perspectives will stem primarily from women and the external primarily from men.

This literary classification, along with its gender-implications, contains a hidden danger of confusion. It evokes associations with categories in research into mysticism which have been the subject of controversy, ardently championed by some and vehemently rejected by others. Here I am thinking, for instance, of the delimitation of a so-called "female mysticism" or "male mysticism", which itself brings into play delicate criteria – virtually impossible to define or prove – in judging the texts. Thus the texts are compared and contrasted with one another with respect to their dimensions of language and experience as well as their authenticity and/or artificiality. Also involved are how much they can be considered subjective and confessional and how much they rely on hagiographical models. The result is a constant struggle between diametrically opposed readings[122]. In the following investigation, I do not intend to provide ammunition to assist either party in their battle. I would rather keep well out of the line of fire and broaden the horizons by considering specifically cases resulting from the model of the erotic relationship. Thus, I view my classification as an attempt consistently to think through the historically-developed, gender-specific valency of the role of the bride of Christ, including those textual documents thought to be intended to encourage people to become brides of Christ, as well as those thought to be written by those who already are. As with all the studies presented here, the attempt at classification constitutes a plea for the indissoluble union of the linguistic-literary dimension and that of spiritual experience. Anything else would mean overlooking the fact that the texts are situated in a theological and anthropological context, where the "Word" is made – and continues to be made – "Flesh".

Inside Views

By literary views from the inside, I mean perspectives of depiction which are either actually or apparently authenticated by experience: as Ingrid Bennewitz

---

[122] For a fundamental account of the controversy surrounding the scholarly hermeneutics of mystical texts, see Alois M. Haas 1996, 9-83; a good critical overview of important sections of the scholarly battlefield is given by Susanne Köbele, 21 ff. – The title of Christine Ruhrberg's work on Christina von Stommeln – "Der literarische Körper der Heiligen" (the literary body of the saints) – highlights the fact that language and vital experience combine (cf. Christine Ruhrberg, chapters 5 and 6); similarly, Walter Simons, in: Sarah Kay / Miri Rubin (eds), 10 ff. and (on Margery Kempe) Karma Lochrie.

puts it, "constructs by the subject or by others, developed according to literary patterns (…), or actual fragments of authentic religious experience"[123]. This type of writing is not necessarily bound to the perspective of the bride told in the first-person singular, which, according to Amy Hollywood, demands a particularly self-assured position of the speaker: "the acquisition of first-person narrative voice requires authority, and confidence in that authority"[124]. Brides of Christ often speak of themselves in indirect speech, in the third-person singular, or in the words of several speakers[125], a device that blurs the internal speaking-position of a bride of Christ. In particular cases, not only do the representational perspectives multiply, but apparently even the possibility for unambiguous designations of authorship also dissolves[126]. Mechthild von Magdeburg's *Das fließende Licht der Gottheit* is one of the works which gives rise to questions like: is it the bride of Christ speaking, or is it her divine beloved? Whose *fließende Licht* is it[127]? This rather obscure authorship leads to a question which is not as dubious as it might appear. Rather it is probably connected with the "attributions of authorship until revoked" which have been observed in Mechthild's work. Are there views from the inside on the part of the bride, but not the bridegroom? In factual terms the question must be answered in the affirmative, since the divine party in the erotic relationship obviously remains silent. If he does speak, what he says is always mediated through a chosen person and is thus prophetic. In the face of this literary fact there can only be one thought to puzzle over: if God, imagined as masculine, is seen as the *auctor principalis* of every erotic relationship with God, as he is portrayed by several of the texts investigated in chapter 3, then, in strict theological terms, he is also the *auctor*, or at least *coauctor* of all Christian bridal mysticism. Although he remains invisible, or at most sketched in the confusing puzzle of someone like Mechthild, he nevertheless stands behind every text in the tradition of bridal mysticism, particularly behind every text founded on experience. God therefore

[123] Ingrid Bennewitz 1994, 417: "Selbst- und Fremdinszenierungen nach literarischen Mustern (…) oder aber doch Fragmente authentischen religiösen Erlebens".

[124] Amy Hollywood, 228, note 23; On Mechthild's narrative alternatives to the first-person perspective, see Amy Hollywood, 60 ff.

[125] Amy Hollywood, 61.

[126] For instance in I, prologue and II,26. From the far poetological and theological horizon, Alois M. Haas speaks of this matter (Alois M. Haas 1987, 245-246, and primarily 1989b); Susanne Köbele sums up the various speaking positions in Mechthild's text (72-73). For the "I" of beguine mysticism (in Mechthild, Hadewijch and Marguerite Porete), see the convincing account by Barbara Newman (1995, 143 ff.) and Amy Hollywood, 61 f. Cf. also Ingrid Kasten 1995, 5 ff. (further bibliography in note 15); Béatrice Acklin Zimmermann 1991, 189; Ingrid Bennewitz 1994, 417; Gisela Vollmann-Profe 1994 and Susanne Bürkle.

[127] Cf. Hildegard Elisabeth Keller 2000.

has a right to the position of an insider, since without him, no text would come about. Mechthild takes account of this *sine qua non* status of the divine bridegroom who primarily remains dumb by amalgamating her bridal perspective with the divine one in several passages. Thus, the initiations of love by the divine bridegroom seem even more deeply internal than the documented literary viewpoint of the bride.

Bridal and Textual Practices

Propagation of the imitation of the bride requires female religious to see themselves in nuptial terms: the *vita monastica* as *imitatio sponsae*. Many hymns, for example, composed by Hildegard von Bingen for weekdays and feast-days in the convent, are animated by the spirit of an erotic relationship with God. For – as has become clear in the context of the consecrated virgins – essentially each and every woman in a convent, as an institutional bride of Christ, can say of herself: "I am Christ's bride". And she is also addressed and encouraged as such by priests. A conscious and gradually intensifying appropriation of the proffered role of the bride by women leading a monastic life can be observed from the high Middle Ages and later among beguines[128]. This can be seen in monastic practices[129], and also in the fact that such texts, written from the first-person perspective of a bride, are produced. If the 'I' tells of her intimacy with a divine lover, then an institutional perspective of the bride of Christ is authenticated in an experience-related sense. It is not really important whether this represents a literary strategy or has a subjective, confessional quality. What is important is that the text is understood as that of an insider – either of her own free will or at the insistence of her divine lover or a priest[130] – writing about her brideship. Obviously this tinge of personal experience, whether actual or fictive, remains such a characteristic feature of the texts that pointing out the relevant hagiographical stylization and models in the background, as Ursula Peters did, can never fully characterize the text. Danielle Régnier-Bohler's remark attests to this lingering uneasiness: "Here [i.e. in the literature of female mysticism], notwithstanding the cautions of Ursula Peters, it is tempting to see individuals turning inward and discovering new ways to

---

[128] Cf. E. Ann Matter 1994. For the Song of Songs as the basic model already in early Christian pastoral care of women, see Peter Brown 1988, esp. chapter 13; Ulrich Köpf 1985 and 1987; Hildegard E. Keller 1993, 101-102; Urban Küsters 1985.

[129] For example those practices which Hildegard of Bingen explains and legitimizes in a letter to Tenxwind of Andernach (see below).

[130] For further information on this, see Ursula Peters, 101-188.

describe their experiences"[131]. In simpler terms – and in light of the reservations about authorship discussed above – one could say that any text which mediates the inside view of a bride suggests a message somewhat like the following: "my text is an account of my personal experience of being a bride of Christ".

In the context of a model propagated by priests for women to identify with, I would like to raise the issue of the links between gender and genre[132]. For after all, it is this constellation which generates the two literary perspectives on the bride which I distinguish. Before we move on to views from the outside, let us therefore consider possible connections between the literary genre, i.e., views of the bride from the inside and the outside, on the one hand, and the gender of their creators, on the other. These connections are part of a broader context which is considered here only from a poetological point of view. Bernard McGinn's demonstration of the theological implications (in brief, the development of what he calls "vernacular theology") is very convincing, because he pays due attention precisely to the Song of Songs and how it was put into practice, both in spiritual and literary terms[133].

Denys Turner asks why the long, male-dominated history of exegesis of the Song of Songs does not include any female exegetes and how one should explain this "absence of women Song commentators"[134]. The immediate answer to this very valid question lies in Church politics. Since the fields of exegesis and ecclesiastical preaching remained theologically denied to women, only "grace" could make kerygmatic authority possible in the conflict between gender and genre. The question must therefore be put more precisely, in light of the continuing hermeneutic uneasiness of male exegetes of the Song of Songs right up to Herder's protest about the undermining of the sense. Caroline Walker-Bynum's studies in the history of devotional piety have made the question more urgent[135]: "It is no longer possible to study religious practice or

---

[131]   Georges Duby / Michelle Perrot 2, 447.

[132]   Barbara Newman (1995, 145 ff.) investigates the way in which Hadewijch plays on this idea in her texts and confronts prose about bridal mysticism with the mystical love lyric. Amy Hollywood (in general 27, ff.; specifically on Mechthild von Magdeburg, 57 ff.) also voices an opinion on this issue (also critical with regard to Bynum). For the gender/genre question, see Sigrid Weigel 1994a, 20 ff.; Jane Burns; Jane Chance (ed.); *Manlîchiu wîp, wîplich man*; Nicole Bériou / David L. D' Avray. For the autobiographical implications of gender and genre in mystical texts see Jeffrey F. Hamburger 1998.

[133]   Cf. Bernard McGinn 1994a, 1-14 and McGinn 1998b; for the Song of Songs, which could be seen as the hermeneutic starting point of this new theology in its relationship to women, cf. McGinn 1994b, 347ff.

[134]   Denys Turner, 37.

[135]   Caroline Walker Bynum 1982; Caroline Walker Bynum 1987; Caroline Walker Bynum 1991; Caroline Walker Bynum / St. Harrell / P. Richman 1986; Caroline Walker Bynum 1995. See also Susanne Bürkle.

religious symbols without taking gender – that is, the cultural experience of being male or female – into account"[136]. To what extent do particular hermeneutic approaches to the system of motifs of the bride constitute a gender-specific application? And what *did* women do with the Old Testament Song of Songs, how *did* they process it, if they did not comment on it at all according to the rules of the theological brotherhood – or, in any case, not in an explicit or professional way? In individual passages as well as in its general structure, Mechthild von Magdeburg's work provides a prime example of non-canonical exegesis of the Song of Songs[137]. She experiments with nuptial experience and language, using both her own brideship and the figurative language of the Song of Songs in a unique way. The very fact that the role of the bride of Christ is assumed by female religious authors shows that the Song of Songs has the quality of an existential and literary inspiration. They do not comment on the bride of Christ as external interpreters, but rather they write of what it means from the inside – whether this occurs in a sustained first-person perspective or in a kaleidoscope of speaking stances. Male priests seem to prefer exegetical commentary or addressing female religious. The relevance of the erotic model in writings for the spiritual guidance of women is striking – an exemplary case is the anonymous *St Trudperter Hohelied*, thought to have been composed by a cleric and dating from the mid-twelfth century. The religious women are encouraged very strongly to be brides; in brideship they should recognize, above all, a quality of experience and identification. The literary procedures for recruiting brides will be discussed below from various points of view.

Accordingly, in both the reception and the production of such texts influenced by nuptial ideas – at least in certain works by women – one finds an understanding of the text characterized by Alois M. Haas as "experimentative rather than interpretative"[138]. It is supported by a Christology which, since Anselm of Canterbury, emphasizes the humanity of Christ. The incarnate God is confronted primarily as human and man, as bridegroom. This tangible humanity makes it possible for the religious to understand their role very literally: "Not surprisingly, however, what had been meant for male virgins allegorically was adopted in a provocatively literal sense by women"[139]. On this basis, the development of another way of interpreting the Song of Songs appears possible: the actual practice of the Song of Songs, in which the incarnate Christ becomes the beloved partner. It is characterized by the general

---

[136] Caroline Walker Bynum 1986, 1-2; see also Caroline Walker Bynum 1991, 191 ff.

[137] Susanne Köbele's account of Mechthild's integration of the Song of Songs is not comprehensive, but gives an overview and examples.

[138] Alois M. Haas 1979, 110, note 7: "mehr experimentierend denn interpretierend".

[139] John Bugge, 92.

inclusion of corporeal dimensions in the text and the attempt to fill the erotic role experientially and give it linguistic and literary form on the basis of the new speaking-stance[140]. For this reason Danielle Régnier-Bohler asserted of certain texts that they communicated in a "'total' language", i.e., a language "that made room for the body "[141].

The Christological background of these speech-acts has rightly been pointed out, for example, in the works of Margery Kempe and Mechthild von Magdeburg: "The revaluation of sensual figurative language is a parallel phenomenon to the revaluation of the bodily, sensual existence of human beings, in so far as their being bound to sensuality is not a deficit in purely spiritual (angelic) existence, but is rather something which brings them close to God in a particular way"[142]. A further characteristic of this radical understanding of the text, which is connected with the discovery of the bride from the perspective of an insider, is the noticeable emphasis on the literal erotic sense of the Scripture[143]. The determination with which a speaking "I" takes over the role of the bride and demands the attention of the divine partner can testify to the particular weighting of the literal sense. This is attested to also by emotive signals such as nuptial forms of address – *ach, geminnete gemahele und brut gottes* (O beloved wife and bride of God) or *ach liebe junge gottes eliche gemahele* (O dear, young, wedded bride of God)[144] – and didactic exhortation in texts of bridal mysticism for women who might become brides of God. On the basis of verbal and non-verbal eroticism, women are really and truly mobilized. They are urged to adorn themselves to suit the taste of the divine bridegroom or to look forward to God as the superlative husband[145]. Representations of the concept of the bride of

---

[140] Alois M. Haas 1988, 359-366. Cf. Caroline Walker Bynum 1987 and 1991, 194 ff., for the incarnational background, particularly of the Song of Songs, see Hildegard E. Keller 1993, 395-451; for sensual vocabulary in the works of Mechthild von Magdeburg, her handling of the Song of Songs, and that of the nuns of Helfta, see Susanne Köbele, 80 ff. See also the article by Walter Simons and Jocelyn Wogan-Browne, in: Sarah Kay / Miri Rubin (eds), 10 ff. and 24 ff.

[141] Danielle Régnier-Bohler (in Georges Duby / Michelle Perrot 2, 433 and 446, respectively).

[142] Susanne Köbele, 80: "Die Aufwertung der sinnlichen Bildersprache ist ein Parallelphänomen zur Aufwertung der leiblich-sinnlichen Existenz des Menschen insofern, als dessen Bindung an Sinnlichkeit kein Defizit reiner Geist-(Engel-)Existenz ist, vielmehr in besonderer Weise an Gott annähert". For Margery Kempe, see the study by Karma Lochrie.

[143] For a differentiated account of the hermeneutics of the figurativeness of the Song of Songs and the importance of its literal sense in Mechthild von Magdeburg, see Susanne Köbele (77 ff.), who draws attention to differences in this respect with regard to the texts of other women (e.g. the nuns of Helfta).

[144] *Der Schürebrand*, 7,15 and 10,9, respectively (cf. section "Offices and Their Authority).

[145] Cf. chapter 2. Barbara Newman (1995, 31) draws attention to the contradictions inherent in such an understanding of the role.

God for personal, practical, everyday use can also be seen as the expression of a very vital transference of brideship. These are phenomena which complement the literary versions of spiritual marriage which have been passed on to us by great mystics. Nuns who remain anonymous – such as those in the convent of Hildegard von Bingen – actually act out the role of bride of Christ in the monastic community. In answer to Tenxwind of Andernach's enquiry about "certain strange and irregular practices"[146], Hildegard of Bingen gives an account of the practice for feast-days in her convent. The nuns go about as brides, wear their long hair down, dress in white with crowns of gold filigree, and wear golden rings. The justification she gives is that the nuns' virginity and their marriage with Christ legitimate all these external signs because the latter signal that they are brides of Christ[147]. The abbess is articulating a concept of the bride of Christ which becomes visible and, through the hymns and antiphons she composed, is made audible to the community celebrating in the convent – *sensus litteralis* in the truest possible sense, since the literal meaning becomes accessible to sensory perception[148].

Outside Views

There are various literary constellations in which a bride is presented from the outside. Within a literary framework, a bride can be described in interaction with her bridegroom or her social environment. If – as in the work by Priester Wernher – this bride is Mary, the mother of God, then the reverential narration of her biography will be a fundamental literary motif. But if she is an impetuous young girl like the one portrayed in Hartmann von Aue's *Der arme Heinrich*, then the suspense-dynamic of the story will be central. There the would-be bride of Christ moves the plot forward by playing secular marriage, and spiritual marriage with Christ off against one another, wishing to sacrifice herself for the protagonist, who is fatally ill. If – and this is the third possibility – the bride is an allegorical woman, such as the daughter of Zion in the verse epic by Lamprecht von Regensburg, then one is dealing with a didactic, schematized account of the mystical progression of a bride of Christ from her awakening to

---

[146] Hildegard von Bingen, *Epistolarium* 52, 12 ff.; trans.: Baird / Ehrman 1994, 127.

[147] Hildegard von Bingen, *Epistolarium* 52r, 17 ff.; trans.: Baird / Ehrman 1994, 129. Where the actual practice of spiritual brideship is concerned, the sacred art in the monasteries and convents is also of central importance. The nuns live out their religious lives in the production and reception of art. See the research of Jeffrey F. Hamburger, esp. Hamburger 1997.

[148] Mechthild von Magdeburg also speaks of the importance of clothes for everyday wear and those for feast-days, but she does so allegorically (*Das fließende Licht der Gottheit*, VII,65).

the final wedding in heaven. Thus: the bride who is portrayed from the outside can be an actual historical person, Mary or another saint; or she may be a religious woman for whose spiritual guidance the author is perhaps responsible or whose biography he is writing; or she could be a fictional protagonist. Especially in (auto)biographical narrative texts one may have the joint work of more than one author, where self-testimonies of a bride of Christ are incorporated into the narrative; then the text shows signs of variation between perspectives from the inside and from the outside. Catherine of Siena and Raymond of Capua, her confessor and biographer, provide an example of this[149].

One also finds literary views on the bride from the outside in exegetical texts for spiritual guidance, in which a religious author gives an allegorical commentary on a bride. In this he peels off one layer of meaning after another. One example of such a didactic text is *Die Hochzeit*. The bride seems like a mannequin in a display-window, a model on whom religious ideas can be pinned at random. At times this is also the case for the encoded lovers of the Song of Songs in the *St. Trudperter Hohenlied*. This is the classical literary situation, in which male theologians mediate between the bride of the Song of Songs and the (frequently female) public, attaching didactic messages to the body and statements of the bride and sometimes to those of the bridegroom. As exegetes looking from the outside, they put words into the figures' mouths as happens in an exemplary sermon by Robert de Sorbon[150]. The public only learns about the bride's inner life through an objectified account, which is intended as spiritual guidance and an introduction into mystical thinking. The bride becomes a model for both individual and collective identification. The listeners are supposed to see themselves and behave as a bridal part of the Church as bride. The basic tenor of such normative texts runs thus: the text shows you what a bride of Christ is, how you can become one, and what your bridegroom will expect of you. This can be related very directly to the appropriate way of life. Thus, monastic rules of behavior, ascetic attitudes, and teachings of virtue may be stylized as the indispensable preparation of a bride of Christ. *Der Schürebrand*, a late-medieval treatise associated with the circles of the Strasbourg Friends of God, which was produced by a priest for two brides of Christ who were not yet eighteen, aims only to lead them to an attitude of "suffering", in the mystical sense[151], so that God may be given full scope to operate. The text explains this

---

[149] See Ann E. Matter 1994, 52-55. For the relations between female religious and their priests, see Ute Stargardt, and (for the case of Heinrich Seuse and Elsbeth Stagel) Jeffrey F. Hamburger 1998.

[150] *Sermo in dominica secunda post Epiphaniam*, ed. (in extracts) by Nicole Bériou / David L. D'Avray, 134-136.

[151] For *Der Schürebrand* see the next section. For the mystical concept of theopathy, cf. Alois M. Haas 1989.

to the young women in erotic terms and introduces them to *stetes minnekosen und heimelich gespreche* [...] *mit uwerme gemahele und gespuntzen Jhesu Christo* (constant and secret love-talk [...] with your bridegroom and spouse Jesus Christ)[152]. Withdrawing in quiet – in a place that is also physically secluded, like a private room or a forgotten corner – the young women should open themselves to the inner word. Then the Holy Spirit will lead them to a conversation of love *one alle gemahte erdihtete gebet* (without artificial, composed prayers)[153].

Offices and Their Authority

Views of the bride of God from the outside – this much should already be clear – often flow from the pens of male authors. Since it is very unusual for them to write from the first-person perspective of the bride themselves[154], they describe the bride as they see her: in the voice of an external, authoritative speaker rather than of a nuptially consecrated women. In this it is quite possible for a male theologian to regret that he has not himself had erotic experience of God. Lamprecht von Regensburg, in his *Tochter Syon*, professes this repeatedly, though this does not stop him at times from also inveighing against the more "easily affected" female sex in the same vein.

This external speaking position, indeed this view of the bride altogether, is basically determined by profession. It befits the office of the theologian, confessor, or priest – the clergy in general, but special mention must be made of the office of bishop. One particular clerical office is the courtship and supervision of the bride – an office which also had social relevance for the contracting of secular marriages and continued to be important long after the Middle Ages[155]. But this is also the office which gives meaning to the ring – the episcopal insignia. The bishop's ring is the double of the bride's engagement ring. First, as the representative of the bride, the Church, the bishop betroths himself with the bridegroom, Christ. Secondly, and more importantly here, the ring singles out the bishop as the one who gives away the bride; it is his task to marry the parish in his charge to Christ, in line with St. Paul's claiming of this office for himself[156]. The wooer of the bride is an ambassador between the bridegroom

---

[152] *Der Schürebrand*, 15,22-26.
[153] *Der Schürebrand*, 15,25.
[154] Cf. also Gabriele L. Strauch, 182 f.
[155] Cf. Giovan Battista Pellegrini, 69 ff.
[156] Similarly, we read in the *Historia Occidentalis* of Jacques de Vitry that the bishop has the ring on his finger so that he can speak in two voices: *Habeat autem anulum in digito, ut dicere possit uoce sponse: "Anulo suo subarauit me dominus noster Ihesus Christus." Non solum autem anulum,*

and the bride, who is part of both a pastoral and literary concept. After all, literary instruction can also be given in the form of the wooing and giving away of a bride. In sermons and other didactic writings of the Middle Ages, where male authors predominate, pastoral bride-wooers are at work[157]. But even without explicitly declaring his task, a pastoral author can undertake the guidance of a counterpart who is imagined as female (an individual or a collective) by addressing "her" as a bride, preparing her for the wedding with Christ, and urging her authoritatively to transform her life to make it more fitting for the bridegroom. In this the priest understands his role as wooing the bride, taking care of the bridegroom's bride, proposing the betrothal and supervising her until she marries or until she moves to the bridegroom's house, preserving her purity.

This office of the Christian wooer of the bride, exercised in writing, was first expressed by St. Paul in 2 Corinthians 11:2. He understands his apostolic calling as the wooing and giving away of a bride, as he explains to his community in Corinth: the men and women of Corinth are the bride of Christ, who is under Paul's care; he has brought about the betrothal, crediting himself with the conversion of the Corinthians. "With godly jealousy", he "espoused" the community "to one husband", so that he may present it "as a chaste virgin to Christ"[158]. These services are felt to enhance his status considerably – probably in line with ancient Jewish opinions[159]. It is partly because of the legal obligations of betrothal that the wooer's task is not yet complete since he must vouch for the virginity of the bride until she moves into her bridegroom's house, i.e., in the case of the community or the Church as bride, until the end of time. Another contributory factor is that the betrothal itself is not fulfillment, the actual wedding is an eschatological event that has not yet occurred[160]. Therefore

---

id est fidei signaculum, in se debet habere, sed insuper animas subditorum uni uiro Christo procuret desponsare, quemadmodum dicit apostolus: "Despondi enim uos uni uiro uirginem castam exhibere Christo."(The Historia Occidentalis of Jacques de Vitry, cap. 35, ed. Hinnebusch, 183,10-15).

[157] Of a group of 45 religious didactic texts (produced between 1075 and 1225 in England, France or Germany), Barbara Newman (1995, 21) ascertains that 43 were written by male authors. On an interesting series of French sermons of the thirteenth century (not explicitly destined to women), in which the preacher acts as wooer, cf. Nicole Bériou / David L. D'Avray. – The Middle English text *The wooing of our Lord* (probably destined to women) attributes the wooer's task to Christ himself.

[158] Cf. Christian Wolff, 210 ff. and Hans Windisch, 320 ff. For the love relationship between Christ and his bride Ecclesia, see Eph 5:25-33.

[159] Moses is seen, in the Jewish Haggada, as the one who gives away the bride Israel (Christian Wolff, 211, note 115). In his first homily on the Song of Songs, Gregory of Nyssa refers to the (Jewish) patriarchs, prophets and law-givers as "wooers of the bride", who brought the gifts of Grace to the bride (Franz Dünzl 1994, I, 128, 24 ff.).

[160] Cf. Christian Wolff, 211 and Hans Windisch, 319. Cf. Mt 25:1 ff; Rev 19:7-9; 21:1 and Eph 5:25-27.

Paul understands his supervisory role with the apostolic word as a didactic one, urging caution. He addresses the community in his charge as a woman, suggests that the Christians of Corinth would be as easily led astray by the serpent as Eve. When he speaks of protecting their chastity, he warns them using an expression common for the seduction and violation of a virgin[161].

Paul's view of himself as having charge of a collective or individual bride of God through the Word – as a nuptial servant – is taken over by pastoral authors from patristic times to the Middle Ages. The authority of the male spiritual guide *vis-à-vis* the *sponsa Christi* seems to be particularly necessary in the case of individual, female brides. Ambrose, for example, renowned for composing treatises on virginity, adopts the office of giving away the bride when, in *De virginibus*, he uses quotations from the Song of Songs to spur on a female 'I' to the life of the bride of Christ. It is not only the numerous imperatives which reveal his wish to help prepare the bride of Christ. His readers also discover it in his open admission of his personal ambition to give away the bride. How he wishes, he sighs, that the virgin could be encouraged by the image of the bee, to be hard-working, modest and abstinent: *quam te uelim, filia (...)*[162]. Ambrose also has to reflect on his success in exhorting women to become brides of Christ. There are objections from third parties that he is constantly preaching about virginity without any signs that this is bearing fruit. Ambrose counters laconically that in other places, in the regions of Bologna and Piacenza or in Mauritania, young women certainly do come forward to take the veil, even if this is not the case in Milan. He does not, however, hold himself responsible: *Sed non mea culpa*[163].

The high-medieval text known as *Die Hochzeit* also shows that a religious author can see himself as giving away the bride. The priest looks after the collective bride of the Church, his tongue warns from the altar through the word of God and prepares the bride for the riches of the bridegroom and for the wedding[164]. A classic example of the literary wooing of the bride is found in late-medieval English literature. Richard Rolle (1300-1349) seems, as a pastoral author, to follow where Paul has led. He gives his views on this in his epistle to a woman, probably a religious, by the title *Ego dormio*. Here, too, a verse from the Song of Songs (5:2) is used so that the author gives the woman into matrimony, not simply as an exegete or a spiritual guide, but as the wooer of the bride. Since he wants to "bring" the woman to Christ's bed, he urges her to be

---

[161] Cf. 2 Cor 11:3 ff. and Christian Wolff 1989, 212 ff. In Col 1:23-29, Paul speaks in general terms of his calling to the service of the Church.

[162] *De virginibus* I,41, Vol. 14 / II, 140.

[163] *De virginibus*, I,57, Vol. 14 / II, 156.

[164] *Die Hochzeit*, 359-374.

awakened to love. He emphasizes expressly that it is not a question of love for him, Richard Rolle, but for the "king of heaven":

> *Mykel lufe he schewes, that never es irk to lufe, bot ay standand, sittand, gangand, or wirkand, es ay his lufe thynkand, and oftsyth tharof es dremande. Forthi that I lufe, I wow the, that I myght have the als I walde, noght to me, bot to my Lorde. I wil become that messanger to bryng the to hys bed, that hase made the and boght the, Christe, the keyng sonn of heven. For he wil with the dwelle, if thou will lufe hym: he askes the na mare bot thi lufe. And my dere syster in Christe, my wil thou dose if thou lufe hym.* Much love He shows, He who is never reluctant to love, but who – whether standing, sitting, walking or working – is always thinking of His love, and is often dreaming of it. For I love you, I vow, so that I might have you as I wish, not for myself, but for my Lord. I will be a messenger to bring you to the bed of Him who has made you and redeemed you: Christ, the King, Heaven's sun. For He will dwell with you, if you will love Him: he asks no more of you but your love. And, my dear sister in Christ, you do my will if you love Him[165].

In conclusion, I wish to present two didactic texts which – in their separate ways – break through the gender structures of this pastoral model, while simultaneously passing on external perspectives on brides of Christ. The unique early Middle High German *St. Trudperter Hohelied* no longer shows the wooing and preparation of a bride as the monopoly of a male priest. Fully in line with the position on teaching by women later adopted by Henry of Ghent, the text itself constitutes "vernacular theology"[166], and urges the nuns to take an active part in the preparation of the brides. The text therefore includes the listening nuns in the dialogue with the bridegroom: "The person doing the explaining here is not the private 'I' of the author. A bridal soul speaks as the guide of the soul, speaks an 'I', drawing the others into a 'We'[167]. The more mature nuns should take the younger ones under their wings. The text sees itself as a literary form of wooing and preparation of the bride: it explicitly states that the aim of the book is to

---

[165] *Ego dormio*, Rolle's first letter in English, ed. Barry Windeatt 1994, 24-25.

[166] Henry gives the following answer to the question of whether a woman could advance to the level of a teacher in theology: she could not attain this rank *ex officio* (like men), but she could certainly *docere ex beneficio et charitate fervore*; she should do this, however, *privatim, in silentio et non in publico et in facie ecclesiae*. (Summae Quaestionum Ordinarium, vol. 1, Art. XI, quaest.11, quoted by Bernard McGinn [ed.] 1994, 1). These remarks from about 1290 establish the sort of theology which Bernard McGinn presents as the third theology of the Middle Ages: alongside scholastic and monastic theology he lists "vernacular theology", which is linked to new, lay-related languages but also to new literary genres. (Cf. Bernard McGinn's Introduction, 4 ff.).

[167] Friedrich Ohly 1995, 105 ff: "Wer hier auslegt, ist nicht das private Ich des Autors. Eine bräutliche Seele spricht als Seelenführerin, holt als Ich die anderen ins Wir".

be a "mirror" for the "brides of almighty God", a means of nuptial self-revelation[168]. The latter appears to be a collective aim, however, since the text explains to the nuns – addressed with a communal "we" – that care for the weaker ones is like sweet milk which will enflame the love for the bridegroom in the less mature sisters. Loving one's neighbor as practiced within the female monastic community is thus integrated into the preparation of the bride and is even declared as such. Like breast-feeding mothers with their babies, brides of God turn their sisters into brides and lead them to the marital bed of their shared bridegroom, Christ:

sô wir sie danne mit listeclicher huote
gelaiten durch ir iugent,
sô müezen sie got deste heizer minnen
unde ir naehesten unde den gemahelen,
zuo des brûtbette wir sie brâht haben,
unde sie ime gezogen haben mit unsereme süezen spunne.

If we then lead them with the skillful supervision necessitated by their youth, they will all the more warmly love God, their neighbor and the husband to whose marital bed we have brought them, and for whom we have raised them with our sweet breast-milk[169].

When, about two hundred years later, a male priest writes the treatise *Der Schürebrand* for two young brides of Christ, his intentions are also spiritual and didactic[170]. As its title suggests, the work aims to fan the flames of the love of God, to feed a fire which is already burning, and to make it blaze:

Dis ist ein nochschüren des minnebrandes, den der heilge geist in uwerre selen het
ungestossen und glünsende gemaht mit dem gnodenrichen inbrünstigen minnen-
füre (…).

This is a renewed fanning of the blaze of love which the Holy Spirit lit and made to glow in your souls with the profound and merciful fire of love [...][171].

---

[168] *St. Trudperter Hohelied*, 145,14-20, but also the joy of the bride expressed in 6,1-8,5. The Song of Songs itself and the Holy Spirit at work in it (love!) are here the actual wooers of the bride.

[169] *St. Trudperter Hohelied*, 125,5-10.

[170] The text, which is transmitted in a total of 6 manuscripts from the areas of Eastern Switzerland and the Alsace, dates from the second half of the 14th century. The treatise originates in the circles of the Friends of God. Cf. Philipp Strauch's study in an appendix to his edition, Kurt Ruh in ²VL 8 (1992), 876 ff. and Andreas Wilts, 349, who suggests (mistakenly, in Kurt Ruh's opinion) that Nikolaus von Blofelden is the author.

[171] *Der Schürebrand*, 4,13-15.

Although the authority of the author in teaching the young women to be brides of Christ is unchecked, at first he speaks modestly – quite rightly, in Ruh's view, since "the mysticism of the 'Schürebrand' is merely literary padding", and "neither understood nor really experienced"[172]. The author's view of himself is in accordance with the title of the work, which is "written from love". He understands not only the work, but also himself as "the one who tends and fans the fire": *[…] so tribet mich doch minne dar zuo, das ich uwer armer unwirdiger schürebrant sin muos alse ein armes küchinbuobelin, des man underwilent ouch wol bedarf in der grossen herren höfe […].* And so love drives me to be your lowly, unworthy fire-tender, like a miserable kitchen boy who is sometimes needed in the courts of the great lords […][173].

Brides Plural and Their Singular Bridegroom

With all these different literary perspectives, we open up a fan to show a variety of brides. In literary and structural terms, the visions of their brideship differ greatly, as I will demonstrate in chapter 3. But there is one thing in common, as constitutive for the Christian erotic relationship with God as it is contradictory: as good brides they should all reach out to the same bridegroom, should devote themselves exclusively to this one husband, and be faithful to him. The bridegroom, on the other hand, is essentially polygamous, but seems to expect total commitment from each individual bride.

As the texts examined later show, the reaction to this structural polygamy depends on the literary perspective of a given text. Certain texts – the *St. Trudperter Hohelied*, for instance – use the divine bridegroom's polygamy to gather the brides of God waiting for their beloved in a monastic community of mourning. Other texts – like the epic texts by Priester Wernher and Hartmann von Aue – circumvent the problem altogether by focusing on the individual loving couple and the fate of the two lovers.

A comparison between two interpretations of the Song of Songs makes clear that the asymmetrical demands for faithfulness can either be voiced or suppressed. The effect in this is subtly different. In his 23rd sermon on the Song of Songs, Bernard speaks of the bedchamber of the royal beloved, who has many dwelling-places. This means that he possesses many brides, Bernard explains, but has a separate, and to a certain extent private, secret with each one[174]. Bernard seeks a conciliatory paradox by speaking up about God's polygamy and

---

[172] Kurt Ruh, ²VL 8 (1992), 878.
[173] *Der Schürebrand*, 4,29-32.
[174] Bernard of Clairvaux, *Sermo 23*, V, 336-339.

relativizing the aspects of it which could be confusing: there is still intimacy within each individual loving couple, the lovers can dwell in one another mutually. Mechthild has a didactic purpose in taking up the motif of the dwelling of the beloved in terms of erotic love[175]. The soul, gradually awakening, asks Love about God's place of residence: *"Eya, nu sage mir, wa sin wonunge si."* (Well, then, tell me where his dwelling is). Love answers with a paradox: *"Es ist enkein herre me, der zemale in allen sinen húsern wone denne alleine er."* (There is no other Lord that dwells in all his castles at the same time but him alone)[176]. This confusing answer is clever, since – in contrast to Bernard – the instructress Love does not mean to hint at the existence of other brides, but rather to highlight precisely the exclusivity of being chosen as bride. The clearest exegetical difference between Bernard and Mechthild is the interpretation of the fact that there are many dwelling-places: Bernard explains it in terms of the multiplicity of brides; Mechthild, on the other hand, refers to allegorized virtues or stations within the same love story. This is consistent, since Love wishes to awaken the soul to the Mysterious, and consequently tells of divine life in the "peace of holy affection" and in the "narrow confines of the soul", trying with sweet and gentle tones to lead the listener to the "bed of love", to the "heights of bliss" and "the exquisite pain" of love[177]. But at another point the text makes no secret of the fact that God will then guard his "pure virgins" jealously: *Er wil si im selber alleine haben* (he wants to have them for himself alone)[178].

Christ's jealous claim to the loyalty of the human brides remains absolute, right into the late medieval texts. So the dialogue-poem *Christus und die minnende Seele*, from the end of the 15th century, speaks explicitly of the bride's desire for possession – she wants to have the divine bridegroom "to herself", but he wishes to keep himself free for all brides. The bride's claim, which is no more absolute than the bridegroom's claim to her, is branded as selfishness (cf. chapters 4 and 5). This remains the only point where criticism could be raised, since the bridegroom's claim to possession is sacrosanct. Christ wants the bride to himself, for as long as she is unspent. For this reason, in another late-medieval dialogue-poem, *Kreuztragende Minne*, he asks the tarrying soul whether she would only turn to him once she had become old and ugly and the world no longer cared anything for her[179]. Incidentally, the polygamous God's

---

[175] Mechthild von Magdeburg, *Das fließende Licht der Gottheit*, II,23 (trans. Tobin, 87-89). The intention of the chapter is pedagogical: Love seeks to awaken the sleeping soul itself and her interest in the *lustlichen got* (vibrant God) – a delicate venture, as Paul Michel's analysis of the dialogue shows (Paul Michel 1995).

[176] Mechthild von Magdeburg, *Das fließende Licht der Gottheit*, II,23,33-35; trans. Tobin, 88.

[177] Mechthild von Magdeburg, *Das fließende Licht der Gottheit*, II,23,36-41; trans. Tobin, 88.

[178] Mechthild von Magdeburg, *Das fließende Licht der Gottheit*, V,24,22-23; trans. Tobin, 204.

[179] *Kreuztragende Minne*, ed. Romuald Banz, 41-44.

requirement for faithfulness would lead to mockery even in the nineteenth century. In his poem *Himmelsbräute* (Brides of Heaven, from *Romanzero*), Heinrich Heine makes Christ a cuckold in the mouth of fallen brides of God[180]. This sort of mockery is only possible against the backdrop of an unchallenged right of possession which applies only to him, never to her.

Conclusion

Relationships between a God who can be experienced personally and a human individual or collective entity develop along the lines of familial or erotic relationships among human beings. These sorts of personal relationships to God, amongst which erotic encounters between divine being and human being stand out, conspicuous and puzzling, form a constant in the history of religion. This is particularly significant for Christian spirituality, which worships a triune, thus "three-personed" God, a God who became human in Jesus Christ. The erotic relationship to a personal God is the spiritual variant which proved especially productive – in terms of cultural history – in the European Middle Ages up to the early modern period. The developmental history of the motif spans pagan and then Old and New Testament concepts of the bride, among which the influence and effect of the exegesis of the Song of Songs, particularly that of the High Middle Ages, is unparalleled. The Judaeo-Christian conglomeration of erotic-religious concepts also enduringly animates literature in the German language, which distinguishes a rich phenomenology of bridal mysticism, and continues to reverberate in Pietistic attempts at revival from the eighteenth century until modern times in the concepts of certain religious groupings.

The erotic relationship with God is constituted in two roles. With regard to medieval bridal mysticism, one can state: the inner structure of the erotic relationship with a transcendent (i.e., either divine or diabolical) partner assigns the male role to the latter and the female role to the human being. The female role is described in erotic, amorous, or matrimonial terms which were common long before the existence of the Christian religion and far beyond it. Early Christian theologians like Origen thus wrestle with redefining the semantics of the erotic terminology, i.e., the same terms that they condemn in a pagan context. This patristic striving to differentiate erotic love towards the Christian God from forms of pagan religious eroticism is very significant for the sexual valency of the motif as a whole: either a female or a male human being can envisage an erotic relationship with God; thus, the motif of the bride of God is supra-sexual.

The motif does not long remain spared from gender-restriction, which is precisely what Origen had opposed. The one-sided female allocation of the

---

[180] Heine has their souls speaking (Heinrich Heine, ed. Klaus Briegleb, vol. 11, 42).

newly-defined role of the Christian bride of God is a fundamental part of the history of the motif – as are, incidentally, the counter-models of an erotic relationship with a transcendent being: "whores of the devil" and "brides of Satan". Although there are a few male brides of Christ, it is women who are pastorally encouraged to slip into the role of the bride and who actually do so. From early Christianity right up to the late Middle Ages, a process takes place which I have referred to here as "sexualization", meaning the increasingly exclusive allocation of the female role to female human beings. Women can be addressed, guided, and presented as brides of Christ.

The reduced valency affects both roles, since it charges them sexually and adds gender-stereotypes to them, as will doubtlessly become clear in the following chapters. In any case, as soon as the female role comes to be associated with the female sex, the sexual marking of both partners becomes impossible to overlook; and it is strikingly absent from the few examples mentioned in which a man describes himself as a bride of Christ. Friedrich Sunder, for example, can observe his soul, represented as a child, marrying an equally childlike Christ in a formal ceremony. Attendant angels and saints form an audience who seem to be watching an amusing game (*unio mystica*, with children playing at weddings?). Men remain woven into the context of bridal mysticism: as priests, they frequently appear to understand their function as the wooing and giving away of the bride. Priests also function as deputy bridegrooms to the Church until the actual bridegroom, Christ, is united with his bride at the end of time. This matrimonial conception of the Church has remained valid until today, as is demonstrated by the very recent controversies over the selection of Roman Catholic priests and the Pope's stance regarding it.

The expression of personal relationships with God has its quirks. These are most noticeable when the roles become gender-specific, which is the case as soon as the motif is sexualized. The female bride of Christ remains bound by the requirements imposed on her sex, when secular marriage and its hierarchy of the sexes is transposed onto spiritual marriage with Christ. Thus, the female role with regard to God unintentionally anchors the bride of Christ within the gender-specific historical constraints of women, whether they live a secular or a religious life. The pull of earthly relations between the sexes gains in influence on the relationship to a God who is imagined as male – the divine and human roles become saturated with male and female gender-stereotypes. This circumstance can be attractive for an approach to the texts – and particularly to the allegorical "men" and "women" active in them – which asks questions relating to cultural history and gender.

Brides of Christ populate the Latin exegesis of the Song of Songs and later literature in various vernaculars as well as sacred art in Europe. That the bride can be described from various perspectives and for different ends contributes considerably to the literary diversity of the brides of Christ. Fundamentally, one can distinguish between portrayals from the outside and reports from the inside, a distinction which tends also to be related to gender. Male authors, who, as theologians and priests, often portray the bride of God *ex officio*, maintain an approach to brideship which is predominantly exegetical and didactic, characterized by distance from the object interpreted. Very often they start with the Song of Songs and its protagonists, then fan out individual dimensions of allegorical meaning, frequently in order to present the distilled message, now didactically processed, to a female audience. The intended effect of this presentation is generally the *imitatio sponsae*: the women addressed should identify fully with the bride as the loving partner of God. Views on the bride of Christ from the outside are also found in narrative contexts in which a bride of God may be the protagonist and is then judged in many varying ways. Views of brides from the inside generally originate as texts by women which are either actual or fictional autobiographies. They take the concept of brideship featured in the Song of Songs or encouraged by priests as an opportunity to experiment and develop a nuptial understanding of themselves with regard to God. As lovers, they slip into the role of the bride of the Song of Songs and assimilate the dimensions of meaning fanned out by the theologians into their own experience of being a bride – whether as a productive (writing) or receptive (reading and contemplating) human being. The role of the bride becomes the matrix which molds new brides of God, of whom more than a few go on, in turn, to reveal literary views of brides from the inside.

Both approaches – that of the male author to his professionally-determined external position, and that of the female author to her charismatically-motivated insider status – develop consistently from the allocation of the concept of the bride of God to women and the instruction in this concept – the wooing and giving away of the bride, so to speak – to men.

Chapter 2
Interfaces: Love and Marriage,
Spiritual and Secular

*(…) semper sponsa, semper innupta, ut nec amor
finem habeat nec damnum pudoris.– Ever the bride,
ever unwedded, so that her love can have no end, and
her modesty can suffer no blemish*[1].

*Felix talium commercium nuptiarum ut homunculi miseri prius uxor nunc in
summi regis thalamis sublimeris. Nec ex huius honoris privilegio priori tantum
modo viro sed quibuscumque servis eiusdem regis praelata* (It was a happy transfer
of your married state, for you were previously the wife of a poor mortal and
now are raised to the bed of the King of kings. By the privilege of your position
you are set not only over your former husband but over every servant of that
King)[2]. No lesser than Peter Abelard – former husband and now a philosopher
leading the monastic life – here subordinates himself as a monk and servant to
the bride of God, Heloise, whom he addresses in his letter as: *Sponsae Christi
servus eiusdem* (To the bride of Christ, from Christ's servant)[3]. Abelard praises
the way of life of the woman who is his former lover and wife, the mother of
his son, and who now lives in the convent as a bride of God and abbess – a successful career development, according to his letters. Only parts of Heloise's
biography – in love and in spiritual matters – can be reconstructed from the
reciprocal correspondence when, across the distance of many years, Heloise
speaks both of her love for Abelard and of her marriage with him[4]. She plays
the two off against each other in her first letter to him, the only man she has
ever loved, when she expresses her unusual priorities where the marriage-bond
is concerned. She explains that she would rather have gone without this bond
in favor of the bond of love which is all-important to her but not legal in the

---

[1] Ambrose of Milan: *De virginibus*, I, 37 ff., Vol. 14/I, 138.
[2] Abelard, *Letter 4*, ed. J.T. Muckle, 83; trans.: Radice 1974, 138
[3] Abelard, *Letter 4*, ed. J.T. Muckle, 82; trans. (adapted from) Radice 1974, 137.
[4] For the extensive and controversial debate on the question of authenticity of the correspondence, see C.J. Mews, 20-26; Barbara Newman 1995, John Marenbon, 82-93, Peter von Moos
1997b. For feminist stylization of Heloise, see Catherine Brown, in: Jane Chance (ed.), 25-51.

eyes of others. Heloise presents her renunciation as selflessness – she welcomed the humiliation of the status of a concubine as necessary to maintain his untarnished reputation:

> *Non matrimonii foedera, non dotes aliquas expectavi, non denique meas voluptates aut voluntates sed tuas, sicut ipse nosti, adimplere studui. Et si uxoris nomen sanctius ac validius videtur, dulcius mihi semper exstitit amicae vocabulum aut, si non indigneris, concubinae vel scorti, ut, quo me videlicet pro te amplius humiliarem, ampliorem apud te consequerer gratiam et sic etiam excellentiae tuae gloriam minus laederem.*

I looked for no marriage-bond, no marriage portion, and it was not my own pleasures and wishes I sought to gratify, as you well know, but yours. The name of wife may seem more sacred or more binding, but sweeter for me will always be the word mistress, or, if you will permit me, that of concubine or whore. I believed that the more I humbled myself on your account, the more gratitude I should win from you, and also the less damage I should do to the brightness of your reputation[5].

Heloise is an appropriate figure to open this chapter, not only because she was intimately acquainted with the discourses of both love and marriage but also because she experienced both turbulently on two levels (spiritual and worldly). She herself makes no secret of the fact that she did not choose the divine bridegroom with the clever planning which characterizes some of the reflections on marriage cited in this chapter. Heloise became a bride of God for the love of her beloved husband – a paradox of which she herself is well aware. Her honesty is never echoed on Abelard's part. He appears to relish taking on the subservient stance of the servant honoring the bride of his Lord Christ:

> *Te vero extunc me superiorem factam intelligas quo domina mea esse coepisti Domini mei sponsa effecta (…).*

[…] you must realize that you became my superior from the day when you began to be my lady on becoming the bride of my Lord […][6].

He is the one who makes an issue of her gain in status, who is ambitious for her spiritual career in matrimonial terms – a level of ambition, moreover, which he rejected for himself. For himself, Abelard hopes to profit from the particular closeness which a bride may achieve with her bridegroom. Abelard would like

---

[5] Abelard, *Letter 1*, ed. J.T. Muckle, 71; trans. Radice 1974, 113. On Heloise's attitude towards her own status, see Michael T. Clanchy 1997, 161-164; Christopher Brooke 1989, 106-118 and 258 ff.; see also the analysis of the letters by Catherine Brown.

[6] Abelard, *Letter 4*, ed. J.T. Muckle, 83; trans. Radice 1974, 137.

to be able to count on his former lover's proximity to God in terms of family law; thus, he commends himself to her prayers:

> *Ni mireris igitur si tam vivus quam mortuus me vestris praecipue commendem orationibus, cum iure publico constet apud dominos plus eorum sponsas intercedendo posse quam ipsorum familias, dominas amplius quam servos.*
>
> So you should not be surprised if I commend myself in life as in death to the prayers of your community, seeing that in common law it is accepted that wives are better able than their households to intercede with their husbands, being ladies rather than servants[7].

These few letters from his or her point of view, respectively, summarize all the elementary threads which the texts of bridal mysticism interweave with various levels of skill: Love and Marriage, on the one hand, and spiritual and secular partnerships, on the other. These, their intersections, and the consequences of such intersections will be discussed in this chapter.

To start with the interface of Love and Marriage: amorous encounters and separations, erotic constellations, professions and breaches of loyalty, wedding and marriage rituals form the expressive repertoire of the literature of bridal mysticism. They are expressions of both affection and power-relations between men and women. As elements in the discourse of relationships, they concern both theological and secular literature in the Middle Ages, as well as social practices. They become specific in particular paradigms: erotic discourse in the Song of Songs as well as in courtly systems of signs – matrimonial discourse in socio-judicial rituals (from the initiation of a marriage to its consummation). These two discourses[8] are closely related in certain ways and certain intentions; the matrimonial and the erotic relationship-models overlap, complement, and contradict one another. The texts themselves interweave the individual elements as a matter of course, as in the little commentary on the Song of Songs which Abelard inserts into his second letter to Heloise. In interpreting the blackness of the beloved in the Song of Songs, he speaks of the mourning worn by the widow who will not see her dead husband (who died on the cross) again until the next world. For that reason the bride of Christ wears the black nun's habit of the *bonarum viduarum* ("good widows")[9]. The Song of Songs' link with the

---

[7] Abelard, *Letter 4*, ed. J.T. Muckle, 83; trans. Radice 1974, 138. See also Michael T. Clanchy 1997, 170.

[8] Here I base myself on a broad definition of the term 'discourse', which embraces a unity of thought and speech which is specific to a given text and provides the answers to the following complex of questions: how, in what textual forms, for what audience does the text speak of the erotic relationship with God as a marriage and/or an erotic secret, respectively? And how does it relate and evaluate earthly and transcendental relationship levels?

[9] Abelard, *Letter 4*, ed. J.T. Muckle, 83; trans. Radice 1974, 138.

theme of marriage can only be discerned in the use of the term "widow", used in marriage and ecclesiastical law[10].

I will outline both discourses by focusing on two contrasting aspects: the implicit time-structure of the relationship (chronology) and the power-relations between the partners (hierarchy) allow one to highlight what is characteristic for each of the two discourses. Particular attention is warranted by the interfaces of the two discourses, i.e., the interplay of two relationship-models with differing chronology and hierarchy between the partners. This embraces all the possibilities listed by Barbara Newman when she investigates "courtly" and "bridal" views of love and the stances of the speakers in the great works of beguine mysticism:

> "What is remarkable about the beguines is that they appropriated both forms of discourse, using them in counterpoint to express contrasting if not contradictory movements in their all-consuming love. Each tradition is in itself supple and nuanced. In juxtaposition, *Brautmystik* and *fine amour* can convey strikingly different views of the lover, the beloved, the emotional and ethical praxis of love, and not least, the community in which the love-drama unfolds, with its carefully defined sets of insiders or outsiders. In combination, the two discourses may reinforce each other or they may work at cross-purposes, almost incidentally conferring dual gender on both the lover and the divine Beloved. It is this dialectic that gives *la mystique courtoise* its characteristic dynamism, broadening its resources to express the loving, volatile self's whole panoply of response to its ineffable Other"[11].

The texts of bridal mysticism are influenced by another interface which appears at first sight to be more obvious. This is the meeting-point of two dimensions in which personal relationships are realized: the spiritual and the earthly planes. In concrete terms, this refers to the presence – sometimes tacit, but often clearly articulated – of secular relationships between men and women when the concept of the bride of Christ is mentioned. For this reason, I would like in this chapter to show how the spiritual and secular dimension of brideship and marriage overlap in the texts of bridal mysticism. How do these interfaces arise, and what is the result? First, I thematize the fundamental evaluation of the two relationship-dimensions: what answer is given to the question

---

[10] A few remarks on the use of the Song of Songs as a wedding song can be found in Franz Dünzl, 61.

[11] Barbara Newman 1995, 138-139. Newman's thesis, which she demonstrates convincingly for the corpus of texts she investigates, is that Hadewijch, Mechthild von Magdeburg and Marguerite Porete did not base themselves exclusively on the monastic culture of the Song of Songs and the discourse of bridal mysticism influenced by St. Bernard, but also experimented with the courtly registers of *fine amour*. This results in an overlap of courtly and bridal-monastic discourse.

'Which of these marriages is the more valuable'? From what perspective is the comparison undertaken? Then I intend to outline the situation in which the discourses of the secular and the spiritual relationship have been contrasted. Which characters are contrasted with one another, who overshadows whom, and with what? Finally, I am interested in one aspect which becomes more striking if one reviews the phenomenology of bridal mysticism throughout the history of the motif. This is the sacrificial status which the bride must take on in order to be ennobled as a bride of God. Viewing these questions collectively should reveal the interfaces between heaven and earth, as well as between unequal and probably uncomparable partners. The motif of the bride of God is anchored in the cultural discourse of the age: a discourse about man and woman, love and marriage, God and the world.

The Discourses of Love and Marriage

The discourse of love, molded above all by the Song of Songs, and the discourse of marriage, shaped more by social history, but also by marriage preaching[12], structure the encounter of the lovers as well as the hierarchical position between them in the literature of bridal mysticism. Both discourses are heterogeneous in nature. One crystallizes out of a literary paradigm that fertilizes centuries of exegesis and religious literature, particularly in the twelfth century, the apogee of the primarily monastic interpretation of the Song of Songs; the other develops around marriage as a social pattern for ordering the relations between the sexes. Marriage is an institution which changes with medieval society itself: from the high Middle Ages it is subject to a huge increase in laws. Questions relating to marriage and sexual law increase in the growing corpus of Canon law in the high Middle Ages. It is not until after 1350 that secular courts begin to erode the ecclesiastical monopoly on jurisdiction over marriage law[13].

Both discourses give rise to movements of advance and retreat, fidelity and breach of faith, action and reaction. This repertoire makes possible the rich game which the literature of bridal mysticism plays with the relationship between husband and wife. I would like to investigate the two discourses, first from the point of view of the time-structure in each case and then with relation to the hierarchical ordering of the partners. The two discourses are presented in their pure forms; only in this way can the collage technique employed in the individual texts become really clear. From a specific and different angle my

---

[12] Cf. David L. D'Avray.
[13] James A. Brundage 1987, 229 ff and 544 ff.; idem 1994; Christopher Brooke 1991; Rudolf Weigand in Rüdiger Schnell 1997, 280-302; Jörg Wettlaufer, 75-105.

investigation integrates into the very lively field of research on the discourses of marriage, love and gender, where one may mention specifically the research project underway in Basel under the leadership of Rüdiger Schnell[14].

Chronology

The Old Testament Song of Songs seems to be a loosely compiled collection of individual texts, giving the impression of an open-ended and fragmentary work. The order of the passages is not definite, the sequence of the events sung about could also be imagined differently, and the "movements of love", as Ricœur calls them, could be arranged in a variety of ways[15]. This unfinished character of the Song of Songs is reflected in the nature of the relationship portrayed: first, the fact that it is only loosely rooted in time and place; the social circumstances of the protagonists can hardly be determined. Secondly, the internal time-logic of the love and passion depicted is also subject to this openness. One cannot establish a linear progression, but rather repetitive, apparently circular movements: seeking, finding, losing again, seeking. This dynamic reflects the vicissitudes, as experienced by the two lovers, of a love-affair. The affair is not regulated, but is made up of brief meetings and partings, without a definite chronological continuity and without reliable finality – either when they are united or when they are separated. This temporariness and unpredictability is the great appeal of the "Song of Songs". It fathoms the poetry of the void, of the lacking, and of the fleeting – bringing the maelstrom between two lovers to the limit of its development. Mystical discourse about the union of God and human being, a union which is fragile and yet always inspires confidence, can be dressed up in such signs. For instance, Mechthild von Magdeburg's *Das fließende Licht der Gottheit*, Lamprecht von Regensburg's *Tochter Syon* and the *St. Trudperter Hohelied* all borrow images of injuring, wounding, illness, and death, although they may not acknowledge this explicitly[16]. They spin out these situations of hurt to illustrate

---

[14] The project ("Darstellung und Reflexion der Geschlechterrollen in deutschen Ehetraktaten von ca. 1470 bis 1580" – The Representation and Reflection of the gender-roles in German marriage treatises from circa 1470 to 1580) has provided the framework for the publication of two collections of essays edited by Rüdiger Schnell (Schnell 1997 and 1998a) and a book by Rüdiger Schnell (Schnell 1998b). The common denominator of the abundant material investigated lies in the methodological focus, the interdependence of text-type and gender-constructs, and in the inter-relation of textual and everday sign-systems. An essential factor in the discourses of gender, marriage and love is the function of a given text.

[15] On the structure of the Song of Songs see Paul Ricœur 1998, here 415 (the term itself is from Origenes); for a history of the research on this subject, see also H. Graf Reventlow, Hoheslied I (Theologische Realenzyklopädie 15, Ann Astell 1990 and Ann E. Matter 1990.

[16] For individual accounts and examples, see chapter 3.

the uneasiness in which God's beloved lives. This unrest, specific to the Song of Songs, is essentially a condition of the chronology of the relationship as expressed in this book of the Bible.

For contracting a marriage and for marriage itself, a series of chronological steps is essential. Firmly rooted in the tradition of Germanic law[17] is the contracting of marriage in the form of *Muntehe* (marriage by purchase). It consists of several public acts of law by which the so-called *Munt* – the power of protection over a woman in family law – is transferred from the *Muntwalt* (the guardian of this *Munt*, generally the girl's father) to the one who is asking for her hand (the bridegroom or his representative, the wooer of the bride). The *Muntehe* is in two parts, one concerned with power (the negotiation of the marriage contract and the fee for the transfer of the *Munt*, or *dos*) and the other with companionship (practices including, for example, the handing over of the bride, the young woman's seating herself on her bridegroom's lap, the bringing home of the bride, or the traditional wedding-feast). These two parts articulate the fundamental juridical structure of the discourse of marriage. Marriage and the contracting of a marriage take place according to a linear chronology, which refers, in the first instance, to legal appropriateness, since one step leads to another until the bridal couple are brought together and remain together. The relative positioning of the woman and the man is directed towards this final goal, which signals a legally defined clarity and finality. The sequence of the individual steps is fixed; the process itself is ritualized and is standard legal practice in each given historical and social context[18].

Accordingly, in the discourse of marriage, socio-historical conditions of the sexes – including the hierarchy between them – are more decisive than the affective or passionate forces of the individuals concerned. If one examines the semantics and etymology of terminology relating to marriage in the major Indo-European languages, Pellegrini says, it is immediately apparent that in each case the (early) medieval concepts of marriage are completely lacking in any relation to emotions, passions or instincts. Rather, marriage reveals its fundamentally legal

---

[17] An excellent overview with further bibliography is provided by Inga Persson, 37 ff.; cf. also 'Ehe', in: Lexikon des Mittelalters, III, especially 1623-1625 and 1629-1630; 'Hochzeit', in: Lexikon des Mittelalters, V; 'Ehe', 'Dos' and 'Munt' in: Handwörterbuch zur deutschen Rechtsgeschichte, I and II.

[18] For the conditions in the high to late Middle Ages, see James Brundage 1987, 176 ff.; Christopher Brooke 1991, Michael Schröter (54-81 and 81-99), Philippe Ariès / Georges Duby 2, 124 ff., Georges Duby 1984 and Jörg Wettlaufer, passim; for early Scholastic teachings on marriage, see Hans Zeimentz and Wilhelm Imkamp, 212 ff. Further bibliography in Georges Duby / Perrot 2, 214-229 and Philippe Ariès / Georges Duby 2, 633-637. – Valuable individual studies on the subject are collected in the 2 volumes Il matrimonio nella società altomedievale, Spoleto 1977.

character: "Thus, as we well know, 'matrimony' was a juridical institution, expressed in varying ways"[19]. Although this categorical statement has to be relativized with regard to the late Middle Ages, even then the legal and institutional aspects seem to be central. Marriage is the legal sealing of dominion, with effect not only within the marriage (as the power of the one sex over the other) but also with respect to third parties. In her status of wife, a bride of God gains her rightful place of honor as the lady of the house. Mechthild von Magdeburg, for example, uses this allegory to assign the human being – seated as divine wife at the side of the Lord of Heaven – a higher ontological rank than the angels[20].

This legal character involves a second temporal aspect: it suggests a longterm validity, which merges into a concept of eternity or even timelessness. The Latin term *matrimonium* – in contrast to concubinage – expresses the idea of a legitimate legal status of motherhood; Old High German *êwa/eha* and Middle High German *êwe/ê* also signify legal facts with a temporal connection: custom, law, justice, covenant or bond (the Old and New Testament in the Bible, in Middle High German also the bond between man and wife). The terms signify "eternally (New High German *ewig*) valid law", and therefore even in OHG can also be used for "eternity" (NHG *Ewigkeit*); MHG *ê* can also mean simply "an endlessly long time"[21].

Third, the contracting of marriage is clearly structured with regard to time. One can distinguish two phases: the first phase is the betrothal (*desponsatio*), through which the woman becomes the *sponsa*, the man the *sponsus*[22]. The woman receives the man's proposal and either accepts it with the consent of her family or rejects it. If she accepts, a marriage contract is drawn up which legally binds the two people to one another. The bride remains under the care of her father until she is given away to the bridegroom at the wedding. She is under obligation to preserve her virginity. This is followed by the second phase, in which the promise given is fulfilled: the contracting of the marriage (*nuptias*) and the handing over of the bride (*traditio*), followed by the wedding feast and the bringing home of the bride by the bridegroom (*deductio in domum*). According to sources from the eleventh and twelfth centuries, various factors could lead to a considerable period elapsing between the betrothal and the wedding[23]. This potential for delay in contracting secular marriage makes the consummation, the final union, something in the future. The ultimate union of the

---

[19] "Il 'matrimonio' era dunque ciò che ben sappiamo, un istituto giuridico, variamente espresso", Giovan Battista Pellegrini, 43-44. He provides an excellent compilation of marriage terminology in the various Indo-European languages.

[20] Mechthild von Magdeburg, *Das fließende Licht der Gottheit,* IV,14; trans. Tobin, 158.

[21] Giovan Battista Pellegrini, 44; Friedrich Kluge, 205, Matthias Lexer I, 715 ff.

[22] Cf. Wilhelm Imkamp's reflections on legal and theological marriage terminology (244).

[23] For possible reasons, see Philippe Ariès/George Duby 2, 127-128.

bridal couple appears bathed in the light of the future, which fits seamlessly with the eschatological connection of the consecration of virgins and has a fundamental influence on the discourse of spiritual marriage[24]. It breaks the boundaries of earthly temporality since the male beloved is no longer of this world. Marriage with Christ and the Christian concept of Salvation as a whole can only achieve fulfillment once Christ has come again at the end of the world.

For the bride of Christ this means that until her death – which in this case corresponds to the *deductio in domum* – she must be vigilant. For third parties, who have been charged with the supervision of the bride, it means a certain authority which goes with the office of giving away the bride. This accrues particularly to the priests, whose texts may have arisen from just such an understanding of themselves and their role, as was discussed in chapter 1.

The mood of the bride of God appears more subdued and melancholic if the matrimonial chronology is presented in such a way that the wedding is understood already to have taken place on earth[25]. There can be various reasons for this: for instance, a marriage contracted from the beginning of all Creation, as is the case with Mechthild von Magdeburg, or where the marriage of a bride of Christ is already lived out in the convent, as in the *St. Trudperter Hohenlied* or Abelard's letter, quoted above. The bride of God perceives herself on earth in the status of a widow since her bridegroom died on the Cross. Her death then signifies not the consummation of the wedding, but a (definitive) reunion with her divine husband. In the case of Heloise, this hope relates to her (earthly) husband Abelard, a notion affirmed by Peter the Venerable: in Heaven Heloise will again be Abelard's bride[26]. These two chronological definitions of the marital status of the woman explain the fact that in the texts – either simultaneously or alternately – there is talk of the joy of hopeful brides and the mourning of sorrowful widows.

Taking the example of the wedding treatise *De quadripartita specie nuptiarum* by Pope Innocent III (1198-1216), I would like to demonstrate how the Christian chronology of Salvation is systematized in the allegory of a marriage[27]. Innocent distinguishes the four senses of the Scripture with regard to the motif of the wedding: on the literal level, there is the (secular) wedding

---

[24] The parable of the 10 virgins waiting for the bridegroom (5 wise and 5 foolish, according to Mt 25:1-3), which has been interpreted with relation to the eschatological wedding with the divine bridegroom, is integrated into the consecration-ritual for early Christian brides of God (Réginald Grégoire, 720 ff.).

[25] Cf. chapter 3 below.

[26] Cf. Michael T. Clanchy 1997, 158ff.

[27] I orientate myself here on the careful study by Wilhelm Imkamp. A further example of a chronology expressed in matrimonial terms is Richard of St. Victor's treatise *De quattuor gradibus violentiae caritatis*.

between man and woman; on the allegorical level, the wedding between Christ and the Church; the tropological sense of the Scripture refers to the wedding between God and the soul, and the anagogical sense, to that between human and divine nature in Christ[28]. For the wedding with Christ, it is of no importance whether this is understood individually or collectively (as referring to the Church), since, in any case, it will only be realized at the end of time. Innocent's model of marriage is also a model of development for a bride of Christ who is, so to speak, preparing herself on two levels for the eschatological wedding. If in Innocent's view the Church fights on earth as the *ecclesia militans*, then all the individual brides fight with it – fortified by the expectation of the wedding feast which is prefigured in the Eucharist. Innocent's typology of marriage links individual and collective/ecclesiastical dimensions in such a way that the idea of the Church as bride must be ratified by each individual 'Christian as a bride'. Individual life on earth undergoes a massive increase in value as a result, since, fundamentally, the spotlessness of the Church must prove itself in each and every soul[29]. Therefore, what is decisive is the *traditio* of the bride at the end of time, the giving away of the bride to the divine bridegroom[30]. The Church, "militant" on earth, then becomes the *ecclesia triumphans*. Each bridal individual can partake of the heavenly wedding feast with the bride, the Church. Christian concepts of Salvation, ecclesiastical or political ideas and spiritual guidance can all be embedded equally well in the chronology of a marriage, from its inception to the bringing home of the bride. This is the view of the papal treatise in question, which reduces individual and collective plans for Salvation and their enactment in time to a single common denominator – a matrimonial common denominator. Further clear or obscure traces of this marital chronology of promise and fulfillment will be brought to light in the textual studies in chapter 3.

In summary, one can recognize that the two discourses give specific form and expression to the erotic relationship with God. Marriage lends itself as an allegory for the temporal achievement of Salvation. It transposes the history of Mankind and the Divine into nuptial images, since the two-phased contracting of marriage provides a place for the linear chronology of Christian salvation: the Church as bride, embodied by all the individual brides, is preparing herself on earth to consummate her marriage in the next world. This culmination is yet to come; it remains in the far distance, but it is a calculable distance, since sure death is an equally sure guarantee of union with the beloved – and then for all eternity. For this reason, the late medieval treatise known as *Der Schürebrand*

---

[28] Cf. Wilhelm Imkamp, 203-267
[29] See Wilhelm Imkamp, 249 ff.
[30] Further examples and discussion of this idea in Wilhelm Imkamp, 246.

reminds the bride of Christ, who is still on earth, of her marital duty of fidelity to her husband Christ, who is already in the next world[31].

The love relationship, on the other hand, molded by the Song of Songs, stands for a different sort of temporariness. It arises from impassioned seeking which can never come to a definitive end, since there can be no definitive finding. Moments of unitive happiness and desolate loneliness always occur in the here and now. One can never hope for the security of lasting possession when one knows that the two lovers have already been possessed by one another again and again. These love-scenarios provide opportunities which the texts take up with varying intentions. The treatise *Der Schürebrand* picks up on this theme in the interests of spiritual didacticism. With reference to the longing of the beloved woman who cannot find her partner, he gives the girls he addresses detailed advice about how to deal with this monastic *acedia*, which is difficult to subdue[32].

Thus, the combination of these two discourses presents opportunities, and the texts are already taking them up if they address their readers as "beloved" or "wife". The circular dynamic of love can burst the chronological banks of the strongly linear discourse of marriage. The latter loses its calculability, its mechanism for consummation, thereby gaining in poetic potential. The married couple can participate in the erotic game of hide-and-seek and put themselves at the mercy of the alternating hot and cold baths of passion. Conversely, the eternal chase of passionate seeking-and-never-truly-finding can be satisfied in an irrevocable bond of marriage. That this level of definitive unity can be realized unconditionally only in eschatological dimensions is all the better as far as Christian bridal mysticism is concerned. It is perhaps one of the most powerful reasons for its combining marriage allegories with the allegorical interpretation of the Songs of Songs.

Hierarchy

Gregory of Nyssa gives a commentary on the bride in his first sermon on the Song of Songs and remarks explicitly that her acting on her own initiative is unusual. The bride anticipates the bridegroom in desire, "in which the longing is not kindled first in the bridegroom, as is the custom among human beings, but rather the virgin anticipates the bridegroom, proclaims her desire publicly, without shame, and bids him satisfy her with a kiss"[33]. This discourse of love in

---

[31] *Der Schürebrand*, 22,15-23.
[32] *Der Schürebrand*, 14,4 ff. To the *acedia* see Alois M. Haas 1995, 93 ff.
[33] English translation based on Gregor von Nyssa, *Der versiegelte Quell. Auslegung des Hohen Liedes*, sermon 1, 34. Cf. Franz Dünzl, 61 f.

the Song of Songs obviously encompasses deviations from gender-specific expectations. Here it is the bride's taking the initiative and approaching her beloved
with desire. What does this have to do with marital and erotic hierarchy?

The Song of Songs presents a love relationship which has the appearance of
a staged duet between a man and a woman. The two sing of their intimacy or
their longing for it. Apart from the two protagonists, only a very limited cast
is mentioned. The dialogue of love takes its course in a symmetry of gestures,
the lovers take turns at making speeches. In terms neither of structure nor of
content can one discern a difference between them that could be interpreted as
a gender-specific hierarchy. The two speak of similar – and equally intense-
passion and do so in similar linguistic registers. The woman and the man each
praise the other from head to toe and back again. Initiative is not the exclusive
preserve of the man; openness and vulnerability are not restricted to the
woman. Both seem powerless in the face of the all-determining power which
forces both lovers into activity or passivity. The discourse of love engendered
by the Song of Songs thus provides a ready-made model of a relationship characterized by equality between the sexes and openness on both sides – an aspect,
moreover, which is recognized again and again as indicative of the uniqueness
of the Old Testament love-song[34].

In complete contrast to this, medieval marriage establishes gender-deter-
mined structures of dominion which preclude any talk of symmetry. Rather, it
gives concrete and juridically relevant form to the hierarchy between man and
wife demanded by society. Its anchor lies hidden in the central concept of Germanic personal law – the *Munt* (right of disposal)[35]. In the tradition of Germanic law, the woman is seen as needing a legal guardian. In this way the man
– first her father, then her husband – possesses guardianship of the woman by
his gender, a situation which is institutionalized to a certain extent. Despite all
theological striving for a measure of equality between the partners, which is
only possible by virtue of the gradual decline in the idea of the *Munt*, marriage
fixes the relation between husband and wife in terms of dominion: she is subordinate to him; he is superior to her. Just how unequal the scope of the sexes
is, is shown most clearly by the way in which the marriage is contracted – a
hierarchical asymmetry which remains little changed even by the gradual
strengthening of the bride's position[36]. The bridegroom approaches the bride's

[34] See, for example, Lucille Day 1995, 259 and 269.
[35] For further bibliography, see Inga Persson, 37-38, and the article 'Munt' in: Handwörterbuch zur deutschen Rechtsgeschichte, for early modern developmental aspects see Heide Wunder.
[36] For the asymmetry and the gradual balancing out, see Michael Schröter (54-81 and 81-99),
for the ritual of contracting a marriage, see Inga Persson, 37 ff. and Philippe Ariès/Georges
Duby 2, 130 ff.

relatives, asks for her hand and effectively for the transfer of the *Munt*, negoti-
ates the dowry, and seals the betrothal. The first step towards the wedding
(*desponsatio*) has been completed. All the subsequent steps (the giving of the
ring and the bride-gift and the signing of the documents) are also reserved for
the man, and it is he who is responsible for the realization of the second part of
the marriage (*nuptiae* and *deductio ad domum*). The husband then takes on the
duty of supervising the woman. In these procedures the woman can – if she is
lucky – *re*-act, by accepting: the proposal of marriage, the ring, the claim to
bring her home, and the wedding. Any other pattern of behavior would go
against gender-specific freedom of movement, thus against social practice.

It is precisely this ritualization, characteristic for the discourse of marriage,
which institutionalizes the hierarchical relation between man and wife. Individual steps with legal significance mark out a path which leads the woman – from
the initiation until the rupturing of a bond – both into subordination with
regard to the man and into the legal obligations of that bond. The palette of
texts which cite such facts from the realm of marriage law and apply them as
allegories of dominion as well as of the dignity of being a legitimate wife
stretches from the Old Testament to the late-medieval literature of bridal mysticism. In this way, the arranging of the dowry, the morning gift to the bride,
the marriage vow, the wife's duty of fidelity, and the concept of adultery can all
become allegorical signals for widely varying messages, as the textual studies in
chapter 3 will show. One example will suffice to show what this can mean: the
Middle English treatise *Holy Maidenhood* changes the function of the indissol-
ubility of marriage and the wife's duty of fidelity, using them as a powerful
argument against marriage in the world. From the perspective of a woman, it
depicts a hypothetical "worst case scenario", which is intended to frighten the
woman addressed off marriage: "Consider, innocent woman: once the knot of
wedlock is tied, even if he is an idiot or a cripple, whatever he may be like, you
must be faithful to him"[37]. This crass example is characteristic of a whole series
of texts which make use of precisely this hierarchy between husband and wife
as established in marriage. This does not always take the form of a polemic
against marriage in the world; sometimes the allegory of marriage can be used
to portray ascetic values such as humility, obedience or the renunciation of the
delights of the world. It is even possible to use both at once, as will be shown
in detail in the example of the late-medieval *Christus und die minnende Seele*
discussed in chapter 4.

Precisely with relation to the hierarchical position and the influence of the
wife in a marriage, medieval discussions of marriage reveal a potential for controversy from the moment the Church begins to strive to enhance the status of

---

[37] *Holy Maidenhood*, ed. Bella Millett / Jocelyn Wogan-Browne, 28,20 ff.

marriage for reasons of sacramental theology[38] and to promote the obligation of bridal consent: "It started essentially as a notable attempt to spiritualize marriage. Its various aspects are well known, from the development of the Marian cult which led to the Virgin mother becoming a symbol of the Church, that is to say, the Bride; to the development of the nuptial theme in mystical literature; and to the relentless examination of texts and their glosses, in order to establish marriage as one of the seven sacraments"[39]. The other party involved in the Church's discussions was the medieval lay nobility, who understood marriage as an instrument of feudal order, at the disposal of the extended family. Gradually, however – according to Georges Duby – a certain concept of a monogamous relationship, instituted by God and thus indissoluble, was increasingly accepted even by the secular nobility. It was based on theological/ecclesiastical values and, from about the thirteenth century, constitutes the 'Christian model of marriage' which persists and holds long into the modern period: a life-long, inseparable, monogamous bond based on the mutual affection and consent of the marriage-partners (*consensus*)[40].

From the high Middle Ages, the theological assessment of marriage opened new perspectives to the benefit of the woman. However, one can scarcely assume that her perspectives on life underwent a substantial change compared to those in the early Middle Ages. Her legal status continued to be limited, and it is only in the rarest of cases that the necessity for consent actually means the freedom to choose one's partner. The fact that brides of Christ, particularly, have to fight for their choice of partner is understood more as a literary or hagiographical topos than as an indication of a changed reality. For this reason, the real value of the freedom of choice for women advocated by the Church is judged critically[41]: "Thus the question of consent in marriage primarily concerned women. A young girl was free in one sense only: to consent to her parents' choice of a mate. Any number of arguments were cited in support of this restriction of female choice: women were sensual, weak-minded creatures; hence their purity was always in danger"[42].

---

[38] For the reverberations in the vernacular epic (in the example of the romance *Mai und Beaflor*, which is transmitted anonymously), see Ingrid Kasten 1993; more generally, Birgitta Maria Faber.

[39] Georges Duby 1994 (Fr. 1988), 17. Preparatory studies in Georges Duby 1984 (Fr. 1981). For early Scholastic marriage doctrine, see Hans Zeimentz, Wilhelm Imkamp, 212 ff. and Georges Duby / Michelle Perrot 2, 214-229 (with further bibliography) and Philippe Ariès / Georges Duby 2, 124 ff.

[40] Cf. Georges Duby / Michelle Perrot 2, 272; Angeliki E. Laiou (ed.), 227 ff. and Jörg Wettlaufer, see index.

[41] See Georges Duby / Michelle Perrot 2, primarily 274 ff.; for the frequently problematized question of female disobedience in the contracting of marriage, see Georges Duby / Michelle Perrot 2, 273 ff.

[42] Paulette L'Hermite-Leclercq in: Georges Duby / Michelle Perrot 2, 218.

In summary: with regard to the hierarchy of the partners, the discourses of love and of marriage also complement each other, although in a contradictory way regarding their value systems. Gregory's contrasting the unconventionally active bride of the Song of Songs with a "normal" bride is evidence of this. This means that, in the position of the bride of the Song of Songs, the woman can take on new and extended room for maneuver in the face of prevailing social standards. The discourse of love provides space for female activity, even aggressiveness, which is however quickly subjected to sanctions (more on this in chapter 5). What the woman may do as a bride of God is not permitted her as the wife of a human or divine husband. In the discourse of marriage, therefore, she finds comparatively narrow, legally fixed (thus reliable, but asymmetric) relations.

The interface between the discourses of love and marriage holds the basic constant of a woman's life, whether secular or monastic. We will continue to bear this in mind during the following section on the qualities of the different husbands. A woman's outlook on life appears to be defined principally in terms of a partner and, in the final instance, pretty well in terms of marriage. Basically, what awaits women is hierarchical subordination, no matter how much the theological and legal position changes to their benefit during the high Middle Ages. Nor does it change because erotic elements from the discourse of the Song of Songs go some way to balancing things out. The spectrum seems restricted to the choice between the subordination of the monastic bride of Christ to a God who is imagined as a superhuman "husband", and the subordination of the wife to her human husband.

Spiritual and Secular Marriage

> *die ehe herrschet über das meer, über alle vögel und gewild (...). Der ehe ist der segen geben, zu herrschen und regieren, zu gebieten und zu handlen, sie haben den segen alles gewalts.– Marriage reigns over the sea, over all birds and wild animals (...). – Marriage is given [God's] blessing to rule and to govern, to command and to act, to have the blessing of all power*[43].

The early Middle High German *St. Trudperter Hohelied* instructs the experienced nuns in the maternal duties they should fulfill with regard to the younger ones. To emphasize this request, their divine husband is involved. Like every secular husband, it is explained, he requires his children to be well looked after.

---

[43] Theophrast von Hohenheim, *De thoro legitimo*, ed. Kurt Goldammer, 224.

Therefore, the question of whether his bride could remain affectionate towards him must take secondary importance: *ir sult wole wizzen, daz dem manne lieber ist daz sîn brût sîniu kint souge unde stille unde habe, danne daz si in zeiner nôte küsse* (you should be well aware that it is preferable to the husband that his bride should feed and suckle his children and look after them, than that she should constantly kiss him)[44]. Already long before the twelfth century, the divine bridegroom can be compared with earthly husbands; the secular and the spiritual marriage can overlap. This close link essentially confirms Brooke's statement on the traditional rivalry between the two marriage discourses: "Thus the central fact about the legal history of marriage in the Middle Ages is that […] it was always in apparent conflict with the celibate ideal, immensely powerful and prestigious between the eleventh and the sixteenth centuries – with a long history before and after"[45]. Particularly behavior with regard to financial questions is seen by Augustine as a meaningful analogy for Christological questions[46], and this also comes to the fore in the *St. Trudperter Hohelied*, since Christ is compared to a wealthy husband. Like the latter, who gives material aid to his noble but impoverished wife, the divine bridegroom acts in the same way from pity, as he "knows well that our soul is noble, but at the same time poor". Generously, therefore, he sends her the bride-gift (*mahelschatz*), without which no marriage can be effected according the law of the world and which symbolizes "good will"[47].

But the human and the divine husband continue to be comparable long after the twelfth century. Both, for example, have an aversion to sour-faced wives, as the late-medieval treatise *Der Schürebrand* relentlessly tries to impress on its two young readers. A bride of God must be forbearing and must fight against melancholy and frustration because it would ill befit the "merciful, noble, almighty King of Heaven" that he should have *ein swermuotig ungelossen muleht bluntzenkar und einen unwurschen zerblegeten bloterkopf […] zuo einer gemaheln und efrouwen in sime ewigen himelschen künigriche* (a heavy-hearted, rebellious and complaining, impatient crock, or a surly, truculent, puffed-up fat-head as

---

[44] *St. Trudperter Hohelied*, 124,18-21. Active love of one's neighbor should be preferred to perfect prayer, analogous to Bernard of Clairvaux's 9th sermon on the Song of Songs (ed. Winkler, VII,9,17-19).

[45] Christopher Brooke 1989, 21-22.

[46] Augustine transposes all the details of the husband's buying of the bride to the incarnate Christ, who, on the Cross, gives his blood for his bride the Church (in his 13th homily on St. John's Gospel, see Martin Herz, 215 ff.). On the topos of the rich husband cf. also Nicole Bériou/David L. D'Avray, 116 ff.

[47] *St. Trudperter Hohelied*, 12,18-24. On the role of will in the *unio mystica*, see Hildegard E. Keller 1993, 326 ff. The treatise *Der Schürebrand* uses the motif of the morning gift in a very similar way (23,5 ff.).

his bride and wife in his heavenly kingdom)[48]. Obviously it was hoped that there was a pedagogical effect to be gained from encouraging the religious women to adapt and subordinate themselves to the predilections of both types of husbands. Before *Der Schürebrand*, Heinrich Seuse had already written a letter urging a spiritual daughter to make herself fit for the court of the King of Heaven: *Gedenk, daz er [Christus] dich im hat gevordret ze einer gemahel, und dar umbe so huet, daz du ût werdest ein havendirnne!* (Remember that he [Christ] has requested you as his bride and wife; therefore, take care that you do not become a kitchen-maid)[49].

In early Christianity, marriage with Christ is accorded the highest rank. It is the fulfillment of all that is merely prefigured by marriage among human beings. Consequently, an erotic union with Christ is unimpeachably the best marriage[50]. It can be argued that this continued long into the Middle Ages. Simultaneously, however, the same respect for marriage with Christ prompts the two relationship-discourses to move subtly closer together. This is the case in the two examples mentioned above, where the subtle and seemingly insignificant parallels between the husbands could almost cause one to forget that here a male human being is being compared with a God who is imagined as male. But there is also a *rapprochement* when Hugh of St. Victor transfers the ideal status of marriage with Christ to the marriage between man and woman. It is only at first sight that this spiritualization of worldly marriage appears paradoxical. Hugh is intent on raising the status of marriage by exposing its sacramental core. This consists precisely in the spiritual union between God and the soul, which places the spiritual and secular discourse on an identical footing.

Although the higher value of the union with the divine bridegroom remains undisputed[51], the ontological difference between the two forms of marriage fades – so much so, that it seems debatable whether the basic difference between the two relationship-discourses is maintained. The extent to which attempting to emphasize the difference actually moves the secular and the spiritual level

---

[48] *Der Schürebrand*, 17,15-19. The expression *bluntzenkar* is a pejorative term for a woman (literally: an ungainly, bulbous vessel), the expression *bloterkopf* is also disparaging (literally: a round, full face) (Philipp Strauch, 67). Kurt Ruh (²VL 8 [1992], 880) views *Der Schürebrand* as above all a monument in linguistic history, whose mystical value is slight. With amazement he remarks, having listed the above expressions: "Es ist eigentümlich festzustellen, daß ein Autor mit so vielen Audrucksmöglichkeiten nicht mehr zu sagen hat" (it is curious to note that an author with such power of expression does not have more to say).

[49] Heinrich Seuse: *Briefbüchlein*, 4th letter, ed. Bihlmeyer, 372, 23-45.

[50] For this eschatological concept, see John Bugge, 67-79 and the comprehensive study by Peter Brown 1988.

[51] Cf. Hans Zeimentz; John Bugge, 84-90, and Nicole Bériou/David L. D'Avray.

closer together is revealed initially by a topos of female biography, particularly of hagiography. It is the situation where a young woman who has rejected an earthly husband and chosen the divine bridegroom must then defend this decision in the face of considerable social pressure, with a high degree of rhetoric. When she argues in favor of a life as a virgin bride of God, she distinguishes it sharply from a life as the bride of a man, since her choice of marriage is *a priori* worth more. Another important topos, which is more common in didactic writings for women, is the drawing up of a balance sheet between the two relationship-discourses, where a male advisor takes stock for a woman; it goes without saying that it comes out in favor of being a bride of God. It is no accident that crucial factors and questions in a woman's life are adduced in the discussion and evaluation of worldly and spiritual marriage. It is even inevitable, if the female role of the bride of Christ is reserved for women and if they are determining the course of their lives by choosing one or other of these husbands, God or man. The overlap of the religious and the earthly sphere as well as of spirituality and relationships between the sexes goes hand in hand with the sexualization of the role of the bride of God.

The following three sections examine the strategies of argumentation of religious writings in favor of the spiritual or worldly marriage option. Most of them are based on the repertoire of characters in the two marriage-discourses, for this lends itself best for paralleling the realities of each marriage and devaluing the one in favor of the other. For one constellation embodies all that is desirable and sacred; the other represents all that is wretched, laborious, and profane. Thus, the original incentive for drawing up accounts between excellent and execrable married couples may be a rhetorical question: who ennobles the marriages, if not the brides and bridegrooms involved?

Bridegrooms Compared

> *Quibus igitur hominem eligere licet deum non licet?*
> *– If they may choose a man, why not let them choose*
> *God?*[52]

The parallels between husbands examined thus far suggest that the texts tend to refrain from making explicit references to an ontological difference between the bridegrooms. Thus, they effectively "hush up" the fact that there is essentially a gaping abyss separating a human and a divine bridegroom. The gap, however, can be expressed; one apt linguistic form is the superlative. It is found in two

---

[52] The words spoken by Ambrose's rebellious bride of Christ (*De Virginibus*, I,58, vol. 14/I, 156).

variants: one positive and applied to the divine bridegroom[53] and the other negative and fitting for the human husband.

First, the former variant: mystical instruction for brides of God praises the bridegroom Christ not only as Redeemer and God but also as the ideal husband. No matter whether it is a question of "wealth in the world, dominion and power or divine nobility", as Ambrose puts it[54], the conclusions are the same: no earthly man can hold a candle to the divine bridegroom. The bridal hymn in the *St. Trudperter Hohenlied* eulogizes all the attributes of the Almighty, who will look after his brides according to all the rules of the art of love – after their life on earth, one notes:

> *si enpfâhet nâch dem ellende aller manne rîcheste.*
> *dâ herberget si aller manne kreftegeste.*
> *dâ troestet sie aller manne gewaltegeste.*
> *dâ minnet si aller manne schoeneste.*
> *dâ wonet si iemer mêre mit aller manne besteme.*

After this [earthly] misery she will receive the richest of husbands.
Then she will shelter the most powerful of husbands.
Then she will comfort the mightiest of husbands.
Then she will love the most handsome of husbands.
Then she will live for evermore with the best of husbands[55].

Here, as in many texts, the superior value of spiritual marriage is revealed particularly in the nature of the husband. The sacral status of the bridegroom is referred to with aristocratic vocabulary. He is the King of Heaven, and Heaven is his palace. Only the young would-be bride of God in Hartmann von Aue's work *Der arme Heinrich* speaks of Christ as a "freeborn farmer" who is asking for her hand. She is probably fitting her choice of words to her situation – what would her parents, who are farmers themselves, think if she were to say that the King of Heaven wanted to marry her?[56]

The protagonist in Priester Wernher's work *Driu liet von der maget* (Three Songs of the Virgin) marks the differences between the two husbands very discreetly. When she comes of marriageable age, Mary, under great social pressure, expresses her fears with regard to a human husband. Fiercely – but unsuccessfully, as it transpires – she opposes marriage in the world. In this she calls attention to the difficulties which a bond with a husband would entail:

---

[53] The same conclusion in French sermons of the thirteenth century on the marriage between the human soul and Christ (cf. Nicole Bériou/David L. D'Avray).
[54] Ambrose, *De virginibus*, I, 65, Vol. 14/I; trans. Shiel 1963, 42.
[55] *St. Trudperter Hohelied*, 106,25-29. Similar sentiments in 8,20-28.
[56] Hartmann von Aue, *Der arme Heinrich*, 775-776.

sie sprah, das sie nien wolte
iemer man geruren.
das werltliche ungefure
duhte sie so chumberriche
daz sie gerne friliche
lebet ane mannes gebende
untze an des libes ende.
got einen hæte sie erwelt,
dem si lip mit sele selt,
daz si wære sin diu und sin brût,
er bediu ir herre und ir trût.

She said that she never wanted to touch a man. Earthly hardship seemed to her so wretched that she would rather remain free and without a bond to any man until the end of her life. She had chosen only God, to whom she had given herself body and soul, so that she might be his maid and his bride, and he her lord and her bridegroom[57].

The nameless girl in *Der arme Heinrich* by Hartmann von Aue constructs a detailed comparison between types of marriage, a comparison important for the story as well as for the relevance of genre[58]. She argues against worldly marriage in justifying to her parents her decision to allow herself to be killed to cure Heinrich's leprosy (so here too the protagonist is under social pressure to justify her choice of marriage). Marriage with Christ, the protagonist believes, would not in many ways distance her from the pleasant side of life, would spare her from things *diu den wîben wirret und sî an vreuden irret* (that distress women and restrict their joy)[59]. She comes to this decision after a comparison between the two husbands and what they have to offer. Her comparison does not differ remarkably from those in monastic and generally pastoral texts; the literary genre seems to be irrelevant in the tradition of this topos of the ideal husband[60]. As the girl imagines it, the divine bridegroom puts all human men – with their conventional, earthly views of marriage – in the shade since Heaven beckons with a truly divine marriage prospect. No earthly happiness could compare with fulfillment at Christ's "court", the girl knows, because it is a place with optimal living conditions, immune to the blows of fate:

[57] Quoted from manuscript D, 1482-1492 (for further information about the work, see chapter 3).

[58] Hartmann von Aue, *Der arme Heinrich*, 767 ff.

[59] Hartmann von Aue, *Der arme Heinrich*, 771-772.

[60] For a very similar result (for French sermons and courtly epic) see Nicole Bériou / David L. D'Avray.

im gât sîn phluoc harte wol,
sîn hof ist alles râtes vol,
da enstirbet ros noch daz rint,
da enmüent diu weinenden kint,
da enist ze heiz noch ze kalt,
da enwirt von jâren nieman alt
(der alte wirt junger),
dâ enist vrost noch hunger,
da enist deheiner slahte leit,
da ist ganziu vreude âne arbeit.
ze dem [Christus] will ich mich ziehen
und selhen bû vliehen,
den der schûr und der hagel sleht
und der wâc abe tweht,
mit dem man ringet und ie ranc.
swaz man daz jâr alsô lanc
dar ûf garbeiten mac,
daz verliuset schiere ein halber tac.
den bû den wil ich lâzen:
er sî von mir verwâzen.

His plough goes very well, his court is full of all provisions. There, neither horses nor cattle die, there, crying children do not bother one, it is neither too hot nor too cold, nobody grows old (on the contrary, the old become young), there is neither frost nor hunger, and no suffering of any kind. There, complete joy reigns without toil. I want to take myself to this farmer, and avoid the sort of farm that is battered by cloudbursts and hail, where floods wash away all that one struggles to achieve and has ever achieved. Whatever one can work up here in a whole year can be lost in half a day. I do not want that sort of farm; a curse be on it from me![61].

The outlook for success speaks clearly in Christ's favor, since no earthly man will have anything adequate to hold up in exchange. The girl sensibly chooses the better part. Perhaps we may wonder – with the girl's parents – that this sort of comparison between marriages and husbands can appear plausible, and make narrative sense. It is even more amazing that this transparent calculation is actually thought to legitimate the sacrifice of a girl, her being put to death for the sake of healing a leper.

I would like to look briefly at what one should understand by the second variant of possible husbands, the epitome of the evils of marriage. A more detailed

---

[61] Hartmann von Aue, *Der arme Heinrich*, 779-798.

example from the late Middle Ages will be presented in its relevant context in chapter 4. In the anonymous Middle English treatise *Holy Maidenhood* from the first half of the twelfth century that is aimed at the instruction of female religious, a woman is presented with an apparently realistic portrait of a hypothetical husband. This husband represents a considerable proportion of all the tribulations of a worldly marriage since the woman has been bought by him and must subordinate herself to him. When he is out of the house, she fears for her breadwinner and her livelihood; when he is at home, he rages, shouts, and crashes about, abusing and beating his wife "like his bought slave and his born serf". Then the text deviously poses the rhetorical question: "What will your relations in bed be like?" What then follows stigmatizes the hypothetical husband completely and degrades him to an instinct-driven animal. The rhetorically skillful text only fleetingly twitches the veil from this superlative beast, before solicitously lowering it again over the worst part of all – sexual acts:

> She must often submit to his will much against her own, in great distress; and
> especially in bed she must put up with all indecencies and his improper games,
> however obscenely devised, whether she wants to or not. May Christ protect every
> maiden from asking or wanting to know what they are (...)[62].

At the point of intersection between worldly and spiritual marriage, there is obviously a central question: what awaits a woman in one or other of these marriages, with one or other of these husbands? There appear to be two possible answers from the woman's point of view: either the divine bridegroom is described as so unattainably illustrious that he casts the darkest of shadows on human husbands or a hypothetical earthly husband is portrayed in such a repulsive and terrifying way that the divine bridegroom stands out as the only – and glorious – alternative for every woman of any sense at all to choose. That the argument can be weighted more strongly towards the well-being of the woman – though without her escaping in any way from the regulatory power of the (human or divine) husband –, is shown by the following sub-section.

Elevated and Degraded Brides

Nubit et plorit. – She weds to weep[63].

Nearly all the texts investigated here (for the exceptions, see the section on the sacrificial status of the bride), with a greater or lesser extent of polemicism and commitment, rank the virgin's life of the bride of Christ above worldly mar-

---

[62] *Holy Maidenhood*, ed. Bella Millett / Jocelyn Wogan-Browne, 28,11 ff.

[63] This is Ambrose's view of the woman in the world (*De Virginibus*, I,25 vol. 14/I; trans. Shiel 1963, 27).

riage. This message is crystal-clear in Abelard's letters to Heloise, commented on at the beginning of this chapter; and it is also the central thesis in English devotional literature for women composed in the twelfth and thirteenth centuries as well as in comparable writings from continental Europe[64]. There it even plays a role in (pro-marriage!) Protestant literature for the education of girls in the sixteenth century[65]. In many of these examples it is remarkable that the question of the marriage options is judged from the perspective of the woman (which is generally more unusual), often by men who use arguments which were formerly used in favor of their own sex: "It is interesting that arguments once employed as negative evidence over the question *'utrum vir sapiens uxorem ducat'* appear in the twelfth-century *Holy Maidenhood* in support of the liberated woman"[66]. Discussing the tribulations of marriage (*molestiae nuptiarum*) – elsewhere classically a mental exercise among men – is obviously one of the most pressing concerns of most male authors engaged in the instruction of women[67].

The purported greater value of marriage with Christ is defended with arguments already used in patristic writings, which undergo a high-medieval renaissance. Two strategies of argumentation are central in this: one arises from an economy of surrender (primarily of virginity), and the other revolves around the enslaving of the woman versus the preservation of her freedom. Usually the two themes are interwoven; therefore, I will examine them in their interdependence.

Ambrose's first writing on virginity, *De virginibus* (composed around 377, probably his first work)[68], treats the two discourses of marriage systematically and weighs them against one another. His verdict is unequivocal: being a bride of God promises the virgin freedom (*sola virginitas libertatem dare*[69]) and dignified self-determination (*feminei principatus*[70]); marriage, on the other hand, means *miserabilis condicio* and slavery, where the wife is not even free to choose

---

[64] See John Bugge, 80 ff.; Barbara Newman 1995, 31 ff.

[65] The praise of virginity derived from early Christian *virgines*-literature is an influence, for example, on Lukas Martini's *Der Christlichen Jungfrawen Ehrenkräntzlein* (Prague, 1580, 3rd chapter). The work is an allegorical educational text – one of the first to be aimed directly at girls. The target readers are here not future nuns, but future married women. Cf. Susanne Barth, 258 ff.

[66] John Bugge, 88.

[67] Examples of male-centered discussion of the *molestiae nuptiarum* are found in Rüdiger Schnell 1982, 169 ff., and in Rudolf Weigand in Rüdiger Schnell 1997; Barbara Newman 1995, 32 (with bibliography), who discusses anti-marriage propaganda written from a female standpoint, giving numerous examples, and R. Howard Bloch, 13 ff.; a few notes on patristic views in Ambrosius, vol. 14/I, 29.

[68] Ambrosius, vol. 14/I 62 ff. – Peter Brown (1988, 341 ff.) gives an exciting account of Ambrose's concepts of virginity within the context of the Latin church.

[69] op.cit., 55.

[70] op.cit., 55.

her master, as might be permitted to an actual slave. And to top it all, a wife has to worry about her market value[71]. Accordingly, the variant chosen by the bride of Christ is clearly the more attractive one, and this becomes a young woman's most powerful argument in the battle for her self-sanctification and self-sacrifice (see below).

The Middle English treatise seems to start from a very similar central question which mingles issues of economics and freedom. It polemicizes against marriage in unusual detail, with a significant strategy of argumentation. In the text, it is a priest who produces the evidence against the supposition of a young woman that there is much joy and happiness to be experienced in worldly marriage and family life. A polemic unfolds, in which the woman is addressed alternately as a potential bride of Christ or as a wife; she is confronted alternately with an attractive or abhorrent hypothetical reality. The polemic against worldly marriage takes up the economic question. It is made clear that virginity has a high value, is actually priceless. Whoever gives it up in exchange for her keep or even wealth from a husband is really "selling herself short" and is cast down severely from the heights of virginity to the depths of subordination and servility to a husband: "But now, first of all, whatever advantage or happiness comes of it, it is too dearly bought when you sell yourself for it, and give up your naked body to be so scandalously abused and treated so shamefully, with such an irrecoverable loss as the honor of virginity, and its reward too, for worldly gain"[72]. Then there is enslavement, turning the woman into the "bought slave" and "born serf" of her husband. The lovingly enumerated hardships of everyday life are intended to illustrate this captivity of the woman: "(…) all the more they show what slavery wives are in, who must endure such things, and what liberty virgins have, who are free from them all"[73].

Marriage with Christ gains in value when worldly marriage is polemically devalued; the central argument in this is the marital degradation of the wife, and in the anonymous treatise this means above all her sexual humiliation, which is described peculiarly vividly. It culminates in the assertion that the husband "treats you disgracefully as a lecher does his whore"[74]. Conversely, in many texts the bride of God undergoes a process of elevation, the extent of which sounds Utopian in the social context of the high Middle Ages[75]. For spiritual

---

[71] E.g. *De virginibus*, op.cit., 55 ff.; 129 ff.; 154 ff. For the late-classical philosophical ideals in the background, see 53 ff.

[72] *Holy Maidenhood*, ed. Bella Millett / Jocelyn Wogan-Browne, 24,3 ff. – John Bugge (88) refers in this context to the writings of Jerome (letters and *Adversus Jovinianum*), but also to classical satire by Theophrastus and Juvenal.

[73] *Holy Maidenhood*, ed. Bella Millett / Jocelyn Wogan-Browne, 34,3 ff.

[74] *Holy Maidenhood*, ed. Bella Millett / Jocelyn Wogan-Browne, 28, 5.

[75] Cf. Rüdiger Schnell 1994, Philippe Ariès / Georges Duby 2, 117 ff.

marriage binds partners whose inequality could not be greater. These essential differences are expressed in terms of social categories, where status and material wealth are decisive, for example, in the treatise where "the very poorest woman who chooses him as a husband is altogether pleasing to him" and therefore attains wealth[76]. In the context of the elevation of the bride of Christ, the repertoire of aristocratic terminology is particularly significant. This is already the case with Ambrose, who promises that as the bride of the *rex aeternus*, the bride of Christ reigns *quasi regina*[77]. The aristocratic terminology is a signal of class differences which are sovereignly disregarded when the bride of God enters into an alliance with a partner who is unattainably above her in ontological terms. The girl in Hartmann von Aue's *Der arme Heinrich* seems to be aware of this. Notwithstanding his social status, she is confident that she will be ennobled by the love of the divine bridegroom, since Christ loves her as a queen:

(...) und ouch zuo mir armen hât
alsô grôze minne
als zeiner küniginne

[...] and loves me too, poor girl that I am, like a queen[78].

Whether, and by what bridegroom, a woman can be ennobled is a fundamental motif in Hartmann's work. Here Heinrich orders that the farmer's daughter, with whom he sets off to Salerno, be dressed in precious materials. This is noted as unusual: for, after all, ermine, velvet, and sable are the preserve of rulers.

That the divine bridegroom's love of the bride can transcend social realities is also marked using aristocratic vocabulary by Mechthild of Magdeburg. Thus she has the soul make a *hovereise* (court visit) to God and speak of the relationship (unthinkable in real life) between the *hoher fürst* (exalted Sovereign) and the *kleine dirne* (little waif)[79]. This same soul – *a priori* a nuptial creature – has the noble title *aller creaturen gôttinne* (the goddess of all creatures) bestowed on her by the divine bridegroom[80].

A clearly differentiated concept of nobility is formulated in letters by Hildegard von Bingen, *magistra sponsarum Christi*, as she is called by Tenxwind of Andernach[81]. In them, she links social, ecclesiastical and ontological categories.

---

[76] *Holy Maidenhood*, ed. Bella Millett / Jocelyn Wogan-Browne, 35,35 ff.
[77] Ambrose, *De virginibus*, I, 37 vol. 14/I; trans. Shiel 1963, 32.
[78] Hartmann von Aue, *Der arme Heinrich*, 810-812.
[79] Mechthild von Magdeburg, *Das fließende Licht der Gottheit*, I,4,6-7; trans. Tobin, 43.
[80] Mechthild von Magdeburg, *Das fließende Licht der Gottheit*, III,9,51; trans. Tobin, 115.
[81] Hildegard von Bingen, *Epistolarium*, 52, 1; trans. Baird / Ehrman 1994, 127. Cf. Elisabeth Gössmann 1995.

When *magistra* Tenxwind critically asks why Hildegard only admits noble and well-respected women into her monastery, she has to give an account of her social concept of nobility. She defends differences of estate both on earth and in the convent as divine ordering. Just as goats, sheep and cattle should not be housed in the one stall, people from different social backgrounds should not live together in the convent[82]. Hildegard insists on the retention of boundaries, which she would like to see recognized as signals of nobility, whether motivated by noble birth, by consecration as a bride of Christ or, in the twelfth century, by both[83]. She militates against religious or social egalitarianism.

Hildegard's concept of the nobility of ecclesiastical status is expressed very clearly in a letter addressed to the Benedictine nuns of Zwiefalten. This is one of the very few examples of a woman adopting a stance towards the bride of Christ in which the two marriage discourses are related to one another and in which the early Christian ideal of virginity shimmers through, if rather less polemically than in the English treatise. Hildegard unsettles the women, who are asking for spiritual guidance, by reminding them of the high rank of virgins consecrated to God. She opens by sketching the scenario of a "noble man" who marries a very beautiful bride who does not in the least want to be a *concubina* or a *saltatrix in habitu meretricio* (dancer who behaves like a prostitute)[84]. The image refers to the bride of Christ and the nobility she earns by renouncing worldly marriage with a "flesh-and-blood" or "earthly" husband. That the honor of receiving a king as husband must be earned by special loyalty, can be illuminated in the context of the sacrificial status of the bride:

> *Cum feminea forma subtrahit se a iunctura mariti propter Deum, nolens uiro copulari, o quam magna nobilitas in illa tunc est, quia ipsam decet desponsatio superni Regis, quoniam carnalem uirum recusauit. Et sic debet amplecti Deum et adherere Domino suo, quia terrenum uirum non habet.*

If a woman refrains from a marital bond with a husband because of God, not wishing to marry a man: oh how great is her nobility! Marriage with the highest king is fitting for her, since she has rejected a flesh-and-blood husband. And therefore she will remain in the embrace of God, her lord, as she has no earthly husband[85].

In the letter to Tenxwind of Andernach, Hildegard explains that the bride of God should be allowed to claim ontological nobility. She is, after all, a virgin, which means here that she is self-determining (*in propria uoluntate sua*). In

---

[82] Hildegard von Bingen, *Epistolarium*, 52r, 40 ff.; trans. Baird / Ehrman 1994, 129.
[83] See Barbara Newman 1995, 37.
[84] Hildegard von Bingen, *Epistolarium*, 250r, 7 ff.
[85] Hildegard von Bingen, *Epistolarium*, 250r, 12-16.

contrast to the virgin, the woman of the world is bound by regulations (*in pre-cepto*)[86] – a contrast between the brides which is represented in very similar terms by Mechthild von Magdeburg: *Ja, si sŏllent ir hŏbet nit mit schemede bedeken als die irdenschen brúte pflegent* (Indeed, they shall not cover their heads in shame, as is the custom for earthly brides)[87]. Consequently, Hildegard sees the quality of virginity as a distinction which the bride of God may wear as a sign of her marriage with Christ. To Abbess Tenxwind, Hildegard puts forward the argument that this virginal integrity is, to a certain extent, paradisiacal:

> (...) *sed ipsa stat in simplicitate et in integritate pulchri paradisi, qui numquam aridus apparebit, sed semper permanet in plena uiriditate floris uirge.*
> "[...]for she [the virgin] stands in the unsullied purity of paradise, lovely and unwithering, and she always remains in the full vitality of the budding rod"[88].

Victima and Sacrificium: The Sacrificial Status of the Bride from a Theological Perspective

The way in which the texts weigh up servitude and liberation as well as degradation and exaltation in the two marriage discourses comes out with a clear balance in favor of the woman and of spiritual marriage. Nevertheless, deciding in its favor is charged with a certain ambivalence. The ennoblement of the bride of Christ is certainly dialectical since it begins with a very essential sacrifice. Thus many texts speak of the risk constituted by the self-sanctification of the bride of Christ. Even the Ambrosian writings on virginity speak of the price of ennoblement, which the woman must be prepared to pay: ascetic self-sacrifice.

After Constantine's official recognition of Christianity as the state religion, virginity, to which the bride of God dedicates herself, is invested with a quality of martyrdom[89]. In his treatise *De virginibus*, Ambrose makes the sacrificial status of the sexually unsullied bride of Christ very clear. He concretizes his concept of the victim in an account of a young woman who has made up her mind to be a bride of God. In contrast to a man, who does not have to use matrimonial arguments to hold firm to his vocation to the religious life[90], this young

---

[86] Hildegard von Bingen, *Epistolarium*, 52r, 24 ff., trans. Baird / Ehrman 1994, 129.

[87] Mechthild von Magdeburg, *Das fließende Licht der Gottheit*, V, 24, 23-24; trans. Tobin, 204.

[88] Hildegard von Bingen, *Epistolarium*, 52r, 24-26; trans. Baird / Ehrman 1994, 129.

[89] For this patristic idea, particularly in Ambrose, vol. 14/I, 51-52. For the connection between asceticism and martyrdom, cf. Peter Brown 1988.

[90] One example from the seventh century is cited by Réginald Grégoire, 719 ff.: Cirano has to oppose a planned marriage and declares that he wishes to remain *devotus in Domino*.

woman has to fight for her decision to live as a bride of Christ. She carries through her decision in the face of parental or (in the case of the young Mary in the work by Priester Wernher[91]) social resistance by vowing herself to the one husband and rejecting the other. Like other young women, Ambrose's star witness finds effective ways to remedy the situation, one of which is to flee from her parental home and take refuge in a church[92]. In other, more entrenched cases, only an apparent sex-change can do the trick. A secondary gender-marker, such as a beard, can save the young bride of God from marriage and the loss of her virginity[93]. The young woman in Ambrose's account flees to the altar to force the issue of consecration. Her spectacularly brave action is reminiscent of the radical measures and imperturbability of the martyrs. Of course, the bishop of Milan does not take exception to this instance of female disobedience, commenting on it instead with understanding, speaking *pro domo*: *(...) quo enim melius uirgo, quam ubi sacrificium uirginitatis offertur?* ("What better place than where virginity is offered in sacrifice?")[94] – Ambrose's disobedient heroine defies the world. She sounds sharp notes which are prototypical and which seem to echo in the behavior of the female protagonist in *Der arme Heinrich* (see below). Aggressive action by daughters with regard to their parents or relatives is not only unusual, but is often given unusual prominence – in the works of Ambrose and in the medieval texts examined. The probable reason for this is that the bride of God can only demonstrate her sacrificial courage if she has to defend her decision with determined resistance. Despite her obvious will for self-determination, it is striking that her parents can be convinced only by a comparison between the bridegrooms (*Sponsum offertis? meliorem repperi*). Does choosing the best entitle you to the last word?[95]

> *Ne is quidem finis audaciae. Stabat ad aram dei pudoris hostia, uictima casti-*
> *tatis, nunc capiti dexteram sacerdotis inponens, predem poscens, nunc iustae*
> *impatiens morae ac summum altari subiecta uerticem: (...) 'Quid agitis uos,*
> *propinqui? Quid exquirendis adhuc nuptiis sollicitatis animum? Iamdudum*
> *prouisas habeo. Sponsum offertis? meliorem repperi. Quaslibet exaggerate diuitias,*
> *iactate nobilitatem, potentiam praedicate: habeo eum diuitias, iactate nobili-*
> *tatem, potentiam praedicate: habeo eum cui nemo se comparet, diuitem mundo,*
> *potentem imperio, nobilem caelo. Si talem habetis, non refuto optionem; si non*
> *repperitis, non prouidetis mihi, parentes, sed inuidetis.'*

---

[91] This work will be discussed in detail in chapter 3.

[92] Réginald Grégoire, 716 ff.

[93] Vilgefortis' virginity was preserved by this trick of nature; see Réginald Grégoire, 772 ff. and Regine Schweizer.

[94] Ambrose: *De virginibus*, I, 65 vol.14/I; trans. Shiel 1963, 41.

[95] Ambrose devotes a lot of space to the discussion between parents and daughter (e.g. *De virginibus*, I, 62-66).

That was not the end of her bravery. Standing before the altar of God, a pure offering, a chaste victim, she even caught the priest's right hand and placed it on her head, demanding of him to say the appropriate prayer. Not tolerating a moment's delay, she bowed her head below the altar and said: [...] My parents and friends, you may stop worrying yourselves about arranging a marriage for me; now my arrangements are over and done with. Perhaps you even have a husband lined up for me. Well, I have found a better one. You may rave about the riches of your choice, boast of his lineage and possessions, but mine is beyond all such comparisons; he has the riches of the universe, he has power over everything, he has heaven for nobility. If you have picked me one equal to him I shall not refuse your choice. If you have not, you are not providing for my good but only depriving me of it[96].

The early-Christian idea of the sacrifice of the bride of God, which replaces martyrdom with virginity and asceticism, is closely connected with the *virgines consecratae*. The sacrifice of their own life and virginity became a substitute for a martyr's death, developing into the wedding with the divine bridegroom[97]. This step in the development of the motif leads it to its first substantial narrowing to the female sex and turns the idea of the sacrifice into an important sub-text for the erotic relationship with God in the Middle Ages. The idea of sacrifice shines through again and again in many and varied ways: the motif of the bride of God as employed in the narrative of *Der arme Heinrich*, for instance, is very different from that in the correspondence between abbesses in which Hildegard of Bingen sets out the nuptial self-understanding of those in the convent.

Brides of Christ, Hildegard replies to Tenxwind of Andernach's question, are *coniuncte in Spiritu Sancto sanctimonie et in aurora uirginitatis. Vnde decet illas peruenire ad summum sacerdotum sicut holocaustum Deo dedicatum* (married with holiness in the Holy Spirit and in the bright dawn of virginity, and so it is proper that they come before the great High Priest as an oblation presented to God)[98]. The sacrifice of one's own virginity and self-sanctification (*sacri-ficium*) are extremely close in more than just etymology. Anyone who wants to be called a bride of Christ must bring an offering; otherwise, the apparent willingness for sacrifice will be revealed as personal ambition and falsehood and will be severely revenged. Making conscious use of topographical images, Hildegard states that if one climbs too high, one will also fall from a great height. Accordingly, the sanctity achieved by the bride of Christ constitutes a constant reminder of her

---

[96] Ambrose, *De virginibus*, I, 65 vol.14/I; trans. Shiel 1963, 41-42.
[97] Cf. Alfred C. Rush, 87 ff.
[98] Hildegard von Bingen, *Epistolarium*, 52r, 31 ff.

obligation to a particular loyalty. The nuns of Zwiefalten who ask for Hilde-gard's advice receive instructions by letter that a bride of Christ should live in seclusion: *in occulto (...) uelut columba in cauerna* (hidden away like a dove in a fissure)[99]. In that way, she can concentrate on her high-ranking bridegroom instead of fleetingly embracing an earthly husband who is not even endowed with human nobility but is simply a *rusticus*.

> *Nam ipsa debet sic permanere ut Eua fuit antequam eam Deus Ade representaret, cum illa tunc non ad Adam, sed ad Deum aspexit. Sic mulier faciat que propter amorem Dei carnalem uirum recusat: ad Deum aspiciat et non ad alium uirum quem prius habere nolebat. (...) Et ideo femina que non uult ire in thalamum carnalis uiri propter dilectionem Dei, debet in spiritali uita mecum esse, qui sum sine initio et fine, nec sit in furtiuis amplexibus rusticum occulte amans. Sed si hec fecerit, non est mecum, quia uipereos mores habet. Quapropter mulier que ita feruet quod non potest seculum relinquere, non uadat in periculum nec altum montem ascendat, ne postea in lacum mergatur, cum mihi prius desponsata fuit et deinde ad carnales amplexus iuit.*

She [the bride of God] should remain as Eve was before God presented her to Adam. Then she did not look to Adam, but to God. This is what a woman should do who rejects an earthly husband because of her love for God. She should look to God, not to another man whom she did not want before. [...] Thus, the woman who does not wish to enter into the chambers of an earthly man because of her love for God should be with me in the spir-itual life, with me who am without beginning or end. She should not give herself over to furtive embraces in secretly loving a common man. If she does do that, she is no longer with me. She is behaving like a viper. A woman who burns so much that she cannot leave the world, should not enter into danger or climb a high mountain, lest she might thereafter be submerged in the depths because she had been married to me and had then given herself over to carnal embraces[100].

Precisely the case of the heartfelt warning to the nuns of Zwiefalten shows what a delicate matter the bride of God's duty of loyalty is when taken seriously. Every bride of God must take account of the nobility of her divine bridegroom – in consideration of his social status, which Hildegard finds imperative, even among human beings. If one is not capable of differentiating, whether with regard to social status or nuptial partners, one does not furnish the *sacrificium* of a bride of God and therefore will not be a *victima castitatis*, but merely a victim

---

[99] Hildegard von Bingen, *Epistolarium*, 250r, 66 ff. This is characteristic also for her career as a visionary. Cf. Christel Meier 1998 and Elisabeth Gössmann.

[100] Hildegard von Bingen, *Epistolarium*, 250r, 16-21 and 31-38 respectively.

of self-pride at best. For this reason, the bride ennobled by her divine bridegroom will experience the opposite of her ascent if she is disloyal to her bridegroom, Hildegard asserts. She will become a *concubina* or a *meretrix* (prostitute),
who is not discerning in bestowing the honors due to a king:

> *Meretrix omnia quasi similia et equalia habet, uidelicet principem ut rusticum.*
> *Qui sic facit, inhonorat me, sapientiam similem faciens ignorantie et pietatem*
> *uanitati ac ceteras uirtutes similes cupro.*

The whore treats all as if they were equal and alike, be they princes or com-
moners. Whoever acts in this way dishonors me. He makes wisdom the
same as foolishness and piety the same as vanity and all other virtues the
same as copper[101].

Concubina, meretrix and *viperei mores* are expressions of a juridically and
morally determined scale of values which differentiates relationships with the
divine bridegroom, or rather, attempts to be worthy of him. This sort of inventory of terms is found in monastic typologies of the bride such as that in the *St.
Trudperter Hohenlied*, which distinguishes *gemahele des almahtegen gotes* (legal
wives of almighty God who have attained the Seven Gifts of the Holy Spirit),
brûte des almahtegen gotes (brides of almighty God, i.e., those who strive seriously and willingly), *adolescentulae* (those who are sluggish, but willing) and
erbelôse kebese (concubines with no hereditary rights, those who are sluggish and
recalcitrant)[102]. This lowest level corresponds to Hildegard's expression *concubina*[103]. However, Hildegard's interpretation of the bride of Christ who is not
prepared to sacrifice herself goes far beyond this sort of typology of spiritual
attitudes. The terms listed above, particularly the viper, signal the context of
Salvation history in which the sacrificial status of the bride is anchored. She
who does not furnish the sacrifice required becomes the victim – the German
term "Opfer" combines both semantic aspects – and degrades both herself and
the bridegroom. This fall of the bride of God is reminiscent of the Fall of
humanity. Hildegard strengthens the echoes of the Fall by mentioning Eve, who
looked steadfastly to God before the creation of Adam, and the "ancient serpent", who finds a victim in the disloyal bride of Christ[104]. If the Fall of Man
is staged as the fall of a bride of Christ (as in Mechthild von Magdeburg's *Das
fließende Licht der Gottheit*), then the reverse, but equally nuptial, connection

---

[101] Hildegard von Bingen, *Epistolarium*, 250r, 52-55.

[102] *St. Trudperter Hohelied*, 147,25-148,5.

[103] Concubinal marriage refers to the conditions by which the Germanic free man, who has
a legal right of disposal over those who are unfree, is permitted to regulate the sexual activities of
his maids and menservants. Cf. Inga Persson, 40 ff.

[104] Cf. Hildegard von Bingen, *Epistolarium*, 250r, 17-23.

between collective and individual Salvation is revealed. In III,9, the human being, created as God's bride, is seduced by the Devil and becomes (in Hildegard's words) his *concubina*[105]. A third, more radical variant of the sacrificial bride who becomes the victim of the Devil and her own weakness occurs in the Middle English treatise mentioned above. This example is reminiscent of the ambiguity of the motif of the bride of Christ, resulting from its sexualization, as discussed in chapter 1. In sum, brides of Christ and brides of the Devil are visibly sisters during the high Middle Ages. It even appears that from the very beginning the polemical commentator expects the bride of Christ to be Janusfaced, since he warns her that she might become the prostitute of the Devil. For if she does not give birth to the "spiritual sons and daughters" (interpreted as virtues) of the divine bridegroom but rather carries all possible sins in her heart, then she is committing adultery with the Devil. Here I quote a passage in which the interconnection between bride of God and bride of the Devil manifests itself with unusual clarity; it not only has overtones of the prototypical jealous husband of the Old Testament, Jahweh, but also accuses the woman essentially of perpetuating the Fall[106]. This is another example of the misogynistic attitude concealed beneath a veneer of promoting women (which is the avowed intention of the whole counseling discussion here):

> But, maiden, although you may have physical integrity, if you have pride, envy, or anger, avarice, weakness of will in your heart, your are prostituting yourself with the Devil of hell, and he fathers in you the children which you bear. When the almighty husband that you are married to sees and understands this, that his enemy is committing adultery with you and that you are pregnant by him with the offspring he hates most, he turns you out of doors at once – and no wonder – and surrenders you completely to the lover you are pregnant by. He does not go halves with anyone, least of all with his enemy[107].

The Sacrificial Status of the Bride in Epic Texts

In narrative contexts, what is important is not success in convincing a woman to become or remain a bride of God, but to provide momentum for the further development of the plot, either hastening or retarding it – in any case, moving

---

[105] Mechthild's representation of the Fall occurs in the context of a vision of Creation conceived in erotic terms(see chapter 3).

[106] Cf. *Holy Maidenhood*, ed. Bella Millett / Jocelyn Wogan-Browne, 34,30 ff., where the threat of prostitution is followed directly by discussion of the birth of Pride (the "eldest daughter" of the Devil) and the Fall of the Angels.

[107] *Holy Maidenhood*, ed. Bella Millett / Jocelyn Wogan-Browne, 37, 20-27.

it along. This is a different framework, these are different conditions in which
to give an account of a bride of God and her sacrificial status. Hartmann von
Aue illustrates the interface between the secular and spiritual relationship discourses in a new way by having two women's lives, in two of his works, revolve
around choosing the correct husband. With his two epic works *Der arme Heinrich* and *Gregorius*, he constitutes the exception mentioned above – an exception not only with relation to the literary genre, but also in his evaluation of the
two discourses.

In his short work, *Der arme Heinrich*, Hartmann relies on the power of the
motif of the bride of Christ to increase suspense, but above all on a variant of a
fundamentally primitive idea of sacrifice. He makes use of the original proximity of self-sanctification and self-sacrifice expressed in the Latin term *sacrificium*. A doctor in Salerno reveals to the leprous Heinrich that only the blood of
a virgin can heal him. A marriageable virgin at least ten years old (*voll manbaere
maget*) would have to be sacrificed for medical reasons, and she would have to
make the decision of her own free will[108]. Heinrich, therefore incurably ill,
resigns himself and seeks refuge with a farming family who cultivate his land.
Three years go by before he tells them of the hopeless prognosis for his health.
The farmer's daughter (eight or ten years old, depending on the manuscript),
who meanwhile has become very close to Heinrich, hears of the necessary self-
sacrifice. Quietly the girl decides to sacrifice her life. After several troubled
nights, matters come to a conversation between the girl and her parents. With
great skill, from a narrative point of view, the girl presents her decision as a
desire to become a bride of God. This sort of self-sacrifice as a bride of Christ
would secure her salvation, since by being killed she would reach the divine
beloved all the more quickly. Her father does not understand or accept this and
mistakenly thinks that his daughter has a radically overdeveloped sense of *triuwe* (loyalty) to their feudal lord[109]. He tries to silence his daughter with
threats. Her mother reminds her of her filial duty of respect and begs her
daughter to relent[110]. But both parents' efforts to change their daughter's mind
are in vain. Finally, they come to view her reasoned words as a sign of spiritual
inspiration and recognize her decision *nolens volens*[111].

This dispute can tell us something about Hartmann's evaluation of the
motif of the bride of God since the attitude of the girl towards both her own

---

[108] Hartmann von Aue, *Der arme Heinrich,* 369-458. Marriageable age varies for girls
between ten (certain clerical positions) and twelve years old (according to Canon Law), for boys
it is fourteen years old. (Paulette L'Hermite-Leclercq in: Georges Duby / Michelle Perrot 2, 217-
218). See also Rüdiger Schnell 1982, 86 ff.

[109] Hartmann von Aue, *Der arme Heinrich,* 573-588.

[110] Hartmann von Aue, *Der arme Heinrich,* 629-663.

[111] Hartmann von Aue, *Der arme Heinrich,* 855 ff.

self-sacrifice and her duty of obedience is significant. The central term of *triuwe*, which the girl uses in her extremely clever self-justification to her parents, is particularly meaningful. The would-be bride of Christ argues with an unwavering determination reminiscent of Ambrose's militant bride of God. She too cannot be moved by parental dissent, although she is fully aware of her duty to obey her parents, also a form of *triuwe*. But immediately she emphasizes this concept in an unusually individual way. It is true that *triuwe* to one's parents should be respected, but for her it is more essential to be true to herself:

ez ist gewisse sîn gebot,
daz ich iu sî undertân,
wan ich den lîp von iu hân:
daz leiste ich âne riuwe.
ouch sol ich mîne triuwe
an mir selber niht brechen.

It is certainly his [God's] command that I should obey you, because I have my being from you. I do this without regret. And yet I should not breach my loyalty to myself[112].

The continuation of the girl's speech reveals her self-centered, even selfish, view of her self-sacrifice. Pointing out that her parents have other children – with the implicit message that they could surely spare one child – seems an insensitive attempt at comfort. On the whole, the arguments sound as though they could come from a modern pamphlet on self-fulfillment. The girl appears to know that her nuptial "pursuit of happiness" will be successful – at all costs.

wie gerne ich iu des volgen wil,
daz ich iu triuwe leiste,
mir selber doch die meiste!
welt ir mir wenden mîn heil,
sô lâze ich iuch ein teil
ê nâch mir geweinen,
ich enwelle mir erscheinen,
wes ich mir selber schuldic bin.
ich wil iemer dâ hin,
da ich volle vreude vinde.
ir habet ouch mê kinde:
diu lât iuwer vreude sin
und getrœstet iuch mîn.
mir mac daz nieman erwern

---

[112] Hartmann von Aue, *Der arme Heinrich*, 816-821.

zewâre, ich enwelle ernern
mînen herren unde mich.

However much I wish to follow you in this, to remain true to you, I must be true above all to myself. If you want to avert my happiness, then I would rather you had to cry a little bit for me, than for it not to be clear to me what I owe myself. I wish to be always where I find full happiness. You have other children: let them be your happiness, and console yourselves about me. Nobody can deter me from saving my lord and myself[113].

Hartmann casts the protagonist's relentless determination and willingness to sacrifice herself in a critical light by making the girl's radical action come to nothing in the further course of the narrative. This is demonstrated above all by four scenes: first, the consultation with the doctor in Salerno, who again tries to change the girl's mind, only to provoke her embittered resistance[114]; second, the veto with which Heinrich intervenes shortly before the killing, which plunges the girl into the despair and fury of one who has been intent only on her own salvation: *'wê mir vil armen und ouwê! (…) muoz ich alsus verlorn hân die rîchen himelkrône?'* ('Alas, poor me, woe is me! […] Have I thus lost the rich crown of heaven?)[115]; third, the intervention of Christ, who can see into all hearts (*cordis speculator*), recognizes the girl's *triuwe* (loyalty) and *nôt* (distress) and effects a miraculous cure on Heinrich, thereby rendering the killing of the girl unnecessary[116]; and fourth, the final wedding between the girl and Heinrich[117]. All these narrative stages show that here no bride of Christ will inscribe her name in the ranks of female hagiography. Certainly the childlike protagonist is given a saintlike aura when she is credited with angelic goodness, or "the greatest good-heartedness that I have ever found in a child". The rhetorical question *welch kint getete ouch ie alsam?* (what child would ever have acted in such a way?) suggests a martyr's status[118]. Nevertheless, because her model of marriage seems too radically oriented towards her own salvation, her obsessive willingness to be sacrificed is alienating. Near the end, the dream of being a bride of Christ dissolves anyway, and a scenario of marriage in the world takes its place. The idea of the bride of Christ becomes a distant memory, a notion which was useful to the narrative at a given point. This result of the narrative

---

[113] Hartmann von Aue, *Der arme Heinrich*, 828-844.
[114] Hartmann von Aue, *Der arme Heinrich*, 1062 ff.
[115] Hartmann von Aue, *Der arme Heinrich*, 1290-1293.
[116] Hartmann von Aue, *Der arme Heinrich*, 1353 ff.
[117] Hartmann von Aue, *Der arme Heinrich*, 1451 ff. For different possible ways of evaluating the eventual marriage, see Marianne Wynn, on the one hand, and David Duckworth, on the other; see also chapter 3 below.
[118] Hartmann von Aue, *Der arme Heinrich*, 464-466 and 520-524, respectively.

use of the motif of the bride of God prompts the question of whether Hartmann von Aue is here ironizing a bride of God. In seeking to answer this question, a glance at Hartmann's *Gregorius* can help.

It seems as if Hartmann likes thematizing the polarity between spiritual and secular marriage. He leads not only a farmer's daughter but also a noble and sovereign lady to this interface between the two discourses. This time the situation is as follows: Gregorius' mother has just buried her dead husband, who was also her brother and the father of her son, and has taken over the administration of his possessions. Already rich lords are wooing the lady, who is praiseworthy in every way[119]. As the text says, she is *guotes mannes wert* (worthy of a good husband). But she rejects all offers because she has made up her mind to marry one who is incomparable, for whom she has prepared herself as a lover, and whom – defying convention – she woos:

Si hete zuo ir minne erwelt
weizgot einen stæten helt,
den aller tiuristen man
der ie mannes namen gewan.
vor dem zierte si ir lîp,
als ein minnendez wîp
ûf einen biderben man sol
dem si gerne behagete wol.
swie vastez sî wider dem site
daz dehein wîp mannes bite,
sô lac si im doch allez an,
sô si des state gewan,
mit dem herzen zaller stunde,
swie joch mit dem munde:
ich meine den gnædigen got.

God knows, she had pledged her love to a strong hero, the most excellent lord that ever was. For him she dressed up, as a loving woman should do for a worthy man whom she wishes to please. And although it is against the custom for a woman to woo a man, she urged him constantly with words and thoughts, as often as she could. By him, I mean the merciful God[120].

Succinctly, the last line provides a solution to the puzzle of the identity of her beloved. The widow is revealed as a woman who has fallen into sin, who wishes to offer a sacrifice in expiation for her incestuous relationship, and who has

---

[119] Hartmann von Aue, *Gregorius*, 853 ff.
[120] Hartmann von Aue, *Gregorius*, 871-885.

chosen the life of a bride of Christ as this atonement. In this, Hartmann presents an unconventional variant of sacrifice and self-sanctification through an erotic relationship with God. Here, too, the woman initially gets her own way, and she is able to make her sacrifice. But she has a high price to pay for her resistance to a new marriage. One of the rejected suitors puts violent pressure on her for many years so that she and her possessions are made the victim of his pillaging attacks. The adult Gregorius, who arrives as an unknown knight, is the first person who can free her from this iron grip[121]. This deed predestines him to become the husband of the lady who rules the land, who, as fate would have it, is his mother. With the approval of her subjects, the bride of Christ, much relieved, decides to enter into a new marriage; of course, nobody knows that this marriage is incestuous[122]. Inevitably, the text suggests, the Devil must have a hand in it. And yet, even amongst these fateful marital developments, there is still place for the praise of worldly marriage:

diz was benamen der beste rât:
wande êlich hîrât
daz ist daz aller beste leben
daz got der werlde hât gegeben.

This [marrying Gregorius] was truly the best counsel, because a legally contracted marriage is the very best way of life that God has given the world[123].

It is significant that the renewed marriage of the widow, who has lived for many years as a bride of God and is now about to marry her son, who was himself conceived through incest, can be praised despite the doomed circumstances. This commentary on marriage should not be understood ironically; rather it reflects Hartmann von Aue's attitude to both worldly and spiritual marriage. He seems to see these as two forms of married life specific to particular social groups: "The praise of marriage in lines 2221 ff. (…), on the other hand, is authorial comment and certainly not irony. – Hartmann's statements generally transcend the situational context, aiming at programmatic ideality; within this ideality, marriage is indeed the Ordo which is well-pleasing to God for *die werlt* (the world), i.e., lay-people"[124].

In summary, one can see that in both *Der arme Heinrich* and *Gregorius*, Hartmann superimposes worldly and spiritual relationship discourses and reveals them as temporary situations in life for the female protagonists. Given this opportunity, the author does more than adopt a highly positive stance –

---

[121] Hartmann von Aue, *Gregorius*, 1838 ff. and 2080 ff.
[122] Hartmann von Aue, *Gregorius*, 2185-2262.
[123] Hartmann von Aue, *Gregorius*, 2221-2224.
[124] Volker Mertens 1978, 68. For widows as brides of Christ, see Réginald Grégoire, 778 ff.

very odd in this context – with regard to the pastoral discourse of worldly marriage of his day. He also makes full use of the narrative potential afforded by the protagonist in her precarious position of being faced by rival marriage options. Hartmann von Aue builds precisely on the rivalry between the marital life-structures of his protagonists, since both temporary brides of Christ help to advance the plot. In both texts, the male protagonists find themselves compelled to act, and this is connected with the status of the bride of God as sacrifice and victim. The fact that the farmer's daughter wishes to sacrifice herself means that Heinrich can travel to Salerno with her and hand her over to the doctor. However, because she fights so fiercely to be killed and is so despairing, Christ, as *speculator cordis*, intervenes and cures Heinrich. In so doing, he creates the conditions for the two to marry, as duly happens. Because Gregorius' mother, as a bride of Christ, opposes her suitors, she is subjected to many years of oppression and can only be saved by her adult son. His superb knightly deeds lead him into the next dilemma, his incestuous marriage with his mother. Hartmann von Aue's brides of God demonstrate humility and courageous self-sacrifice, which certainly befit a bride of God but which are equally desirable for a wife in the world. And it is to this final destination of married women that Hartmann leads them, along winding narrative paths, almost as though – in *Der arme Heinrich*, at least – one could hear the concluding applause.

Conclusion

In this chapter I have aimed to demonstrate the collision, in the texts of bridal mysticism, of the spiritual and the secular dimensions, on the one hand, and the discourses of love and marriage molded by the Song of Songs, on the other. Strangely enough, this occurs precisely when there is a question of distinguishing spiritual marriage with Christ – often praised as an option for life in its own right – from marriage with a human partner. This gives rise to an interface between a relationship with God imagined in erotic terms and an earthly relationship between the sexes. At these points of intersection, elements combine and overlap which complement each other in ways which are sometimes contradictory, which are sometimes in ideal harmony, and which – at best – can reciprocally transcend their individual limitations. This appears to me to be the case in the clash between the erotic discourse of the Song of Songs and the social and legal discourse of marriage, both of which contribute different aspects to the repertoire of expression of mystical discourse.

I have sought to capture this by looking at certain aspects of the chronological structure and hierarchy of the partners in each case. The erotic discourse emphasizes transient fulfillment in love, which is always already characterized by imminent withdrawal and calls to mind the consuming vortex which is born of just this knowledge of the fragility of the union. The discourse of marriage stresses a regulated bond, one which is defined by social rituals. In this bond, the known factors are the contractual conditions, the hierarchical ordering of the partners, and the horizons of its temporal fulfillment. Because of the chronological linearity of the spiritual concept of marriage, one can foresee a time when the human bride (or widow) will see her divine bridegroom or departed husband (again). Until then, she will wait as an obedient bride, or a patient widow.

But there are also interfaces where the colliding elements benefit each other very little, if at all. This comes to the fore particularly when they are compared in a common light, for example, in the comparison between the spiritual and the secular relationship. The fundamental impetus which maintains the momentum of comparisons between the two forms of marriage is undoubtedly the question of the optimal choice of partner – a question posed from a (constructed or authentic) female perspective and seldom lacking propaganda-related ulterior motives. Through the comparison between a relationship with a transcendent partner and with a human husband, the woman is meant to be presented with criteria to choose a relationship. Marriage with the divine bridegroom, celebrated in heaven, is intended to seem a convincing and glowing alternative to the ordinary life of a woman. The higher value of marriage with Christ can then become a powerful argument in the public self-defense of the young virgin Mary, who denies herself to a human husband in order to become the bride and mother of Christ, or the case of a farmer's daughter who wishes to have herself put to death. Since Christ is a divine bridegroom, in all texts and genres, *a priori*, he is above human husbands. He is a super-man, in the etymological sense, whose domicile cannot indeed be reached before death.

This contains a promise of nobility for the woman who sacrifices herself by dedicating herself to God. Her social and ontological increase in value is the reason and basis for the particular status-consciousness which emerges, for example, in Hildegard's letters to other religious women.

The ascetic, sacrificial status of the bride of God, which is apparent in early Christianity, shines through again in a very archaic way in the texts. A woman sanctifies herself through the ascetic sacrifice of her Self, whether this is in the works of – to name but a few – Ambrose, Hildegard von Bingen, Abelard, or Hartmann von Aue. This motif of selflessness is found in great variety from the purest of brides of Christ to less blameless examples. The farmer's daughter in her nuptial pursuit of salvation – the product of a male imagination – can also be suspected of selfishness. But male priests are particularly insistent on drawing attention to the unique opportunity to escape much of the hardship of a woman's lot by taking up the option of a divine bridegroom. This is not only found in the Middle English treatise discussed above but will also be encountered in the late-medieval *Christus und die minnende Seele*. Both texts radicalize the interfaces between love and marriage, but particularly between spiritual marriage and marriage in the world. Both, not coincidentally, propagate the way of life of a bride of Christ as the optimal way to less toil and more comfort. There is the bizarre depiction of the *molestiae nuptiarum* of a wife who becomes the victim of marital violence, but also – astonishingly enough – in the more recent text, the victim of her divine husband. In matrimonial allegories of mystical catharsis, the archaic idea of the ascetic self-sacrifice of the bride of Christ is rediscovered and expressed with that disturbing naturalism that had already come to the fore in the much older treatise.

So what remains of the question of sacrifice and the associated comparison of ways of life for women? Perhaps a plain and simple balance: ever since Ambrose's definition, being a bride of Christ is a *holocaustum*, a burnt offering; this status of sacrifice and victim is also cherished and cultivated by the late-medieval texts, partly because it implies a particular nobility. Certainly, the woman in the world also leads a self-sacrificing life with many cares and anxieties, even a life where she is the victim of her husband's violence, as at least two of the texts assert at great length. Accordingly, the sacrificial status of the woman appears to be the basic model for the relationship between husband and wife, whether spiritual or worldly – the level on which it is realized merely determines whether the sacrifice exalts the bride to the heights of sanctity, or brings about her downfall.

It is more than questionable whether the conclusions drawn from the discourse of relationships in the world are really applicable to spiritual discourse. For that reason, I would like to cast a critical glance over the comparisons between spiritual and secular marriage in religious literature. They are actually intended to emphasize the ontological difference, on principle, of marriage with Christ. Precisely the most exaggerated variants give rise to doubt about whether this goal can credibly be achieved in this way. Perspectives on marriage which are inherently incommensurate are lined up for comparison, brought to muster, and inspected in a petty *via comparationis*. Even if the focus is on increasing the value of one and decreasing that of the other, the two discourses are still being brought into line with one another. The intended exaltation of one set of brides and/or bridegrooms and the diminution of the other sets up a competition of everyone for himself/herself. The effective result of this competition is less a differentiation than a leveling of all differences. For would human brides and human and divine bridegrooms line up against one another otherwise? Would it otherwise be possible to play off one type of marriage against the other?

In the course of such competitions, the plane of the spiritual relationship assimilates components from the earthly world of the sexes. The divine partner suddenly becomes the prototype of an ideal earthly husband; the latter, in his turn, can achieve the dubious distinction of being caricatured as the superlative domestic monster. All the texts presented make one conclusion inevitable: the bride of Christ makes a more fortunate marriage, which is tactically wiser and shows more consideration for herself, than the woman in the world. Because – and this seems to me to be the bottom line of this almost obsessive weighing up of marriage here and marriage there – a woman cannot in any case avoid a (matrimonial) bond with a male partner, be he divine or human.

In the face of this situation, the texts in fact communicate little that is encouraging, although some of them profess to do just this. Sometimes – and I am thinking here, for instance, of the girl in Hartmann von Aue's narrative, the treatise *Holy Maidenhood*, or the polemicized Christ in *Christus und die minnende Seele* – the suspect accounting of matrimonial fulfillment is dusted down and spelled out. But in this mundane cost-benefit analysis, there is no longer any trace of the supremely different quality of that which is risked by the *sponsa Christi* without any budgetary considerations. The more doggedly the difference between the forms of marriage is pointed out and the more the two dimensions of marriage overlap, the more the fundamental difference claimed between heavenly and earthly marriage pales into insignificance.

Chapter 3
Brides of God: A Synoptic View

Ibi videt invisibilia, audit
ineffabilia, quae non licet homini loqui.[1]

In English, Bernard's words read: "There she sees the invisible, hears the ineffable, of which a human being is not permitted to speak". "There", is the chamber of the king, which is how the Song of Songs refers to the innermost sanctum. "She" who is permitted to see and hear is the bride of God who, as the divine beloved, shares in a secret and defends it from outside knowledge with protective words: *Secretum meum mihi, secretum meum mihi*[2]. Being human, she neither may – nor can – have any part in this secret, as Bernard of Clairvaux makes clear. Being a bride, however, as several literary works seem to suggest in giving accounts at this point of just such exquisite mysteries, she must have a part and report back about it[3]. The way she can do this depends on the text, its function and public. For some brides, this can be contrived hermeneutically through allegorical commentary on their robe and/or bridal attributes, without any other secrets being revealed than the mysteries of faith. Other brides are forced into a tight corner by the narrative situation, so they have to reveal the decisions hidden in their hearts. Then they surrender their visions of the divine bridegroom and, should the need arise, fight bitterly for them. And there is yet another group of brides who tell of their love-secret in a monologue or dialogue, seeking that subtle balance between veiling and unveiling which Bernard's words and their office as "secretaries of God"[4] seem to imply.

The medieval literature of bridal mysticism, both in Latin and in the vernaculars, inclines one to see the *invisibilia* and *ineffabilia* as that which – despite all scepticism about speech and all obligations to silence – is and must be spoken. This chapter focuses on a number of brides of God and their secrets, secrets sometimes whispered or blurted out to the reader and sometimes withheld altogether.

---

[1] Bernard of Clairvaux, *De gradibus humilitatis et superbiae*, VII,23, ed. Gerhard Winkler, II, 78.

[2] Is 24:16, quoted in Bernard of Clairvaux, *De gradibus humilitatis et superbiae*, VIII,23, ed. by Gerhard Winkler, II, 82.

[3] This verse is quoted (in this context) by, for example, Walter Hilton, St Bridget of Sweden and Margery Kempe (cf. Barry Windeatt 1994, 166 and 228).

[4] Cf. Diane Watt and Hildegard Elisabeth Keller 2000.

So the main concern is how – in a given literary type of text – brides speak of their God, whom they experience as a lover, as well as of how they are made to speak or remain silent.

The title of this chapter – 'A Synoptic View' – should be understood etymologically. I would like to bring various literary brides of God, from texts which will be introduced briefly in the first section, into view simultaneously. This manner of presentation has a dual purpose: first, to provide a sort of general survey of the literary motif of the erotic relationship with God; and second, to reveal the individual development of a given erotic relationship with God in each of the texts. For this reason, from the second section onwards, I present the development in four sequences, which extend from the initiation of the relationship, through its fulfillment, and on to its possible darker sides. The first sequence ('The First Move – Masculine') is concerned with the eroticization and activation of the lovers; the reaction of the other is treated in the second sequence ('Female Responses'). The third sequence ('Becoming One') revolves around possible varieties of union. The pain, longing, and separation suffered by at least some of the brides are the subject of the fourth sequence ('Tribulations').

Following the connecting thread of these stages, one can show, in the first instance, how the loving couple's relationship is constituted, how it can be successful, and how it can be weakened or even broken down. Second, a synoptic view crystallizes the differences; these are determined essentially by the genres and intentions of the texts as well as their literary representations of the bride of God. Third, each of the four stations of the synopsis reveals the phenomenology of the brides of Christ and their secrets. Gaps and omissions are also particularly informative instances where certain texts shift the focus away from the drawbacks of being a bride of God, whereas other texts give precisely these same drawbacks particular weight because love seems to be intensified by suffering, and desire by hardship.

For this synoptic view of brides of God I will focus on a manageable number of texts chosen according three criteria: first, they give central importance to the motif of the bride of Christ; second, they were produced within well-defined temporal and geographic boundaries; and thirdly, they belong to different genres. This last is particularly important since the differences among the loving couples and their relationships are partly determined by the genre-specific context, as has become clear already. With this in mind, I have selected the following six works of literature in German, written within just under a hundred years of each other (I list them in chronological order):

1. *St. Trudperter Hohelied* (*The St. Trudpert Song of Songs*, anonymous, circa 1160)

2. *Die Hochzeit* (*The Wedding*, anonymous, circa 1160)

3. Priester Wernher, *Driu liet von der maget* (or *Maria*) (*Three books of the Virgin*, 1172)

4. Hartmann von Aue, *Der arme Heinrich* (*Poor Henry*, circa 1200)

5. Lamprecht von Regensburg, *Tochter Syon* (*Daughter of Zion*, between 1240 and 1250)

6. Mechthild von Magdeburg, *Das fließende Licht der Gottheit* (*The Flowing Light of the Godhead*, between 1250 and 1282).

The corpus of texts chosen includes texts of bridal mysticism in the strictest sense of the word, i.e., the witness of an author who understands herself as a bride of God (Mechthild von Magdeburg's *Das fließende Licht der Gottheit*), as well as an anonymous text which aims to train women as brides of God and constitutes a sort of literary escort of the bride (*St. Trudperter Hohelied*). A third work, Lamprecht von Regensburg's *Tochter Syon*, shows a strong courtly influence but is probably aimed at religious women; despite its epic character, it has much in common with the first works mentioned: dialogical structure and a profoundly dramatic quality, on the one hand, and spiritual didacticism, on the other. The range of bridal mysticism is extended considerably if one includes catechetical literature. This is one of the reasons for including Priester Wernher's text in my selection: it has a strong pastoral intent and employs the motif of the wedding in instructing the congregation in the principles of the Faith, as well as being an example of the early Marian epic, which belongs to the courtly culture of the nobility. There is also a short narrative by Hartmann von Aue, one of the most representative authors of the courtly epic.

Six Brides for Six Literary Works

I will start by introducing the works listed above in the context of their genre, composition and reception. I highlight the extent to which the motif of the bride of God dominates the work in question, and how the meaning of the motif varies in each case.

Mechthild von Magdeburg: Das fließende Licht der Gottheit

The most recent of the brides of God presented here is also one of the best known in the Christian bridal mysticism of Europe, if one measures her prominence by her presence in medievalists' publications on mystical literature[5].

---

[5] Here I mention but a few bibliographical references to Mechthild's bridal mysticism (more comprehensive bibliography in Gertrud Jaron Lewis, Kurt Ruh 1993, 246-247, and, especially

Mechthild von Magdeburg was probably a beguine as a young woman; subsequently, she lived in the Cistercian convent of Helfta[6]. She is the author of a work known as *Das fließende Licht der Gottheit*, which was originally composed in Middle Low German, though it survives only in a Latin translation and an Alemannic transcription. The estimated date of its composition is between 1250 and 1282[7]. In this work, the author lends a voice to a determined and articulate *gotes brut* (bride of God) who speaks, caresses, prays, praises, dances, and laments. Here an erotic relationship with God is illuminated from within, though there is still the odd dark corner or two concealed from the reader. In all seven books, the theme of the bride is developed from the point of view of one who has had this experience, but this occurs with particular intensity in the first three books. From a great variety of literary perspectives, including first-person narrative, the readers encounter a human being who tells of a fire of love which flares up and blazes and who shows her bridal face in numerous encounters with other allegorical figures. The readers are the silent eye- (and ear-) witnesses of this being.

The short dramatizations[8] and various dialogues between the bride and diverse allegorical personifications (the human body, virtues, Lady Love or persons of the Godhead) are particularly interesting against the background of medieval images of the nature of Man, according to which it is difficult to come to know the *invisibilia* of a human being, his or her thoughts or secrets. Mechthild takes up a common technique of medieval poetics for visualizing these *occulta* or *secreta cordis*: she personifies the forces, so that they, as moving and speaking *homines exteriores*, act out the invisible[9]. Lamprecht von Regensburg, whose work is the next to be introduced, follows his source in practicing this same technique, sometimes like a virtuoso puppeteer.

---

for English literature, Frank Tobin 1994 and Barbara Newman 1995): Bernard McGinn 1988, 222-244 and passim, Frank Tobin 1994, Barbara Newman 1995 passim, Amy Hollywood, 57 ff., Frances Beer, 78-108, Margot Schmidt, in: Margot Schmidt / Dieter Bauer (eds) 71-133; Margot Schmidt 1987, 100-125; Margot Schmidt, in: Dietrich Schmidtke (ed.) 61-88, esp. 67-80; Ursula Peters 1988; Marianne Heimbach 1989; Kurt Ruh 1993, 245-295; Marianne Heimbach, in: Béatrice Acklin Zimmermann (ed.), 83-106 and Susanne Köbele 1993, 71 ff.

[6] On the subject of Mechthild's biography, see Kurt Ruh 1993, 247 ff. and Bernard McGinn 1988, 222f.

[7] For Mechthild and her work, see Hans Neumann, [2]VL 6 (1985) 260-270, here 261-263. – For the dating of composition and redaction, see Hans Neumann's essays (bibliographical references in Hans Neumann, [2]VL 6 [1985], 268-9) and the account of Mechthild's life and the history of the text in Kurt Ruh 1993, 247 ff.

[8] Successful dramatizations are found, for example in I,44, III,1 and III,9. Cf. Paul Michel 1995.

[9] CF. Lionel J. Friedman. A poetic variant of this procedure would be the describing and interpreting of those signs (mimic and gestures) which can be read from the "external being" – On this, see above all Horst Wenzel 1995 passim, and Peter von Moos 1995, 1996 and 1997a.

The frequent use of dramatization and dialogue in Mechthild's work is in line with the structure written into the Song of Songs. Origen already noted that dialogue was a decisive factor in determining the genre of that book of the Bible[10]. It has been granted the author (Mechthild) by God that Solomon's words, and not his "dark deeds", will be one of the five "lights", or "prophets" which illumine *Das fließende Licht der Gottheit*. Mechthild also mentions both the love-intoxicated bride and the bridegroom, who is compelled to admit his love to her[11]. Thus, the Song of Songs is accorded the status of a sort of spiritual or literary patron: it serves as a model, above all in its passionate dynamic of seeking and finding[12]. However, when Mechthild wishes to thematize the binding, but fragile, bond between God and Man or the eschatological communion of the blessed, marital concepts come to the fore.

But, even more essentially, all the scenic narration and all the dialogues are anchored in the authorial confessions of an 'I'[13], as recent research by Jeffrey F. Hamburger has shown in detail for Seuse's *Exemplar*[14]. It is the extraordinarily kaleidoscopic witness, almost impossible to categorize, of a bride who tells about, and comments on, herself: "We will have to forgo all further attempts to classify Mechthild's writings in any sort of typology of genres. Designations on the basis of content, such as 'Diary', 'Psychological Narrative', 'Fragments of an Inner Biography' and other such terms are inadequate, since from the point of view of modern literary typology they give the impression that these writings can easily be compared with modern works. Designations on the basis of form, on the other hand, invariably apply only to the particular literary feature, such as dialogue, or rhyming or narrative techniques, without giving a comprehensive description of the phenomenon as a whole. The matter is further confused by the fact that Mechthild employs every possible stylistic register and form of genre, from everyday speech, through short story, legend and dialogue, discourse of inspiration, revelation, vision, prayer, hymn, liturgical and above all biblical resonances, right up to affective and lyrical discourse"[15]. Accordingly,

[10] For this, see Friedrich Ohly, Zur Gattung des Hohenlieds in der Exegese, in: Friedrich Ohly 1995, 95 ff.

[11] Mechthild von Magdeburg, *Das fließende Licht der Gottheit*, III, 20, 14-17; trans. Tobin, 126-127. Mechthild mentions Moses, David, Solomon, Jeremiah and Daniel.

[12] Susanne Köbele 1993, 91 ff., discusses several key passages which show how Mechthild weaves the wording of the Song of Songs into her own text.

[13] Cf. Mechthild von Magdeburg, *Das fließende Licht der Gottheit*, III,25.

[14] Cf. Jeffrey F. Hamburger 1998.

[15] Alois M. Haas 1987, 247: "Man wird darauf verzichten müssen, Mechthilds Aufzeichnungen irgendwie gattungstypologisch einzuordnen. Gehaltliche Bestimmungen wie Tagebuch, Seelengeschichte, Fragmente einer inneren Biographie und andere mehr sind unzureichend, weil sie von der modernen literarischen Typologie her den Eindruck allzu leichthändiger Vergleichbarkeit mit heutigen Werken erwecken. Formale Benennungen dagegen betreffen immer nur das

and very much in the spirit of the five Old Testament "lights" of her work, this playing with "genre interference" is a constituent feature of Mechthild's writing[16]. This first-person bride is the only one in the synoptic view taken here who, by her own account, speaks autonomously. She therefore provides a literary view from within of a bride who, as a nun and a beguine, has led a troubled life as a female religious.

St. Trudperter Hohelied

This monastic prose text is marked by Alemannic and Bavarian dialectal features and was probably composed in Admont in the early sixties of the twelfth century[17]. It is the "earliest purely vernacular, complete interpretation of the Song of Songs from the Middle Ages", and was composed, in Friedrich Ohly's opinion, by an anonymous cleric: "I imagine the author to be a monastic priest responsible for the spiritual guidance of a convent of nuns, a man who dedicated himself to serving the spirituality of the community of women in his charge, for whom he composed this work"[18]. A skillfully crafted prologue and epilogue frame the prose commentary. Its basic motif is that of brideship as choreographed in the Song of Songs. The words of the latter are interpreted by

---

literarische Detail, etwa den Dialog, die Reim- und Erzähltechnik, ohne doch eine umfassende Beschreibung des Phänomens zu liefern. Irritierend kommt die Tatsache hinzu, dass Mechthild alle möglichen Stilebenen und Gattungsformen verwendet, von der Alltagsrede über Kurzerzählung, Legende und Dialog, Eingebungsrede, Offenbarung, Vision, Gebet, Hymne, liturgische und vor allem biblische Reminiszenzen bis zur affektiv-lyrischen Rede".

[16] Susanne Köbele 1993, 71-73, provides a very helpful systematization of the literary styles involved and points to the Old Testament figure of King David, called on in III,20,12-13, where he is said to teach, lament, plead, warn, and praise God.

[17] Friedrich Ohly, Das St.Trudperter Hohelied, in ²VL 9 (1995) 1089-1106, for the dating 1091 f., for Admont as the place of composition, see Friedrich Ohly, ibid., 1092 f. (with select bibliography to 1980, full bibliography from then on), for St.Georgen as the place of composition, see Urban Küsters 1985, 88 ff.; Kurt Ruh 1993, 24 f. and Dieter Kartschoke 1990, 253-257. – More recent works which give detailed treatment of the St.Trudperter Hohenlied: Urban Küsters 1985; Irene Berkenbusch, in Dietrich Schmidtke (ed.), 43-60; Hildegard Elisabeth Keller 1993; various essays in Friedrich Ohly 1995; Bernard McGinn 1994, 347 ff., Hans-Jörg Spitz 1999. – All quotations from the Middle High German text are taken from the edition by Ohly; the English translations are based on Ohly's translations into modern German and the wealth of commentary in his edition.

[18] Friedrich Ohly, Das St.Trudperter Hohelied, in ²VL 9 (1995) 1089-1090: "die früheste rein volkssprachige, vollständige Auslegung des Hohenlieds aus dem Mittelalter. [...] Als Autor denke ich an einen Mönchspriester und geistlichen Betreuer eines Nonnenklosters, der sich in den Dienst der Spiritualität der ihm anvertrauten Frauengemeinde stellte, für welche er das Werk verfasste".

the text according to the spiritual senses of the Scripture, with the Mariological and tropological interpretation[19] of the bride in the foreground.

The female listeners, addressed as *geistliche menneschen* (spiritual people) and *brûte des almahtigen gotes* (brides of Almighty God), are supposed to experience, in the interaction of the lovers of the Song of Songs, their own individual sense of what it is to become a bride. For this reason, it is *ein lêre der minneclichen gotes erkennüsse* (a teaching about the loving knowledge of God)[20], it is a sort of literary escort of the bride. This is the first vernacular writing directed at women intended to introduce them to the idea of being brides of Christ as individuals. Despite all its emphasis on the monastic community, the work is characterized by internalization and tries to attune the nuns to this using carefully chosen, emotionally-charged language. Emotive exhortations and appeals are designed to arouse "the right sort of love", not the *stinkende[] minne der vûlichen bôsheit* (the stinking love of putrid evil)[21].

Besides affective appeals which create a sense of identity, specific patterns of interpretation are characteristic. Here it is a matter of interpretative structures which draw the audience into the process of bridal mysticism. Friedrich Ohly demonstrates these sorts of procedures in a comparison with Williram of Ebersberg's (German-Latin) paraphrase of the Song of Songs, the only commentary on the Song of Songs "of which one can say for certain that the author of the *St. Trudperter Hohelied* was closely familiar with it"[22]. It is precisely in these procedures that one can see the individuality of the work: whereas Williram makes extensive use of personal interpretation of the Word, with a self-assurance which is cautiously expressed but nonetheless unmistakable[23], the *St. Trudperter Hohelied* exercises great restraint about making the speakers (Christ, the bride, etc.) mouthpieces for authorial exegesis. But that does not mean that the author does not trouble to address the audience directly. It is rather that he chooses different literary perspectives – not the internal, somewhat fictitious view of the bride or even the bridegroom, but a discourse in the first-person plural, a 'we', where the female listeners learn to join in speaking the words of the bride's role. They also learn "to address Christ in the intimate second person singular, in a form rich in content and artistic value"[24]. The work presents, so to speak, a performative

---

[19] Friedrich Ohly relativizes the Mariological interpretation (in favor of an interpretation relating to the soul), Das St.Trudperter Hohelied, in ²VL 9 (1995) 1100 f.

[20] *St. Trudperter Hohelied*, 145,12-13.

[21] *St. Trudperter Hohelied*, 7,19 ff; cf. also 11,5-10.

[22] Friedrich Ohly 1995, 103: "von dem mit Sicherheit zu sagen ist, dass der Autor des TH mit ihm genau vertraut war".

[23] Williram relies on the effect of increased authority of all those parts of the commentary which are put into the mouth of Christ or the Church (as bride), (cf. Friedrich Ohly 1995, 103 ff.).

[24] Friedrich Ohly 1995, 106: "Christus auch in kunst- und inhaltsreicher Duform anzusprechen".

inside view; in this way it immediately draws the women into empathy with the bride: "The nuns, as a community, repeatedly come to enjoy the word of God addressed to them individually, and this direct appeal creates a great sense of nearness to him. The achievement of this author is thus that of converting an eschatological or Mariological exegesis into one orientated towards individual souls"[25].

Lamprecht von Regensburg: Tochter Syon

Between 1240 and 1250, Lamprecht von Regensburg, probably of aristocratic origin and later a member of the Regensburg Franciscan convent, wrote a work of over 4000 lines in rhymed couplets, known as *Tochter Syon*[26]. This is the distinguished title bestowed on the protagonist and also the name given to the account of her search for a beloved, whom she eventually finds, and marries, in the person of the King of Heaven. Here too the career of a bride of God is the central motif of the work. The core narrative links numerous quotations from the Song of Songs[27] and depicts the Daughter of Zion's process of self-discovery, during which knowledge is imparted by various personifications, most of whom are female. The lady who governs over all these allegorical women in the castle of the heart, and the true director of proceedings, is Lady Love (*vrouwe Karitas*). The events are narrated in a linear fashion: The soul, recognizing the necessity of love, sends out a scout (*Cognitio*, alias *bekanntnisse* – Knowledge) to find a worthy object for her affections. The lack of success of his venture is a

---

[25] Friedrich Ohly 1995, 106: "Die Nonnengemeinde gelangt damit wiederholt in den Genuss eines ihr eigen zugewandten Wortes Gottes, dessen unmittelbarer Zuspruch eine grosse Nähe zu ihm schafft. Es ist die Leistung dieses Autors, eine heilsgeschichtliche oder mariologische Exegese so in eine seelengeschichtliche zu überführen".

[26] For Lamprecht von Regensburg and his work, see Joachim Heinzle in [2]VL 5 (1985) 522 f.; Margot Schmidt, Lambert de Ratisbonne, in: Dictionnaire de Spiritualité 9 (1976) 142-143; Helmut de Boor [11]1991, 364; Max Wehrli [2]1984, 686-687; Joachim Heinzle 1984, 89-93 and 102 ff. – Nothing is known about Lamprecht as a person except what can be gleaned from his works; his first is *Sanct Francisken Leben* (*The Life of St. Francis*, which is included in the edition, by Karl Weinhold, which I cite for *Tochter Syon*). Edith Feistner observes that the biographical legend of St. Francis and the (later) *Tochter Syon* relate to one another as "Absicht und Einlösung" (intention and implementation): in the first work Lamprecht expresses his wish to become a Franciscan, and he is already a member of the Franciscan order when writing the second work (Edith Feistner 1995, 202). Feistner finds no historical evidence for the (oral) source, Gerhard (Feistner 1995, 202, note 432). She interprets the comments by the author, which are often of a personal nature, as Lamprecht's stylization of himself as a Franciscan preacher, who, by being unlettered, treads in the footsteps of the unlettered St. Francis (Feistner, 204 ff.).

[27] Cf. Lamprecht von Regensburg, *Tochter Syon*, 1924 ff., 2008 ff., 2030 ff., 2636 ff., 3741 ff., 4038 ff., 4175 ff., 4271 ff.

cruel blow for the soul, who now begins to suffer at the vanity of all earthly things. She receives active support and advice from a succession of allegorical figures. In Lamprecht's work – in contrast to the *Alemannische Tochter Syon*[28] – Lady Love, who caused the severe lovesickness of the soul, takes on the role of matchmaker between the soul and God. Her action is successful, so the narrative of *Tochter Syon* concludes, rather abruptly, with the wedding in heaven; a prayer brings the work to a close.

Lamprecht's *Tochter Syon* is the most detailed and unconventional vernacular variant of all the many *Tochter Sion* compositions in verse or prose. These are based on several versions of a Latin treatise from the first half of the thirteenth century[29]. Lamprecht cites a certain Gerhard, who has been identified as the minister for the Franciscan province of Alemannia Superior in the South-West of Germany, as guarantor for *die materie und den sin* (the material and the meaning), i.e., for the orally-transmitted source of the work[30]. On the basis of this name, the work is dated between 1246 and 1252, the documented period in office of a Provincial of that name.

In light of the teachings on asceticism at the beginning of the text and in the excurses and the mention of *geistliche liute* (religious people) in the conclusion[31], one can assume that Lamprecht is probably writing his work for an audience of religious. He has an unconventional narrative technique, often interpolating didactic parables or autobiographical snippets which break up the linear narration. The personal authorial comments seem frank and original[32]. In them, Lamprecht often expresses his pain and sorrow that he cannot experience for himself what he writes about, since no mystical grace has been granted him. So he is fully aware that he can only approach the bride cautiously from the outside, by means of his source, and cannot show any sort of authentic view of her from within.

An introductory section, consisting of a prologue (invocation of the Holy Spirit[33]) and a lesson on human love[34], reveals the function bestowed on the erotic relationship with God. For this reason I will give a brief presentation of

---

[28] These variations are related to their use of different sources. On this, and the *Alemannische Tochter Syon*, see Dietrich Schmidtke, Tochter Sion-Traktat, in: ²VL 9 (1995) 950-954.

[29] All the German and Latin versions are listed by Dietrich Schmidtke, Tochter Sion-Traktat, in: ²VL 9 (1995) 950-960.

[30] Lamprecht von Regensburg, *Tochter Syon*, 48-62 and 289-293.

[31] Lamprecht von Regensburg, *Tochter Syon*, 4290 ff.

[32] Joachim Heinzle highlights the documentary value of Lamprecht's frank statements about himself with relation to our conception of medieval individuality (²VL 5 [1985] 523).

[33] *Tochter Syon*, 1-51 (striking use of spatial symbolism).

[34] A sort of theoretical introduction explains the meaning of love in the battle between the body and the soul (63-288). Cf. my remarks at the beginning of the chapter (short presentation of *Tochter Syon*). Cf. Hildegard Elisabeth Keller 1998b.

it. – The author outlines a monastic view of human nature, according to which (the male) body and (the female) soul (each with his/her own desires) do battle with one another: *sus ist ein strît under in*[35]. In this competitive relationship, the soul, with her "mission" and "longing", is felt to be in a weaker position than the body (for after all, he only wants "what he can see and hear")[36]. And this is when religious Eros moves into the fray and becomes indispensable in the battle of asceticism. For no sooner is the soul compelled by Love, making her long for the beloved, than she receives strength and "gains the upper hand"[37]. Love enables the soul to see the beloved from the inner watchtower of the heart, to spy out her enemies and to reflect divine love. The soul, once an "unfired tile", has now become the "mirror of love" and is honored with the title 'Daughter of Zion'[38]. The subtle gentleness which shines forth from *Jesus der alsô suoze zartet* (who caresses so sweetly)[39], also reconciles the inner and the outer being, the *lîp* no longer conflicts with the *sêle*. Thus, at this early stage the longing for the divine beloved is a substantial aid along the path of asceticism[40].

This theoretical introduction is provided with a narrative illustration in the form of the 4000-line biography of Tochter Syon. The erotic motif is thus, in a unique way, taken into the service of monastic psychology. It seems as though the omnipotence of love, mentioned as if in passing and dramatized by Lamprecht in violent images, is the true didactic content which is treated in a psychological and theological manner: Lady Love, who is secretly one with God, seems to be the secret mover of all, from heaven (driving God down to the world) to earth (mobilizing the soul against the body)[41].

In many respects, *Tochter Syon* forms a link between all the works investigated here. As in the *St. Trudperter Hohenlied*, *Das fließende Licht der Gottheit*, and *Die Hochzeit*, the bridal relationship between God and the soul is the central motif of the whole work. The autobiographical authorial comment and certain other rhetorical techniques – the high level of dialogue and Lamprecht's

---

[35] Cf. 63-101. This concept belongs to the Christian tradition of asceticism and the Psychomachia. For the tradition of monastic thought with regard to the relationship between *lîp* (body) and *sêle* (soul), see Hildegard E. Keller 1993, 59-173.

[36] Lamprecht von Regensburg, *Tochter Syon*, 63-110.

[37] Lamprecht von Regensburg, *Tochter Syon*, 102-110, here 104.

[38] The basis of this name is a stylization of the daughters of Babylon and those of Zion; the former are followers of the world (the allegory of the tile, 268 ff.), the latter group follow God (252 ff.). For Lamprecht's double interpretation of the name Zion, see Weinhold's notes on lines 135, 497 and lines 268, 499, and Gudrun Schleusener-Eichholz, in: Verbum et Signum, vol. 1, 283 ff.

[39] Lamprecht von Regensburg, *Tochter Syon*, 112.

[40] The contemplation of the Passion also provides this sort of reinforcement (cf. 237-248).

[41] Cf. the way in which Love dramatizes Salvation history (Lamprecht von Regensburg, *Tochter Syon*, 3050-3118).

skilful use of his source, where personifications act out scenes[42] – are reminiscent of Mechthild's work, which was composed at about the same time. The didactic approach to *geistliche liute* associates it with the *St. Trudperter Hohenlied*, and it has its precise, detailed passages of didactic allegorical interpretation in common with the texts for religious instruction. The lavish delight in narration and the clear understanding of what creates entertainment bring it close to Hartmann von Aue's epic *Der arme Heinrich*, but particularly to Priester Werner's *Driu liet von der maget*, which is also the result of the reworking of a Latin source. Finally, there is also an affinity with *Christus und die minnende Seele* (see chapters 4 and 5), a text written about 200 years later. Both texts have recourse to what seems to be a popularized version of the motif of the bride, with the aim of mediating ascetic material; but the earlier one – and this is the remarkable part – does so with erotic motifs borrowed from the Song of Songs, whereas in *Christus und die minnende Seele* the ascetic catharsis is dramatized in a marital context, i.e., as the disciplining of a wife by her husband. In Lamprecht's *Tochter Syon* it is noticeable that the motif of marriage, if it comes to the forefront at all, is portrayed in terms of a passionate relationship or the festive wedding between heaven and earth, in which the legal connotations of marriage are entirely absent. This is not true of all works in the *Tochter Syon* tradition: the *Alemannische Tochter Syon*, for example, depicts the precise legal bond constituted by the vow of fidelity and the exchange of rings[43].

Die Hochzeit

One of the early vernacular texts which shapes the motif of the bride and above all of the contracting of marriage is the anonymously transmitted work known as *Die Hochzeit*, which dates from about 1160[44]. This didactic text, 1089 lines long, is "the first freely-invented allegorical poem in the German language"[45]. It

---

[42] Lamprecht often mentions the Latin and German designation of the allegories simultaneously, making it clear that he is translating and reworking the text. Cf. *Cognitio* alias *bekanntnisse* 303-5; *frou Misericordia* alias *Barmherzigkeit* 3320-3321; *Oratio* alias *Gebet* 3480-3492. The occurrence of allegorical figures representing inner-human authorities follows in the tradition of Prudentius 's *Psychomachia*.

[43] *Alemannische Tochter Syon*, 536 ff.

[44] Cf. Peter Ganz, ²VL 4 (1983) 77-79; Peter Ganz 1974; Dieter Kartschoke 1990, 377-380; Gisela Vollmann-Profe 1986, 71-73; Walter Haug's commentary, in: Frühe deutsche Literatur, 1515 ff. – Inga Persson examines *Die Hochzeit* (and two other early Middle High German texts) on the basis of legal and literary history, producing a study which is both competent and comprehensive from the point of view of my own investigation. See Inga Persson, 93-135.

[45] Walter Haug, in: Frühe deutsche Literatur, 1515: "[das] erste frei erfundene allegorische Gedicht in deutscher Sprache".

was composed by a cleric who is conscious of his education[46], for an audience "on the borderline between the monastic and the lay sphere"[47]. He certainly seems to be familiar with the exegesis of the Song of Songs but does not lean explicitly on this famous literary model, turning instead – perhaps inspired by the equivalent accounts in epics about wooing a bride[48] – to the contracting of marriage under Germanic law. The ritual of contracting a marriage "acts as a bracket which holds together the course of the narrative, on the one hand, and the allegorical conception, on the other"[49], and occurs, therefore, at the center of the *spell* (play) in the text. This play concerns a potentate living in a moun- tainous region whose servants rise up against their master. He banishes the guilty servants to a dark abyss, but they continue to stir up unrest among the ruler's people. Then he hears about a wonderful woman. Immediately he decides to marry her and sends out someone to woo her on his behalf. He orga- nizes all the necessary steps for the wedding and for bringing the bride home. At this point, there is an initial exegesis of the play. It explains the basic tenets of the Christian faith and tells of the omnipotence of God, of baptism, of the word of God propagated by the priest. It treats of the sacraments, the works of compassion, and the human senses (on which human salvation is dependent). It considers confession and the three situations in life in which it can be made, as well as the Last Judgment and the purity which is necessary for the kingdom of heaven. A second exegesis praises the beauty of Mary and tells of the neces- sity for the Redemption. It recounts the birth of Christ, his miracles, his Pas- sion, and his descent into Hell. It explains that those Christ saved then are now with him in paradise and celebrate an eternal wedding for ever and ever and that anyone who wants to take part must fulfill the requirements of being a bride.

The two allegorical interpretations are evidence that *Die Hochzeit* is a text with a clear purpose. It aims to instruct and bears the didactic traces of a sermon in rhyme; the spiritual sense of the play is explained in two rather unsystematic processes[50]. The first, tropological exegesis depicts the relationship between Christ/God and the human soul – and this is explicitly taken to mean either *man oder wîp* (man or woman)[51]. The second exegesis, in terms of Mariology or

---

[46] *Die Hochzeit*, 6-7 and 40-42, and Ernst Hellgardt.

[47] Inga Persson, 141-142: "im Grenzbereich zwischen monastischer und laikaler Sphäre".

[48] According to Walter Haug, in: Frühe deutsche Literatur, 1515.

[49] Inga Persson, 121: "wirkt wie eine Klammer, die einerseits den Erzählverlauf, andererseits die allegorische Konzeption zusammenhält"; the *spell* (play) encompasses lines 145-324.

[50] Cf. Gisela Vollmann-Profe 1986, 71-74, who examines *Die Hochzeit* in the context of the nuptial interpretation of the simile of the cave. – For the question of genre, see the helpful account by Inga Persson (60-63).

[51] Cf. *Die Hochzeit*, 325-776.

Salvation history, presents the Christian Redemption in the guise of the motif of marriage[52]. Both explanations draw attention again and again to the eschatological wedding-feast at the end of time. The text urges its audience to prepare themselves to take part in it, but without extending an explicit invitation to the addressees to become brides themselves.

In this respect, *Die Hochzeit* is different from the clearly monastic didactic text, the *St. Trudperter Hohelied*, although the two texts are almost contemporary and both use allegorical interpretations as the vehicle for religious knowledge. The *St. Trudperter Hohelied* appeals to the emotions of its female listeners and aims to guide them to an internalized spirituality, extolling the gestures of love in the Song of Songs to this end. *Die Hochzeit*, on the other hand, hands down Christian truths in sober exegesis, giving an allegorical interpretation of the ritual steps of the legally-regulated preparation of a marriage up to the wedding itself and thus teaching the cornerstones of a Christian perspective on life and the world.

The story of the wedding recounted at the beginning of *Die Hochzeit* shows the contracting of a marriage in the world, and this process is then transposed to a spiritual level. The bride is presented from a literary, external viewpoint and her attributes are commented on from a distanced position. The same is the case with the bridegroom. The bride does not speak either to the bridegroom or to those who are supposed to emulate her; she is presented as a passive figure against a marital and legal background. She is a model whom the pastoral commentator can use to present his collection of successive spiritual messages. He surveys her body and clothing, looking up and down and interpreting each step in a twofold manner – almost as though he were creating a bilingual legend about a statue. Inga Persson has suggested that this allegorical didactic text is evidence for the change in the twelfth century in people's conception of marriage: the transition from the Germanic *Muntehe* (marriage by purchase) to the marriage of consent propagated by the Church.

Priester Wernher: Driu liet von der maget (Maria)

The work known as *Driu liet von der maget* (or sometimes as *Maria*), written only a few years later (1172) by Wernher, a priest who was probably working in Augsburg, is an early poem concerning Mary[53]. In *driu liet* (three books), it

---

[52] Cf. *Die Hochzeit*, 787-1061.

[53] On the question of genre, see Achim Masser 1969 and 1976; for the *Driu liet* in general, see Kurt Gärtner, [2]VL 10 (1998) 903-915, with bibliography 913-915; Hans Fromm, Priester Wernher, in: Walter Killy, Literaturlexikon, vol. 12, 1992, 263-264; Jan Gijsel 1978; Max Wehrli [2]1984, 174-175 and Nikolaus Henkel 1996. – For Augsburg as the place of origin, see Norbert Hörberg and Nikolaus Henkel.

recounts the story of Mary's parents as well as her birth, childhood and adolescence up to her marriage with Joseph (an old man). It recounts the Annunciation, Mary's pregnancy and the birth of Christ, his presentation in the Temple, the flight to Egypt and the return. An appended concluding section tells the story of Christ's miracles, Crucifixion and Ascension as well as the Last Judgment. This account of the life of Mary and of her son is framed by an epilogue and a prologue in which the author, thoroughly self-aware, calls on Mary with great adoration to be his helper in the task of translation. She must help him to produce the book in the German language so that all who want to be children of God – whether they be ordinary lay-people or noble and sovereign ladies – may read it[54]. There is a remark between the 2nd and 3rd *liet* (book) which gives some indication of the possible audience intended. There the work recommends itself to a female lay audience "as a relic with healing power" which should be kept carefully and read, and applied in practice when a woman is in labour, for the protection of the newborn child and for the general happiness of all the residents in a house in which the book is kept in good faith[55].

As the author reports in the epilogue, in 1172 a priest called Manegold invited him for a visit, familiarized him with the *materje* (material), and urged him to write. This genesis is reminiscent of that of the text by Lamprecht von Regensburg. Both Lamprecht and Priester Wernher base their works on an orally-transmitted Latin source, the details of which are not known. In the case of the *Driu liet*, this must have been the Pseudo-gospel of Matthew[56]. – The transmission of Wernher's text is problematic. As yet, attempts to reconstruct a text close to that of the author, on the basis of the seven surviving manuscripts from the early thirteenth and mid-fourteenth centuries, have not led to a satisfactory solution[57].

---

[54] Priester Wernher, *Maria,* C 136-149, A 134-145 (with an additional reference to *phaffen*), D 136-149.

[55] Kurt Gärtner, ²VL 10 (1998) 905. – For Mary's function as a helper during childbirth, see Britta-Juliane Kruse, passim.

[56] On the much discussed question of the source see Kurt Gärtner, ²VL 10 (1998) 909-911, on the author's use of the source 909. – A more detailed account of the contents of the text, which does not constitute a complete life of Mary, see Kurt Gärtner ²VL 10 (1998) 907-909, and Dieter Kartschoke 1990, 329-331; Nikolaus Henkel 1996 draws attention to an interesting general narrative complex around 1200.

[57] Kurt Gärtner summarizes the decades of dispute about the evaluation of the two complete manuscripts and the fragments, which flared up over the question of what was original and what was a revision or a free adaptation (Kurt Gärtner 1974, 103 ff.). On the manuscripts, see Kurt Gärtner, ²VL 10 (1998) 905-907, and also Carl Wesle's introduction to the first edition; Hans Fromm's foreword to the second impression; Kurt Gärtner 1974; Dieter Kartschoke 1990, 328 and Gerd Pichler / Hermann Reichert; Nikolaus Henkel 1996 comes forward with new reflections about the history of the text; for the illuminated manuscript D, see Regensburger Buchmalerei,

It is above all the second book of the three that concerns us since it is there that the motif of the bride of God comes to bear on the narrative. It tells of the adolescence of Mary, the lengthy wooing of the bride, and the publicly enforced marriage ceremony. Then follows the Annunciation, where Wernher extends the account in the source considerably, mainly with relation to the dialogue between Mary and the angel Gabriel[58]. Furthermore, above all in the second book, and particularly in MS D[59] – in contrast to the Latin tradition, which does not yet apply the motif of the bride to Mary – Mary appears as the exemplary bride, on whom the vehement love of her divine bridegroom is bestowed[60]. The erotic model of the relationship is reserved for the adored mother of God and her biography. Sporadic insertions in the 'we' of the first person plural obviously aim to move the readers to contemplation and asceticism, but above all to the adoration of Mary. In prayer-like passages she is recommended as a helper[61], especially at difficult births; in one instance she is called on as an intercessor, that God might kindle "us" in love[62]. Only once is the term *hochzîte* directed to the readers[63], but here it means not "wedding", but the feast of Christmas, which is extolled to the faithful.

If one follows Nikolaus Henkel's convincing exposition concerning the history of the various versions of the text in the case both of Wernher's *Maria* and of biblical apocryphal works at this time, then the reception-history of this text shows it to be anchored in a narrative world relating to Mary and Christ. This means that the themes about the bride are also integrated into a religious, didactic narrative complex which – like the self-establishing world of the courtly romances – was "part of the literary culture of the nobility at this time"[64]. The literary representation of the bride is in accordance with this purpose. Her dramatic career is portrayed from an external perspective, which furthers adoring

---

57-58 and fig. 122. – I quote the text according to the complete manuscripts A and D as printed by Wesle, and the version reconstituted by Wesle from the fragmented MS C, noting the appropriate sigla in each case.

[58] Hans Fromm 1955, 47 f. and 57.

[59] Instances of this will be discussed below. This manuscript is dated about 1220 and constitutes a very stylistically-aware adaptation of the *Maria*; see Nikolaus Henkel 1996, 7.

[60] Cf. Hans Fromm 1955, 56. For the motif of the bride in Wernher's work, see Hans Fromm 1955, 179.

[61] Examples of prayer-like passages, apart from the prologue, are A 3623-3634 and 5707-5840; ascetic exhortations in *Maria*, A 3899-3904; D 4449-4462.

[62] Priester Wernher, *Maria*, C 1462-1466.

[63] Priester Wernher, *Maria*, C 4143.

[64] Nikolaus Henkel 1996, here 20-21. In terms of methodology, Henkel follows the school of research, influentially promoted by Kurt Ruh, which emphasizes the transmission history of the text, and he therefore takes a critical view of the previous classification of the Marian epic by literary historians (cf. primarily Nikolaus Henkel 1996, 1-4).

contemplation, but not *imitatio*. The aspect of dialogue, which is skillfully intensified by Wernher (in the Annunciation scene, for example) increases the entertainment value, but does not aim to have an explicit pedagogical appeal as in *Tochter Syon*, *Das fließende Licht der Gottheit* or the *St. Trudperter Hohenlied*.

Hartmann von Aue: Der arme Heinrich

The short narrative work *Der arme Heinrich*, written only a few years later, tells of a unnamed female protagonist who temporarily comes forward with a wish to become a bride of God, but in the end marries the male protagonist, Heinrich. Hartmann von Aue's late work (probably written in about 1200)[65] has proved its enduring influence in literary and musical adaptations to the present day – as a recent instance of literature in German, one could mention Markus Werner's novel *Bis bald* (1992).

Little is known about Hartmann as a person – in this he is no different from the authors of the other works whom we know by name: Mechthild von Magdeburg, Priester Wernher and Lamprecht von Regensburg. The name Hartmann von Ouwe and the indirect statement about himself and his social background – that he belonged to the class of the *ministeriales*: *der was Hartman genant, dienstman was er zOuwe* – are known from the first verses of the prologue to *Der arme Heinrich*. The possible geographical identifications of this Ouwe are all in the area of southern Germany or northeast Switzerland, i.e., in the former duchy of Swabia[66]. Hartmann received a thorough schooling, which can be assumed to have included philosophical and religious education. His period of literary creativity probably began in about 1180 (or shortly afterwards) and ended after 1200[67].

No source is known for the religious tale *Der arme Heinrich*, but various motifs seem to derive from the sphere of saints' legends, fairy-tales, and magical or religious practices[68]; according to Kurt Ruh, two types of leprosy legend

---

[65] For the chronology of Hartmann von Aue's literary works, see Christoph Cormeau, ²VL 3 (1981) 501-2.

[66] An overview of this list of places is given by Christoph Cormeau, ²VL 3 (1981) 500-1.

[67] On Hartmann von Aue and his work, see Christoph Cormeau, ²VL 3 (1981) 500-520 and his collection of essays, Hartmann von Aue, also Christoph Cormeau / Wilhelm Störmer ²1993. Cf. also Helmut de Boor ¹¹1991, 64 ff.; Max Wehrli ²1984, 281-194 and passim; Joachim Heinzle 1984, 173 f.; for an overview of the critical literature, see Ursula Rautenberg's edition (Stuttgart 1993); a good introduction to *Der arme Heinrich* in English is provided by Susan L. Clark, 121-165. Further material and illustrations relating to the transmission can be found in Ulrich Müller 1971.

[68] Cf. Christoph Cormeau ²VL 3 (1981) 513-514 and Leslie Seiffert; for the question of virginity, see Maria E. Müller 1995, 267-291, for its magical aspects particularly 278 ff.

can be blended to give two narrative models[69]. But first an outline of the contents: a baron, Heinrich, who has contracted leprosy, resigns himself in the face of his poor chances of recovery and retires to the most remote farm on his estate, where he arranges to be looked after by the family of the farmer in charge. Three years go by before he reveals how he may be healed, according to information given him by a doctor in Salerno. What is required is the blood of a virgin who would sacrifice herself of her own free will. The farmer's daughter promptly makes up her mind to sacrifice herself for her feudal lord. But this must be legitimated for Christian morality: it must not be possible to classify this voluntary death as a death-wish or a desire to commit suicide, but rather as martyrdom. Second, the girl has to convince those from whom she has her being – *wan ich den lîp von iu hân* (818) – of her wish to sacrifice herself.

Here then – and essentially only here – the idea of the bride of God comes into play. The girl presents her death-wish as a longing for the divine bride-groom, and her death as the wedding with Christ. As in a marriage in the world, the girl needs her parents to agree to her unusual marriage-plans, and uses a comparison of types of marriage and a specific definition of *triuwe* in her argument (see chapter 2)[70]. This explains the fact that the female protagonist only once speaks in detail about being a bride of God in front of her parents and does not speak of it to the doctor in Salerno[71].

Having gained the consent of all parties involved, the pair can travel to Salerno, where a doctor will put the girl to death. But just as the physician is about to exercise his difficult office, Heinrich glimpses the naked girl through a crack in the wall, experiences a sort of conversion, and immediately intervenes; he is willing to accept his fate as a man who is incurably ill. The girl is greatly saddened at being saved against her will, as the *cordis speculator*, who looks into her heart, sees. Therefore, as the two make their way home, Christ heals and rejuvenates Heinrich, *daz er vil gar worden was als von zweinzic jâren* (so that he became like a twenty-year-old)[72]. The story ends on a festive note: the protagonists marry, though this marriage does remain a controversial issue[73].

---

[69] Kurt Ruh 1971.

[70] For the themes of marriage and the comparison between types of marriage, see chapter 2, and also Martin H. Jones' article (it came to my knowledge after completion of this book). For the way the motif of marriage is commented on in *Der arme Heinrich* cf. Kathryn Smits, 433-449; Eva Maria Carne, 48-55 and 114 ff.; Shari Holmer, 5-13; Eva Tobler; Maria E. Müller 1995. For Hartmann von Aue's concept of marriage in *Erec*, which develops an ideal picture of a Christian marriage-partnership, see Kathryn Smits 1981, 13-25.

[71] For the scene with the doctor, cf. 1076 ff.

[72] *Der arme Heinrich*, 1376-1377.

[73] Maria E. Müller 1995, 288, suggests that the two characters are "nicht final auf die Ehe hin strukturiert" (not ultimately constructed to tend towards marriage). Marianne Wynn interprets the ending in marriage essentially very skeptically, seeing marriage as a punishment, a corrective

It is here the girl who is at the center of the erotic relationship with God and moves the plot forward at a particular point by professing a wish to become Christ's bride. This motif is unthinkable without the self-sacrifice of the female protagonist, which seems to be completely in accordance with the early Christian tradition[74]. In this story as in his *Gregorius,* Hartmann uses the motif of the bride of God for the rhetoric of the female protagonist, who is called on to legitimate a life-decision. The motif is neither a spiritual model for the audience to identify with nor the essential attribute of a woman who is worthy of all adoration. Rather, I think it is primarily a narrative tool for speeding up the action and secondly a counter-model in a discourse on marriage which is subtly dressed up in narrative clothing. But one cannot dispute that the identity of the bride of God is here also reserved for women who wish to lead a *vita religiosa* or, at least, who no longer wish to lead any form of earthly life[75].

The First Move – Masculine

(…) for my lofe is evyr redy to the![76]

To begin with a preliminary conclusion: in all the texts selected, it is the masculine party who initiates matters. God, represented as male – or possibly a personification of his love, who behaves in a masculine way despite being female – makes the first move, even if the reasons for wooing the bride are not reflected on or revealed. No matter how passionate she is, the woman or the soul imagined as female always has the obligation of responding. This will come into the picture in the subsequent section.

The King's Bidding

Right at the beginning of the *spell* section, *Die Hochzeit* has a scenario representing a Germanic marriage ceremony[77]. In the *spell,* God is allegorized as a feudal "lord" who has heard of a matchless *maget guote* (good maiden) and her

---

measure for the female protagonist. David Duckworth, on the other hand, judges the finale optimistically (see David Duckworth's position in note 6, 119).

[74] Cf. the discussions of the sacrificial status of the bride in chapter 2.

[75] Cf. chapter 2. Incidentally, Kathryn Smits 1984 already comments on the narrative function of the image of marriage (436).

[76] *The Book of Margery Kempe,* chapter 36, Barry Windeatt ed. 196.

[77] Inga Persson, 121 ff, discovers numerous divergences from the strict Germanic concept of marriage (in favor of the consensual pattern).

many qualities[78]. This praise of the bride arouses the ruler's thoughts of imperial politics, of conceiving lawful heirs to maintain dominion over the realm, and thus, by extension, also of marriage[79]. He decides to marry the exceptional young woman:

Do chom im do in sinen muot,
daz im diu maget wære guot.
do wolde do der guote chneht
gehiwen umbe daz reht,
daz er einen erben verliezze,
den nieman sines riches bestiezze,
der mohte sin ein chunich ane sorgen
ubir dei telir unde ubir die berge.

Then it occurred to him that the girl would be a good wife for him. Then the noble hero wanted to marry so that he would leave an heir, whom no one from his realm could drive out, who could be king over the valleys and the mountains without cares[80].

The man seals a marriage contract, true to the necessary ritual: in accordance with the tradition in Germanic law, he sends a messenger to woo the woman. She herself can become involved in the negotiations, but there is no direct discussion between the two who wish to marry[81]. After the woman has consented on the advice of her relatives, the ring (representing the *dos*) is handed over and arrangements are made for bringing the bride to her new home. This concludes the part concerning affairs of state[82].

Until the second part – companionship – can begin (bringing home the bride and the wedding feast, which constitute the official announcement of the marriage), the relatives take over the interim supervision of the bride. Then the bride is summoned to dress herself for the wedding; her father bathes the girl, dresses her in white, and adorns her. Accompanied by a magnificent wedding procession, the bridegroom leads his radiantly beautiful bride home, and there the celebratory feast begins[83]. The legal and official character of this wedding

---

[78] For the praise of the bride, see *Die Hochzeit*, 196-205.

[79] For this decision to marry, see Inga Persson, 122-123.

[80] *Die Hochzeit*, 208-215.

[81] According to Inga Persson, though this does not prove that this is a case of a Christian marriage of consent, it is true that the Germanic concept of the *Muntehe* is already toned down, since there a woman would not be able to negotiate for herself (Inga Persson, 37 and 124).

[82] The terminological distinction between the first part, to do with affairs of state, and the second part, to do with companionship, is based on Siegfried Reicke, Geschichtliche Grundlagen des deutschen Eheschliessungsrechts, quoted by Inga Persson, 37.

[83] *Die Hochzeit*, 216-324.

scenario has an influence on the marriage allegory, whether it is related tropo-
logically to a human believer, to Mary, or to the life to come. The ritualized
legal bond between two partners which *Die Hochzeit* depicts and interprets
casts God's marriage proposal in a very imperious light. The divine wooing is
more like a command through which God accomplishes his plan for individual
and collective Salvation, so the human being must submit.

This is made clear by the first exegesis, which explains the relationship
between God and the individual soul. For the feast is said to signify the *mæren
gotes chraft* (the wondrous strength of God), with which God disposes everything in heaven and on earth as he sees fit. The plan for Salvation came first; its
implementation was secondary[84]. This corresponds with the presentation of the
bridegroom as omnipotent. He reigns as the almighty God in the kingdom of
heaven with its four gates, holding life and death in his hands with unrestrained
sovereign power.

> *an deme wirt wol schin,*
> *daz er ein herre wil sin,*
> *der ubir al si uf habente*
> *daz ie wart lebente.*
> *an sinner gehuhte*
> *sint daz mer joch die lufte,*
> *elliu apgrunde*
> *unde daz ist dar unde.*
> *er phliget vinstir unde lieht,*
> *ane in ist niht.*

In this it is revealed that he wants to be lord over all that was ever alive. In
his thoughts he holds the sea and the air, all abysses and what is below them.
He keeps watch over darkness and light; without him there is nothing[85].

This last line, *ane in ist niht*, formulates the theological basis for the fact that
even as a partner in a relationship God acts alone in the cosmos. He continually makes approaches to his human bride, again and again making the "first
move", initially through the Holy Spirit *der in daz mennisch chumet* (who enters
into the human being)[86]. He who is with the Holy Spirit to the end will live in
God, but he who separates from it will die[87]. Further, the bridegroom draws
near to his bride in baptism, where he honors *daz wenige chint, daz diu muotir*

---

[84] *Die Hochzeit*, 331-338.
[85] *Die Hochzeit*, 473-481. From 407-481 the four gates of heaven are interpreted allegorically,
each according to the entrance of the blessed.
[86] *Die Hochzeit*, 339-343. My translation of 343 diverges from that of Walter Haug.
[87] *Die Hochzeit*, 344-346.

da gebirt (the lowly child which the mother brings into the world)[88] with his gifts – the engagement ring is an allegory of the christening-robe.

Thus, even before the elements of a Christian life, which actually belong to the vigorous response of the bride, are explained, the text highlights how important the initial two "first moves" are for the entire concept of the bride of God. When he or she is finally resurrected, the "child" will wear the christening robe (i.e., the engagement ring) *unde ouch diu gotes gemahelin immer ewich schule sin* (and will be God's spouse for ever and ever)[89]. The pastoral intention of the text influences both the bridegroom's manner and his offer of marriage: this does not have an individual character, but it *is* directed to the individual, who has to know for certain about "life and death" and must be aware of the possibilities for a Salvation which is to be mediated by the Church[90].

The second exegesis follows and concentrates on Mary and the plan for collective Salvation which is connected with this bride. When the still imperious God sees how the *heimwarten liute* (people at home, 807) keep a look out for his lovely bride, he is moved towards reconciliation. He is willing to make sacrifices and now wishes to save the rebellious servants he had previously banished to the abyss in fury, as in the Old Testament[91]. He decides to lay aside his anger (*do wolde er werden ane zorn*)[92] – a change for the better visualized in the allegory of a bird[93] – and sends a messenger to woo a bride who could reconcile "the angels and humanity" with the Creator[94]. The confidant – who is called simply *der engil* (the angel) – is required to bring her this message:

daz si das chint gebære,
daz da mite versunet wæren
die engil und diu loute
mit der gotes broute.

that she would bear a child, so that the angels and the people would be reconciled through the bride of God[95].

This extremely abbreviated Annunciation scene, which does not even wait for the bride's answer, is the sparest of the four very different variants of the

---

[88] *Die Hochzeit,* 350-351.

[89] *Die Hochzeit,* 357-358.

[90] This is the sense of the lines that lead into the Mariological interpretation (*Die Hochzeit,* 787-790).

[91] This rebellion relates to an element in the *spell* (166-189), which alludes to both the Fall of the Angels and the Fall of Man.

[92] *Die Hochzeit,* 818.

[93] The allegory of the pelican, a topos for the Incarnation, is adduced for the idea of deliverance (819 ff.).

[94] *Die Hochzeit,* 891.

[95] *Die Hochzeit,* 889-892.

Annunciation in these texts, all of which derive from interpretations of the betrothal of God and Mary. Priester Wernher's *Driu liet*, the *St. Trudperter Hohelied* and *Das fließende Licht der Gottheit* introduce an intensity into this core scene which corresponds to the intentions of the text in each case.

Walter Haug refers to the Annunciation as "what must be the most famous declaration of love through a messenger"[96], and – one could add in this context – it turns out to be a sort of prime instance of the "first move" in the erotic relationship with God. Priester Wernher dramatizes it so that it really sparkles. In his *Driu liet von der maget* he adapts his apocryphal source in such a way that the Annunciation to Mary becomes the central scene in the whole work: "The Annunciation is accorded decisive importance in Wernher's work. It is the external and internal center of the 'Maria', and all that happens is grouped around it"[97]. Priester Wernher gives little emphasis to aspects concerning marital law, telling instead of a startlingly intimate secret between two lovers, in which a third person (the angel as messenger) is involved.

After a mysterious account of Mary's childhood and a meeting between the angel and Mary at the well, which constitutes a sort of pre-Annunciation[98], the text leads the idea of the bride of Christ out of its prefatory stage. Here too the Annunciation takes place in a chamber – in two senses, since Mary has already long been familiar to the reader as *die kamere des wâren sunnen* (the chamber of the true sun)[99].

Gabriel joyfully comes down to earth from the kingdom of heaven, walks into the ladies' chamber, and startles Mary with his brightness[100]. As in the medieval iconography[101], she almost drops her spinning in shock. Without hesitating, Gabriel passes on God's declaration of love, which could not be clearer[102] and – particularly in MS A[103] – does not really do much to set Mary at her ease:

[96] Walter Haug, in: Horst Wenzel (Ed.) 1997, 33: "die wohl berühmteste Liebeserklärung über einen Boten".

[97] Hans Fromm 1955, 83: "Der Annunciatio kommt in der Dichtung Wernhers entscheidende Bedeutung zu. Sie ist äusserer und innerer Mittelpunkt der 'Maria', und alles Geschehen ist um sie herum gruppiert".

[98] After the gospel of Pseudo-Matthew, chapter IX. – The events which precede Mary's becoming a bride will be discussed in the following section.

[99] She receives this title during the scene at the well (Priester Wernher, *Maria*, C 2429, A 2043, D 2321). Cf. Hans Fromm 1955, 83 f.

[100] Priester Wernher, *Maria*, A 2111 ff., C missing, D 2397 ff.

[101] See Hans Fromm 1955, 86 and the references by Walter Haug, in: Horst Wenzel (Ed.) 1997, 34, n. 12.

[102] The transmission of the Annunciation scene is unfortunate, because MS C is very fragmented from line 2459 onwards, and A and D differ greatly from one another, so the original wording can hardly be reconstructed. Since D adds extensively to the text at certain points, I will quote from A.

[103] On this Austrian manuscript from the mid-thirteenth century, see Wesle and Fromm, VII ff.

'*Aue Maria,*
die deine wambe freya
die wil got besitzzen
mit geistlicher hitzzen.
ein vollev genade dv bist:
ia wil der himilische Christ
von dir werden geborn:
dar zů hat er dich erchorn. [...]
dv solt ze broutbette gan
in dem himele obene:
des wirst dv ze lobene.'

'Ave Maria, God wishes to possess your free womb with spiritual heat. You are a fulfilled grace, since the heavenly Christ wishes to be born from you. He has chosen you for this. [...] You must go to the bridal bed up in heaven. For this you will be praised'[104].

What is striking about this angelic greeting is the forthright expression of burning desire, the anatomical precision with which the divine beloved takes aim at his bride, and the commanding tone of this divine bridegroom. His proposal seems to be less an offer of marriage than a command to the bride to comply with his orders in love. In both cases the angel uses few words to convey a message which fits Walter Haug's dictum on the Annunciation in Lk 1:35 perfectly: "A declaration of love which is overwhelming and steeped in power, allowing only obedience for an answer and admitting no discussion"[105]. – The metonymy for the Holy Spirit (*hitzze*) is, incidentally, a key term in mysticism, covering both negative and positive semantic aspects; in all the texts investigated here, apart from *Der arme Heinrich* and *Die Hochzeit*, it has a more or less important place[106].

Both *Die Hochzeit* and Priester Wernher's *Maria* have demonstrated a particular type of male initiative: the sending out of messengers with proposals of marriage. The *St. Trudperter Hohelied* depicts a more immediate variant of this declaration of love, probably partly because it aims to guide its listeners to a

---

[104] Priester Wernher, *Maria,* A 2133-2148, C breaks off here, D is greatly altered.

[105] Walter Haug, in: Horst Wenzel (ed.) 1997, 33: "Eine machtgesättigte, überwältigende Liebeserklärung, die nur Gehorsam als Antwort erlaubt, kein Gespräch zulässt".

[106] Cf. Cant. 8:6. A few examples from the *St. Trudperter Hohelied* (in a negative sense 1,11 ff., 145,22; 145,24; in a positive sense for heat which is assigned to the Holy Spirit and the soul gripped by love: 1,8 ff. and Friedrich Ohly's commentary; cf. Friedrich Ohly 1953; Hildegard E. Keller 1993, 39 ff.; 158-59 and 372-394); in works by Lamprecht von Regensburg, *Franziskenleben*, ed. Weinhold, 3698; positive in *Tochter Syon*, 3996. – Numerous examples of heat as a pneumatological term are listed in Lexer I, cols 1307-8.

mystical attitude to life. The fact that conversation between the lovers is super-
fluous is an indication less of the blind obedience of the bride than of the devotion of which she is capable. The scene evolves into a wordless encounter
between the one who kisses and the one who is kissed[107].

Mechthild von Magdeburg also depicts an Annunciation without a mediating angel, using a different literary form. From her own viewpoint, Mary tells
how the original marriage between God and humanity has been destroyed, and
cries out for restitution. In this text too, Mary becomes the highest-ranking
bride. Aware of this, she says that the wise *godhead* has decided to allay the
father's sadness and anger about the loss of the beloved created:

> *"Do únsers vatter jubilus betrůbet wart mit Adames valle, also das er mûste zúr-*
> *nen, do underfieng dú ewige wisheit der almehtigen gotheit mit mir den zorn.*
> *Do erwelte mich der vatter zů einer brut, das er etwas ze minnende hette, wand*
> *sin liebú brut was tot, die edel sele; und do kos mich der sun zů einer mûter und*
> *do enpfieng mich der helig geist ze einer trútinne. Do was ich alleine brut der*
> *heligen drivaltekeit und mûter der weisen und trůg si fúr gottes ǒgen, also das si*
> *nit versunken ze male, als doch etliche taten [...]."*

"When our Father's *jubilus* was saddened by Adam's fall, so that he had to
become angry, the Eternal Wisdom of the almighty Godhead intercepted the
anger together with me. The Father chose me for his bride – that he might
have something to love; for his darling bride, the noble soul, was dead. The
Son chose me to be his mother, and the Holy Spirit received me as his
beloved. Then I alone was the bride of the Holy Trinity and mother of
orphans, and I brought them before God's eyes so that they might not all
sink down, though some did [...]"[108].

Being Human, Being a Bride

Mary is a unique bride and mother of God. But the *St. Trudperter Hohelied* and
Das fließende Licht der Gottheit do not set her apart but anchor her exemplary
case in a suprasexual concept of Creation. This concept is radical since to be a
human being means to be created and intended as the bride of God. A divine

---

[107] 8,30 ff. as an interpretation of the kiss in the Song of Songs (Cant 1:1). Cf. the section
'Becoming One'.

[108] Mechthild von Magdeburg, *Das fließende Licht der Gottheit*, I,22,43-50; trans. Tobin, 50-
51. – The fact that Mary, the new bride, can soothe the divine anger is also mentioned by the
St. Trudperter Hohelied, 52,7-9.

authority – the Trinity or one person of the Trinity[109] – acts as Creator and
bridegroom. The human being is the bride, so to speak, *per creationem*. Both
works contain Trinitarian dialogues which are distinctive "theological myths":
"The two scenes do not correspond to anything in the Bible and are among the
theological myths, as I would like to call them, which run alongside elevated
theology; they were devised and developed by well-known theologians and
entered into theological preaching in literature as well as in the visual arts. They
should not be weighed in the precise balance of dogma"[110]. These conversations
among the various persons of the Trinity center on the Creation of human
beings (the counsel of Creation) and on their Redemption after the Fall (counsel of Redemption)[111] respectively. Both works describe the existence and status
of humanity before God as a passionate love-relationship and marriage, which
is not immune to the vicissitudes of love between human beings. Both texts
portray a Holy Spirit who takes the initiative, who – as divine love – speaks up
in favor of the creation of human beings. And both – in this passage at least –
devise a concept of the bride of God which is not restricted to the female sex.
Rather this concept posits the fundamental meaning of human existence in the
erotic relationship with God.

The dramatic dialogue in the *St. Trudperter Hohenlied* is an early composition[112] and is characterized by a "laconic succinctness" which demands quite a
lot of the audience[113]. The Holy Spirit pleads – against the two other more
reserved persons of the Trinity – in favor of the creation of human beings who

---

[109] In the *St. Trudperter Hohenlied* one finds the indication of the Holy Ghost as the beloved
(e.g. 21,18), but the first or second person of the Trinity, and the Trinity as a whole, also occur
as the bridegroom (e.g. 13,4-21).

[110] Friedrich Ohly 1994, 242: "Beide Szenen sind ohne einen Anhalt in der Bibel und zählen
zu den neben der hohen Theologie hergehenden theologischen Mythen, wie ich sie nennen
möchte, die, von namhaften Theologen erfunden und entwickelt, auch in die theologische
Verkündigung der Literatur wie der Bildkünste eingegangen sind und nicht auf der Goldwaage
der Dogmatik gewogen werden möchten".

[111] In the *St. Trudperter Hohenlied* these are treated separately in 2,17-23 and 132,6-24; *Das
fließende Licht der Gottheit* unites the two in III,9.

[112] "Es überrascht, dass es im 12. Jahrhundert allein in der deutschen Sprache zu einem
dramatischen Redewechsel der trinitarischen Personen beim Erschaffungsrat gekommen zu sein
scheint: hier im TH und dann im Anegenge" ("It is surprising that in the twelfth century it only
seems to have been in the German language that one found a dramatic exchange between the persons of the Trinity in the counsel of Creation: here in the *TH* and then in the *Anegenge*",
Friedrich Ohly 1994, 248) – "Als erster hat anscheinend der Autor des TH die Personen der
Trinität zu einer mit Redewechsel geführten Beratung über die Erschaffung des Menschen ver-
bunden" ("Apparently the author of the *TH* was the first to link the persons of the Trinity with a
consultation through dialogue about the creation of human beings", Friedrich Ohly 1994, 252).

[113] Friedrich Ohly 1994, 252: "lakonische Prägnanz".

would partake in divine reality[114]. As in the *St. Trudperter Hohelied*'s counsel of Redemption[115], in the Spirit's plea for Creation no nuptial notes are sounded as yet, either in the form of a "you" or a "we": "It is a liturgical 'we', transcending time and space, of all human beings towards God between the Creation and the end of time; the eternal 'we' of humanity before God, who have in common all that befalls them in Salvation history from the Creation and the Fall right up to the Last Judgment"[116]. It is in the exegesis of the kiss in terms of Salvation history, immediately after the prologue[117], that there is first mention of the concept of humanity as God's bride, who went astray in the Fall and whose position was mediated back to humanity through Mary. The exalted highest rank of Mary[118] thus does not consist in her being the unique – or even the first – bride, but rather in her winning back the "grace of the kiss"[119]: *si hât uns allen hulde gewunnen ze küssenne* (for all of us she won the gracious permission to kiss)[120]. To disregard this interpretation of the kiss is to overlook the erotic meaning given to human existence, which is anchored here – as in Mechthild's work, but with different accentuation – in the beginnings of Salvation history. There is really only a single sentence in the *St. Trudperter Hohelied*'s outline of the Creation[121] which mentions the original unity of the kiss between humanity and God:

---

[114] God the Father declares himself against an extension of his power, Christ wishes to abstain from a maximization of wisdom (*St. Trudperter Hohelied*, 2,17-23). Friedrich Ohly (1994, 254-258) puts forward patristic and high medieval evidence for this concept of a God who is modest in his demands.

[115] According to Friedrich Ohly, the counsel of Redemption in the *St. Trudperter Hohelied* (132,6-24) is one of the earliest examples and differs "more radically from all the other examples from that century than they differ amongst themselves" ("radikaler von allen anderen Zeugnissen des Jahrhunderts als diese voneinander abweichen", Friedrich Ohly 1994, 277). Useful further bibliography and text samples from the 12th century in Friedrich Ohly 1994, 258 ff. and 277 ff.

[116] "Es ist ein Zeit und Raum überschreitendes liturgisches Wir aller Menschen gegenüber Gott zwischen Schöpfung und Weltende, das ewige Wir der Menschheit vor Gott, der alles Geschehen der Heilsgeschichte von der Schöpfung und dem Sündenfall bis zum Eschaton gemeinsam widerfährt". In the prologue Friedrich Ohly also discerns a "collective 'we' of contemporaries" ("Gruppen-Wir von Zeitgenossen", Friedrich Ohly 1994, 258).

[117] After Cant. 1:1a: *Osculetur me osculo oris suo* ("Let him kiss me with the kisses of his mouth"). See Friedrich Ohly 1993, 9-31, here 16.

[118] Cf. 10,16-22. The *St. Trudperter Hohelied* visualizes Mary's high rank not only in bridal motifs, but also often in imagery of the body: she is the neck that links the body of humanity with the divine head (cf. 23,16 ff.; Hildegard E. Keller 1993, 210-214), or she embodies the eyes in the body of Christ, with which God looks towards human beings (78,18 ff.; Hildegard E. Keller 1993, 265-278).

[119] Cf. Kurt Ruh 1994, 44-45. For the exemplariness of Mary for brides of God in this work and for the concept of Creation cf. Hildegard E. Keller 1993, 224-253 and 455-467.

[120] *St. Trudperter Hohelied*, 10,32-11,1.

[121] *St. Trudperter Hohelied*, 8,9-14,2.

waeren wir volstanden, sône waere der munt, unser willen unde unser minne nie vone sîneme munde genomen, daz sîn güete unde sîn genâde ist.

If we had kept faith [with God], then the mouth of our will and our love would never have been separated from his mouth, that is his goodness and his grace[122].

Until the Fall, mankind was mouth to mouth with God, so to speak: human will and love were connected to divine goodness and grace[123]. Thus the first kiss was actually given in the creation of mankind and was broken off by the Fall. The second kiss – between Mary and God[124] – is an allegory of the Incarnation, which reconciled heaven and earth and extended the invitation to the divine kiss to all.

The detailed dialogue among the persons of the Trinity in *Das fließende Licht der Gottheit*, where there is a general consultation about the Creation and Redemption[125], reveals a God who is unmistakably erotic in his thinking and needs human beings. In unconventional and concise chronology, Mechthild gives an account of Salvation history (Creation and Fall of the angels, Creation of Man, Fall, Incarnation, Christ's sacrifice of death) and bathes them in a radically erotic light. In this she distances herself from the doctrine of the choirs of angels, which teaches that humans exist thanks to the fall of the tenth choir of angels. She stresses the necessity of human beings in Creation[126]. There is an expressly erotic motivation for their being, as is revealed by the divine internal counsel on Creation. The proactive Holy Spirit appeals to divine fertility and encourages the idea of creating angels and human beings. The suggestion gains a hearing with God the Father, since he is positively bursting with love[127]:

---

[122] *St. Trudperter Hohelied*, 8,14-18.

[123] This demonstrates the original situation of the *unio mystica*. Cf. the section 'Becoming One', in this chapter.

[124] For the kiss of Mary, cf. Ruh 1994, 40 f.

[125] Mechthild von Magdeburg, *Das fließende Licht der Gottheit*, III,9, 86-89; trans. Tobin, 116. For the motif of Redemption, cf. Friedrich Ohly 1994, 253; Margot Schmidt's commentary in her translation of this passage (369, n. 127); Marianne Heimbach 1989, 66ff.; idem in Béatrice Acklin Zimmermann (Ed.), 88 ff; for Mechthild's narrative processes, see Ingrid Kasten 1995.

[126] Cf. Mechthild von Magdeburg, *Das fließende Licht der Gottheit*, III,9,13-20 and 67-71; trans. Tobin, pp. 114-115.

[127] For the translation of God's statement *ich donen al von minnen*, cf. the commentary volume, 55-56. Here one should not imagine a musical conception of the Trinity (cf. Mechthild von Magdeburg, *Das fließende Licht der Gottheit*, III,9, 86 (trans. Tobin, 116) and Schmidt 1990, 80 ff.).

Do sprach der vatter: "Sun, mich rúret óch ein kreftig lust in miner gótlichen brust und ich donen al von minnen. Wir wellen fruhtber werden, uf das man úns wider minne und das man únser grossen ere ein wenig erkenne. Ich wil mir selben machen ein brut, dú sol mich grússen mit irem munde unde mit irem ansehen verwunden, denne erste gat es an ein minnen."

The Father said: "Son, a powerful desire stirs in my divine breast as well, and I swell in love alone. We shall become fruitful so that we shall be loved in return, and so that our glory in some small way shall be recognized. I shall make a bride for myself who shall greet me with her mouth and wound me with her beauty. Only then does love really begin"[128].

The Holy Spirit takes on the duty of giving away the bride, who must first be called into being; he is prepared to bring her to the Father's bed[129]. The Son also gives his agreement although he is already aware of the fatal price he will have to pay for this act of love. The Godhead begins the work of creating Adam and Eve, and the text dwells briefly on their paradisiacal constitution[130]. This would mean that a bride is created intentionally for the loving Godhead[131]. This ontological "first move" is followed by the explicit address and institution of the bride. God the Father addresses his beloved in the tones of a bridegroom. He delivers a legally-binding marriage vow which prepares the way for the later interpretation of the Fall as adultery. Particularly the term *hanttrúwe* is important here, as in marriage law it denotes the fact of the bride-price or dowry[132]. The marriage vow begins in the following way:

---

[128] Mechthild von Magdeburg, *Das fließende Licht der Gottheit*, III,9,25-29; trans. Tobin, 114-115.

[129] Mechthild von Magdeburg, *Das fließende Licht der Gottheit*, III,9,30-31; trans. Tobin, 115.

[130] For the anatomical implications of Mechthild's interpretation of the creation of human beings and their fall in III,9, see Hildegard Elisabeth Keller 1995.

[131] In Mechthild's work it is impossible to allocate the role of the bridegroom consistently to any one person of the Trinity, since it is taken on by the Holy Ghost (I,44,71-74; trans. Tobin, 61), God the Father (III,9,25 ff.; trans. Tobin, 114), Christ (I,22,6; trans. Tobin, 49) or the Trinity as a whole (I,43; II,22,15; trans. Tobin, 58 and 87).

[132] Under the lemma *arra* (most frequently meaning dowry, morning gift) Diefenbach refers to *hanttrúwe* in 2 manuscript glossaries, and under the lemma *dos* (in the plural also with the meaning of dowry, morning gift) he refers to a glossary from the 15th century (*hanttrowe*). The commentary volume to *Das fließende Licht der Gottheit* (36) points out that in the Latin *Revelationes* it is misleadingly translated as *pactum* because the term *hanttrúwe* represents a marriage vow by God with regard to the soul. But what is apt about this translation is that handing over the bride-price is viewed as the sign of a "true contract of marriage" (primarily in an aristocratic marriage). Cf. Michael Schröter, 83ff, esp. 88ff., Handwörterbuch für deutsche Rechtsgeschichte, I, article "dos". – For the repudiation (*verkebsen*) of the wife after the Fall, see the final section in this chapter.

"Ich bin got aller gótten, du bist aller creaturen góttinne und ich gibe dir mine hanttrúwe, das ich dich niemer verkiese [...]."

"I am the God of gods; you are the goddess of all creatures, and I give you my solemn assurance that I shall never reject you [...]"[133].

The subsequent references to the staff who will serve the bride (angels and the Holy Spirit), to Free Will, and to the only command in the Garden of Eden, confirm that the human being is legally established as wife and that the marriage ceremony has been completed, without the bride's being able to consent in any way. In God's timelessly *spilender minnevlút* (playful flood of love)[134], two things are fundamental: first, humanity exists; second, it does so in the status of a 'bride from all eternity'[135] – a concept of creation which is also outlined by Mechthild von Hackeborn, another nun from Helfta[136]. The bond with God is sealed under unambiguously matrimonial circumstances; human consent is perhaps concealed in the reference to Free Will. The human soul remains a bride of God by rejecting other offers (such as that of an erotic relationship with the devil). In quite a different way from worldly love, this is also a counter-model to the concept of the bride of God, which is staged as a confirmation of that concept[137].

Delivered Up

The activity of God, imagined as male, is manifest: his very being is initiative. As a feudal potentate or simply a man who wishes to marry, God sends out messengers in search of brides or procures them for himself directly, so as to unite himself with them in the original kiss[138]. Scarcely ever is the bride actually required to answer. She seems always to have her *fiat mihi* already at the tip of her tongue. Perhaps being a bride is absolutely all she can do.

This dynamic is asymmetric and corresponds to the contracting of marriage in the world, which is the basic allegory spun out in several texts. But sometimes this asymmetric relationship is also considered in theological terms. Certain of the works investigated here do reflect on the fact that the initiative is

---

[133] Mechthild von Magdeburg, *Das fließende Licht der Gottheit*, III,9,50-52; trans. Tobin, 115, with a note commenting on the term *hanttrúwe*.

[134] Cf. also Margot Schmidt in: Margot Schmidt / Dieter Bauer (eds.), 71-133.

[135] Mechthild von Magdeburg, *Das fließende Licht der Gottheit*, I,44,74; trans. Tobin, 61.

[136] Mechthild von Hackeborn, *Das Buch vom strömenden Lob*, 86. See McGinn 1988, 267 ff.

[137] Cf. Mechthild von Magdeburg, *Das fließende Licht der Gottheit*, IV, 2. For the motif of the bride of the Devil, see chapter 1.

[138] Cf. my remarks on the fundamentally polygamous structures in chapter 1 ("Brides Plural and Their Singular Bridegroom").

exclusively male, that is, divine. Since God cannot contain himself, Mechthild calls him a 'flowing spring that no one can block'[139], and Eckhart credits him with an ebullient nature (*ebullitio*)[140]. The effect of this excessive nature is particularly strong in what, according to John 4:16, God himself is – Love. As Mechthild puts it, God creates human beings because he is powerless in the face of his own nature as Creator – *do got nit me mohte sich enthalten in sich selben* (as God could no longer hold himself back)[141]; he must be able to love. This natural compulsion is the actual neediness of God which is spoken of in numerous images[142] and which in Mechthild's work is declared by the divine lover himself:

Das ich dich sere minne, das han ich von miner nature, wan ich selbe bin die minne. Das ich dich dikke minne, das han ich von miner gerunge, wan ich gere, das man mich sere minne. Das ich dich lange minne, das ist von miner ewekeit, wan ich ane ende bin und ane aneginne.

That I love you passionately comes from my nature, for I am love itself. That I love you often comes from my desire, for I desire to be loved passionately. That I love you long comes from my being eternal, for I am without an end and without a beginning[143].

It cannot surprise us that God is eroticized within the Trinity[144] and allows himself to be chastised with wounds of love by an allegorical authority[145]. With amazing consistency and in accordance with medieval theology[146], Lamprecht von Regensburg shows how powerless God is with regard to love. For the allegorical figure of Lady Love is secretly the director of Christian Salvation history. She hurls God out of his heaven, down through several levels onto earth, into

[139] Mechthild von Magdeburg, *Das fließende Licht der Gottheit*, V,26,9-10; trans. Tobin, 207.
[140] The concept of *(e)bullitio*, with the image of God as the *bonum diffusivum sui*, belongs to a doctrine of Creation which is influenced by Neo-Platonism. Further references in Alois M. Haas 1989a, 259 and 455, n. 82 and Meister Eckhart, Werke, ed. by Niklaus Largier, Index (*bullitio, ebullitio*).
[141] Mechthild von Magdeburg, *Das fließende Licht der Gottheit*, I,22,35-36; trans. Tobin, 50.
[142] For example, Mechthild von Magdeburg, *Das fließende Licht der Gottheit*, I,19 and IV,12,32-33 (trans. Tobin, 48 and 153); as a fire without beginning which burns of its own accord, III,4,27 (trans. Tobin, 111); as (incurable) lovesickness, III,2,15 and I,4,8-10 (trans. Tobin, 108 and 44).
[143] Mechthild von Magdeburg, *Das fließende Licht der Gottheit*, I,24, 1-5; trans. Tobin, 52.
[144] For example, cf. Mechthild von Magdeburg, *Das fließende Licht der Gottheit*, V,27,4-11; trans. Tobin, 208.
[145] See chapter 5, section "An Archeress" and Hildegard Elisabeth Keller 1998b.
[146] Margot Schmidt (in her translation of Mechthild von Magdeburg, 348, n. 14a) points to a reference, among others, in the *Glossa Ordinaria* to Mt 1,20, PL 114,71 which describes love as the original force behind the Creation and the Incarnation.

the manger, and then onto the Cross[147]. Only right at the very end is it revealed that Lady Love is a hypostatization of divine love, and is thus mysteriously identical with God:

got und diu minne sint al ein,
dehein scheidunge ist an in zwein.
diu minne ist got, got ist diu minne,
einz ist in dem andern inne.
sie zwei hânt beide einen site:
swar sie in warf, dar viel si mite,
swâ er ist, dâ ist ouch sie.
ûf erde in himel und in helle
geliez si in und er sie nie,
sie was ie sîn geselle
und immer ist dort unde hie.

God and Love are all one, nothing separates them. Love is God, God is Love, the one is in the other. They both behave in the same way: wherever she threw him, she landed too; wherever he is, she is. On earth, in heaven and in hell he never left her and she never left him, she always was his companion and always is, there as here[148].

It has to do with this powerful, even violent, female allegory that only *Tochter Syon* deviates – in literary terms at least – from the principally male initiative in the erotic relationship with God[149]. Here there is no wooing bridegroom. The soul seems of her own accord to urge *daz si etswaz solde minnen und daz ir minneclicher schîn niht âne minne mohte sîn* (that she should love something and that her lovable appearance should not remain without love)[150]. One of the personified Powers of the Soul is supposed to identify a fitting object of love in the world; her mission, however, yields depressing findings[151]. Ladies in the service of Lady Love (personifications of Faith and Hope) then put the seeking soul on the right track with long monologues about Christ[152]. Gradually she develops the symptoms of severe lovesickness, which can only be

---

[147] Cf. Lamprecht von Regensburg, *Tochter Syon*, 3084-3118.

[148] Lamprecht von Regensburg, *Tochter Syon*, 3190-3200.

[149] By this I mean, of course, only the works investigated here; another possible exception one could consider is the dialogue between Love and the impassive soul in *Das fliessende Licht der Gottheit*, II,25 (see the following section on this).

[150] Lamprecht von Regensburg, *Tochter Syon*, 296-297.

[151] After exhaustive reconnaissance in the world, the power of cognition returns home with the insight that all earthly things are nothing, and delivers a didactic speech about contempt for the world (Lamprecht von Regensburg, *Tochter Syon*, 301-369).

[152] Lamprecht von Regensburg, *Tochter Syon*, 594 ff..

helped by the great mistress, Lady Love, in person. As a proactive mediator, she travels to the divine beloved and undertakes the decisive steps since both loving parties are in her hands – not least because she is one and the same as the divine bridegroom.

Indubitably, the author of *Tochter Syon* raises a narrative song of praise to Lady Love: she is the potentate who reigns over all that is created, as well as over God himself, who pervades and moves everything; but she is also the recommended therapy for the individual's struggle on earth[153]. That is one of the core messages of all the mystical texts investigated here, however they transmit this from a literary point of view. The texts seldom lack references to the foretaste of eternity[154] which Love is, or to the healing effect of the word which tells of love – the Song of Songs holding obvious pre-eminence[155]. When Mechthild, for instance, formulates a prayer of supplication for love[156] or distinguishes between *ungebunden* (unbound) and *gebunden minne* (bound love)[157], it is reminiscent of the ascetic praise of love in *Tochter Syon*. Only if one remains strengthened and bound by love will one survive earthly life unscathed:

> *Swelch mensche alsust gebunden wirt mit der gruntrůrunge der kreftigen minne,*
> *dem kan ich enkeinen val zů den hôbtsúnden vinden, wan dú sele ist gebunden,*
> *si můs ie minnen. Got müsse úns alle alsust binden!*

I cannot imagine a person bound by the deepest stirrings of powerful love falling into serious sin; for the soul is bound, she has to love. May God thus bind us all![158]

In this employment of love, it is not important whether the bride speaks herself or whether an authorial figure who is present to a greater or lesser degree comments on the brideship. Love, flowing forth from the divine lover and into the human being, and the identity accorded her – that of God's bride – appear as a mode of coping with life which is vital for all levels of Salvation history.

---

[153] Cf. my remarks at the beginning of the chapter.

[154] C.f., for example, Lamprecht von Regensburg, *Tochter Syon*, 1088 and n. 174. *St. Trudperter Hohelied* 2,10-17; 7,31-33; Mechthild von Magdeburg, *Das fliessende Licht der Gottheit*, V,31 – For the timelessness of love and love as a foretaste of eternity, see, for example *St. Trudperter Hohelied*, 74,30-31 or Hadewijch's 12th letter.

[155] C.f., for example, *St. Trudperter Hohelied*, 6,5-7,32; 15,6-14; 80,26-81,32.

[156] Mechthild von Magdeburg, *Das fließende Licht der Gottheit*, I,23.

[157] Mechthild von Magdeburg, *Das fließende Licht der Gottheit*, II, 24,65-87; trans. Tobin, 92. Cf. the note on this in Margot Schmidt's translation, 363, n. 85 and Amy Hollywood, 67-72.

[158] Mechthild von Magdeburg, *Das fließende Licht der Gottheit*, II, 24,84-87; trans. Tobin, 92.

Female Responses

> *"(...) that gret charite that is in the; and yet I am*
> *cawse of that charite myself (...)".*
>
> *"O herre, das ist úbergros, das dú ist din*
> *minnegenos, dú nit minne an ir selben hat, si werde e*
> *von dir beweget."– "O Lord, that is too much that she*
> *be your partner in love who has no love in her, unless*
> *she is moved by you."*[159]

Until now a dynamic has emerged which *a priori* places the female bride of God in a position in which she can or must always respond to a first move which comes from someone else. It is in this other's initiative that a nature flows which is "always ready to love", as Christ says to Margery Kempe (in the motto which heads chapter 1 above). One concept which is characteristic of this phenomenon goes back to Dionysius the Areopagite: "Theopathy", which means experiencing God "through suffering" (in the sense of "incurring suffering"), thus experiencing him at the point of surrender, in devotion[160]. This mode of experience is also reflected linguistically[161], and sometimes sudden awareness may result in an incisive turning-point, for instance, Heinrich Seuse's experience of the rag and the devastating recognition that this brought: "take as your example that rag, worried between the teeth of a dog in the cloisters, and suffer all that is required of you (by God) as patiently and silently as that"[162]. In the mystical mind, human behavior should be fundamentally suffering and accepting. Passivity and receptivity, devotion and subjection with regard to a divine impetus are thus not primarily gender-specific.

---

[159] The first quotation is taken from *The Book of Margery Kempe*, chapter 36, ed. Barry Windeatt, 197; the second is from Mechthild von Magdeburg, *Das fließende Licht der Gottheit*, I,44,41-43 (trans. Tobin, 60). The two mottos express the same theme from two different viewpoints: in the first, Christ speaks to his bride, Margery, in the second, the bride responds to her beloved.

[160] For the concept of 'Theopathy', see Alois M. Haas 1989a, 50 ff., 127 ff. and 404, n. 87.

[161] An important feature here is often the link back to the Passion of Christ. For the term *erliden* for Mechthild von Magdeburg, see *Das fliessende Licht der Gottheit*, IV,12,44-45, VI,1,105 (trans. Tobin, 154 and 226-227). – For mystical passivity and the attitude of suffering, see Amy Hollywood, 173 ff.; Barbara Newman 1995, passim; for the fundamental concepts, see Alois M. Haas 1989a, 127-151; Alois Haas 1996, 411-445 and 446-464; for the term *gelâzenheit* (detachment) and its links with the idea of suffering, see Alois M. Haas 1995, 247ff. and Meister Eckhart, Werke, ed. Largier, vol. II, index *gelâzenheit* und *abegescheidenheit*. For mystical passivity, cf. also Paul Mommaers, 49 ff. and 77ff.

[162] Heinrich Seuse, *Vita*, chapter 20, ed. Bihlmeyer 58,3 ff. Cf. on this Alois M. Haas 1995, 125-147; 179-222 and Jeffrey F. Hamburger 1998.

But if this impetus comes from a God who is imagined as male or even as a sovereign husband, then the attitudes of the female party may be amalgamated with the gender of the female audience or author. Then this mere 'loving back', which is only possible by virtue of that love by the other (both the bridegroom and the bride demonstrate this in the two mottos at the beginning of this section), is not characteristic of the human being who is obviously inferior to God. Rather, this situation of merely being able to react comes to distinguish a female bride with regard to a male God, and one can already discern slight changes of emphasis and shifts between the sexes which alter and restrict the motif of the erotic relationship with God.

We will see that the brides' responses vary starkly. This is explained in several ways: first, by how widely or narrowly the idea of the bride is conceived; secondly, by the genre, the associated intention as well as the literary representation of the bride involved, which can be demonstrated particularly clearly in the very varied portrayals of Mary; thirdly, by the consideration that strongly matrimonial conceptions require different responses from a bride than those required by an erotic *spil* (game), as can be revealed in a comparison between *Die Hochzeit* and certain passages from *Das fließende Licht der Gottheit*.

The (Dis)Obedient Yes of the Bride

Now we come to flesh-and-blood women in the texts and their zigzagging biographies. How do they respond to the moves made by the bridegroom? A woman's life in the world, as a wife and mother, constitutes a basic model from which both the girl in *Der arme Heinrich* and the Mary of the apocryphal gospels and Priester Wernher's text deviate already in childhood. This factor is essential in determining their unconventional life-stories, both from their own internal perspective and from an external perspective. Both guard, for a varying length of time, a personal secret, the revelation of which necessarily entangles them in disputes with their social or family surroundings. From an onlooker's point of view, they are odd, disobedient and impudent although in their own views they are obeying an inner callings and obediently responding to the divine bridegroom. Both aspects – their obedience to their calling and their disobedience towards social demands – play a decisive role in the narrative process.

Since the bride, notwithstanding her passionate nature, is always simply obliged to respond (verbally or non-verbally), it is quite unexpected that it is actually the girl in *Der arme Heinrich* who introduces the concept of the bride of God into the text. The motif is integrated into the dispute about the healing of Heinrich, i.e., about the girl's self-sacrifice. Just how central the passage is which opens with the stating of the conditions for a cure and ends with the protagonist's declaration that she will sacrifice herself is demonstrated by its length of 435 lines (of a total of just 1521)[163]. Part of this passage is the prolix response of the imagined bride of God she would like to become. It is the longest, most rhetorically-polished, and perhaps the most spontaneous of the responses discussed here because it seems to be born of necessity within the argument[164]. After a short while, during which the girl keeps hidden her decision to sacrifice herself for the leprous Heinrich, it comes to a night-time discussion between daughter and parents in their shared bed. Although the girl suspects that she will have difficulty in obtaining permission[165], she admits that she wants to be put to death for Heinrich's sake. Her father threatens and her mother implores; neither of them will hear of it. In vain the daughter redoubles her efforts with a contemptuous lament about the vanity of this world. Without the text telling of a divine love-proposal (so there is no explicit 'first move'), the eight- or ten-year-old girl suddenly declares that a 'freeborn farmer' (an allegory of Christ) is courting her and she wishes to accept his proposal:

mîn gert ein vrîer bûman,
dem ich wol mînes lîbes gan.

A freeborn farmer desires me and I gladly wish to give myself to him[166].

Eloquently, she speaks out against marriage with an earthly man and informs her parents (and in fact also the divine bridegroom in the next world) of her willingness to marry; her father and mother eventually give in since they believe the girl's speech, which is all too reasonable, must be inspired by the Holy Spirit. The question of whether this determined resistance against her parents' ban and her hard-won self-determination in matters of marriage – female disobedience, in the medieval view – is judged ambivalently, has been discussed above in chapter 2. But it is certain that the further progress of the story, specifically the involvement of two protagonists, corrects the radical nature of the would-be bride of God.

Priester Wernher too shows the socially-determined redirecting of a disobedient bride of God in the life of another real woman. He too tells at length of a conflict about the unconventional arrangement of her (love-)life. No sooner has the girl Mary reached so-called marriageable age, than she finds herself in great trouble which also stems from hiding a secret. Her previous history, which

---

[163] Hartmann von Aue, *Der arme Heinrich*, 467-903.

[164] The effect of the bride's response is even greater if one considers the importance of the motif of the bride of Christ, which is only partial in this narrative. For this, see the remarks in chapter 2.

[165] Hartmann von Aue, *Der arme Heinrich*, 533-538.

[166] Hartmann von Aue, *Der arme Heinrich*, 775-6.

is told by Priester Wernher carefully following his apocryphal source, must be unfolded briefly to make clear that from the very beginning Mary is a bride of God, who responds in both word and deed.

Mary is chosen already in the womb – a 'first move' by the bridegroom. An angel informs her mother Anne that she is *swanger* [...] *cheiserlicher burde* (pregnant with an imperial burden)[167], that the daughter in her womb is blessed and unique among women and will be chosen as the queen of all the heavenly hosts, the mother and dwelling-place of God. The tiny bride cannot respond otherwise than vitally to this question: she is born, as it says consistently, as *brûte* (bride)[168]. There follow two further lively responses when she is a small girl: from childhood she prepares herself for being a bride of God – in the form of a life not of childlike laughter and chatter, but of diligence and ascetic virtue, which she understands as wifely preparation for the *himelischen wirte* (lord of heaven) who wishes to marry her and live with her[169]. But Mary also prepares herself through intimate and loving contact (*tougenliche minne*[170]) with the angel Gabriel. She is greatly concerned to keep the evening encounters secret, but to the community of women in which she lives *waz ez unverborgen* (it was unconcealed)[171]. It is Wernher's addition that Mary guards her contact with the angel as a secret and shields it from the knowledge of others[172]. A similar way of protecting her intimacy is invoked by Mechthild's bride of God: *die brúte mûssent alles nit sagen* (brides may not tell everything they experience)[173].

This previous history proves that inwardly Mary has long ago given her response to her divine bridegroom. Before this 'yes' can be realized in the (again very private) Annunciation scene, however, it must first be tested publicly, perhaps for two reasons: Mary will fulfill a very public and thus particularly testing task as a bride of God; and a young woman unwilling to marry and thus disobedient is very fertile ground from a narrative point of view. In any case, the testing of her connection with a bridegroom who is not of this world reveals itself as a stony path. It begins when the rich Abiathar spies her beauty and immediately makes up his mind *daz er die maget gewunne sînem lieben sun ze*

---

[167] Priester Wernher, *Maria*, C 613-14, A 549-550, D 619-620.

[168] This is the first time that Priester Wernher calls Mary a bride (*Maria*, C 1078, A 962, D 1048). Later her bridal status is referred to more clearly, e.g., *sie ist des himels frouwen unde brût* (she is the lady and bride of heaven) (C 1313, A missing, D 1257) and, in MS D only, twice again near the end: *des himels brut* (the bride of heaven) (D 3225, C missing) and *die lieben gotes brut* (the dear brides of God) (D 3429, A missing).

[169] Priester Wernher, *Maria*, C 1477 ff., A 1277, D 1403 ff.; for her moderation in laughing, see C 1516 f.; in eating, see C 1390 ff., for her industriousness, see C 1358 ff.

[170] Priester Wernher, *Maria*, C 1402-1403, D 1350-1351, A 1218-1219.

[171] Priester Wernher, *Maria*, C 1399, A 1215 ff., D 1346.

[172] Hans Fromm 1955, 56.

[173] Mechthild von Magdeburg, *Das fließende Licht der Gottheit*, II,19,33; trans. Tobin, 82.

wunne (that he will acquire the maiden for the delight of his son)[174]. But the father hardly has a chance to file his claim, because Mary interrupts him with a vehement rejection. In at least one manuscript, she declares her allegiance to her divine bridegroom for the first time; she does not want a connection with any other man:

> *sie sprah, daz sie nien wolte*
> *iemer man geruren.*
> *daz wertliche ungefure*
> *duhte sie so chumberriche*
> *daz sie gerne friliche*
> *lebet ane mannes gebende*
> *untze an des libes ende.*
> *got einen hæte sie erwelt,*
> *dem si lip mit sele selt,*
> *daz si wêre sin div vnd sin brût,*
> *er bediv ir herre vnd ir trût.*

She said she never wanted to touch a man. Since worldly hardship seemed to her so full of cares, she would like to live free and without being bound to a husband until the end of her life. She had chosen only God and had dedicated herself to him body and soul so that she might be his maid and bride, and he her lord and beloved[175].

The case becomes public knowledge when the disgusted wooer of the bride buys the support of the community and wants to purchase no other bride but her for his son, by any means whatever. Her second, public parrying speech is even more uncompromising:

> *'wes mûet ir ivh, herren min?*
> *lat dize umbescheiden spil sin,*
> *wand ich niemer man gwinne*
> *ze wertliker minne!*
> *ir ne schult mih niht reizzen.*
> *ia han ich got entheizzen*
> *min sele unbewollen:*
> *mag ich daz eruollen,*
> *daz ist der beste rat*
> *da min gedinge anstat.'*

---

[174] Priester Wernher, *Maria*, C 1539 ff., here 1545-6, A 1329 ff., C 1465 ff.
[175] Priester Wernher, *Maria*, D 1482-1492; (abbreviated) C 1554-1560, A 1344-1350.

'Why are you going to these lengths, my lords? Let this bold venture be, as I will never take a husband in worldly love! You should not provoke me, for have I not promised my pure soul to God? If I can fulfill this, it is the best goal I can hope for'[176].

The case of the disobedient woman intensifies. A bribed bishop tries to order her into marriage with theological arguments (marriage and motherhood have been woman's lot since Eve): *frŏe la uarn dinen spot: nim den man ze e* (My Lady, give up your contempt and marry the man)[177]. In a last eloquent speech of resistance Mary shows her sound knowledge of the Bible (she points to her forerunners Abel and Elijah) and prophesies to the gentlemen they could better squeeze water from a stone than move her to marriage[178].

The *kindiske wibe* (childlike woman, D 1601) angers the men who are present, and, consumed by fury, they decide on a trial by ordeal. Once more the rod of Aaron is called on to arbitrate a dispute: whose bride should Mary be?[179] The old widower Joseph, too, for whom marriage would be extremely unwelcome, brings along a dry twig out of pure obedience. Well, we know the outcome: Mary and Joseph, heavy-hearted, bow to the divine sign at least as much as to public opinion[180]. Despite Joseph's sincere opposition, they insist that he *die maget ivnge in sinen gewalt næme* (should take the young maiden into his power)[181]. Mary, on the other hand, clarifies that she is prepared to obey the distribution of power and the hierarchy between the sexes ordained on earth, but that she will not be coerced sexually[182]. In accordance with the ritual, she accepts the wedding ring and bride-gift from the hand of her future husband, who is luckily also very unwilling to marry. He is already afraid that he will not be able to fulfill his marital duty of surveillance, for which reason five women from Mary's previous entourage are sent with her as keepers.

This doggedly imposed marriage between two people is of course interesting from the point of view of the narrative. It is not lacking in comedy or at least tragi-comedy. In none other of the works investigated here are the personal premises and social complications of the parties involved narrated with such

---

[176] Priester Wernher, *Maria*, D 1519-1528; (with slight deviations) C 1588-1598, A 1372-1382.

[177] Priester Wernher, *Maria*, D 1544-1545; the whole speech by the bishop: C 1604 ff., A 1385 ff., D 1531 ff. – Wesle's reconstruction of manuscript C, which has been cut up, stops after the bishop's speech and does not start again until the Annunciation by the angel; manuscripts A and D (very vivid) keep back the dispute until Mary's marriage to Joseph.

[178] Priester Wernher, *Maria*, D 1560-1598, A 1412-1444.

[179] Priester Wernher, *Maria*, D 1666, A 1502.

[180] Priester Wernher, *Maria*, A 1790 ff; D 2020 ff.

[181] Priester Wernher, *Maria*, D 1908-1909, A 1702-1703.

[182] Priester Wernher, *Maria*, D 2062-2102, A 1824-1864.

relish as they are in manuscript D of Priester Wernher's *Maria*. This is determined on the one hand by the source (apocryphal texts, for the first time in
German vernacular literature) and the genre; this life of Mary is carefully
worked out so that God's plan for Salvation and marriage shines through here,
all the more triumphantly since the divine bridegroom must find the Ariadne's
thread in the labyrinth of the social ordering of the sexes. On the other hand,
this purely legal, and thus feigned, marriage makes it possible for the young
bride of God to respond to the husband of her choice despite all public ani-
mosity, and – in her repeated rejection of other husbands – to repeat her 'yes'
to him continually.

And yet all these affirmations – like the pre-Annunciation at the well[183] –
essentially belong only to the background because it is only with the Annunciation that Mary becomes a fully-fledged bride and mother of God. The declaration of love which takes place in the ladies' chamber leaves no room for an
explicit response since the bridegroom wishes to occupy his beloved as a
dwelling-place[184]. This is what the angel informs her; Mary ponders what it
may mean, and the angel then states it more precisely: she will give birth to a
son[185]. Emboldened, she begins to analyze the message: where will the child
come from, since she is, after all, a virgin, and has always "zealously" ensured
that she has remained "without all knowledge of union with a man"[186]. The
Holy Spirit will, the angel reassures her, cause God to be able to "be with her".
This explanation allows her not only to hope and believe but also to take on her
task. For the last time, she now gives her definitive answer – her extended *fiat
mihi*:

> *si sprach in ir gemuete:*
> *'got mвzze mich behвten.*
> *als ich dich herre hore jehen,*
> *also mvezze mir geschehen:*
> *al nach deinen worten*
> *wil ich genade warten [...].'*

She said in her soul: 'May God take care of me. Let it happen to me as you
have said, lord: fully in accordance with your words, I will await
grace[...]'[187].

---

[183] Priester Wernher, *Maria*, C 2428 ff., A 2041 ff., D 2321 ff.
[184] Priester Wernher, *Maria*, A 2133-2148, C breaks off here, D greatly altered.
[185] Priester Wernher, *Maria*, A 2149 ff., C breaks off, D 2432 ff.
[186] Priester Wernher, *Maria*, A 2167 ff., C missing, D 2446 ff.
[187] Priester Wernher, *Maria*, A 2209-2214; C missing, (more briefly) D 2488-2490.

The Silent Yes of the Bride

The responses of the bride considered until now have been characterized by
the juxtaposition of worldly and spiritual marriage. They reject the one form
of marriage and fight for the other. Thus their response is consistently active,
eloquent, and self-determined. Nevertheless, all their lives they remain within
the social sphere of influence of marriage, whether this binds them to a
human husband or to a God who is represented as male. The sexualized motif
of the bride of God is tailored to the female sex, to the way of life imposed on
it, and to the power differences between husband and wife. But what do the
responses of a bride look like if the text does not narrate a female biography,
but rather intends to provide collective or individual behavioral guidelines for
a monastic bride of God or one who represents humanity as a whole? Then –
this is the first thing which becomes apparent – the nuns or believers (men
and women) addressed must first learn how to respond themselves, participating in the intimate process. They can only do this if they identify with the
bride, slip inside her skin, and learn to speak from her internal perspective.
The following texts devote themselves to this didactic goal using various literary means.

We have already seen that the *St. Trudperter Hohelied* addresses primarily
monastic women as brides of God. However, it also understands the soul of
every human being and humanity as a whole as an eroticized being. This is
particularly apparent in the key-scene, already mentioned, where humanity is
kissed by God. The text therefore calls the audience to be brides – once the
possibility of the kiss has been reinstated by Mary[188]. The emotive tone and
the use of emotive imperatives – together with a more differentiated, even
innovative, vocabulary of love, and a rich language of tender, particularly
maternal gestures – appeal to a longing to be kissed oneself, to be a bride oneself[189]. It aims to arouse by promising a warm heart and a body free of lust[190].
The promise demonstrates that the brides addressed do not live in the world
and among men but belong in the a priori bridal category of virgins consecrated to God. The erotic pleasures promised are alluring because they com-
pensate for the joys of love that have to be forgone in this world – a premise,
moreover, which also lies behind the profession of fidelity of Mechthild's

---

[188] *St. Trudperter Hohelied*, 10,30-11,1.
[189] From 11,5 there is a build-up of imperatives directed towards the audience. On the language and its affective exhortations, cf. Friedrich Ohly 1993b and Friedrich Ohly 1998, passim;
on the vocabulary, see Ingeborg Sauer-Geppert, passim; Hildegard E. Keller 1993, 453 ff. in general, on gestures of maternal gentleness, see 220-253.
[190] *St. Trudperter Hohelied*, 11,13-14.

bride: *din brust und min ist ein, ungedrukt von allen mannen sunder dich alleine* (Your breast and mine are one, not caressed by any man but you alone)[191].

> *Nû gêt zuo ir iuncvrouwen, ir dâ nie mit girde gekusten.*
> *nû singet ir schoenesten, ir der welte mit vlîze nie gesunget.*
> *iuwer brüste werdent von gote gehalsen, wan sie nie nehein man bevie.*
> *nû singet ir liebesten, wan ir nie heiser enwurdet von weltlicheme sange.*

So set to it, you virgins, who have never been kissed with desire. Sing now, you beauties, who have never eagerly sung of the world. Your breasts will be embraced by God, since they were never yet touched by a man. Now sing, o dearest ones, because you have not yet been made hoarse by worldly songs[192].

Through exhortation, the *St. Trudperter Hohelied* beckons the women it addresses towards brideship and leads them into an internalized spirituality using erotic terms. This didactic mysticism occurs in the interaction between the text and the nuns addressed, as is the stated intention of this text of devotional instruction[193].

So how is the bride aroused and made to respond? The same question is put in very different literary terms when *Das fließende Licht der Gottheit* presents the laborious awakening of the "impassive soul" in dialogue form. Here it is not primarily a text which is trying to bestir its readers but an allegorical figure which tries to sensitize another figure within the text to the divine bridegroom[194]. Can this figure of Love instruct the readers by allowing them, more or less as voyeurs[195], to listen in on the dry, pedagogically crafted dialogue in the text? In any case, the readers observe the emotive to-ing and fro-ing from the outside, seeing not only how Love pesters the soul with questions[196] but also how she converts and awakens it: "The awakening of the soul is not reported, but rather occurs in and through the dialogue itself. The dialogue performs what it speaks about: conversion"[197]. The sluggish willfulness of the soul

---

[191] Mechthild von Magdeburg, *Das fließende Licht der Gottheit,* II,25,138-139; trans. Tobin, 96. Hans Neumann reconstructed these two lines from the Latin *Revelationes* (see his commentary, 45); Margot Schmidt did not translate them – cf. also I,42 and I,43.

[192] *St. Trudperter Hohelied*, 11,5-10.

[193] Cf. *St. Trudperter Hohelied*, 145,12-13.

[194] Mechthild von Magdeburg, *Das fließende Licht der Gottheit,* II,23. Cf. Paul Michel's analysis of the dialogue (Paul Michel 1995).

[195] Paul Michel 1995, 63 f., summarizes the pedagogical dialectic.

[196] The parts of the dialogue often begin with the interjections *eya* and *owe*; there is also no shortage of qualifying adjectives when one party addresses the other.

[197] Paul Michel 1995, 64: "Es wird nicht vom Aufwachen der Seele berichtet, sondern dieses ereignet sich im und durch den Dialog selbst. Der Dialog macht das vor, wovon er spricht: die Konversion".

– *"Las mich ungewekket, ich weis nit, was du mir sagest."* ("Let me sleep, I don't know what you are talking about.") – as well as the stubborn missionary zeal of Love – *"Eya liebú, nu la dich wekken."* ("Ah my love, let me awaken you")[198] – are part of this.

If the bride is to become active, she must be informed of what a response to the offer of love from the divine bridegroom could involve. The *St. Trudperter Hohelied* concretizes what it means to become a bride in an emphatic program of virtues. The centerpiece of this is self-examination: *Nû sih wes dir gebreste.* (Now look what you may be lacking.)[199]. It is easy to recognize this general human deficit since humility, obedience, and patience, on the one hand, and love, faith, and hope, on the other, were gambled away by Lucifer, Adam, and Eve. Ever since then, Man's being in the image of God has been disrupted unless every individual person tries to win back these virtues[200]. This is the precondition for *unio mystica*. And only then does it come to marriage: *Nû gêt ez an die brûtloufte*[201]; only then is the human being led into the bedroom, into himself or herself, and into God[202].

This struggle for monastic or Christian virtues makes possible a more universal understanding of what it means to be a bride and helps to overcome the sexual fixation of the bride on the female role-pattern. The bridal soul can live in either a female or a male body, if – in accordance with the wedding allegory – the divine bridegroom grants her the "good will" for the wedding. This bridal gift corresponds to the consent of the bride required by marriage law: *âne den enwirt niemer nehein brûtloufte ioch nâch der welte ê* (Without it [the will] there can never be a marriage at all, even according to the law of the world)[203].

Das fließende Licht der Gottheit also presents the virtues as "that which leads to marriage". It personifies Faith, Love, and Hope as well as Humility, Chastity, and the seven Gifts of the Holy Ghost, and has these figures give away the bride. Accordingly, perfecting herself in these virtues constitutes the bride's active response. Mechthild lets the bridal procession pass by before the eyes of the reader and interprets it in minute detail[204]. Male, female, and animal participants in the princely procession personify virtues, human senses, powers of

---

[198] Mechthild von Magdeburg, *Das fließende Licht der Gottheit*, II,23,6-7 and II,23,33; trans. Tobin, 87-88.

[199] *St. Trudperter Hohelied*, 12,29.

[200] *St. Trudperter Hohelied*, 11,32-13,3; Hildegard E. Keller 1993, cf. index, s.v. Tugend).

[201] *St. Trudperter Hohelied*, 13,4.

[202] *St. Trudperter Hohelied*, 18,7 ff. Cf. the section "Becoming One", in this chapter.

[203] *St. Trudperter Hohelied*, 12,24-25.

[204] Mechthild von Magdeburg, *Das fließende Licht der Gottheit*, I,46.

the soul, passions, or bodies. It is a review of puppets, interpreted mechanically, a didactic agenda dressed up in a stiff wedding-dress.

Die Hochzeit shows the bride's response in relation to the catechism. In the play, a young woman is said to agree to a proposal of marriage. This certainly deviates from the Germanic tradition of contracting a marriage; on the other hand, it does not quite constitute consent in the sense of the ecclesiastical teachings on the subject[205]. In the first, tropological, interpretation, this response of the bride is equivalent to an exemplary Christian life. The individual Christian responds as a bride by accepting baptism and the assistance of the Holy Spirit as well as by living with the Christian message of Salvation. He obeys "those who woo the bride" (the priests) and "the bride's relatives" (the sacraments) and walks in communion with all those who wish to attend the wedding (those who do works of mercy). The bride purifies herself by taking a bath, adorns herself with the golden bridal brooch (the detailed teachings of Confession), and puts on her wedding-dress (the purity of the Blessed)[206] – a model example of a successful Christian life, allegorized as bridal happiness.

The second explanation shows Mary's 'yes' to her task. It is, amazingly, wordless. It is a contractual agreement which commits a virgin, who is prepared to carry it out, to a plan for Salvation; there is no sense in which an intimate event is gloried in for the sake of the narrative, as is the case in Priester Wernher's *Maria*. The bridegroom sends out the *engil* (angel) to woo the bride. The Annunciation is reported briefly[207] as preparing the way for a marriage which – fully in accordance with the Middle High German terminology – also means a legal covenant (*diu niuwe ê*, the New Testament). The bride does not give an explicit response; it is merely said that all people would be reconciled through the bride if the virgin did what the angel asked her to. Mary's silent response was known to all[208].

---

[205] *Die Hochzeit*, 221-222. In the Germanic *Muntehe* (marriage by purchase) the woman is not one of the parties to the contract (these are the wooing husband and the guardian, normally the father), but is rather the object of negotiation. Since in *Die Hochzeit* there is no discussion of consent, however, one cannot speak of Christianization. Thus the work is based on several different concepts of marriage (cf. Inga Persson, 37 ff., 124 and 141 ff.)

[206] Cf. on the Holy Spirit, 339-346; baptism, 347-358; the priest, 359-374; the sacraments, 375 ff.; the escorts, 482 ff.; the teachings on Confession, which includes the interpretation of the bridal brooch and of other similes, 580-709; purity, 777 ff. – on the bride's bath, see Inga Persson, 107-108, on the teachings on Confession, 109-112, on the wedding-dress, 112-113.

[207] *Die Hochzeit*, 879-892.

[208] *Die Hochzeit*, 887-892.

The Vehement Yes of a Passionate Bride

A third variety of responses articulates an unbridled vehemence which moves the brides of God outwardly and inwardly and drives them into expressing their views from within. Its effects are cryptic but not unfathomable. This impression no doubt arises partly because the bride of God envelops her passion in a mystery connected with the limits of what one is able to say. But before she erects this sort of barrier of silence, the bride – inflamed by love – speaks, calls, and shouts. One example of this is the "Lament of the Loving Soul" who, in her dialogue with her beloved God[209], exhausts every device imaginable – even feigning serious illness[210] – and will not be deterred by either self-humiliation (she begs for the mercy that would be granted to any loyal dog[211]) or aggrandizement. Suddenly she threatens her beloved, with the combined vehemence of both Lady Love, with her bow and arrows, and the seeking bride of the Song of Songs[212]:

> *Ich jage dich mit aller maht.*
> *Hette ich eines risen kraft,*
> *dú were schier von mir verlorn,*
> *keme ich reht na dir uf das spor.*

I pursue you with all my might. If I had the strength of a giant and if I got onto your trail, still I would quickly lose your tracks[213].

In another case, in similar language, Love is first praised in the abundance of her power; then a passionate first-person narrator goes on to tell the beloved not only of the ineffable greatness of her longing but also of all other gifts from God. Presumptuously, the bride states that all Creation, animate and inanimate, could not share "my heart's pursuit" and "intensity of my longing" – the passion of a passion[214].

The bride's longing is also expressed in actual movement. Journeys take place in Lamprecht von Regensburg's *Tochter Syon*; traveling brides occur twice in the *Alemannische Tochter Syon* and *Das fließende Licht der Gottheit*. They

---

[209] Mechthild von Magdeburg, *Das fließende Licht der Gottheit*, II,25.

[210] Mechthild von Magdeburg, *Das fließende Licht der Gottheit*, II,25,8-24; trans. Tobin, 93.

[211] Mechthild von Magdeburg, *Das fließende Licht der Gottheit*, II,25,29-38 and II,25,90-95; trans. Tobin, 93 and 95.

[212] Cf. chapter 5. Mechthild is even more sovereign in her statements about Christ, with whom, she says, she can do whatever she wants (II,22,18-19; trans. Tobin, 87).

[213] Mechthild von Magdeburg, *Das fließende Licht der Gottheit*, II,25,25-28; trans. Tobin, 93.

[214] Cf. Mechthild von Magdeburg, *Das fließende Licht der Gottheit*, V,31,12-31; trans. Tobin, 213.

accept the offer of love and fly immediately to heaven with their answer. In two passages, Mechthild shows how skillfully she can handle both the interpretative and the expressive sides of allegory, whether together or separately[215]. Whereas earlier the wedding-procession showed interpretative allegory, now the opposite procedure, that of expressive allegory, can be seen. Mechthild personifies a Middle High German term (e.g., *gerunge*, longing) as a male or female figure according to the grammatical gender of the word and has these allegorical personages act out what happens to the soul. Longing, hitherto merely a detail in a stiff wedding-allegory, can now fly to the bridegroom and give the bride's response. This is a dramatized 'yes' which initiates erotic events. On the instructions of the Holy Spirit, the bride then approaches the young man. Both are moved and they even dance; then she wishes to cool herself. With their soothing words, the chamberlains (the senses) provoke her resistance: "*(...) Ich bin ein vollewahsen brut, ich wil gan nach minem trut.*" ("I am a full-grown bride. I want to go to my Lover.")[216]. The senses are afraid of the blazing Godhead; the bride turns her back on them and, almost wolfishly, pursues her way to the beloved. She enters into *die verholnen kammeren der unsinlichen gotheit* (the secret chamber of the invisible Godhead)[217]. The bride's tone changes suddenly once again when she stands before the beloved, who, with the power invested in him as God and husband, commands her to undress so that he may fill her *grundelose girheit* (boundless desire) with his *endelose miltekeit* (limitless lavishness)[218].

On a second journey, too, the longing soul gains access to her beloved and forces her way in the face of the angels' resistance. Interestingly, the forceful behavior of the bride, or the soul, is reminiscent of the courtly balance of power. A noble lady exercised command over those in her service[219], but where her marriage was concerned, she was subject to the undiminished power of her lord and husband: "The authoritarian and imperious behavior of women of the aristocracy, which is confirmed by other sources, seems at first to stand in stark contrast to the picture of the subordinate wife just developed. Yet it should be recalled that in such instances they are acting not in their capacity as wives, but as members of their class toward family retainers or the poor"[220]. In addition, this sort of journey reveals the extent to which Mechthild's bride-figures oscillate between self-aggrandizement (towards the angels) and obsequiousness

---

[215] Cf. the analysis of IV,12 in Susanne Köbele, 94-96.

[216] Mechthild von Magdeburg, *Das fließende Licht der Gottheit*, I,44,63-64; trans. Tobin, 61.

[217] Mechthild von Magdeburg, *Das fließende Licht der Gottheit*, I,44,78-79; trans. Tobin, 62.

[218] Mechthild von Magdeburg, *Das fließende Licht der Gottheit*, I,44,79-88; trans. Tobin, 62.

[219] It is not only III,9 which makes clear that the angels must serve the soul and bride of God (cf. the section "Becoming One").

[220] Claudia Opitz, in: Georges Duby / Michelle Perrot 2, 279.

(towards the divine bridegroom). A journey to the beloved obviously helps one to recognize and defend one's own, human, place in Creation.

As in Lamprecht von Regensburg's work, messengers are first sent to the court of heaven. In Mechthild's work, the soul sends Longing (*gerunge*), who is "by nature swift", as a messenger to her beloved. The message is urgent: that the bride desires him. Once she has arrived on high, Longing asks to be admitted and gives the heavenly lord of the household a very vivid account of the soul, who has been left literally high and dry:

> *"Herre, ich kúnde dir, min vrŏwe mag nit lange alsust leben; wŏltistu vliessen, so mŏhte si sweben, wan der visch mag uf dem sande nit lange leben und frisch wesen".*

> "Lord, I report to you that my lady cannot live much longer in her present condition. But if you were to flow, then she could swim. A fish cannot remain alive and stay fresh long on the sand"[221].

God's prompt answer is scarcely surprising: *"Var wider, ich lan dich nu nit in, du inbringest mir die hungerige sele, der mich lustet ob allen dingen."* ("Go on back. I'm not going to let you in unless you bring me the hungry soul that I desire more than anything else".) The soul, delighted with the invitation, now sets off herself, soaring heavenwards on the wings of desire. When two angels meet her on the way and insistently ask her to account for herself – *"Vrowe sele, was wellent ir sust verre? Ir sint ie noch gekleidet mit der vinsteren erden."* ("Lady Soul, what are you doing way up here? You are still clothed with dark earth")[222] –, she immediately assumes the imperious tone she uses towards the chamberlains. She reveals the self-assurance of an imperious noble lady and rebukes the angels, who are also apostrophized as "Lords", for not greeting her. Then she counters the angels' reservations about the ascent of the earth-clad soul. Without any inhibition, she relativizes the sanctity of the angels:

> *"Ir herren, swigent des alstille und grússent mich ein wenig bas, ich wil varen minnen. Ie naher ir dem ertrich sinkent, ie me ir verbergent úwer sússes himmelbliken, und ie hŏher ich stige, ie klarer ich schine."*

> "Ye Lords, be completely quiet about that and see that you extend to me a better greeting. I am going loving. The closer you sink to earth, the more you hide your celestial splendor; And the higher I climb, the brighter I shine")[223].

---

[221] Mechthild von Magdeburg, *Das fließende Licht der Gottheit*, III,1,8-11; trans. Tobin, 101.
[222] Mechthild von Magdeburg, *Das fließende Licht der Gottheit*, III,1,16-17; trans. Tobin, 101.
[223] Mechthild von Magdeburg, *Das fließende Licht der Gottheit*, III,1,17-22; trans. Tobin,

Immediately, the angels join her obediently and escort her to the gates of heaven. The context in which such wranglings over rank take place is an erotic one. This basic model of a journey up through all the stages of being to the very highest is repeated in Lamprecht von Regensburg.

The bride in *Tochter Syon* must wait over 4000 lines before she can journey to her beloved, during which time she undergoes first a process of realization and then one of suffering[224]. It takes place against the backdrop of the castle of the heart[225], which seems to be a school for all the allegorical "neighbors" and "residents" of whom Lady Love is mistress. The Daughter of Zion's biography of love, intended after all as a narrative illustration of the doctrine of love in the introduction[226], tells of her response, which slowly but surely becomes more and more ardent. This story begins with the search for a worthy object to love, which already turns out to be quite an effort[227]. But it only really becomes strenuous when the heart flares up (with love for Christ!) and the spirit *wüete in sanfte tuonder tobeheite* (rages in agreeable love-frenzy[228]). Suggestive comments by the author stylize these affective side-effects of the therapy of love as grace: *Ich wolde gerne, ob ez got wolde, daz mîn sêle ligen solde in solher jâmerschricke an dem selben bette dicke* (…) (I would gladly wish, if God so willed, for my soul to lie often in the same bed in the same pangs of love […][229]). The equally suggestive didactic speeches[230] of Faith and Hope gradually give the soul an intimation of approaching though at first it is merely dream-like[231]. The Daughter of Zion warms visibly, above all thanks to the exegete of the Song of Songs, Lady Wisdom. It is she who teaches the soul to say the words of the bride of the Song of Songs, and explains them to her[232]. The soul, already considerably aroused, calls out to Wisdom:

"sô wol smeckt dîn rede mir,
daz mir nû zwir alsô wê

101.

[224] This main part includes anthropological and theological themes such as the relationship between body and soul, the powers of the soul, the Trinity, contemplations on the Passion, and eschatological questions.

[225] Cf. Lamprecht von Regensburg, *Tochter Syon*, 400-430.

[226] A sort of theoretical introduction explains the significance of love in the struggle between body and soul (63-288). Cf. my discussion at the beginning of the chapter (short presentation of *Tochter Syon*).

[227] Lamprecht von Regensburg, *Tochter Syon*, 294-399.

[228] Lamprecht von Regensburg, *Tochter Syon*, 448-449.

[229] Lamprecht von Regensburg, *Tochter Syon*, 376-399 (on the disappointment of love) and 450-479 (on the frenzy of love).

[230] Cf., for example, the enticing depiction of participation in the divine mystery (829 ff.), of the frenzies of love (872 ff.) or of the reinforcement of the powers of the soul (944 ff.).

[231] Cf. Lamprecht von Regensburg, *Tochter Syon*, 869-870.

nâch mînem liebe ist dan ê.
ei süezer got, wie wol mir wirt,
sô mîn minne fruht gebirt
von mînem friunt dem süezen manne!
wie gesih ich in od wanne?
ôwê daz ich niht ûz enmac! [...]
heiâ hei dan, wer bin ich,
sô ich die himelkrôn sol tragen?
daz enkan ich niemen nû gesagen."

"Your words are so delicious to me that I now long for my beloved twice as much as before. Ah, sweet God, how happy it will make me if my love bears fruit from my friend, my dear husband! How will I see him, or when? Alas, that I cannot get out [of this body]! [...] Who am I, that I should wear the crown of heaven? I cannot tell anyone about it now"[233].

As yet the bride does not turn directly to her beloved. In increasingly torturous pain, she sends further messengers to the authority immediately above them in the hierarchy of being: *senunge* (Desire) and *gerunge* (Longing), for instance, are sent not directly to the beloved, as in Mechthild, but to Lady Love[234], who, as the highest in rank, is then in turn sent to God. It is only thanks to this mediation that union eventually does come about.

The journeys, as well as the messages brought back by the messengers, show that in this case the way of the bride is a long one. It is more a path of learning than the way of the imperious journeying bride in Mechthild von Magdeburg's work. Lamprecht mediates the encounter with God in two senses. On the level of the narrative, this occurs – as in his Latin source – through the conversing allegorical women. On the level of reader – text communication, the excurses by the author explain how many spiritual steps have to be gone through on the way to God – provided that God even permits the journey in the first place[235]. Moreover, Lamprecht has personal reasons for not showing a bride who forces her way to her beloved irresistibly and immoderately. This would be too great a contradiction of his creed of *mâze* (moderation)[236]. Even

---

[232] Lamprecht von Regensburg, *Tochter Syon*, 1822 ff., above all 1925 ff.

[233] Lamprecht von Regensburg, *Tochter Syon*, 2093-2123.

[234] Lamprecht von Regensburg, *Tochter Syon*, 2902 ff. Together with Mercy and Prayer, Love is then sent to heaven and before God (from 3325 ff.). She does not bring back a message from God directly intended for the soul, but instead four drops as a therapeutic treatment (3770 ff.).

[235] Lamprecht often deals critically with the fact (a painful one for him) that the mystical experience of love is a question of Grace and thus cannot be forced (discussed repeatedly, and sometimes polemically, 2711-3040).

when she arrives in heaven for her wedding, his Daughter of Zion is restrained, though inwardly glowing. Only after the actual 'yes', does the bride become immoderately impatient. When Lady Love informs her that "sun and moon and stars and subject" to her beloved, the bride is seized by a haste which is not unknown in the other brides[237].

> *"frowe", sprach sie, "nû wol dan,*
> *dâ wirt vürbaz niht bîtens an.*
> *ich wil ze im, er bîtet mîn,*
> *ine mac ân in niht langer sîn.*
> *île, wirn suln uns niht sûmen,*
> *ich wil dise gegent rûmen,*
> *wand ich muoz varen in sîn lant,*
> *dâ bin ich baz dan hie bekant."*

"My Lady", she said, "come now, let there be no more waiting. I want to go to him, he is waiting for me, I cannot do without him anymore. Hurry, we should delay no longer, I wish to leave this place; I have to go to his country, I know my way around better there than here"[238].

The soul can no longer be pacified and faints from such fires of love *daz sich daz herze in der brust erschutte und erkrachte* (that the heart in her breast shattered and split with sighs)[239]. Standing near the bride, dumbfounded at this last response, is Lady Love, who smiles mischievously with secret pride, for she has consciously contrived all:

> *sie smielte unde lachte,*
> *wand sie ir seneden ungemach*
> *mit süezer rede machte.*

She smiled and laughed, because she had caused these pangs of longing with her enticing words[240].

[236] Cf. Lamprecht von Regensburg, *Tochter Syon*, 2994 ff.

[237] Lamprecht von Regensburg, *Tochter Syon*, 3960-3965; the 'yes' of the bride occurs in 3966-3972. Cf. the scene at the doctor's in Salerno (*Der arme Heinrich*, 1107 ff.); the *St. Trudperter Hohelied* warns, from a quite different perspective, against being over-hasty in wishing to die (120,12 ff.; see below for more details).

[238] Lamprecht von Regensburg, *Tochter Syon*, 3973-3980.

[239] Lamprecht von Regensburg, *Tochter Syon*, 3998-3999.

Becoming One

> *Therfore most I*
> *nedys be homly wyth the and lyn in thi bed wyth the.*[241]

What has to happen for the lovers to come together, and what actually happens when things get that far? This question opens up the full panoply of the semantics of the erotic *unio mystica* and also – perhaps unexpectedly – the semantics of death. Death is dyed in erotic and matrimonial colors, since death opens the eternal wedding-feast. However, as far as bridal happiness which can be experienced already on earth is concerned, one can see that veiling and unveiling hold each other in the balance. Secrets are exclusive, as we readers come to discover.

Heavenly Inclinations

Those texts which assume a sort of erotic original state, a primal kiss between the Creator and humankind, show the *unio mystica* in its cosmic dimensions: heaven leans down to earth. This is also the case if there is talk of the Incarnation or of Mary as the bride of God in the mission of Salvation history.

The Annunciation, as Priester Wernher's *Maria* narrates it according to the apocryphal gospel, combines several contradictions in a single event. This time-lapse results in the well-known Christian paradox, which does not even make sense to Mary herself at first[242]: Mary, married to an old man, becomes pregnant by another (divine) bridegroom, whose bride she has secretly been for a long time, yet she remains a virgin – *maget ân ende, mûtir ane meil* (unendingly a virgin, mother without blemish)[243]. Once Mary can trust the angel who tells her of the circumstances in which she will become pregnant, *von des glôben samen wart sie zehante swanger* (she immediately became pregnant from the seeds of faith)[244]. The cosmic image for the union of the lovers corresponds to this unusual brideship:

da wart der himel genæiget,
als uns div scrift zæiget,

---

[240] Lamprecht von Regensburg, *Tochter Syon*, 4001-3.

[241] Christ addressing the soul, in: *The Book of Margery Kempe*, chapter 36, ed. Barry Windeatt, 196.

[242] Cf. Mary's reaction to the angel's message, in C 2417 ff. and 2133 ff. (Section on female responses).

[243] Priester Wernher, *Maria*, D 2536 (missing in C and A). – Joseph's inner conflicts with his situation are shown in the 3rd book; an angel stands by him.

zuo der erde; daz ergie
do in unser frŏe umbevie
mit mæitwesentem libe.
div nîe wart ze wibe,
sie ist mit der erde gemeinte,
zu der sih alsus uereinte
der himel ioh des himels wirt.

Then, as the Scriptures tell us, heaven leaned down to earth. This happened when our mistress embraced him with her virginal body. She who never became a woman is designated by the earth, which unified itself with heaven, even with the lord of heaven, in just this way[245].

In the *St. Trudperter Hohenlied* there is an initial primal kiss between humanity and God, which is interrupted by the Fall of Man. Originally, "the mouth of our will and our love" lay on the mouth of God – "his goodness and his mercy"[246]. This formula is all there is to say until two dissimilar beings can unite to reconstitute this lost unity – naturally in the terms of that same formula. The kissing God and the kissed Mary wordlessly put their lips together:

der munt dâ mite si kust, daz was ir wille und ir minne. der was gestecket an
sîne güete unde an sîne genâde. der munt ist zuogetân küssende, er wirt ûfgetân
sprechende. er hete si ê geküsset ê er ir zuo spraeche.
er was der küssende, sie minnende.
si was diu gekuste, in minnende.

The mouth with which she kissed was her will and her love. It was fixed on his goodness and his mercy. The mouth is closed in kissing, it is opened in speaking. He had already kissed her before he spoke to her. He was the one who kissed, loving her. She was the one who was kissed, loving him[247].

Afterwards, God says "a word" to the one he has kissed, which is *ze vleische worden und wonet in uns* (made flesh and dwells within us)[248]. The kiss signifies Christ. From now on, the allegorical formula of the kiss between heaven and earth reveals that primal unity which is a fundamental concern of the text on both a collective and an individual level and which is consummated in the *unio mystica*. In this way, the erotic registers are integrated into the *St. Trudperter*

---

[244] Priester Wernher, *Maria*, D 2496-2497, A 2220-2221, C missing.
[245] Priester Wernher, *Maria*, D 2525-2333 (again in D 3811-3816). MS D gives much more detail here and explains the figurativeness, whereas A keeps it very brief (A 2229-2231), C missing.
[246] *St. Trudperter Hohelied*, 8,15-17.
[247] *St. Trudperter Hohelied*, 8,29-34, on Cant. 1,1a.

Hohelied's repertoire for speaking about mystical union[249]. The nuns are taught again and again to practice this union, very much as the personified Faith instructs the Daughter of Zion in Lamprecht's text[250]. No matter whether this lesson is given to the readers directly by the commentator or occurs within the text between individual figures, it is always grounded in the Augustinian doctrine of the three powers of the soul which make a human being fit for God (*capax Dei*), and which can therefore be linked with the divine Trinity or its attributes[251]. This formula for unity was already discernible in the primal kiss, and since Mary's atonement it has been valid for all heaven's leanings towards the human brides of God.

Das fließende Licht der Gottheit also presents the erotic original wedding between the divine bridegroom and his created bride, i.e., humanity. The nuptial interpretation of Genesis[252] tells in one breath of the creation of the bride and of union with her. Although this brief union lasts only until the Fall, it is a given fact from the beginning and needs no explanation. On the other hand, Mechthild also dramatizes the erotic encounters of one individual soul. In the latter scenario, it is not a question of heaven inclining to earth but of brides beginning to journey, as impetuously as the one whose passion drives her directly before the divine beloved. There the bride stands and speaks, and there the narrator stops at the ineffable:

> *"Herre, nu bin ich ein nakent sele und du in dir selben ein wolgezieret got. Únser zweiger gemeinschaft ist das ewige lip ane tot". So geschihet da ein selig stilli nach ir beider willen. Er gibet sich ir und si git sich ime. Was ir nu geschehe, das weis si, und des getröste ich mich.*

"Lord, now I am a naked soul and you in yourself are a well-adorned God. Our shared lot is eternal life without death". Then a blessed stillness that both desire comes over them. He surrenders himself to her, and she surrenders herself to him. What happens to her then – she knows – and that is fine with me[253].

---

[248] *St. Trudperter Hohelied*, 9,1 and 10,13-14.

[249] These modes of expression can be accounted for by the Song of Songs: liquefaction and transformation, anatomical or nutrition-related concepts of unity (e.g. the ecclesiastical body of Christ in the *St. Trudperter Hohelied*, 75,18-90,5-8; cf. on this, Hildegard E. Keller 1993, 253-314).

[250] Lamprecht von Regensburg, *Tochter Syon*, 794 ff. The ultimate transformation of the human soul by the Trinity is eschatological, as one would expect from the messenger Fides (907-977).

[251] In summary, the soul's power of memory (*gehugede*) is linked with Might (God the Father), the power of insight (*vernunst*), with Wisdom (Christ), and the will (*willen*), with Goodness and Mercy (Holy Spirit). The human being in the image of God is echoed in this triad of powers of the soul.

[252] Cf. Mechthild von Magdeburg, *Das fließende Licht der Gottheit*, III,9.

On another occasion, the bride, who had held her own against two angels on her journey, stands bewildered before God and subordinates herself to the beloved as to a lord and husband, glorifying him and humbling herself graciously as though before a ruler. This is a relationship-dynamic which corresponds to the mysterious alternation between humiliation and aggrandizement and to the ordering, manifest in this alternation, of all that has being; it shapes *Das fließende Licht der Gottheit* both as poetry and as theology[254]. Humiliation and enhancement always intertwine, even during the amorous gestures, when the fatherly beloved draws the humble bride up to himself, embraces her, and carries her up high above all that is created:

Do nam er si under sine gotlichen arme und leite sin vetterliche hant uf ire brúste und sach si an ir antlút. Merke, ob si do út wart gekússet? In dem kusse wart si do ufgeruket in die höhste höhi über aller engel köre.

He took her in his divine arms and laid his fatherly hand on her breast and looked into her face. Well, was she kissed at all? In the kiss she was drawn up to the most sublime heights above all the angel choirs[255].

Lamprecht tells how heaven inclines to the Daughter of Zion's castle of the heart. An extremely festive wedding takes place, both as a social occasion and as a very intimate encounter. The preparations for the wedding form the prelude.

After even the divine bridegroom suffers from life-threatening wounds of love and calls out the appropriate verse from the Song of Songs[256], the waiting soul can assemble the wedding-procession. She must reject all the menial maidservants (the vices) and position herself in the circle of her lady companions (the virtues)[257]. The bride, impatient to the point of illness, has to be given a medicine[258]; then the bringing home of the bride can begin – in a dreamlike way that is difficult to pin down:

[...] daz si viel zuckende an
den briutegamen, dem sie
den hals mit halsen umbevie

---

[253] Mechthild von Magdeburg, *Das fließende Licht der Gottheit*, I,44,88-92; trans. Tobin, 62.

[254] Cf. Mavi Rinaldi; Alois M. Haas 1996, 248 ff. and 279 ff., Marianne Heimbach 1989, 57-66, Susanne Köbele.

[255] Mechthild von Magdeburg, *Das fließende Licht der Gottheit*, III,1,31-34; trans. Tobin, 102.

[256] After Cant. 4:9 (Lamprecht von Regensburg, *Tochter Syon*, 3741-3744).

[257] The menial servants who are not worthy of heaven are feelings such as anger, hatred, quarrelsomeness, unwillingness, grief and other forms of 'letting oneself go' (Lamprecht von Regensburg, *Tochter Syon*, 3822 ff.). The companions who are agreeable to the bridegroom are the virtues already introduced (3844 ff.)

[258] The four drops taken by Lady Love from the wounded beloved (Lamprecht von Regensburg, *Tochter Syon*, 3766 ff.).

und druht in an ir herze.
do gelac ir sâ der smerze
und der kumber, der ir war.
sie kust in aber und aber dar.
ei wie rehte wol ir was!

[...] so that she fell against the bridegroom, enraptured, fell about his neck in an embrace and pressed him to her heart. That stilled her pain and cares. She kissed him again and again. Ah, what great well-being she felt![259]

A careful exegesis of the kiss[260] also prepares us for what is to come: both heaven and the intimate chambers of the heart open up to one another – *des himels und des herzen tür was weder slôz noch rigel vür* (neither heaven's door nor that of the heart had either a lock or a bolt on it)[261]. Since the two rooms are connected to one another, all the servants of heaven and of the heart (the angels and the allegorical women, respectively) move animatedly up and down[262]. Reciprocal gestures of love, familiar from the secular love lyric as well as from the passages from Mechthild's text discussed above, herald a long-awaited happiness:

die wîl ist ungescheiden
der wille in in beiden,
sô wehselt sich ir zweier gir,
sie ist in im und er in ir.
ei welh süeziu wehselunge
wirt von ir zweier gerunge!
er gert ir sie gert sîn,
sus wirt ir lieb einander schîn.

All the while [= while they are together], their wills are united, their desire is exchanged, she is in him, and he in her. Ah, what sweet exchange there is in their longing! He desires her, she desires him; in this way their mutual joy becomes apparent to each other[263].

Death as Homecoming and Wedding

Death separates lovers. Without this tragic topos, the secular discourse of love would be bereft of many of its most famous exponents. This is equally true of

---

[259] Lamprecht von Regensburg, *Tochter Syon*, 4023-4030.
[260] Lamprecht von Regensburg, *Tochter Syon*, 4031-4104.
[261] Lamprecht von Regensburg, *Tochter Syon*, 4113-4.
[262] Lamprecht von Regensburg, *Tochter Syon*, 4110-4126. The wedding takes place in the private chambers of the heart (4110 ff.), from 4134, however, the soul and her entourage move into heaven.
[263] Lamprecht von Regensburg, *Tochter Syon*, 4188-4195.

the religious discourse of love and marriage but paradoxically the converse is also true – not only from an eschatological point of view: death unites lovers. Precisely in the coming together of the human bride of God and the divine bridegroom, death plays a decisive role.

Even the Song of Songs already links death and love with that compelling logic which inspires Mechthild to metaphors for *unio* such as: *Wer von minnen stirbet, den sol man in gotte begraben* (Who dies of love shall be buried in God)[264]. The contracting of a marriage can also be used as an allegory of dying and can overlay death with an idea of homecoming and unification. Thus, in the first instance, Christ's death on the Cross was understood as a betrothal or wedding ceremony: the betrothal (*desponsatio*) of the one bridegroom with his collective bride (the Church) and thereby with his many individual brides (souls). Traces of this sort of erotic or matrimonial theology of the Cross are found in the *St. Trud-perter Hohenlied*, in formulations by Mechthild von Magdeburg[265], as well as in the interpretation of the kiss of Judas given by her fellow-Cistercian, Mechthild von Hackeborn. In the latter's *Liber specialis gratiae*, Christ says of Judas: "In this kiss my heart felt such love that, had he only repented, by the strength of that kiss I would have won his soul as my bride. For in that moment, I took protection of all those whom I had predestined to brideship from eternity"[266].

It is Lamprecht von Regensburg, however, who, in his *Tochter Syon*, gives the most penetrating depiction of how closely *passio crucis* and *passio amoris* are intermingled[267]. On the Cross Christ reveals his passionate love for the bride, which is why Lamprecht depicts Christ's martyrdom twice, in erotically suggestive terms. In the humiliation of Christ, heaven once more bows down "to the valley"[268], again as a revelation of love. Christ was so full of love, we are told, that he allowed himself to be pierced with nails, spear, and thorns, *daz sîn minne binnen muoste ûz im rinnen* (so that his inner love had to flow out of him)[269]. The Incarnation and, above all, the Crucifixion appear to be the descent of the wooing bridegroom to the bride who could never have made it to the beloved by her own strength[270]. That Christ does not send someone to

---

[264] Mechthild von Magdeburg, *Das fließende Licht der Gottheit*, I,3,28-29; trans. Tobin, 43. – Cf. Cant. 8:6.

[265] *St. Trudperter Hohelied*, 68,2-4; Mechthild von Magdeburg, *Das fließende Licht der Gottheit*, I,22,4-5; trans. Tobin, 49.

[266] Mechthild von Hackeborn, *Das Buch vom strömenden Lob*, 86.

[267] See also chapter 5; and Mechthild von Magdeburg, *Das fließende Licht der Gottheit,*, III, 9, 73-79.

[268] Lamprecht von Regensburg, *Tochter Syon*, 1483-84.

[269] Lamprecht von Regensburg, *Tochter Syon*, 1458-9.

[270] Lamprecht von Regensburg, *Tochter Syon*, 1489-1504.

woo the bride but bears all the vividly depicted suffering unto death himself is a sign of the majesty of this wedding through the Cross:

in twanc ir minne zuo der gir
daz er sie selbe holte
dârumbe er dicke dolte
manigerslahte smâheit
mit kumberlîcher arbeit.
er lie sich hungern unde dürsten,
dem himelischen fürsten
wart dicke kalt unde heiz,
in badete manec angestsweiz,
wand als schier er wart geborn,
dô wart den juden ûf in zorn
und vârten sîn unz an den tac
daz er tôter vor in lac,
und alrêrst, dô er erstarp,
zuo einer brût er sie erwarp.
von Syon tohter nû sich,
wie tiure er hât gemahelt dich!

Her love forced him to desire to fetch her himself, for which reason he suffered manifold disgrace with sorrowful tribulation. He allowed himself to be starved and left to thirst; the prince of heaven was often cold and hot, he was bathed in the sweat of fear, because as soon as he was born he attracted the anger of the Jews, who pursued him until the day that he lay dead before them. Now, only with his death, he won her [the soul] as his bride. Now see, Daughter of Zion, at what high price he married you[271].

This erotic Christology is linked with a second way of connecting death and the love union, this time on the level of the individual. Several of the texts show that the individual death of a human being is often overlaid with the idea of homecoming or unification. In the medieval view, and still today in the language of death notices, dying is 'going home' or 'being called home'. With regard to the motif of the bride of God, death has the additional meaning of at last being able to get married and celebrate the bliss of being together with the beloved in his house, one's own home. There is, moreover, not only a Christological, but also a sacramental reason that death can appear as the prelude to a marriage. This reason is given by only one of the texts, *Die Hochzeit*. In its first interpretation, aimed at the faithful, this catechetic text recalls the general bridal concept of Christian life. Being a bride is not a question of one's place

---

[271] Lamprecht von Regensburg, *Tochter Syon*, 1506-22.

within the Church nor of one's sex, but of baptism. In their white baptismal garments all baptized men and women wear their wedding dresses, which they will need after the Resurrection of the Dead. This is an idea, already known in Patristic writings[272], which is constantly present in *Die Hochzeit*:

> *so bezeichent daz vingerlin*
> *den westerhuot sin,*
> *den daz chint ouffe hat,*
> *als ez ze jungist erstat,*
> *unde ouch diu gotes gemahelin*
> *immir ewich schule sin.*

Thus the ring signifies the christening-robe which the child wears when he or she at the last arises to be the wife of God for ever and ever[273].

The temporal structure which, in chapter 2, I identified as characteristic for the marriage allegory, is specific to the bridal coloring of death. The contracting of a marriage (wooing the bride, betrothal, bringing home the bride, wedding) becomes an allegorical chronology of the life of a bride of God right up to the end. The human being on earth can be interpreted either as the betrothed before the wedding or as a wife or widow whose husband awaits her in the next world. In the first understanding, death means the wedding and bringing home of the bride[274]; in the second, it is the reunion of the married couple, which convention places in the house of the divine husband. In this way, the asymmetry of worldly marriage imprints itself on the relationship with God: the human being can no more determine his own death than the bride can determine when she will be brought home by the bridegroom. It is he who decides when an individual bride will "enter into the bridal chamber", i.e., will die; he also determines when his wedding with the collective bride, viz., the end of time, will take place. Sometimes a miniature matrimonial *ars moriendi* can be constructed on the basis of this idea. Lamprecht von Regensburg, for instance, visualizes the proper attitude to death in erotic terms and encourages the bride to prepare to leave her place on earth when the beloved requests her to: *dû ensîst alle zît bereit gegen sîner heimlicheit.* (be always prepared to be brought home and to be intimate with him)[275].

---

[272] Cf. Alfred C. Rush, 86 ff.

[273] *Die Hochzeit*, 353-358.

[274] For the period of time between *desponsatio* and *nuptiae* in the high Middle Ages, see chapter 2.

[275] Lamprecht von Regensburg, *Tochter Syon*, 1525-6. This imperative follows on from the wedding on the Cross explained before. – The fact that the death of a human being means the bringing home of the bride by the beloved, is also reflected in 1532-1541 and 3957 ff. – For the concept of *heimelicheit*, see below.

The "character as a sign"[276] which death has in the Middle Ages cannot be
specified more closely from the perspective chosen here. Physical death means
the certainty, first, of going to a place where one is at home and, secondly, of
being "fetched home" by the bridegroom[277]. Death is not only the end of one's
time in exile on earth, but also the beginning of definitive love-fulfillment:
"The eschaton for all elect is decidedly bridal"[278]. Christian death thus acquires
a familiar, comfortable -and erotic- countenance. This sort of death lures many
a bride of God into its arms. The protagonist in *Der arme Heinrich* aspires to it
with a stunning directness which is rivaled only by the early Christian martyrs.
Pelagia, for example, is supposed to have drowned herself to protect her virginity, wearing a wedding dress because she was going to her bridegroom[279].
Whilst the nameless girl in Hartmann's work declares that she wishes to go
home to her divine bridegroom by being put to death for medical reasons, her
parents see her as *zem tôde sô gâhen* (hasty for death)[280]. Later, just in time, the
narrator extends the girl's life. With Christ as the *deus ex machina*, he releases
both protagonists from their sufferings, and there is no longer any obstacle to a
marriage between them[281]. The foiled bride of God becomes Heinrich's wife.

The idea that the pull of this attractive, even homely image of death should
be withstood is also mirrored in didactic works. Lamprecht has the personification of love pronounce an admonition of patience. When the extremely impatient soul wishes to go immediately to the beloved, she is urged to wait calmly,
for the moment to die has yet to come:

> *'schône frowe schône,*
> *frou tohter von Syone,*
> *ir müezet bîten eine wîle.*
> *die wîl und ir mit fleisches kîle*
> *alsô sît verzwicket,*
> *sô ist iu der wec verstricket,*
> *der iuch dâhin leiten sol.*
> *lât iu mit gedanken wol*
> *mit im sîn in der zît*
> *und ir sô beslozzen sît.'*

'O most beautiful mistress, Lady Daughter of Zion, you must wait yet
awhile. So long as you are still bound to the keel of the flesh, the way that

---

[276] Alois M. Haas 1984, 149.
[277] *Die Hochzeit*, 775 ff.
[278] Alfred C. Rush, 92 and 100-101 (with examples primarily from Greek patristic writings).
[279] Ambrose of Milan, *De virginibus*, 3,7,4; quoted in Alfred C. Rush, 89.
[280] Hartmann von Aue, *Der arme Heinrich*, 856.
[281] Hartmann von Aue, *Der arme Heinrich*, 1356 ff.

will bring you there is closed off to you. Content yourself with thoughts of him so long as you are still locked in [in the body]'[282].

Das fließende Licht der Gottheit also shows a prayer-like preparation for death, in which erotic requests are directed towards Jesus (among others). May he "then" receive the soul like a "most dearly beloved bridegroom", as noble suitors do when they give rich wedding gifts to their brides; may he "then" take her in the arms of their love and cover her with the mantle of his longing[283].

Other works give a direct recommendation to their audience to await death, or their being brought home, with humility. This Christian attitude takes account of the fact that death is as unpredictable as it is unavoidable. *Die Hochzeit* awakens hopes of the eternal wedding feast; on the other hand, it calms the impatient with the reminder that the feast never ends and the celebrations will wait for all those who are still in this world. This is comforting: no one can be too late for the feast of the Blessed[284]. Like Lamprecht, the *St. Trudperter Hohelied* warns of the dangers of actively wishing for death, even if it does bring release[285]: those who "wish to die before God wishes it" are depriving God of his power, for he alone knows when it is time to deliver human beings from the "wilderness of their earthly wanderings" (*ellende*)[286].

In accordance with Rev. 19:9, the brides of God experience their superlative wedding-feast in the next world. One bridegroom celebrates with his many brides – endlessly, as *Die Hochzeit* promises[287]. Both literature and the visual arts, such as a late-medieval painting from the circle of Simon Marmion (circa 1467-1470), picture this heavenly nuptial bliss in flowery terms[288]. What is being promised here – as in Albert the Great's treatise on the Resurrection – as a nuptial event, is the blessed life in the world to come. With Albert this nuptial concept of eschatological glory becomes generally accepted. In his treatise *De resurrectione* he puts forward the view that the human being receives, from God the Father, a dowry (*dos*) which can be differentiated into essential qualities of the body and of the soul. These *dotes* as a whole make up the state of glory of the bride, i.e. of the human being. The soul receives especially the four gifts of the *dos impassibilitatis, subtilitatis, agilitatis* and *claritatis*. As one might expect,

---

[282] Lamprecht von Regensburg, *Tochter Syon*, 3983-3992.

[283] Mechthild von Magdeburg, *Das fließende Licht der Gottheit*, VII,35,36-40; trans. Tobin, 304. – Apart from Jesus, various authorities are called on (as "father", "mother", "friend" etc.) to lend assistance at the moment of death. – Another passage which connects dying with the bringing home of the bride is II,25,97 ff.; trans. Tobin, 95.

[284] *Die Hochzeit*, 1062-1075.

[285] See, for example, *St. Trudperter Hohelied*, 134,24-25.

[286] *St. Trudperter Hohelied*, 120,12-16 and 25-28.

[287] *Die Hochzeit*, 1062 ff.

[288] Cf. the catalogue of the exhibition *Le Jardin Clos de l'âme*, 111, also 105, 109-110, 115 and 14.

Albert parallels this ensoulment with the material transactions in an earthly, worldly marriage, which also harbour a sort of equilibration of unequal partners. For (just as with an impoverished bride) the *dos* allows a free marriage between the lowly creature and her creator; in this way the *dos* is not simply ornamental, but the alleviation for the bride of the burden of marriage: *Et quod dos sit ornatus, cum dos non sit ornatus, sed potius dos est sublevamen onerum matrimonii*[289].

Images of the crowning of the bride or the wedding dance of the virgins in heaven are similarly ecstatic. The soul, it is promised in the *St. Trudperter Hohenlied*, will be led "into her father's kingdom, to her brother's inheritance in her beloved's palace", to erotic fulfillment:

> *dâ wirstû gesetzet in den barm dînes vater,*
> *dâ halset dich dîn bruoder mit sîner zesewen,*
> *dâ minnet dich dîn briutegome êweclîche, wann dû in hie minnest.*

There you will be placed in your father's lap. There your brother will embrace you in his right arm. There your bridegroom will love you eternally as you love him here [on earth][290].

This legitimate entry into the house of the divine husband is the grand finale of a successful life, as *Das fließende Licht der Gottheit* also illustrates twice. The visionary 'I' sees Hildegund, who has died, standing before God like a bride who has been brought home by the bridegroom: *Da stûnt Hiltegunt vor dem trone des himmelschen vatters, gezieret als ein nûwú brut, die der kúnig geholet hat ze huse.* (There stood Hildegund, before the throne of the heavenly father, adorned as a new bride whom the king has brought home)[291]. In full bridal adornment, crowned seven times, she justifies herself and her chosen path and gives allegorical interpretations of her splendid wedding clothes. The choirs of angels pay homage to her and to another soul, who, with the full legal status of *husvro* (lady of the house), sits at the side of the *ewige wirte* (eternal lord of the household). In this second example, the ordering of Creation, particularly the rank of angels and human beings, is under discussion. The journeying brides' perception of their ontological status with regard to the angels and God is exactly the way they fare once they have definitively arrived. As a wife, the soul is her husband's equal, and this status gives her final proof of the superiority of human beings over the angels, who are servants in heaven[292].

---

[289] Albertus Magnus, *De resurr.* q 1 a 10 S 1 contra 2, quoted in Hermann J. Weber, p. 317, n. 259. For the eschatological concepts of Albert the Great and others, see Hermann J. Weber.
[290] *St. Trudperter Hohelied*, 134,32-135,1.
[291] Mechthild von Magdeburg, *Das fließende Licht der Gottheit,* II,20,7-8; trans. Tobin, 84.
[292] Cf. Mechthild von Magdeburg, *Das fließende Licht der Gottheit,* IV,14,40-44; trans. Tobin, 157-158.

The cosmic wedding-feast in Lamprecht's *Tochter Syon*, placed above under the motto of heavenly inclinations, can neither be assigned clearly to the temporal sphere nor recognized definitely as a representation of eternal bliss. For it is the four drops of divine blood, acting as *pars pro toto*, which start off the whole process. Is the ambiguity of the text meant to show that the experience of union possible on earth anticipates the wedding in the next world? Certainly the wedding itself remains an after-death event[293].

Das fließende Licht der Gottheit also concurs with this. And Mechthild also emphasizes – similarly to Lamprecht, but more strongly – the communalization of the final wedding company. There is no more talk of intimate private happiness. When all the brides come together for the eschatological wedding feast, the structural polygamy of the erotic concept of the bride of God is revealed. The many brides celebrate with the one bridegroom, who, in addition, is constantly mutating between God the Father and God the Son. However, neither the polygamy nor the Trinitarian face of the bridegroom constitutes an impediment or a damper. On the contrary, Christ, who had taken on the task of restoring the repudiated bride, moves into his father's abode after the Last Judgment with all the brides for the "eternal feast". The Father makes a speech, including the entire staff of heaven (angels, saints, the Mother of God) and welcoming the virginal brides of God as the undoubted elite of the Blessed. The distinction between the *virgines* and "those who are not pure virgins" is elitist and separates virginal monastic brides of God from the other brides. In the crowning of the brides, too, one can perceive a consciousness of the elite status of virginity: married and widowed souls are crowned by a seated God; the virgins, by a God who rises to his feet respectfully, "standing like the son of an emperor"[294]:

> "*[...] Mine lieben brúte, vröwent úch iemer me, vröwent úch in miner ewigen luterkeit, verclagent nu sanfte alles we und alles leit. Min heligen engele sunt úch dienen, mine heligen sont úch eren, die múter mines sunes menscheit sol úch mit lobe si bereit, das ir ir geselle sint. Vröwent úch, lieben brúte, min sun sol úch al umbevan, min gotheit sol úch al durgan, min helig geist sol úch iemer me leiten in wunnenklicher ögenweide nach allem úwerem willen. Wie möhte úch bas gelingen? Ich wil úch selber minnen. Die nit lutere megede sint, die söllent dise hochgezit besitzen und besehen und gebruchen als verre es múglich mag gesin*".

> "[...] My dear brides, be joyful for ever, rejoice in my eternal purity; let all pain and all suffering softly disappear. My holy angels shall serve you; my saints shall honor you; the mother of my Son's humanity shall be ready with praise

---

[293] Cf. Lamprecht von Regensburg, *Tochter Syon*, 3881 ff. – On the temporariness of human beings' experience and knowledge of God, cf. 3913 ff.

[294] Mechthild von Magdeburg, *Das fließende Licht der Gottheit*, IV,24,13-20; trans. Tobin, 168.

for you because you are like her. Rejoice, dear brides, my Son shall embrace you warmly; my Godhead shall permeate you totally; my Holy Spirit shall lead you evermore, all according to you wish, to a delightful feast for your eyes. Could your success ever be greater? I myself shall love you. Those who are not pure virgins shall share and observe and enjoy this feast as far as possible"[295].

Cohabitatio: Living With/In One Another as Man and Wife

The passages of text just mentioned, like many others in the majority of the texts investigated here, suggest that the bliss promised in the next world is based on a familial or marital model of living. If the soul journeys to her divine bridegroom, this is actually a journey home – a journey from earth to heaven, from exile (*ellende*) to her home country. When she arrives in God's country, she is immersed in nuptial glory, all memory of suffering is erased, the homecomer is crowned and greeted "inwardly" and "outwardly". The fact that the Blessed live in a peaceful household community is confirmed also by visionary glimpses of the next world[296]. The *St. Trudperter Hohelied* seems to see matrimony in the next world in just this way: the bride of God then lives in the *himelischen herberge* (heavenly home)[297].

This model builds as a matter of course on the spatial conception of heaven which emerges, in the idea of the "heavenly Jerusalem", as the paradisiacal dwelling-place of the Blessed, an idea suggested by Apoc. 21:2. This is (in both senses of the word) a Christian topos which shaped art and literature from early Christianity onwards, with particular intensity during the high Middle Ages[298]. In all the texts investigated here, God "sits enthroned" and "dwells" in heaven, in his town with its many towers and in his palace to which the bridegroom brings his bride. *Das fließende Licht der Gottheit* as well as *Die Hochzeit* interpret this residence or individual parts of the building allegorically[299]. Lamprecht,

[295] Mechthild von Magdeburg, *Das fließende Licht der Gottheit,* VII,37,24-33; trans. Tobin, 308-309.

[296] Mechthild von Magdeburg, *Das fließende Licht der Gottheit,* IV,24,7-8 (trans. Tobin, 168); III,1; I,44 and passim. For the journey home, see *St. Trudperter Hohelied,* 120,12-16 and 25-28. – On the iconographical context, see Jeffrey F. Hamburger 1997, 138 ff.

[297] *St. Trudperter Hohelied,* 106,31 and 134,30-31.

[298] Cf. the article "Himmlisches Jerusalem", in *Lexikon des Mittelalters* 5 (1991), 28-29 and the article "Jerusalem", 351-359. – References to the iconography, for which the heavenly Jerusalem is central, in the article "Jerusalem, Himmlisches", in *Lexikon für christliche Ikonographie* 2,394-399.

[299] Cf. Mechthild von Magdeburg, *Das fließende Licht der Gottheit,* IV,24, where the three-dimensionality of the conception of heaven is affirmed and simultaneously deconstructed by the allegorical interpretation of the gates. – *Die Hochzeit,* 407 ff. (entrance gates); the girl in *Der*

too, uses the architecture of heaven, above all of the divine throne room, for theological statements. He does so, though, in a particularly amusing way by having a fictional eavesdropper secretly peep into the throne room and – to the malicious delight of the readers? – swoon, overwhelmed[300].

Lamprecht's three-dimensional staging of the wedding shows how the shared life of the happy couple can begin. Heaven opens wide as does the chamber of the heart. Between the rooms, which symbolize the two lovers, the presence of the one now floods radiantly into the other[301].

> *Nummer dumen âmen.*
> *dô sie zesamen kâmen,*
> *was iht hôhzît aldâ?*
> *wer zwîfelt dâran? zwâre jâ,*
> *diu hôhzît wart dâ sô grôz,*
> *daz sich der himel entslôz*
> *gegen des herzen kemenâten,*
> *dâ sie die brûtlouft inne hâten.*
> *des himels und des herzen tür*
> *was weder slôz noch rigel vür.*
> *si stuonden ûf gegen ein,*
> *ietwederz in daz ander schein,*
> *ein wec von eime anz ander gienc.*

Nummer dumen amen [in nomine domini amen]. When they came together, was there a wedding-feast? Who could doubt it? Truly yes, the wedding was so great that heaven opened wide to the private chamber of the heart in which they celebrated the wedding. The door of heaven and that of the heart had neither lock nor bolt. They stood open to one another. Each radiated into the other, and the one path led from one to the other)[302].

In this large-scale social occasion, the guests from the two spheres also transcend entire worlds. One has to imagine a broad stream of heavenly and earthly wedding-guests in both directions, since both protagonists have a considerable number of escorts[303], and the festive delight of the whole company expresses itself in a great desire to move about:

arme Heinrich tells of the "court" of her divine beloved (780); *St. Trudperter Hohelied*, 106,24-29; 134,30-31and passim.

[300] Lamprecht von Regensburg, *Tochter Syon*, 3518 ff. (Oratio) and 4153 ff. (Voluntas, Ratio).

[301] Lamprecht von Regensburg, *Tochter Syon*, 4130 f.

[302] Lamprecht von Regensburg, *Tochter Syon*, 4105-4117.

[303] Angels, in the case of the divine bridegroom; in the case of the bride, the allegorical "women", the virtues, resident in the castle of the heart.

daz gesinde ienez enphienc.
swaz in des herzen klûse
gesindes was ze hûse,
die·sprungen frôlîche
über sich ze himelrîche,
die von himel mit in hernider.
sus fuoren sie vür unde wider
in einer gemeinen wal
ensamt ûf und ze tal.

The serving staff of the one [lover] received those of the other. The servants who were at home in the cell of the heart jumped joyfully over one another on their way to heaven; those from heaven then in turn jumped back down with them. In this way, they all traveled back and forth and up and down together in a common flow[304].

Until now, I have illustrated only one of the aspects of meaning of the *cohabitatio* mentioned in the title of this sub-section, that of eternal living with and in God and the corresponding Christian spatial concepts. In a spiritual impetus towards internalization, mystical literature and the visual arts systematically extend this idea of dwelling together in the one space to include human beings still alive on earth. God dwells in the human being, who is his temple; the human heart is the house of God and, according to a fundamental concept of mysticism, also the birthplace of Christ[305]. Spatial conceptions of mutual cohabitation articulate elements of exclusion and inclusion in experiencing God – which are particularly important in the erotic context of being a bride of God. Jeffrey F. Hamburger suspects, on the basis of pictorial sources from the women's convent of St. Walburg (Eichstätt, Southern Germany), that one can discern a gender-specific affinity in this and speaks of "this image of interiority and, it might be added, 'feminine' domesticity"[306].

The second semantic aspect of *cohabitatio* is linked both with the exegesis of the Song of Songs, especially those verses which center on intimate inner rooms or interiors[307], and with the Annunciation to Mary. Elaborating on the Song of

---

[304] Lamprecht von Regensburg, *Tochter Syon*, 4118-4126.

[305] After Eph 2:2; 1 Cor 3:16 and 6:19; 2 Cor 6:16. – Cf. Friedrich Ohly, "Haus III", in: *Reallexikon für Antike und Christentum* 13 (1986), 905-1063; Friedrich Ohly, *Cor amantis non angustum*, in Friedrich Ohly 1977; Gerhard Bauer, and, with copies of the very original drawings from St. Walburg, Jeffrey F. Hamburger 1997, above all 134 ff. and 168 ff. For more detailed reflection on these domestic concepts, see also Marjorie O'Rourke Boyle, Hildegard Elisabeth Keller 1997c and Hildegard Elisabeth Keller 2000.

[306] Jeffrey F. Hamburger 1997, 169.

[307] One thinks here primarily of Cant. 1:3 (*cellaria*) and 1:16 (*lectulus floridus*). On the latter, see Karin Lerchner, esp. 45 ff.

Songs' verse *introduxit me rex in cellaria sua*[308], the *St. Trudperter Hohelied* shows God leading his bride into the interior of the house through an allegorical topography of paths and forecourts. He leads her all the way to the bedchamber, thus right into the innermost part of her soul, the place where – according to a paradox formulated already by Augustine[309] – God sleeps and lives: *unser sêle ist sîn gadem unde sîn liebester himel* (our soul is his bedchamber and his dearest heaven)[310]. It is part of the mystical link between subject and object that the delimitations between the two become blurred, even dissolve, and that in the end it is difficult to determine who is whose resting-place, home, and bedchamber. In any case, the lovers are *allein*, i.e., alone and all one[311]. They live and sleep in one another and with one another: the one in the other and the other in the one.

This reciprocal dwelling in one another can be determined more closely in the example of the Mother of God. In her case, one can discern who claims and occupies whom as a living-space and with what consequences. In other words, she in whom the Eternal first conceives and then dwells reveals two things: first, that inhabiting, occupying, and having sexual relations overlap[312]; second, that expressions such as "living together" or "cohabiting" can blend erotic and spatial meanings. The bride and mother of God is a human being who has become one with God and who is praised and characterized spatially in this capacity. This is evidenced by her many spatial epithets (e.g., hall, chamber, house, tent, tabernacle, temple)[313]. Mary is called a "sealed chamber"; in the Annunciation scene she is shown in an isolated room and is there converted into the original dwelling-place of God[314]. Mary's isolation

---

[308] *St. Trudperter Hohelied*, 18,7/-34. For detailed commentary on this passage, see Urban Küsters, 278 ff; Hildegard E. Keller 1993, 469 ff.

[309] *Deus interior intimo meo* (Conf. III,6,11). In the twelfth century, the idea is phrased: *Veni intus, interius, et plane intrinsecus supra te ad me* (Hugh of St.Victor, PL 176,990; quoted in Urban Küsters 1985, 279). Mechthild von Hackeborn gives a similar statement by God: "Because I lie deeper down in you than all your innermost things within you" (*Das Buch vom strömenden Lob*, 79). Cf. also Bernard of Clairvaux's 23rd sermon on the Song of Songs, with many spatial metaphors for God and living in him, and Mechthild von Magdeburg, *Das fließende Licht der Gottheit*, IV,12,1 (trans. Tobin, 152). Further bibliography in Hildegard Elisabeth Keller 1997c.

[310] *St. Trudperter Hohelied*, 18,19. See the commentary in Ohly's edition, 623 ff.

[311] *St. Trudperter Hohelied*, 18,26-27. Cf. Urban Küsters 1985, 280. – The spatial concepts in the scenes of union in *Das fließende Licht der Gottheit* (I, 44 and III,1) seem to me to be comparable.

[312] Friedrich Ohly is very illuminating on this whole connection (*Cor amantis*, in Friedrich Ohly 1977, 143-144, and the commentary in his edition of the *St. Trudperter Hohelied*, 546, 553-556 and 597-598).

[313] On this fixed inventory of formulae in Marian hymns, cf. Anselm Salzer, 8 f., 18 ff., 36 ff. and passim, and, from a visual point of view, Gregor Martin Lechner, passim.

[314] Cf. also Bernard of Clairvaux, *In laudibus virginis matris*, 2nd homily, IV, 50-51 and the Christmas sermon of Johannes Tauler.

embodies an initial message which I wish to term ascetic, for it refers to the closeting of the human being within himself (or herself). He should not let himself be distracted by earthly things and should hide within himself, as Johannes Tauler says[315].

A second message can be called mystical to the extent that it points to the Incarnation and the birth of God in each individual human being. But this message follows rather from Mary's openness, which makes it possible for the human being to be an inhabitable space, a *receptaculum* which can be filled by forces which are other than human. God lives and fertilizes within the interior of the human being. This message is conveyed by Priester Wernher's work. In rapid succession, his Annunciation shows the request to go to the bridal bed of heaven followed by Mary's being made pregnant, which is circumscribed in spatial terms again and again throughout the work[316]. The angel explains little to her – only that she will become the "hall of God", that God "wishes to occupy her womb with spiritual heat"[317]:

> *'dine sorge du verla!*
> *gesegent bistu vor allem weibe:*
> *got hat in deinem leibe*
> *im erwelt einen sal [...]'.*

'Abandon your cares! You are blessed above all women: God has chosen a dwelling-place for himself in your body'[318].

The angel gives another explanation which is valuable for us: that God would *mit seines geistes towe wone bey* (live / sleep with her with the dew of his Holy Spirit)[319]. Promptly Mary becomes pregnant "through the seed of Faith"[320]. The images of interiors – buildings and bodies – and erotic union merge into one another; the concepts of "living in" and "having sexual relations with" one another can scarcely be distinguished.

How and whether the representation of a Mary occupied in this way influences the literary depiction of the unions of other brides of God is a delicate question[321]. Certainly, the idea of Mary as a human dwelling-place and a vessel for the transcendental serves as an example for mysticism. Sources of a mainly iconographical nature lead Jeffrey F. Hamburger to very similar

---

[315] Ed. by Pfeiffer, V 1, 11,27-29.
[316] Priester Wernher, *Maria*, A 2146 ff.; D 2428 ff.
[317] Priester Wernher, *Maria*, A 2133 (missing in C and D).
[318] Priester Wernher, *Maria*, A 2155-2159; D 2437-2441.
[319] Priester Wernher, *Maria*, A 2192-2193; D 2470-2471 (missing in C).
[320] Priester Wernher, *Maria*, A 2220; D 2496 (missing in C).
[321] See Jeffrey F. Hamburger 1997, 169 ff.

insights: one can imagine conceptual connections between certain human or specifically female interiors (abdomen, or uterus, and heart). In view of the sources, these sorts of mystical conceptions of an interior in which God and the human being meet, live in one another, and have sexual relations do not seem out of the ordinary[322].

It is equally certain that the density of meaning demonstrated in the spatial symbols flickers again and again in the texts about brides of God, sometimes in a single word. The opening motto for this sub-section comes from an intimate dialogue between Margery Kempe and Christ, who reveals to her that what he needs most is for her to lie in bed with him and for them to be *homly*[323]. This term corresponds to Middle High German *heimelich*; from the point of view of their etymology, both are spatial terms and the role they play varies in importance from text to text, particularly in mystical literature. *Homly* and *heimelich* here mean in a familiar, intimate, tender, erotic, sexual way[324]. And if Lamprecht speaks of constantly holding oneself in readiness for the wedding (for him this means being brought home, thus dying), then he uses the corresponding substantival formulation *heimlicheit*, which is also used as an equivalent for Latin *secretum*, saying: *dû ensîst alle zît bereit gegen sîner heimlicheit.* (Hold yourself constantly in readiness for his intimacy and intimate company [i.e., to die and go to him])[325]. The three aspects – going home to heaven, living with God as a wife and being intimate with him as a lover – are inextricably connected in this concept of union[326].

---

[322] Cf. Jeffrey F. Hamburger 1997, 170 ff.

[323] *The Book of Margery Kempe*, ed. Barry Windeatt, 196, 2944. – Barry Windeatt's translation (1985, 126) gives *intimate* as an equivalent of the Middle English *homly*.

[324] The Middle High German term *heimelich* is an adjective derived from *heim*, a concept which is spatial as far as its etymology is concerned, and which in Old High German already meant the enclosed court, the home, the known and indigenous, and therefore, the familiar. The meanings of the Middle High German adjective *heimelich* and its corresponding noun *heimlicheit* extend beyond the intimate and intimate bonds (betrothal, marriage) to include that which is withdrawn from others' eyes, secluded (also places), secretive, thus also the taboo (sexual matters, sexual intercourse, bodily excretions) (Lexer I,1216 ff.). In mystical literature, Middle English *homly*, Middle Dutch *hemelijk* (e.g. in Hadewijch) or Middle High German *heimelich* (in all the texts investigated here with the exception of *Die Hochzeit*) serves as a key term for intimacy with God as the bearer of secrets and divine beloved. Thus the term points to erotic union, personal intimacy, but also mystical penetration into the divine mysteries. – Cf. also chapter 4, and Hildegard Elisabeth Keller 2000.

[325] Lamprecht von Regensburg, *Tochter Syon*, 1525-6. For the translation of the term *heimelicheit*, see also the preceding note.

[326] The manuscript apparatus in Weinhold's edition is informative. On one occasion, he notes *haimlait* (G), *haim lait* (P) and *himelait* (L), which seems to support the above interpretation of death as a heavenly homecoming.

The Silence of the Brides

In all the texts we have seen that the bride or those who report on her may suddenly fall silent. The explanations given for this silence have been various.

First there is the case of quietness as a result of resting in God: a mystical *otium*, which often comes to the fore in discussions of the sleeping bride in the Song of Songs (Cant. 5:2) or other occasions. This is also reported in dialogues which are suddenly interrupted by the comments of an outside narrator: *So geschihet da ein selig stilli nach ir beider willen* (Then a blessed stillness that both desire comes over them)[327]. This sort of falling silent may also be thematized from a didactic point of view, saying of mystical union that *si sol mit stille verstanden werden in der süezen bewegede libes unde sêle* (it should be understood and experienced with stillness in the sweet movement of body and soul)[328].

Secondly, there is a silence which is really the bride withholding what she experiences in the chamber of her beloved, in his bed, and in his arms. This kind of secrecy is common to both religious and secular discourses of love. If the bride speaks of *secretum mei mihi*[329], then she means primarily the secret of her love, which she guards from her social environment. She has this protective gesture in common with many literary brides of God, for example, with Priester Wernher's Mary, who joins the angels in an unsuccessful effort to conceal her *tougenliche minne* (secret love) from those around her[330]. The intimacy of two lovers has to be shielded from the knowledge of others, as chapter 4 will illustrate from a different perspective[331]. The female narrator in *Das fließende Licht der Gottheit* grants this privacy to the two, who meet secretly. They surrender to one another, but what the bride experiences remains unsaid: *Was ir nu geschehe, das weis si, und des getrôste ich mich.* (What happens to her then – she knows – and that is fine with me)[332].

Mechthild employs not only the voice of a narrator but also personifications to present deliberate silence as an adequate social reaction to an erotic experience. In the dialogue, an allegorized authority helps to draw up the boundaries

---

[327] Mechthild von Magdeburg, *Das fließende Licht der Gottheit*, I,44,90-91; trans. Tobin, 62.

[328] *St. Trudperter Hohelied*, 18,33-34.

[329] Is. 24:16, quoted in Bernard, *De gradibus humilitatis et superbiae*, VIII,23, ed. Gerhard Winkler, II, 82. On the *secretum* in the texts of *Christus und die minnende Seele*, see Werner Williams-Krapp; on its MHG equivalent, *heimlicheit* in Mechthild von Magdeburg, see Alois M. Haas 1996, 248-269; Marianne Heimbach-Steins in: Claudia Brinker et al. (eds.), 71-86, and Hildegard Elisabeth Keller 2000.

[330] Cf. the section "The Couple and the Others" in chapter 4.

[331] Priester Wernher, *Maria*, C 1402-1403 and 1399 respectively, D 1350-1351 and 1346 respectively, A 1218-1219 and 1215 ff. respectively. – According to Hans Fromm 1955, 56, this discretion is not accounted for by Wernher's source.

[332] Mechthild von Magdeburg, *Das fließende Licht der Gottheit*, I,44, 90-93; trans. Tobin, 62.

of what can be known, tantalizingly by learning nothing. In this way, Mechthild creates problems for the literary procedure of using personal allegories to project the "inner person" and its secrets outwards[333]: the bride, who is supposed to report back, will not let out her secret. So Mechthild cuts off the story of the *herzeheimelîcheiten* (*occulta cordis*) before it has really begun, as happens when Lady Knowledge (on behalf of the reader?) tries to probe the bride's intimate secrets (*heimelîcheit*) and comes up against precisely this boundary set by the bride:

> "*Eya vro brut, went ir mir noch ein wortzeichen sagen der unsprechlicher heimlicheit, die zwúschent gotte und úch lit?*"
> "*Vrôwe bekantnisse, das tûn ich nit. Die brúte mússent alles nit sagen, was in beschiht. dú helig beschŏwunge und dû vilwerde gebruchunge sont ir han von mir, die userwelte bevindunge von gotte[334] sol úch und allen creaturen iemer me verborgen sin sunder alleine mir.*"

> "Mistress Bride, would you say a word to me about the ineffable intimacy that exists between God and you?"
> "Lady Knowledge, that I shall not do. Brides may not tell everything they experience. Holy contemplation and precious enjoyment you shall learn about from me. My privileged experience of God must always be hidden from you and from all creatures except for myself")[335].

There is a third motivation for the bride's keeping silence, one which leads back to the motto at the start of this whole chapter and the *invisibilia* and *ineffabilia* mentioned in it. Here it is a question neither of the bride's falling silent in peaceful contentment nor of her consciously keeping secret an intimate privacy. Rather it is the speechlessness of one who looks into the innermost mystery of God, as though peering into a room – a throne room in *Tochter Syon*[336], a chamber with exclusive rights of entry in *Das fließende Licht der Gottheit*[337], and an intimate bedchamber in the *St. Trudperter Hohelied*[338]. Some of the

---

[333] Medieval poetics visualizes the invisible inner life of a human being, the *occulta* or *secreta cordis*, in two ways: first, by describing the signs which can be read from the "outer man"; secondly, by personifying inner forces so that they manifest the invisible as speaking and acting *homines exteriores*. Cf. Lionel J. Friedman, Horst Wenzel 1995, Sarah Kay/Miri Rubin (eds.), Peter von Moos 1995, 1996 and 1997a and also – for other texts – Rüdiger Schnell 1998c and Christel Meier 1998, from a more general point of view see Walter Haug 1995.

[334] The Latin translation of Mechthild's work renders this as *mihi singulariter infusa*.

[335] Mechthild von Magdeburg, *Das fliessende Licht der Gottheit*, II,19,31 ff; trans. Tobin, 82. – With Margot Schmidt's additions from the Latin *Revelationes*.

[336] Lamprecht von Regensburg, *Tochter Syon*, 3518 ff.; 4153 ff.

[337] Mechthild von Magdeburg, *Das fliessende Licht der Gottheit*, I,44, 78-79; trans. Tobin, 61-62.

[338] Cf. *St. Trudperter Hohelied*, 18,18-20; on the motif of the *tougene chamere* (hidden chamber), see 46,13.

personifications in *Tochter Syon* experience for themselves how overwhelming it can be to see God; Oratio can only stammer: *terribilis est locus iste et cetera* before losing consciousness[339]. The brides themselves at that point come into contact with something that exceeds all that they have ever perceived and articulated, as one of them specifically states. Even though she admits that despite the help of wise people and angels, she is not capable of articulating what she sees[340], she never gives up the struggle to communicate; for she still speaks continuously – though essentially always about her speechlessness:

> *Dú minste warheit, die ich da han gesehen und gehôret und bekant, der gelichet nit dú hôhste wisheit, dú in disem ertrich ie wart genant. Ich han da inne unge-hôrtú ding gesehen, als mine bihter sagent, wan ich der schrift ungeleret bin.*

The least truth that I saw and heard and understood there was incomparably more than the loftiest wisdom ever uttered here on earth. I saw there things never heard before, my confessors tell me, for I am ignorant of reading or writing[341].

For the bride, then, the union means that she enters a room which is normally taboo – the *verholnen kammeren der unsúnlichen gotheit* (the secret chamber of the invisible Godhead)[342]. What she experiences there goes beyond the limits of her comprehension: *ineffabilia* and *invisibilia*, as Bernard puts it. Second, this exclusivity bestows on the bride a special status with regard to the outside world and her social context[343]. Bernard recommends silence (*non licet loqui*), and the situation is no doubt intensified for those whose sex denies them a theological education and its consequent authority to speak about the mystery. To safeguard herself against hostility, Mechthild hints at how impertinent it might be thought for her to see divine wonders and speak about them[344].

Lamprecht illuminates this specific kind of silence and secrecy from the perspective of social psychology. Too much unruliness in those who had experienced an *unio mystica* would arouse jealousy and self-doubt in those who were excluded. For this reason he fondly urges discretion and measured silence on those blessed in this way[345]. Accordingly, it becomes apparent that *sacrum*,

---

[339] Lamprecht von Regensburg, *Tochter Syon*, 3527-3528.
[340] Mechthild von Magdeburg, *Das fließende Licht der Gottheit*, III,1,153; trans. Tobin, 106.
[341] Mechthild von Magdeburg, *Das fließende Licht der Gottheit*, III,1,34-37; trans. Tobin, 102. Similarly, VII,59 (trans. Tobin, 328).
[342] Mechthild von Magdeburg, *Das fließende Licht der Gottheit*, I,44, 78-79; trans. Tobin, 62.
[343] For monastic circles, the relationship between the individual and the monastic community was always a delicate question. On this, see Urban Küsters, chapter V, and Thomas Lentes.
[344] Cf. Mechthild von Magdeburg, *Das fließende Licht der Gottheit*, III,1.
[345] Lamprecht von Regensburg, *Tochter Syon*, 2943 ff.

secretum, and *silentium* are mutually dependent across the spectrum of mystical union, all the more so where an *unio mystica erotica* is concerned[346].

Tribulations

> *What mai I seie? (…) bothe his comyng and his goyng. This is the game on love.*[347]

The conditions of brideship examined thus far make it clear that the portraits of brides of God presented by the six works differ greatly, both quantitatively and qualitatively. One text may scarcely waste a word on a particular facet whereas another may deal with it at length, treating it as its very core. These differences of emphasis are one of the most fundamental things which this synoptic view of the brides shows because they give a profile of the literary faces of the brides and bridegrooms. This process of differentiated reading of the texts will now be applied again, more starkly than before. Not all the texts concern themselves with the sorrowful aspects of the erotic relationship with God which, in all six texts, is definitively fulfilled according to the visions of the end of time outlined above. Some of the texts prefer to dwell on the light already shimmering through from the next world and leave out the darker sides of being a bride of God, which is why this sub-section is the shortest. But overcast moments – elements of pain, suffering, and general deprivation – are inevitable *in statu viae*, and sometimes seem even to be provisions for the journey along the earthly way. Thus there are texts for which the hurt is an essential, though not definitive, part of the basic experience of passion, of being a bride.

Brides in Bliss

The fact that in *Der arme Heinrich* no gloom of any kind impinges on the nuptial dream of the would-be bride of God is surely explained by the narrative perspective and the intentions of the argument. She paints a picture of radiant,

---

[346] The close relationship between *sacrum* and *secretum* can be demonstrated particularly clearly in the semantic field of *heimelich*. Sometimes manuscripts show *heimelich* (secret) and *heilig* (holy) in an almost interchangeable relationship. This is the case in the first chapter of Heinrich Seuse's *Minnebüchlein*. In the sentence *O sele min, gang ein willi in dich, in die heimlikeit dines hertzen* (O my soul, go into yourself for a while, into the secrecy of your heart), in manuscript z one finds the word *heiligkeit* instead of *heimlichkeit* (Bihlmeyer, 538, 1-2 and note). Cf. Hildegard Elisabeth Keller 2000.

[347] *The Prickynge of Love*, chapter 26, quoted in Barry Windeatt 1994, 177.

frictionless oneness with the beloved which excludes all suffering[348]. The glory which the protagonist depicts to her parents dissipates all fear of dying or being put to death, though this is described fully, with suggestive intentions, by the doctor. The only crisis she experiences is caused by the "trepidation" of the doctor and Heinrich, and it manifests itself in her excessive impatience in the operating room[349]. The only negative side, insofar as there is one, is the forced bringing home (i.e., putting to death) of the bride and the suffering of her parents. Suffering is transferred to her social surroundings.

Die Hochzeit, a completely different sort of text, does equally little to dim the splendor of being a bride of God. The brides on all levels of the exegesis are elevated to eschatological marital status after the appropriate marriage ritual. The only shadows possible would be on the wedding-dress, interpreted as levels of purity of the faithful[350], or the inferiority of the bridal adornment, interpreted as varying attitudes in confession[351]. The Mariological interpretation reveals an immaculate bride who has been relieved of all tribulations[352]. With a glimpse of the eschatological wedding-feast which *nimmir zergat unde immir ewich stat* (never ends and continues for ever), *Die Hochzeit* abruptly cuts out[353].

Priester Wernher shows Mary as a different bride of God. With great narrative staying power, his text expounds a woman's biography which is certainly atypical but which can constitute an exemplary way of life for a female bride of God with regard to the turbulence surrounding an unwanted marriage. This bride of God knows no moments of alienation from her divine bridegroom. This sort of difficulty seems to be as alien to her as to the brides in *Die Hochzeit* or *Der arme Heinrich*. Nevertheless, she still has her troubles. Her worries are socially determined. On the one hand, they are connected on with the expectations to which a woman who has reached marriageable age must conform; on the other, they are concerned with her loyalty to her divine beloved and her bridal calling. Only when the forced marriage with Joseph is inevitable does she weep in desperation[354]. In a far more dangerous situation, however, neither Mary nor Joseph's cheerfulness can be dampened in the least. They remain calm when the Jews bring charges against Mary, who has become pregnant in an unusual way, and Joseph, who has neglected his duty of surveillance, and subject

---

[348] Cf. the accumulation of negations, Hartmann von Aue, *Der arme Heinrich*, 781-798.

[349] Hartmann von Aue, *Der arme Heinrich*, 1105 ff.

[350] *Die Hochzeit*, 777-786.

[351] After the interpretation of the bride's bath as the *conversio* of the faithful, there follows (in 622-695) an account of varying attitudes towards penance and the sacrament of confession.

[352] *Die Hochzeit*, 791 ff.

[353] *Die Hochzeit*, 1062-1065.

[354] Priester Wernher, *Maria*, A 1818 ff.; D 2054 ff.(C missing).

the two to a trial by ordeal[355]. Doubtless the shadows on Mary's bridal bliss can be seen as the social suffering of a female bride of God, but the integrity of the bride remains as untouched by them as does her bond with her divine beloved. This is very different for the brides of God in the mystical texts.

Brides as Refugees and Exiles

The world in which the human bride of God lives is an *ellende* (exile), a miserable stopover and certainly not her true home[356]. Even the most fulfilling bridal bliss on earth is really only dreamlike and pales in the face of the reality in the next world. This, in any case, is how the mystical texts see it[357], and they call for the brides to distance themselves from the world. That the world may also force a distance between the lovers is discussed in two of the texts with regard to verse 8:14 of the Songs of Songs. The variations between these two interpretations of separation and repudiation show different conceptions of mystical union.

At the end, the *St. Trudperter Hohelied* has the brides themselves say and interpret this verse: *Fliuch von mir, mîn wine* (Flee from me, my beloved)[358]. Four times the bride dismisses her beloved, rejecting all comforts of an earthly and a heavenly nature. The bride exchanges "the gentle words of your present affectionate talk" for the "sharp, bitter words of your enemies", the "gladdening sight (of God)" for the "bitter sight of your henchmen", and the "present well-being of all bodily rest" for "everything that you have suffered here in exile, all the punishment of human beings who are damned"[359]. Just as urgently as the didactic mirror of the brides of God initially encouraged the listening women to "sing" and kiss[360], it now invites them to follow Christ one last time in his suffering – this time as sorrowing, weeping widows and orphans, who may

---

[355] Cf. Priester Wernher, *Maria*, A 2815 ff.; D 3201 ff.; above all A 2857-2863; D 3254-3261 (C missing).

[356] On the concept of life on earth as life in *ellende* (exile), see Hildegard E. Keller 1993, 140 ff. For a general study on monastic *acedia* and melancholy see Alois M. Haas 1995.

[357] This is true particularly of knowledge of God, which is very limited here on earth (cf. Lamprecht von Regensburg, *Tochter Syon*, 3915 ff.; for life on earth, see Lamprecht von Regensburg, *Tochter Syon*, 4278 ff.; *St. Trudperter Hohelied*, 30,28-29; 35,14-15; Mechthild von Magdeburg, *Das fliessende Licht der Gottheit*, VI,20,6 ff. and VII,7,31 ff.; (trans. Tobin, 249 and 281). For the motif of the dream, see Urban Küsters 1985, 288 ff.

[358] *St. Trudperter Hohelied*, 143,31. Cf. Urban Küsters 1985, 319 ff; Hildegard E. Keller 1993, 482 ff.; Friedrich Ohly 1995,106 ff. (particularly on the technique of self-exegesis).

[359] *St. Trudperter Hohelied*, 144,6-19.

[360] *St. Trudperter Hohelied*, 6,22 ff.

lament and pine for their bridegroom (*beati qui lugent*)[361]. For after all, he left them at the Ascension and waits for them in the next world. For that reason, as they themselves say:

> *von dannen ist uns mêre ze suochenne weinen danne singen unde ze suochenne*
> *eine mendende unvröude denne eine bittere vröude, diu in weltlicheme gewerbe*
> *muoz sîn. nû nemac unser weinendiu mandunge niemer voller werden denne*
> *daz wir sprechen ze unsereme trûte: fuge a me.*

For that reason we would rather seek weeping than singing, and joyful unhappiness rather than bitter joy in worldly activities. Now our tearful joy cannot be fuller than if we say to our beloved: flee from me[362].

The oxymorons (*mendende unvröude, weinendiu mandunge*) provide a link to negative experiences in *Das fließende Licht der Gottheit*, which are also thematized in the context of the command from the Song of Songs. In a sort of didactic conversation between the soul and the bride of the Song of Songs, at first the command to flee does not (as above) constitute an exemplary attitude for the bride. The soul asks the bride of the Song of Songs why she had asked her beloved to flee since she herself would rather die in pure love than send her beloved away voluntarily[363]. The experienced bride explains her behavior in terms of her increasing drunkenness (Cant. 6:5), which gives love unlimited power over her and allows her to experience the depths of God. This didactic exegesis of wine – it means and suffering abuse and pain as well as sinking below all created things – inspires the soul towards *imitatio sponsae*, which essentially amounts to *imitatio Christi*[364]. The succinct conclusion closes with a combination of suffering, love, and desire which is typical for Mechthild: *Swer mit dirre not wirt bevangen, der mûs iemer me ungelôst in gotte seleklîche hangen* (Whoever becomes entangled in longing such as this must forever hang blessedly fettered in God)[365].

Both the *St. Trudperter Hohelied* and *Das fließende Licht der Gottheit* teach the bride the right attitude of love, using the same speech from the Song of Songs. The former immediately places the words of the Song of Songs together with its appropriate interpretation in the mouth of the female audience in order

---

[361] *St. Trudperter Hohelied*, 143,18 ff.

[362] *St. Trudperter Hohelied*, 143,24-25.

[363] Mechthild von Magdeburg, *Das fließende Licht der Gottheit*, III,3,5-11; trans. Tobin, 108-109.

[364] Cf. Mechthild von Magdeburg, *Das fließende Licht der Gottheit*, III,3,25 ff. (trans. Tobin, 109) – For the concept of the omnipotence of love, see the section 'Delivered Up' in this chapter, and chapter 5.

[365] Mechthild von Magdeburg, *Das fließende Licht der Gottheit*, III,3,46-47; trans. Tobin, 110.

to lead them to adopt the attitude of the bride. The latter weaves the discussion of the dismissal into a didactic dialogue between a soul who still flees from all darkness and the bride of the Song of Songs herself, permeated by love. Perhaps it is an indication of the didactic success of this conversation between two brides that the soul herself later dares to direct the command *fuga a me* to the beloved, and then goes through the most overwhelming alienation: *"Eya, entwich mir, lieber herre, und la mich fürbas sinken durch din ere."* ("Oh, leave me, dear Lord, and let me sink further for your honor!")[366].

Hurt and Alienated Brides

Let us dwell for a moment on the deeply emotive concept of alienation in *Das fließende Licht der Gottheit* and on the specific term associated with it, *gotzvrömdunge*. Brides of God are fundamentally alienated. They have become estranged from the world, from themselves, and from their beloved – and seem to attain their highest level of fulfillment in this[367]. This paradox makes it difficult to assign numerous passages in Mechthild's work – as well as Lamprecht's *Tochter Syon* and the *St. Trudperter Hohelied* – to a particular station of this synoptic view. For the question of whether a bride of God experiences deprivation **or** fulfillment when she speaks of suffering does not arise: the texts view these two aspects as inseparably intertwined. How does this paradox arise?

The experience of love in *Das fließende Licht der Gottheit* is molded to the highest possible degree by vicissitudes: love is an abyss, as the soul is told by Lamprecht von Regensburg and – in Mechthild's text – by the prototypical authority, the bride of the Song of Songs. Rejection (as well as *suessikeit* and *bekanntnis* – sweetness and knowledge) is one of the principal ways in which love is experienced[368]. In the face of *der minne wandelunge* (the vicissitudes of love), one has to reckon with sudden changes: the game breaks off at the most exquisite moment[369]. What the soul experiences subjectively as ups and downs, is in fact the surging up and sinking back down and the heating up and cooling down of *der minne zuge* (the maelstrom of love)[370].

---

[366] Mechthild von Magdeburg, *Das fließende Licht der Gottheit*, IV,12,46-7.; trans. Tobin, 154.

[367] Mechthild von Magdeburg, *Das fließende Licht der Gottheit*, IV,12,64 ff.; trans. Tobin, 154-155. On the linguistic aspects of this paradoxicality, cf. Susanne Köbele, 94-95. On the aspect of suffering, cf. Alois M. Haas 1989, 130 ff., Marianne Heimbach, 72 ff., Amy Hollwood, 173 ff., Barbara Newman 1995, 158 ff; for the term *gotzvrömdunge* (= strangeness of God, alienation from God) Alois M. Haas 1979, 113 ff., Marianne Heimbach, 50 ff.; Barbara Newman 1995, 137 ff.

[368] Mechthild von Magdeburg, *Das fließende Licht der Gottheit*, VI,20,11-13; trans. Tobin, 249.

[369] Mechthild von Magdeburg, *Das fließende Licht der Gottheit,* IV,12,69-70 (trans. Tobin, 154) and I,2,21-22 (trans. Tobin, 41), respectively.

[370] One example of the many passages with a vertical dynamic is *Das fließende Licht der Gottheit,* V,4, especially 24-41 and 65-69 (trans. Tobin, 183.

This power and violence of love is reflected not only in addresses to love itself: *o minnebant, din süssú hant hat den gewalt, si bindet beide jung und alt* (O Fetter of love, your tender hand is strong. It binds both young and old)[371]. Even the language used to describe the effects of love manifests its violence: in the texts of Mechthild and Lamprecht, but also in the *St. Trudperter Hohenlied*, the lovers sustain injuries and illnesses, and their suffering is often unalleviated and incurable[372] although – in Mechthild's work at least – they in no way suffer in silence. Deprivation drives them to communicate. One of the most astonishing dialogues between the two lovers opens with the love-lament of the bride. Using forceful imagery, she makes several attempts to receive an answer to her torment. The bridegroom urges patience and comforts her with the promise that he is preparing her a bed in the *bŏmgarten der minne* ("orchard of love") and will surrender himself to her[373]. This sort of distress seems to be the bride's daily bread, which she takes in and assimilates, giving it literary shape from her innermost erotic identity, a result unimaginable for texts like *Die Hochzeit*, Priester Wernher's *Maria* or Hartmann von Aue's *Der arme Heinrich*.

Passio amoris is Janus-faced and blends suffering and passion even as far as the Creator. The Creator creates himself a bride with Christ's agreement, although the latter already knows the high price he will have to pay: *"Vatter, du weist es wol, ich sol noch sterben von minnen, iedoch wellen wir dieser dingen in grosser helikeit vrŏlichen beginnen"* ("Father, you well know that I shall yet die for love. Still, we want to begin these things joyfully in great holiness")[374]. Later the loving God is driven down from heaven to earth and death, as Mechthild and Lamprecht von Regensburg depict[375]. This divine readiness for passion sets the highest standard for human beings and incorporates archetypical suffering in love. From now on Christ's Passion and the love-passion of the soul are inter-twined and are fulfilled – in the case of Mechthild's original and famous vehe-mence – even to the extent of sinking under Lucifer's tail[376]. In this the bride

---

[371] Mechthild von Magdeburg, *Das fließende Licht der Gottheit,* V,30,6-7; trans. Tobin, 211.

[372] In Mechthild von Magdeburg's *Das fließende Licht der Gottheit,* dense allegories and depic-tion of the pangs of love of the bride in I,3, II,25 and III,10; cf. also V,4,49 ff. (trans. Tobin, 183) and V,31,10 ff. (trans. Tobin, 213); Lamprecht von Regensburg, *Tochter Syon,* 3595 ff. (bride-groom), 3993 ff. (bride); *St. Trudperter Hohelied,* 74,3 ff. (illness of the soul) and 143,19 ff. (dis-tress at being abandoned). See generally the article "Blessure d'amour" in *Dictionnaire de Spiritu-alité,* I, 1724-1729; on linguistic images and the pictorial language of love in Italian Renaissance art, see Victoria von Flemming.

[373] Mechthild von Magdeburg, *Das fließende Licht der Gottheit,* II,25,97-130; trans. Tobin, 95.

[374] Mechthild von Magdeburg, *Das fließende Licht der Gottheit,* III,9, 31-33; trans. Tobin, 115.

[375] Mechthild von Magdeburg, *Das fließende Licht der Gottheit,* I,3,11-13 and VII,56 (trans. Tobin, 42 and 325), on Lamprecht, see the first section of this chapter, and chapter 5.

[376] Mechthild von Magdeburg, *Das fließende Licht der Gottheit,* III,10 and V,4,52 (trans. Tobin, 117-119 and 183).

models herself and her love on the beloved, not only in suffering but also in salvation[377]. For in the descent of the bride ("the ultimate extreme of love",
according to Margot Schmidt[378]), a sort of homeopathy takes effect, where like
is healed by like: Christ must apply himself as a remedy to the love-wound he
himself has given. This is the message which the soul gives the angel Gabriel in
a sort of inverse Annunciation, drawing on the lovesickness mentioned in the
Song of Songs[379]. But this is also the therapy used by Lady Love for the fatally
ill Daughter of Zion: she trickles four drops of divine blood into the uncon-
scious bride and gives her an infusion of grace, where the medicine (God) is
simultaneously the cause of the illness (God): theopathy and theotherapy[380].

Repudiated Brides and Concubines

Mechthild's passionate version of Creation (III,9) reads like the biography of a
bride and wife of God in the Old Testament sense. The Fall destroys the newly-
established bridal relationship; the marital bond between collective humanity
and its Creator is shattered. The bitter lament of the soul, which is really an
accusation to God, has recourse to legal terminology just as was the case in her
institution as a legitimate bride:

> *Do schrei dú sele in grosser vinsternisse manig jar nach irem liebe mit ellender*
> *stimme und rief: "O herre liep, war ist komen din überstíssú minne? Wie sere*
> *hastu verkebset din elich kúneginne! Dis ist der propheten sin. O grosser herre, wie*
> *maht du erliden dise lange not, das du nit tötest únsern tot? Jo wiltu doch werden*
> *geboren; mer, herre, allú dinú getat ist doch vollekomen, also ist öch din zorn."*

"Then for many a year the soul cried out in great darkness for her Lover. Her
voice filled with misery, she cried: "O Lord, dear One where has your most
delectable love gone? How bitterly have you called your wife and queen a
whore! That is the meaning of the prophets. O great Lord, how can you bear
this endless distress and do not give the death to our death? If only you were
to be born. But, Lord, since all your deeds are perfect, so is your wrath[381].

---

[377] In the last books of Mechthild's work, mysticism of the Passion and of atonement comes
to the fore. Cf. Mechthild von Magdeburg, *Das fließende Licht der Gottheit*, IV,12,64 ff.; VII,4;
VII,21,31 ff. (trans. Tobin, 154, 279 and 293-294).

[378] Margot Schmidt 1989, 75: "ein äusserstes plus ultra der Liebe".

[379] Mechthild von Magdeburg, *Das fließende Licht der Gottheit*, VII,58 after Cant. 2:5 and
5:8.

[380] For the four drops, of which one is indeed called *gratie infusio* or *genâden inguz* (infusion
of Grace), see Lamprecht von Regensburg, *Tochter Syon*, 3768 ff.

[381] Cf. Mechthild von Magdeburg, *Das fliessende Licht der Gottheit*, III,9, 61-66; trans.
Tobin, 116.

The expression *elich kúnegin* highlights the high position of the human soul as the bride of God and this is a marker for the idea of ennoblement discussed in chapter 2: the soul, as wife, is a queen. The lament, on the other hand, demonstrates the danger of falling, which was also mentioned. Both – rise and fall – are expressed in terms which define the status of the woman with regard to her husband. The title *elich kúnegin* (royal wife, or lawfully wedded queen in the sense of a noble lady of the house, here parallel to Latin *regina* in Cant. 6:7-8) applies to the soul because God has given her his *hanttrúwe* (oath of conjugal loyalty), and accordingly it forms the opposite to *kebse*. In the high Middle Ages, the term *kebse* (Latin *concubina*, as in Cant. 6:7-8) should be taken to mean a concubine who is far below the wife in terms of marriage and inheritance law. In Germanic marriage-law, concubinal marriage also meant that, by virtue of his legal right of disposal, the Germanic free man could arrange the sexual relationships between his male and female servants and could, for example, claim a maid for his own needs[382]. The word *kebse* designates this kind of relationship, which contrasts sharply with the high medieval theology of marriage. The term *kebse* could then be used as an instrument for ranking the brides of God, as is illustrated by the *St. Trudperter Hohelied*, the literary escort of the bride[383].

The term used by Mechthild, *verkebsen*, means in the first instance to make a woman one's (extramarital) lover. Further – and this is along the lines of the Old Testament tradition of Jahweh repudiating his adulterous bride, Israel – *verkebsen* means that the husband breaks his marriage vow and expels his bride or wife from her rightful position as lady of the house[384]. What Mechthild refers to as the *verkebsen* of the soul corresponds, moreover, to the transformation of the male and female sexual anatomy made necessary by the Fall, as she had discussed a few lines earlier[385].

This disruption in Salvation history can only be restored by Christ's Passion and wedding on the Cross. Then the soul will be allowed to be his legitimate bride again and may hope that she will be brought home at the end of time to sit at her husband's side as the *husvrouvwe gottes* (God's wife and the lady of the house). If one reviews this development of a marriage, then one can discern that Mechthild extends a sort of matrimonial baldachin over the concept of the

---

[382] According to Paul Mikat, in his article "Ehe", in: Handwörterbuch zur deutschen Rechtsgeschichte 1, 809-833, who also points out that *Kebsehe* and *Friedelehe* (marriage by mutual consent) are indistinguishable.

[383] The interpretation of the *concubina* refers here to possible reprehensible attitudes of monastic brides of God, particularly the sluggish, proud or complaining nun (very sharp in the *St. Trudperter Hohelied*, 97,33 ff., more conciliatory in 148,4 ff.). – Cf. Christopher Brooke 1989, 64 ff.

[384] Cf. Lexer I, 1533-34.

[385] Cf. III,9,58 ff.; Hildegard E. Keller 1995.

bride of God[386]. Not only in *Das fließende Licht der Gottheit*, but also in the *St. Trudperter Hohenlied* and *Tochter Syon*, all the violent tendencies and all the vicissitudes of love are kept safely within the horizon of the household in the next world. My synoptic view shows that the very idea of the turbulence of earthly existence, of the careworn, and of those who are consumed by love and mysteriously still living a fulfilled life, is not shared by all six works. What they do have in common – and not one of the six texts is silent on this – is the perspective on the future communion of the embraced, and this satisfies their every wish.

---

[386] In my view, it also spans the courtly characteristics of the motif identified by Barbara Newman (Barbara Newman 1995, 139 ff.).

Chapter 4
Privation and Privacy: One Late Bride of God

In Chapter 3 it became clear that the literature of bridal mysticism visualizes relationships between men and women as in a showcase. Step by step the readers follow the approach and alienation of the two unequal partners in both erotic and marital circumstances. This chapter will treat of a work which uses erotic and marital allegories as a means to orientate human beings towards God by fitting them into a certain power structure. The main protagonist in this process is Christ, who acts on a "soul" which is portrayed as feminine. This explains the succinct title of the work – *Christus und die minnende Seele*, Christ and the loving soul – a dialogue of love dating from the late fifteenth century. It has received little attention from researchers[1]; it is addressed here because it is radical and bizarre. The process of the drawing together of God and Man is schematized far more strongly than in the works which have been considered thus far in terms of the relations between the sexes and the associated power structure. This late example of bridal mysticism drawn from German literature uses its subject to visualize and legitimize the hierarchical difference between the lord and husband, who is omnipotent, and his wife, whose duty is to be obedient. Illuminated manuscripts demonstrate in text and image how erotic and matrimonial discourses as well as religious and secular relationships can complement one another in this sense, which is suddenly very much profane. Such transpositions between earthly and heavenly relationships are revealed above all in the comparisons between marriages and husbands drawn much more sharply by the divine bridegroom in this late medieval example than in all those presented in Chapter Two above. Unexpectedly, a textual source thus opens up a surprising perspective on a familial world in the late medieval town, seen through the distorting mirror of the polemics of bridal mysticism[2].

[1] Since the edition by Romuald Banz, this work has been largely ignored in the development of research, although the question of the socio-historical position of the work could be reopened with regard to its production and reception. Apart from the odd mention in histories of literature and the *Verfasserlexikon*, investigations have centered on the study of sources within the tradition of picture-cycles (Hellmut Rosenfeld 1953, 66-75). Taking a recent discovery as his starting point, Werner Williams-Krapp, 350-364, takes a new look at the relationship between the individual examples of text and illustration which survive.

[2] Attempts to probe the factuality or fiction of a work are legitimate, indeed unavoidable from the point of view of the reader. Basic questions regarding the relationship between the

The illuminated text of *Christus und die minnende Seele*[3], 2112 lines long, was transmitted anonymously and probably originated in the area around Constance[4]. This means that it belongs to the body of late bridal mysticism for women[5] which originated in the Southern German area. If one understands the concluding lines as a statement by the author, then the category of mystic confessional texts must be excluded: *Ich han min leben laider als hailclich nit verschlissen, das mich got sin haimliche laß wissen* (sadly, I have not lived my life in a saintly enough way for God to let me know his secrets)[6]. This statement can be interpreted as the author-figure's admission that he/she cannot lay claim to mystical experience. Thus the "Soul" of the title does not represent an authentic first-person perspective.

In terms of its sources the work is thought to be the textual augmentation of an unknown picture-cycle belonging to the late medieval tradition of picture-cycles associated with bridal mysticism[7]. The rigid schematization and linearity of the depiction of the encounter between Christ and the soul is probably connected with this origin[8]. It gives the work a didactic effect. The relationship

---

history of literature and actual relations between the sexes are, between "texts" and "reality" in general, formulated by Rüdiger Schnell 1994a, 114 ff., and his introduction Text und Geschlecht, in: Rüdiger Schnell 1997, 9-46.

[3] Edited by Romuald Banz (quotations with line-references). Cf. Hellmut Rosenfeld, *Christus und die minnende Seele,* in [2]VL 1 (1978) 1235-1237.

[4] Banz suggested Constance as the area of origin because of the provenance of the manuscripts (3 of the 4 manuscripts are from Constance). As to the question of whether it originated in the Dominican convent of St. Peter or by commission of the patrician Margarete von (Ehinger-) Kappel, Banz decides in favor of the latter (cf. Banz, 6 ff., Rosenfeld [2]VL 1 [1978] 1237). My thanks to Bernd Konrad for his interest in corresponding on the Einsiedeln Codex and Rudolf Stahel's illuminations in the Donaueschinger Codex. For Rudolf Stahel see Bernd Konrad 1989 and 1997.

[5] Werner Williams-Krapp (as earlier Banz and Rosenfeld 1953) assumes that picture-cycle mysticism originated in the context of the female mysticism which flourished in the South West in the fourteenth century.

[6] 2099-2100. These lines in the last section of the dialogue are at first designated as the speech of the soul. Seamlessly, the discourse takes on the aspect of prayer, which permits the interpretation of the concluding lines also as an authorial statement (similarly Banz, 39).

[7] For a brief orientation in the tradition of picture-cycles on the theme of bridal mysticism, I would recommend Werner Williams-Krapp, esp. 350-352, for the Einsiedeln codex 710 (322) see Niklaus Largier and Jeffrey F. Hamburger 1998, Franz Reitinger, 101-118; Amy Gebauer is working on her doctoral thesis on the manuscripts and their connection to the devotional culture in the fifteenth century.

[8] Strong schematization of the stations of love is typical of the pedagogical tradition of the picture-cycle. The mystical experience should become a sort of training schedule for the less blessed (Hans-Friedrich Rosenfeld / Hellmut Rosenfeld, 186).

between Christ and the soul is also strongly pedagogical[9], at least in the first half of the work. This accords well with the intention of the text: each reader can – from the perspective of the work, even, should – herself slip into the pupil's role of the erotically aroused soul.

Who wrote *Christus und die minnende Seele*? And for whom? Romuald Banz, the editor, attributed the work to a female author; and despite the objections of Philipp Strauch, this has been accepted by subsequent research. This attribution has been narrowed down: one should see the author as a female religious who wrote for beguines in the area of Lake Constance[10]. It is not clear to me why the work is supposed to belong in beguine circles. Neither the text nor the pictures show any distinctive features which would point specifically to beguine spirituality. In all the illuminated manuscripts the female figure wears a monastic habit, either Cistercian or Dominican[11]. In my opinion the literary and historical position of the work should be re-investigated from three angles: from the point of view of the sources of the work[12], of its origin, and of its reception. Little definite can be said about the origin of the work since the scribes, author, and illuminators are never named or identified. More promising is the question of the reception of the work. If one considers the manuscript which is now in Einsiedeln (Cod. 710 [322]) and its record of former owners, the recipients of the work should be sought among the circles of religious and secular women of the aristocratic class of Constance[13]. Did the circle to whom the work was primarily

---

[9] This pedagogical effect is conveyed by the question-and-answer structure, by Christ's strict didactic tone, particularly at the beginning (e.g. section VI, 706ff.), as well as by the soul's statement that she will take Christ as a *schuolmaister* (710 t.).

[10] For Banz's construction of a female author, cf. 33 ff. and 180-181; for Strauch's contradiction of this, see his review in Anzeiger für das deutsche Altertum, 52 (1910), 256-257. Thomas Cramer, 175, and Hedwig Heger's revised version of Hans Rupprich's literary history (De Boor / Newald IV/1, 330-331) also agree with Banz; the latter would see the author as part of the monastic milieu: "the work was written by a woman (belonging to an order in Constance?), probably for one of the beguine communities on lake Constance" (330).

[11] The question of whether it is indeed Cistercian, as Banz argues, or Dominican, which is suggested not only by its appearance but also by one of the owners recorded in Cod. Einsiedeln 710 (322) – the Dominican sisters of St. Peter in Constance – must remain open.

[12] The social satire *Des Teufels Netz* can be demonstrated to be at least a partial source. Cf. Hildegard Elisabeth Keller 1997b.

[13] An owner-record in the main manuscript (Einsiedeln Cod. 710 [322]) points in the direction of a private commission by the aristocratic Margarete Ehinger-Kappel. The coat of arms in the front was interpreted by Banz, in accordance with Einsiedeln codices 283 and 752, as indicating ownership by Margarete Ehinger-Kappel, a married noble woman of Constance (Banz, 6-23 and my correspondence with Bernd Konrad). If this record refers to the first owner of the work, then it would have been produced as a devotional work for private reading. The other record of ownership in this codex names the Dominican sisters of St. Peter, Constance.

addressed comprise quite wealthy secular women (the patrons), one of whom gave the devotional work to her own daughter who was entering a convent or left it to a convent later? It is true that the history of the motifs, the illuminations, and one of the records of ownership might suggest the latter[14]. But the question of the social relations among the women of Constance would remain an open one. Were the aristocratic ladies of Constance accustomed to reading the same material as their sisters or sisters-in-law who were brides of Christ? Can one imagine a local, and obviously class-related, reading community among women? That gives rise to another whole series of questions. How could the motif of the mystic marriage of the soul with God extend beyond its home territory in the monastic realm to encompass married women and mothers in the world? What conditions were necessary in the first place for the opposing marriage paths (as a bride of Christ or the bride of a human man respectively) to become a common theme in the pastoral care of women? The textual analysis which follows will at least provide some initial answers. One can be certain in any case that *Christus und die minnende Seele* should be seen in the context of late medieval literary production for a female public (and that means the wives of divine as well as of earthly husbands).

Let us cast a glance over Banz's arguments in his identification of the gender of the author since they are relevant to one of the main themes of this book, the triangle between the erotically conceived relationship with God, those who fill the roles in it, and its literary representation. The fact that a Christ who is conceived as male confronts a soul which is portrayed (in both text and illustration) as female is for Banz a compelling indication of a female author, who depicts, as it were, her own role in relation to God. He understands the apportioning of gender roles as an indication that the soul reveals the voice of a woman. Thus, like Heinrich Seuse[15], he assumes that the soul speaks from authentic experience. For him, the authenticity – and consequently the femininity – is confirmed by

[14] It depends on the situation in which the work was produced and its reception, whether the motif really does leave the specifically ecclesiastical sphere, where it is limited to nuns, to be applied to married women and mothers in the world (which would be the case if the work were owned first and commissioned by Margarete Ehinger). The development of the motif within the work, and above all the pictures of the soul in a monastic habit (second half of the work), however, lead one to conclude that the application of the concept of the bride of Christ to the religious sphere remains intact and that it is not transferred to women in secular marriages.
In the case of a monastic readership, the reform of the Dominican convents is fundamental in stimulating women's wish to read, and thus also their need of reading matter.

[15] Banz draws his considered conclusion about the authorship of the work from comparisons with Heinrich Seuse's experience of love (33) and completely blocks out the history of the motif of the bride of Christ and the gender restriction of the soul to the female sex. The Einsiedeln Codex 710 (322) contains Seuse's *Exemplar*. Cf. the two recent studies on receptional questions by Largier and Hamburger 1998.

the tone of the bridal mysticism as a whole; he feels that it is so completely based on a female outlook and feeling that one could only conclude that its author was a woman[16]. He sees particularly the drastic depiction of marriage and other representations from a female viewpoint as directly related to the female sex of the author. Where the female soul laments, he hears the voice of the female author. Although Banz determines correctly that Christ is masculinized and the soul feminized[17], his conclusions reflect the scholarly attitudes of his time. Banz assumes that the gender constructions of the early twentieth century can build seamlessly on those of the fifteenth century. Thus, he does not question the female portrayal of the soul and can assume all the more naturally and innocently that a woman speaks through the soul. It is clearly unthinkable that a male author would speak both through a female soul and through a male Christ; it is equally unthinkable that a male recipient could recognize himself in a female figure – and Christ is here hardly conceived as a figure one could identify with.

The motif of the bride of Christ is written into both text and illuminations. First, in the matter of the iconography: the title of the treatise refers to the relationship between Christ and the *sel*, his *gemahel* (spouse), but that the soul in question cannot be the soul of a man is also demonstrated by the illumination directly underneath as well as by all twenty of the remaining illustrations[18]. The illumination shows a female figure in a green dress kneeling beside a bed, an angel standing opposite her. The woman, who, until section 11, appears before the ascetically dressed bridegroom in a variety of very fashionable garments and hairstyles, is the soul. Another complete change of costume does not occur until section 12, once the soul has accomplished a form of withdrawal from the world. From then until the end, the soul only appears on

---

[16] 33-34. This statement refers to passages from the poem *Kreuztragende Minne* (KM), but since Banz assumes a female author for both texts, his argumentation reveals his conception of the female sex. The passages in question are the soul's statement: *Ich bin jung, zart, edel und krank: Wie möcht ich dulden solchen gang?* (I am young, delicate, fine and weak: how could I suffer such things?), KM, 13 f.; and Christ's statement: *Wilt du dich erst keren zü mir, Wenn die welt nicht me hat uff dir, Und alt und ungestalt bist worn?* (Do you wish to turn to me only once the world has no more use for you and you have become old and disfigured?), KM, 41 ff.

[17] This can be established on a textual basis in a manner which would be more acceptable today. In a passage which is not adduced by Banz, the soul is unambiguously denoted as female: Christ clearly addresses the soul as a woman when he states that the exemplary soul no longer bears any trace of her descent from Eve (182-186).

[18] I take manuscript E (Stiftsbibliothek Einsiedeln, Codex 710 [322]; cf. Banz, 223 ff.) as my starting-point. Aside from the title-page, the illumination in question is the first in the treatise (Banz's fig. IV). The individual depictions at the beginning of each section illustrate the title and the first quatrain under the picture. In the first section this mentions angels, which is why the soul is accompanied by an angel.

the scene in a Cistercian habit, which is intended to signal her progress along the path of religion[19]. It is true that the changing costume of the soul is entirely plausible as a visual sign of the mystical path. But does it agree with the logic of the text? Since it is made known as early as the end of the first section that the soul has been "involved" with Christ for many days and years, it seems that the decision in favor of a divine husband has already been made. On the other hand, one would then have to ask oneself why such an extremely harsh picture is presented of secular marriage (since it has already been rejected). Perhaps the pictures use the varying clothing merely to show, and in this case *with* the text, that the taming of the shrew is not yet complete and that she still has not fully made up her mind between the world and withdrawal from the world. It is not until the middle of the work that Christ can bring home his bride and welcome her to his house (the convent?)[20]. No matter whether the clothing is monastic or secular, what is abundantly clear is that the soul is characterized as a woman and that the appurtenances of the figure of Christ, though sparse, are definitely male.

The way in which the bridal mysticism in the work plays with gender roles, leading to a violent typology of the relationship between man and woman, has led researchers to view *Christus und die minnende Seele* as a popularizing epigone[21]. This judgment is certainly not unjustified. Undoubtedly the work goes far beyond the standard set by medieval literature in German in the hermeneutics of bridal mysticism – an observation which should be judged from the history of the origin and reception of the work. There is a lot more worth noting than merely the drastic comparison of types of marriage at the beginning of the work. From a constructed female perspective, this permits a glance into a small, private cosmos which has gone badly awry. Horrendous scenes of worldly marriage are revealed. Altogether, very secular models of the private lives of two partners prove to constitute the overriding structure of the work. Love and marital relations are put to use to tell a story which basically transcends sexual differences: what is introduced as hypothetically "realistic" everyday life in the family or as the amorous intimacy of a couple is in fact a sign of a non-earthly reality.

[19] The *Rothschild Canticles* also show the bride of Christ as a woman wearing both worldly and monastic dress (cf. Jeffrey F. Hamburger 1990).

[20] Banz assumes that in the original cycle the soul always appeared in the same clothing. His explanation is that the variations are motivated by aesthetic considerations and by the idea of mystical progress (235). With great attention to detail, Banz describes many individual features of the woman's clothing, headcovering, and hair-styles (234).

[21] The rigid schematization of the mystical development and the crude marriage passage in the first section led to the low estimation of the text in the context of mysticism. Although, according to Max Wehrli, it is not simply a token of shameless crudity, but much more an example of late medieval variation and parody (Max Wehrli [2]1984, 690-1), it is still thought of as popularized, even vulgarized bridal mysticism.

In the course of the following pages I center the discussion around the radically realized relationship between Christ and the loving soul as a couple. This
means that I reverse the order of argumentation used hitherto. What was formerly one of the reasons to dismiss the work will here take center stage. I am
expressly interested in the whole reservoir of gender relations: the ways in
which they were put to use, the hierarchy they portray, and the intimacy that
was thought possible or impossible. Undoubtedly, *Christus und die minnende
Seele* carries the nuptial model to extremes. This radicalization is what makes
the showcase of the text so promising if one is interested in the connections
between concepts of intimacy and gender. My reading is guided by curiosity
about how the categories of gender, marital dominion, and erotic intimacy are
articulated in this late work. It is certain that the discourse of love and that of
marriage are juxtaposed for contrast as well as integrated into one another.
Thus, three basic dimensions become apparent, though these overlap again and
again: secular marriage, spiritual marriage, and erotic love. Questions take
shape: What variety of bridal mysticism does one see here in text and picture?
What late medieval form of discourse of love and of marriage does one see? And
to what extent are they determined by genre and the function of the text? What
is it that makes the matrimonial sphere the source of negative images, but the
erotic love-relationship the source of positive intimacy? These questions surrounding a couple which is formed of a divine "husband" and a human "wife"
are relevant to the controversial debate which is conducted intensively in the
study of high and late medieval as well as early modern literature: the discussion about the relationship between the discourse of love and of marriage in the
relations between human men and women, the interrelation of these concepts
and how they relate to reality[22].

Gender Discourse as Structure

Until now, the structure of *Christus und die minnende Seele* has only received
attention in that repeated reference has been made to the "muddle" of the individual scenes, which vary in number and order within the picture-cycle tradition. According to Banz, the "female" author frequently loses the thread[23]. In
his comparison of this work with others in the same tradition, Williams-Krapp
determines that the order is "greatly distorted" and is surprised that the author
did not appear to be at all disturbed by this "illogical order". She must have
been so "intent on the individual scene" that she lost sight of the coherence of

---

[22] Cf. chapter 2, section "The Discourses of Love and Marriage".
[23] Romuald Banz, 37.

the work[24]. Obviously the elements which determine the structure in *Christus und die minnende Seele* have eluded researchers[25]. I intend to introduce one of these – for me the most important one – step by step: the model of the matrimonial and the erotic relationship.

The mystical dialogue depicts the relationship between a soul, represented as female, and a Christ who is portrayed as male. This story is told in two main sections, which can be distinguished as much by iconographic characteristics as by the fundamentally different fields of reference of man and woman[26]. The first half of the work reveals a matrimonial pattern of relations between the sexes, in which the wife is subordinate to the husband. This marriage allegorization serves as a symbol for rulership, thus leaving the asymmetry of husband and wife untouched. Just as the human husband is expected to secure his dominant position, the divine husband also takes over the scepter without any hesitation. In this, the first half of the work is conducted in terms of a structurally violent model. Accordingly, the secular and spiritual perspectives on marriage do not represent union, but rather – in a surprisingly violent way – they furnish the necessary preconditions for it.

It is not until the second half of the work that matters even out between the protagonists in the love scenes, which are partially interwoven with motifs from the Song of Songs. In contrast to the ascetic marriage-allegory, these are familiar

---

[24] Cf. Werner Williams-Krapp, 363 and 364. Largier does not discuss this question, but concentrates on the process of reading the text and images in the codex.

[25] In sections 4 and 5 or 8 and 9, various techniques used to connect scenes show evidence of an awareness by their designer of the mystical process. Thus, scenes are not simply transposed in respect of the tradition of the picture-cycle; they are interpreted differently.

[26] With, and sometimes contrary to, the text, the way the woman is dressed is an attempt to bring order to the mystical process. Although the soul professes allegiance to Christ from the beginning – 12 f. (*ainig* should be understood here as a mystical term [alone with me], but also as a nuptial term [become one with me]); in 106-107, the soul states: *Ich han es mit dir getriben manig iar und tag, Das du mir nie antät sölich clag* (I have been involved with you for many a year and a day now. You never made such a complaint to me) – the spiritual marriage appears only to be established after the soul assumes the dress of a Dominican nun (from section 12). Lines 1642 ff., when the theme of laying aside worldly clothing re-occurs, are probably a flashback. Like the change from secular to monastic clothing, the change in furniture (as noted already by Banz, 233) seems to provide visual confirmation of mystical progress. Essentially, I suggest a twofold division of the work on the basis of the changing relations between the protagonists. But this division should not be taken too far. First, the text also draws on other relationship-models (Man as a servant of God in 488-490, 1040 and 1695); second, dominion of the one over the other is also legitimized by factors other than matrimonial ones (such as Christ as *schuolmaister* in 710 ff. and as lord over the world to come in 555 ff.); third, through the adaptation of the motif of the love potion, a station which is taken from the discourse of courtly love finds its way into the marriage allegory. In this, attempts at integration are apparent, above all in the fact that drunkenness here becomes the allegorical means through which the husband subjects his wife fully to his dominion.

and are well known among the constituent features of this literary genre. Contrapuntally, in terms of an erotic encounter, they show the protagonists in a symmetrical relationship to each other: the woman can become active and can hold her opposite in her power; the man becomes passive, which means, in this case, enduring suffering. Gradually, an amorous bond develops. The intimacy of dancing together, whispering together gently, kissing, and embracing outweighs the one-sided asceticism of marriage.

The importance of a wider circle of people, of the general public, in the broadest sense of the words, also changes with the relationship of the couple. In the first half of the work, the "world" can be present since the matter under discussion is social and religious alienation between people. In the second half, an antinomy gradually builds up between the loving couple and the rest of the world because if these others knew the details, it would endanger the social reputation of the woman, that is to say, the soul. A two-phase process becomes apparent, in which spiritual marriage structurally absorbs the discourses of secular marriage and love. The mystical threefold schema of *via purgativa, via illuminativa,* and *via unitiva*[27] is reduced to a twofold series of relationships. This makes it possible to parallel the discourses of secular and spiritual marriage. In addition, the discourse of marriage is thus also linked with the discourse of love. Marriage, where the emphasis lies on domination, becomes an allegory for catharsis whereas the reciprocal gestures of love come to represent unitive processes.

These allegories intensify the typology of gender relations to extreme degrees. On the one hand, secular and spiritual gender relations confront each other. Their antinomy is grounded in the discrepancy between the two husbands. On the other hand, the power hierarchy of marriage is opposed to the lack of domination of the erotic relationship. Finally, between the matrimonial rituals of domination and the erotic, increasingly self-sufficient relationship of two lovers, there arise hermeneutic tensions within and between the literal and allegorical dimensions of meaning. In the comparison of types of marriage at the beginning of the work, the constructed feminine perspective is striking. Here the tendency discussed in the first two chapters is all too clear and is fundamental for the development of the motif. When Christ speaks to the soul, life counseling and marriage counseling are one and the same thing. That the counselor is not unbiased need hardly be stressed here. Christ's comparison between the secular and the religious life is the comparison between two marriages, above all between two husbands, of whom *he* is one. Then Christ, the

---

[27] Sections 1 or 2 up to and including 11 correspond to the first step of the classical mystical path, the *via purgativa*; this is constituted by marriage. The *via illuminativa* and the *via unitiva* occur in the second half of the work, where they are drawn together under the theme of love.

alternative husband, proceeds to take the marriage – in text and image – to precisely that bitter conclusion which, right at the beginning, he had painted to the allegorical wife as the ideal option.

Marriage and Privation

The first half of the work is dominated by marriage, which includes the violent subordination of one sex by the other. That each and every element of happiness is negated and that separation becomes more important than union is in keeping with the ascetic curriculum. Familial and marital privacy is to be understood as a symbol of privation. This reveals a hierarchy of the sexes which determines the relationship between Christ and the soul. First, I discuss the opening of the work and the glance it permits us into the domestic world of a married couple. My next section is devoted to the shock tactics of this picture of secular marriage, after which I introduce the first allegorical dimension. From then until the middle of the work, marriage serves as an allegorical ritual of individual asceticism, the subject of my last section.

Secular Marriage as Shock Tactics

The first of the 21 parts of varying length into which the work is divided, completely removes this dialogue from the sphere of religious literature of love[28]. This first part is singular and stands out immediately from the point of view of its sources since it incorporates elements which are textually and iconographically foreign to the genre and integrates them through formal means[29]. The most important innovation is the inclusion of secular marital relations[30]. The

---

[28] Each two-line title in red ink is followed by a miniature which illustrates the interchange between Christ and the loving soul immediately below it. For the pictures in the Einsiedeln codex, see Banz, 223-249; for those in Donaueschingen, codex 106, see the fundamental work by Bernd Konrad 1989, 57-92, esp. 69-70; Bernd Konrad 1992 and 1997, with reproductions (KO 37, 83 and 85).

[29] The associated illumination shows the praying figure of a woman and an angel, which leads Banz (231) to situate it in the tradition of the Annunciation. The scene of a pair comprising a human and an angel around a bed is unique, as all the other pictures show both protagonists of the work together. The scene which comes first in the picture-cycle tradition shows Christ beside the bed where the figure of the woman is lying – in *Christus und die minnende Seele* this is the second picture (for the theme of the night-prayer, cf. Rosenfeld 1953, 73). For the intertextual links with the social satire *Des Teufels Netz*, which were noted already by Banz, see Hildegard Elisabeth Keller 1997b.

[30] The contrasting opposition of the two types of marriage or even any kind of thematization of a woman's life in the world is completely lacking in the other versions of the same material (for

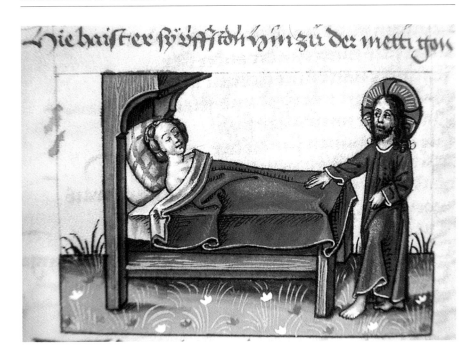

short flashlit domestic scene proves, however, to be less erratic than it appears at first sight. Rather, in the further course of the work there ensues a synthesis of the motif of marriage, which proceeds from the sharp contrast of two discourses of marriage (secular and spiritual) on the one hand and, on the other hand, of the discourse of love and of marriage. The two contrasting pairs have been illustrated in chapter 2.

Into the intimate sphere of the bedroom, in which the figure of a woman, kneeling beside her bed, says her nightly prayers in the presence of her guardian angel, Christ enters as a third person. He forcibly demands the attention of the sleepy, mildly reluctant woman who is identified as the "soul" and his "bride". In the subjunctive mood, he tells her about secular marriage, more like a horror story than a bedtime story. For no sooner is a human husband present than the nightmare for the woman begins: *Mit dem müstist tag und nacht übil zit han* (with him you would have an awful time both day and night)[31]. Terrible days and nights, cursing and scolding from her drunken husband, and her own unhappiness – all would have to be suffered in silence by the wife.

---

an overview, see Banz, 43-52 and 124 ff.). Cf. Williams-Krapp's schema, in which he compares and contrasts the order of the stations within the individual works in the picture-cycle tradition (Williams-Krapp, 361 ff.; Banz, 46).

[31] *Christus und die minnende Seele*, 23.

Villicht keme der man
Umb mitternacht gan
Von dem win
Trunkner und völler dan ain schwin;
So hebt sich denn ain schweren und ain schelten.
Dess müstest denn engelten.

Perhaps your husband would come home around midnight, more drunk and full from wine than a swine; then the cursing and scolding would begin. You would have to put up with it[32].

Her children too would suffer deprivation. If she protested and answered back, she would be made to atone for it with brutal clarity.

'[...] ich müß dir es anders sagen;
Gelt, ich mache dich aber klagen!'
Und schlüg dich denn in das mul
Und mit dem har umb das fur,
Und müstist für in zitrind ston
Und sprechen: 'ich hab unrecht geton,
Du solt es dür got mir varen lon' –,
Und müstist im denn zarten
und siner begird warten.

'[...] I'll have to tell you again; Huh, I'll give you something to complain about!' And then he would beat you in the face and [drag] you around the fire by the hair, and you would have to stand before him quaking and say: 'I did wrong. For God's sake, you should forgive me' –, and then you would have to make up to him and wait on his desires[33].

The physical violence exerted by the husband continues in verbal form when the wife asks for a penny for bread. Her husband accuses her of always wanting to be "full", and professes to be surprised that she "guzzles" all day and is still "scrawny and skinny". Her weeping provokes his aggression[34] still further:

Und er spräch: 'gelt, ich mache dich grennen und grainen!
Müß ich aber an dir zerschlahen die hend?'

---

[32] *Christus und die minnende Seele*, 30-34.
[33] *Christus und die minnende Seele*, 45-51. Cf. also 30-44.
[34] The cynical comments of the husband reflect the maxims of the disciplining of his wife expected of a husband, which could certainly take the form of physical violence. This is also apparent in the view that the wife would "improve" in measure with the number of blows dealt her by her husband.

Und stieß dir den kopf umb die wend
Und mit dem knú in den ruggen;
Das müstist du als vertruken.

And he would say: 'Huh, I'll make you roar and cry! Do I have to beat you again with my hands?' And he would bang your head against the wall and knee you in the back; All this you would have to tolerate[35].

The wife, in her passive role, has no right to defend herself. Nothing – not resistance, not humble self-effacement, not compliant ingratiation – can alleviate her distress. She cowers in her existence in the shadow of a tyrannical husband who exerts his unilateral law of might and pulls out all the stops of aggression. His violence has a legal and a temperamental side which his wife cannot escape in her personal living space[36]. Christ's depiction suggests that violent, almost sadistic, tendencies are fundamental to the male nature. This cannot be questioned as a medical concept since the theory of the four humors, which was valid for medicine in the Middle Ages and for popular medicine well into modern times, views the choleric as a bile-driven, pugilistic brute. "Pugilistic" means that the husband beats his wife, as numerous late medieval picture sequences show. The woman serves merely as an attribute which helps to explain the nature of the male.

The legal subordination of the wife to the husband is a constituent feature of the medieval concept of marriage. Violence on the part of the marital overlord is correspondingly well attested, and drew particular attention in the fifteenth and sixteenth centuries[37]. The Constance deed-book of 1436 therefore refers to the husband as the wife's *rechten vogt* (true guardian). As such he had rights and duties which, interestingly enough, were defined in terms of an external and an internal aspect. Against the outside, in legal trials and the like, he had to protect her and had to grant her legal rights before the court in the first place[38].

---

[35] *Christus und die minnende Seele*, 59-63.

[36] Physical abuse was an important argument in anti-marital polemics aimed at women. Cf. the polemical comparisons of marriages discussed in chapter 2 above. For the physical abuse of married women, see Erika Uitz, 145 ff.; Urte Bejick, 114-121; more generally, Christiane Krausch, 447-454, Rudolf Weigand in Rüdiger Schnell 1997 and Heide Wunder.

[37] Even the early medieval poem *Vom Rechte* (circa 1150) makes clear that the husband takes the wife "into his power by way of the law", i.e. through marriage (387-398, Hg. Walter Haug / Benedikt K. Vollmann, Frankfurt, 1991). Marriage includes the right of disposal of the husband and overlord over the welfare of his wife and also his right to dispense corporal punishment. For the marital rights situation in Constance, see Hartmut Eisenmann, 29-85. – More generally on this subject, Michael Schröter, particularly chapter 1,2. Cf. Rüdiger Schnell 1994a, 97 ff., with further bibliography, and Rüdiger Schnell 1998b, especially 217ff. and 277ff.

[38] Hartmut Eisenmann, 30-32.

Within the home, he should guarantee her upkeep and had the right to inflict corporal punishment, though this was only permitted him under two conditions: first, the woman had to have done something wrong; second, he was not allowed to punish her in secret. However, since the records of the council of Constance note only one case of this kind – Peter Ruprecht swears before the mayor that he will *[sine] ehelich wirtine (…) nit ubel handeln, noch schlahen, noch mit beschlossen turen straffen (…) darumb er si ouch vor den luten offenlich und nit haimlich straffen sol* (not mistreat, nor beat his wedded wife, nor punish her behind closed doors, so that he would punish her publicly in front of people and not secretly)[39] –, it is not really possible to establish whether this statement is generally valid. Here public opinion works for the wife as a positive control mechanism, which is not in force in *Christus und die minnende Seele*. There the man treats his wife badly behind closed doors and then interprets her diffident verbal defense as "blame". There is no sign of public opinion as an informed body, which exerts control over or shows solidarity with either of the parties involved. The image revealed is that of a fully sound-proofed and sealed family sphere, in which the wife, robbed of her voice, speaks solely through her silence. If one adds to the marital situation other hardships ruthlessly depicted by Christ, such as the sufferings of a mother, then the semantic range of the Middle High German word *arebeit* is shown to be applicable in full[40].

> *So denn würde umb die mitten nacht,*
> *Und du gern hetist rüw und gemach*
> *Und weltist gern ze bette gon,*
> *so welti dich das kind nit lon,*
> *Und vienge denn an ze grinen und grainen.*
> *So hübist denn och an ze wainen*
> *Und das ze sogen*
> *Bis dir vergiengint die ogen,*
> *Und das kind ze wiegint*
> *Und mit im ze kriegint*
> *Und es uff heben*
> *Und andrest nider legen.*
> *Villicht het es under sich geton:*
> *So müstist denn wúschen und wäschen gon,*
> *Und würdest ain stinkende metti hon.*
> *Deß bist du von mir alles erlon.*

[39] Ratsprotokoll 1376/91, fol. 193, quoted by Hartmut Eisenmann, 33, note 21.
[40] The depiction of motherhood is impressively gloomy (cf. the nightly duties of breastfeeding and changing diapers. 76-91). The mother's lack of sleep finds its sharpest expression in the idea of the "stinking matins".

Then it would come to pass at about midnight, when you would gladly have peace and comfort and would really like to go to bed, that the child would-n't let you go and would start up its crying and yelling. Then you would give it the breast, and you too would start to weep until your eyes wore out, cradling the child and struggling with it, picking it up and then putting it down again. Perhaps it will have soiled itself: then you would have to get down to wiping and washing, and would have a stinking matins. All that you would be spared by me[41].

There is no longer any doubt that secular marriage presents nothing but one sad lesson in life for the woman: she learns only *vertruken* (to endure) and *in allen schmiegen und lernen liegen und triegen* (to subjugate herself in all things, she becomes adept at lying and deception) – nothing but *angsten und sorgen* (fears and worries) and *steken und worgen in der weltlichen e* (weltering and suf-focating in marriage in the world)[42]. In the last rhyming couplet, Christ's cri-tique of marriage tips over into derision. The penultimate line refers to the cleaning of the child with the metaphor of the "stinking matins". This term for the first of the hours in the monastery, prayed while it is still night, moves the theme of marriage into the religious sphere. In the last line, Christ, with his skill in rhetoric, draws attention to himself as the completely different husband. But he only praises the advantages of marriage to *him* very briefly and with ref-erence solely to himself: he would deliver the listening woman from all the troubles depicted. Certainly, the bride of Christ would also have to get up for matins, thus early. She, however, would be able to sleep on *e daz bettli recht erkalte* (before her bed had even got cold). If all went well, he would give her such joy that she would not want to go without his love for anything in the world: *Also wol wurd dir mit mir sin* (you would be so content with me)[43].

The metaphor of the "stinking matins" (90) is a signal for the metamorpho-sis of the marriage motif. Christ, of course, does not wish to expose marriage itself[44], but rather to highlight the discrepancy between secular and spiritual

---

[41] *Christus und die minnende Seele*, 76-91.
[42] *Christus und die minnende Seele*, 71-74.
[43] *Christus und die minnende Seele*, 92-101.
[44] Secular marriage in itself could be a "direct way to God", but this opportunity is unfortu-nately often wasted, Christ is sorry to say. For this reason, one is better off to leave it alone from the start (732). The image of marriage presented in the first section from Christ's mouth is dif-ferentiated little in the course of the work. From lines 730-740 it becomes apparent that Christ cannot intend a general condemnation of marriage, since he mentions it in the context of the seven sacraments. Marriage in itself is also a way to God if it is lived according to his command-ments. But he says that unfortunately this happens very rarely, and he gives adultery as the rea-son for this. He advises the soul to stay away from *weltlichen e*, as it "causes suffering to men and women".

marriage[45]. The noteworthy aspect is how this occurs: Christ asserts that there is a difference between the *husbands* and introduces this difference with the scornful matins metaphor. It might seem surprising even at this stage that Christ is able to convince the soul of his difference as a husband. Obviously the horrendous picture of marriage does not miss its target: the soul is frightened off secular marriage. The hypothetical reality causes the woman, the soul, to take a step towards the heavenly bridegroom: she would rather be dead and buried than abandoned to such a "filthy world", she says. And also in all the time she has been involved with him she has never been given any cause for complaint[46]. And why shouldn't she believe Christ since he describes the *toben und wüten, das man und wib mit ain ander hond* (the turmoil and rage which man and wife have with one another) in her interest, to protect her from it: *Siech, da vor wil ich dich behüten* [...]. (Look, I want to protect you from all that [...])[47]. Nothing at all would lead one to suspect that the divine husband could show even the slightest similarity with the earthly husband.

Secular Marriage as an Image of Alienation

With his gloomy picture of domestic life, Christ propagates more than just spiritual marriage. In a double devaluation, he targets also a more general public: the Christian human race, the "world" as such. The soul introduces the second, collective dimension of meaning of the image of marriage when she speaks of the degenerate world which slanders Christ[48]. Now the Christ whom she has addressed reveals his further purpose. Directly following his depiction of marriage, Christ speaks of a collective alienation between people and, above all, between believers and himself. In this there are echoes of the collective meaning of the marriage allegory in the Old Testament[49]. Christ's mode of

---

[45] Negative characterizations of marriage are found in the pragmatic and fictional marriage literature of the early modern period, for instance in Fischart's depiction of the domestic sphere, which (without any particular intention to warn women) portrays an idyll which (for the woman) is extremely ambiguous (cf. Pia Holenstein, 224 f., for a methodological comment cf. Rüdiger Schnell 1998b, 18-20). – In *Christus und die minnende Seele* the negative portrayal of the relationship between husband and wife is given a strikingly different function. Another notable absence is the theme of the *böse wîp*, which is prevalent particularly in the 13th and 14th century. Cf. Kyra Heidemann, 47-78, here 57 f.

[46] *Christus und die minnende Seele*, 102-107.

[47] *Christus und die minnende Seele*, 108-112.

[48] *Christus und die minnende Seele*, 102-105.

[49] The prophets Hosea, Jeremiah, Ezekiel and Isaiah feel a mission to proclaim the marriage bond between the divine male partner (Jahweh) and the collective female partner (the people of Israel), to call it to mind if they break away from Jahweh (= adultery), and to threaten the revenge

speech suggests an implicit link[50]: this leads from the individual dimension of marriage to the collective dimension of the relationship to God of those who are disposed to be hostile to him. The soul, i.e., the bride of Christ, then takes on the quality of an opposite and exemplary figure. Christ directs an ideal psychological profile of the loving soul to the guardian angel. Several mystical virtues and topoi are woven into it: humility, patience, seclusion, charitable activity, readiness to provide a "storm shelter" for Christ and to give oneself to him as a resting place, temple, and birthplace for God. This outline anticipates the final state of the soul, but first she must suffer the ascetic preparatory phase[51].

Christ complains about the people who relate to him *in kainer süßikait* (without sweetness) or have never got to know him inwardly. There are some whose knowledge of him has "completely perished in the impure world", so that they do not keep his commandments and swear and curse by his name. Anyone who does not yet know the Our Father properly is also guilty of this[52]. He has redeemed many a one on the cross, who would scarcely "remove his shoe for him"[53]. For all that he has done for her, the world rewards him with nothing but ingratitude. The soul's question of whether anyone could mediate between the estranged parties receives a skeptical answer from Christ. In theory his "dear friends" would be capable of doing this, but in public they were always just shouted at: *Sähint sy ain über das feld oder· straß her gan, Den schruwintz als ain wolf an* (if they see one of them walking over the fields or along the street, they shout at him as though it were a wolf)[54]. Christ assures her immediately that for one *dienestman*, true servant, he would save a thousand degenerates[55].

---

of the jealous husband. Hosea is even compelled – as a substitute divine husband, as it were – himself to take a slave as his wife and to father children with her, who are all given telling names: "Unloved one", "Not my people". Cf. Hos 1-3; Ezek 16; Jer 31:31-32; Is 54. – The idea that the relationship between husband and wife is a reflection of the relationship of humanity to God lives on in Christianity, explicitly, for instance, in Petrarch's Latin reworking of the theme of patient Griseldis (which, strikingly, is again fashioned on the obedience of the wife). There Griseldis, who is a helpful subject to her husband, should encourage other women to be as dutiful to their Lord God as one would be to a husband. Cf. Kyra Heidemann, 54 f.

[50] An attitude which would correspond to the Old Testament image of marriage would be that of the cheated husband speaking jealously to the adulteress – i.e., to the collective female figure "Christianity".

[51] *Christus und die minnende Seele*, 177-220.

[52] *Christus und die minnende Seele*, 113-124.

[53] *Christus und die minnende Seele*, 139-141.

[54] *Christus und die minnende Seele*, 134-135.

[55] *Christus und die minnende Seele*, 138-153.

This criticism of the times makes it clear that more than the private cosmos has gone awry. In his arguments and speech[56], Christ links the microcosm between the sexes with the macrocosmic relationship between God and humanity. Thus, the discord between man and wife reflects in a nutshell the rupture between the human race and its redeemer. The bemoaning of marriage finds its continuation in the bemoaning of the world and – building on the traditional Judaeo-Christian marriage allegory – the image of marriage attains its first allegorical significance. A further dimension is significant for the individual, a tropological marriage allegory I now take up.

Secular Marriage as an Allegory of Asceticism

The works based on the tradition of the picture-cycle relate principally to the Old Testament Song of Songs and the mystical interpretation of it as an allegory. The marriage ceremony and marital power relations between man and wife are not a theme for them[57]. Unlike these works, *Christus und die minnende Seele* recognizes the ordering force of earthly marriage structures. For this reason the work merges scenes of worldly marriage with spiritual marriage. This occurs with shocking directness between the second and eleventh sections. Partly explicitly and partly on the basis of structural links, the text uses the relations between the sexes within marriage as an allegory. In itself this is nothing new, and we have encountered it several times in the texts investigated. What is surprising here is the message of the marital allegory: catharsis, asceticism, and subjugation to the divine bridegroom. *Christus und die minnende Seele* uses the hierarchy of the sexes in marriage as a tropological model of asceticism considered as a penal system. If the focus before was on the image of naked violence in secular marriage, now, in a remarkably complementary manner, there emerges that of a husband whose *gewalte* is unbroken: in this capacity Christ imposes ascetic privation on his bride, the soul. In text and picture this results

---

[56] Here this is achieved through the repetition of lines, a feature of *MS* that Banz establishes (as a deficiency) without investigating its effect. A rhyming couplet which is repeated twice links the bemoaning of marriage and of the world: the rhyming lines 33-34 (*schweren und ain schelten / engelten*, [cursing and scolding / put up with it]) relate first to the rage of the husband, which the wife must endure and atone for, but then, with the gender roles reversed, to the cursing world which turns away from Christ (117-118). This reveals a parallelism between the relationship between the sexes, on the one hand, and of God and Man, on the other hand, which is also reflected in line 23 and 138.

[57] See chapters 1 and 2 for a basic overview; for *Christus und die minnende Seele*, cf. Werner Williams-Krapp, 350 and 355-358. In one instance the text Mz even gives a reference to the relevant passage in the Song of Songs (13th picture, Cant. 4,9).

in a striking amalgam of the passion of the way of the Cross and the way of marriage: the stations of asceticism are depicted as the stations of a marriage. In concrete terms, this means that Christ disciplines humanity as a husband does his wife, so spiritual marriage bears an amazingly close similarity to the martyrdom of secular marriage. In this, the hermeneutic foundations are laid for understanding the sequence between the second and eleventh sections: the violence and power of the husband and overlord, on the one hand, and the ascetic *imitatio Christi*, on the other, mold the behavior of a protagonist who unites two functions within himself: that of husband and that of redeemer.

This is not the first time, however, that skepticism arises about the alleged difference between the two husbands. From the beginning, Christ's speech[58] and particularly his admonitions to obey show an active, domineering attitude toward the woman, who should listen and be obedient: *Und los was ich dir sag* (and listen to what I tell you)[59]. Until the middle of the work, Christ takes over the undisputed legal position of the husband and overlord and thus the asymmetry of the parties involved. Christ has also internalized what is probably the most propagated warning against the reversal of the hierarchy of sexes within marriage: *Es stünde ainem man übel an, Wölte er sich sin wib zwingen lan* (it would befit a man ill if he allowed his wife to order him around)[60]. Later on the woman realizes that she has not accorded Christ the status he deserves: *Ich handlet in als ainen husknecht, Deß man dik wol enbär* (I treated him as a domestic servant one could quite easily do without)[61].

But just how different is everyday life within spiritual marriage? This much can be said in advance: the program of asceticism provides the explanation for the semantic elements which make the first half of the work so unpleasant that it makes one wish to believe it was intended as parody. For ascetic imitation does not mean a form of voluntarily experienced withdrawal for which the individual herself accepts responsibility: I, bride of Christ, loose myself from the world for the sake of my beloved. Rather, withdrawal from the world occurs as a process which is identical to the gradual consolidation of the husband's marital power over his wife. Accordingly, Christ as the husband imposes asceticism on the soul as his bride: I, divine bridegroom, loose you, bride of

---

[58] Even in interactive processes between the two parties (dialogue, unification), Christ uses the active first person form, but gives the other a passive or even object status (*sid du mir bist ainig worden / so schaff ich mit dir dinen frommen* [since you have become united with me, I create your spiritual improvement with you], cf. 11-17). Christ's certainty, expressed in his mode of speech, that he can ordain over the woman/soul, is found until the end of the work (cf. 1810 f. and 1870 f., very clearly in 950-966, 1069-70).

[59] *Christus und die minnende Seele*, 17, 228, 783, 954 and 1070.

[60] *Christus und die minnende Seele*, 512-3.

[61] *Christus und die minnende Seele*, 1247-8.

Christ, from everything which separates you from me. Christ cuts her off from everything and shatters everything about her which attaches her to the world. In this way he "privatizes" her in both senses of the word, i.e., he takes her into his own personal sphere of influence and deprives her of all which is individual to her.

The asceticism begins with sleep deprivation. Christ wakes his bride rudely for matins. In this night prayer she should immerse herself in the story of his passion, which is depicted in gory detail[62]. In both marriages, consequently, one has to reckon with matins filled with *passio*: in the first case, of the kind referred to mockingly as *stinkende*; in the other, of one whose significance is beyond question. But a purely meditative re-enactment of Christ's passion is not the end of it. As early as the third section, the bride of Christ's own body is involved. According to text and picture, Christ deprives her of food, drawing on the example of the apostles. They had often "to live without meat and wine" and "also to go hungry" when they followed Christ. In contrast to her male predecessors, the woman, i.e., the soul, cannot *in frömde lande varn* (travel to foreign lands). Christ keeps his wife in the domestic sphere: *So wil ich hier haimen dich bewarn Mit essen und trinken Und wil dir self in schenken.* (I want to keep you here at home with food and drink, and want to pour for you myself)[63]. Despite the illustrious examples held up to her, the soul complains strongly that Christ does not allow her enough to eat: *Er wil mich hungers töten.* [...] *Du spisest mich zemal claine; Mir schlotret di hut umb das baine.* (he wants to make me die of hunger [...] You give me too little to eat; My skin is flapping around my bones)[64]. True, the wife's answering back does not provoke the husband, but Christ does remain impervious to her complaints. Since she is not the only one who is hungry, he is interested only in the ascetic success of the diet: *Ich fürcht, du würdest mir licht ze gaile, Dät ich dir die spis wolfaile.* (I fear you might become too cheerful if I gave you an abundance of food)[65].

Accordingly, both variants of marriage demonstrate an analogous situation of initial physical privation of the wife. Through necessity, ineptitude, or ill will, the secular husband keeps his wife on the most meager of rations and brutally smothers her complaints. Her hunger is thus but the daily suffering of one who is helpless. It is true that the resistance of the bride of Christ is equally fruitless, but at least she suffers hunger in accordance with apostolic example and in the

---

[62] *Christus und die minnende Seele*, 221-380.

[63] *Christus und die minnende Seele*, 396-399.

[64] *Christus und die minnende Seele*, 390-1; 386 or 400-1.

[65] *Christus und die minnende Seele*, 403-405. For Christ's didactic argumentation, see 406-458. The separation from worldly things is central, so that the human being can *höhes gaistes pflegen* (cultivate the higher self).

furtherance of higher aims. Thus, although Christ states the mystagogical objective of what he imposes on his wife, the relations between the sexes remain structurally the same in both marriage discourses: both husbands have their brides firmly in hand – as Christ very decidedly confirms: *Ich lon sy uß minen züchten nicht, Wie ir ioch dar umb beschicht.* (I will not release her from my disciplining, no matter what happens to her because of it)[66].

> *Hie wil er kestgen iren lib*
> *Das sy dest minder in der welt belib.*

Here he desires to chastise her body
So that she stays in the world even less.

---

[66] *Christus und die minnende Seele,* 448-449.

The parallels become clearer as soon as there is talk of disciplining. Then the rod is never far away. Already in the fourth scene we hear the wife complaining: *Du schlechst mich also ser, Ich mag es nit liden mer.* (you beat me so much, I cannot bear it anymore)[67]. Here too the allegorical strokes of the rod are meaningful: he has to "chastise her flesh so that he may live within it". For this, she has to cut herself loose from the world[68]. A passive construction would be more suitable in place of the reflexive one used here, since it is not the figure of the woman, but her husband who carries out the chastisement. His justification, that she would not be capable of it on her own[69], does nothing to lessen the conspicuous similarity to the marital violence depicted in the introductory scenes. In Christ there speaks a husband who wishes to subdue his rebellious wife and force her into the place ordained for her, so as to secure his power as husband and overlord. He seems to have made the grade as an exemplary husband and knows the ways and means to fulfil his duty to control his wife. The following passage takes up the early modern theme of the marital battle of the sexes. Christ seems to be familiar with the warnings to husbands to subjugate their wives. If the husband did not do this, he would find himself subjected to mockery and his social reputation endangered: "One cannot dispel the impression that from the 14th/15th century onwards the husband was under enormous pressure from the expectation that he should exercise unlimited authority within the home"[70]. Christ reaches the decision to make her repellent to the world through various illnesses, since:

Ich han mit dir ain gaistlich e,
Du müst liden wol und we;
Es sol nach dinem willen nit gan,
Du müst volgen dinem man.
Du woltest mich schier vertruken:
Darumb wil ich dich hie buken
Und dir din ruggen beren.
Des magst du dich nit erweren.
Es stünde ainem man úbel an,
Wölte er sich sin wib zwingen lan.
Da mit erzaig ich min kraft,
Das nútz ist wider min macht:
Ich mag wol tün was ich wil,
Ich nim und gib wem ich wil [...].

---

[67] *Christus und die minnende Seele*, 463-4; cf. also 473 f.
[68] According to the title-lines and the explanation of the picture (459-464).
[69] *Christus und die minnende Seele*, 478 ff.
[70] Rüdiger Schnell 1994a, 98.

I have a spiritual marriage with you. You must endure well-being and pain; it will not go according to your will, you must follow your husband. You wanted almost to overthrow me: that is why I will bend you here and beat your back for you. You cannot defend yourself. It would befit a husband ill if he allowed himself to be forced by his wife. In this I demonstrate my strength, that nothing is equal to my might: I can do whatever I will, I take from, and give to, whom I will [...][71].

This profession of belief in the husband's dominance over the wife, i.e., the soul, simultaneously constitutes evidence of divine omnipotence over humanity. Thus for the second time, Christ links the discourse of marriage with the relationship between God and the world. What is happening here, though, is more than a transference of secular marital dominion onto the religious sphere. The relation of the sexes within marriage becomes a model of a power structure, which is universalized and thus made applicable to every area of reality. The dominion (as well as the submission) of the husband extends itself into the world as a universal sign[72].

In the next scene[73], Christ "lames", "blinds", and "tames" the bride and thus forces her concentration onto himself. Christ's answer to the question of why he can tame her only through physical injury is revealing. Since she did not like going to church, she will now have her very own private temple in her heart and receive Christ there. If he did not blind her, "her eyes would run round and round"[74]. But this restlessness of the eyes[75] would drive him out of her. For this reason he destroys her senses and her ability to take her own steps. Later too the wife is told that her place is in the home. When Christ undresses the soul, she complains: she cannot possibly go to church naked[76]. Without further ado, Christ points her to the bench by the stove, which is just as good for her as going to church: *Gangist nit zu der kilchen, so belib dahaim Und sitz zü dem ofen uf den stain.* (If you don't want to go to church, stay at

---

[71] *Christus und die minnende Seele*, 504-517.

[72] This aspect shows that the theme of male marital domination over the woman, which was becoming an issue in the 15th century, could easily be functionalized for other interests than those concerning marriage. For the topos of the powerful woman in art and literature see Susan L. Smith.

[73] *Christus und die minnende Seele*, section 5, 569-704.

[74] *Christus und die minnende Seele*, 609.

[75] These *umb und umb loffenten ogen* belong here in the husband's sphere of control. Berthold von Regensburg warns in his 32nd sermon – *Von des libes siechtuom unde der sêle tôde* (Of the sickness of the body and the death of the soul) – of the danger of mortal sin for man and woman from *spaehen öugeln* (roving eyes). 2 Pet. 2:14 could be to blame for Christ's radical solution in *Christus und die minnende Seele*.

[76] Cf. *Christus und die minnende Seele*, 858-965.

home and sit by the stove on the stone bench)[77]. Christ bases his argument here too on the distraction of people in church: they might well *be* there physically, but they were thinking of their goods and belongings. This is his reason for taking everything away from the soul, this way she will no longer have anything which could distract her from him[78]. Again he asks her to be his dwelling place and temple: *Du bist doch selb der tempel rain, Den ich selber mir main Von himel herab dar in ze komen* (for you are the pure temple which I myself intend to come down into from heaven)[79]. That is why the husband Christ does not look, as other men do, at the woman's "red mouth", which will soon turn to ashes, but wants her instead as an inner sanctum[80]. His claim to possess her is basically a claim to occupy her. In order for this to happen, the wife must also surrender her spinning equipment, so that she turns herself to him "completely": *Ich wil nit, das man nu ain stündli on mich vertribe: Ich wil ain gantzes 'bi im beliben'.* (I do not want you to pass even a short hour without me: I want a complete 'remaining with him')[81]. This does at first meet with resistance from her because she doubts his earnestness[82]. But soon she complies with what is imposed on her[83]; she later also accepts the fact that only the claims of the husband on the wife, and not the reverse, will meet with fulfillment[84].

That the divine bridegroom subjugates his bride more and more possessively, manifests itself also in the structure of the dialogue. Communicative speech-acts, such as the appellative *gelt*, reinforce the link between the ascetic preparation by Christ and the male brutality of the secular marriage. Christ addresses his opposite using the same *gelt* as that with which the secular husband mocks his wife before beating her: *Gelt, ich werd dich also an griffen, Das du mir nit*

---

[77] *Christus und die minnende Seele*, 896-897.

[78] *Christus und die minnende Seele*, 904-910.

[79] *Christus und die minnende Seele*, 900-902. He repeats that the bride of Christ should serve him as a dwelling-place in 1173-1175.

[80] *Christus und die minnende Seele*, 669-676. In the dialogue poem *Kreuztragende Minne*, which is also printed by Banz, the Christ figure argues in a different vein. The soul hesitates to give herself to Christ, so that he asks her if she would only turn to him when she was old and ugly and the world no longer cared anything for her (40-44). – The same absolute claim to the bride marks the relationship between God the Father and "his virgins" in Mechthild von Magdeburg's *Das fließende Licht der Gottheit*: *Er wil si im selber alleine haben* (he wants to have them to himself alone), V,24,22-23. Cf. chapter 1, section Brides Plural and Their Singular Bridegroom.

[81] *Christus und die minnende Seele*, 852-853.

[82] Cf. *Christus und die minnende Seele*, 777-796.

[83] From 803, she retracts all her complaints and praises her situation in the highest terms.

[84] From 1324 ff., Christ resists when the bride tries to lay exclusive claim to him. It would be nonsense if she wished to lock him up in her heart since everybody wants to have something of him. He will not stoop to such a foolish demand: *Und woltest mich allain han, So wär ich wol ain doracht man* (and if I you wanted to have me to yourself, I would be a foolish man), 1340-1341. Cf. also 965.

mugist entwichen (Well, I will grip you in such a way that you will not be able to escape me)[85]. Conversely, the complaints of the soul are not just an indication of her unwillingness to suffer but also a reflection on the violence of the husband. Thus, several times she laments Christ's hardness: *O herr, du bist ain herter man* (O Lord, you are a hard man)[86], and *Wie bin ich mit dir überhertet so gar!* (how extremely harshly I am treated by you!)[87].

The literal relinquishing of the world culminates in the gallows on which the divine bridegroom hangs his bride in the ninth section. What appears on the level of the pictures to be a punishment by the gallows is in fact a hanging which models itself on the act of the Crucifixion. There are echoes of the realistic depiction in the second section of the passion of Christ: her hands and feet are not yet *wund* (wounded), and her body is still *gesund* (healthy); her arms are not yet *zerspannen* (stretched out), and she is not yet truly

---

85 *Christus und die minnende Seele*, 640-641.
86 *Christus und die minnende Seele*, 972.
87 *Christus und die minnende Seele*, 928.

erhangen (hanged)[88]. Again the meaning of this allegory can be determined so simply that it is almost direct: the bride should be raised above the earthly: this will perfect her love for her divine husband[89]. Three sentences with the stereotypical address *O herr* (O Lord)[90], document the success of the husband's training. At first she complains, then she falls silent. The bride, or the soul, achieves uniformity with the will of her husband, or Christ. Promptly Christ then releases the bride from her suffering: *Gang her ab, won es ist zit, di liden ich nit lenger an dir lid* (Go down from here, for it is time; I will no longer suffer this suffering in you)[91].

The last scenes of the catharsis form a transition to the theme of *minne*, love. In the tenth section the husband hands his opposite the love potion to feed the flames of love which were already kindled on the gallows. Taming here means only weakening, so in the eleventh section the husband can bring his bride completely within his power. The soul, whose transformation is expressed in an appeal for atonement, claims: *O herr, ich geflúh dich niemer mehr, Deß setz ich dir lib und sel.* (O Lord, I will never flee from you again, I promise you that with body and soul)[92]. The preparation of the bride is at an end, and her relationship with Christ gradually emerges from the ascetic shadows of the marriage discourse. The fact that from the following picture she appears in monastic dress seems to confirm that this is the right order. The bride's new clothes herald the resurrection of the *sponsa Christi*. In contrast to the secular wife, who, in her senseless suffering, remains in the status of the dejected subject, the bride of Christ can rise again as a subject capable of encounter. This thesis seems bizarre in light of the outrageous manner in which the text and pictures proceed. It must be tested in the second *cursus* of the work.

But before that, I take one last look at the unpleasant, violent marriage discourse: the physical mutilation of the soul by Christ and the allegorization of this ritual between husband and wife cannot and should not be separated. The

---

[88] On the one hand the wife must "repay" him his sacrifice; on the other, she should have a taste of his suffering on the Cross (983-993). Cf. 233 ff.

[89] What is going on here is an exercise of atonement (cf. 1024 ff.) and mystical meditation on the passion (cf. 984). MHG *galge* means both "wooden framework" (over a well, as a gallows) and "cross" (Lexer I, 727-8). The relevant illumination shows a gallows in the form of a framework of tree trunks, as could also stand at the head of a well; the woodcuts, however, show a cross, on which the bride of Christ hangs, nailed or bound (see fig. 16, below). Banz (228) mentions here the influence of the "Kümmernußbilder", the iconography of Vilgefortis, here of course without beard. Cf. Lexikon der christlichen Ikonographie VII, 353-355 and Regine Schweizer.

[90] *Christus und die minnende Seele*, 972, 994 and 1000.

[91] *Christus und die minnende Seele*, 1024-1026.

[92] *Christus und die minnende Seele*, 1094-1095. For this reinterpretation of the scene as far as the tradition is concerned, see lines 1156 ff. *Christus und die minnende Seele* does not include the sleep scene from the Song of Songs, which is present in Mz (Williams-Krapp, 356).

suprasexual religious action dresses up in the allegory of the marital model of the sexes. The socially regulated power structure between the sexes is not meant to be extracted from this, but to be used in a suitable way. The late medieval dialogue does this in a singular way. Thus, a marriage discourse which is taken very literally depicts the relationship between God and humanity with outrageous directness. The domestication of the wife by the husband occurs in a multiple sense: the woman, i.e., the soul, is tamed, made domestic, relegated to the home, and required to be herself an inner sanctum for a God who demands all this as his right as a husband. Is it not just a very small step to think that behind Christ there stands a husband who acts like God? Structurally, therefore, the question arises whether the divine nature of the husband is supposed to ennoble spiritual marriage (along with the rulership structure which it incorporates) or whether it is rather that the corset of marital domination is intended to schematize and authenticate the mystical dialogue. From the perspective of the work either seems plausible.

Erotic Love and Intimacy

Besides the relentlessly consolidated dominion of one over the other, there is still something missing for the *unio mystica*, which, of course, is yet to come: gestures of cautious affection, of erotic attraction, and of amorous, reciprocal passion. Perhaps in the meantime one would scarcely think them possible. But the second part of the work responds to the desire for images of positive intimacy between man and woman. The counterbalance to the crude *via purgativa* is found at least partially in that canonical reservoir of the erotic imagery of bridal mysticism, the Song of Songs. From the twelfth section, together with other literary topoi of love, it proves – in quotations almost painfully literal – to be a source of imagery for the *via illuminativa* and the *via unitiva*. A metamorphosis now takes place which is crystallized in the clothing of the figure of the woman, in the tone of the two protagonists, and in their roles as well as in the quantitative division of speech. In sections 15-18, 20 and 21 Christ speaks only the first couplet in each case while the rest is carried by the female protagonist. This balances out the apportioning of speech in the first part of the work and also shifts the didactic emphasis: if at the beginning it is above all Christ who instructs the soul, increasingly the soul takes over this position. Naturally, her teaching is directed not towards Christ but to the reading public. This is an explicit strengthening of the already dialogical character of the work, even of the whole codex[93]. But it also extends the dialogue

---

[93] Cf. Jeffrey F. Hamburger 1998, who develops the connection between *imitatio* and dialogicity for the Seuse-part of this codex (esp. 443ff.), and Niklaus Largier (on all three texts in the codex).

beyond the margins of the text, since in the second part of *Christus und die minnende Seele* the sermon-like passages draw the recipients more firmly into the didactic love-dialogue.

The Woman and the Restoration of Balance

After her transformation (11), the woman / soul is prepared for being alone. Now Christ eludes her, leaves the scene, and positions himself behind a curtain. For the first time, the woman herself becomes active: she searches for him. A new tone dominates the female speech from now on: the lamenting tone of literary brides, be it that of the searching *sponsa* of the Song of Songs or that of a female voice in the context of courtly *Minne*: *Ach got, wie sol es mir gon, Das ich min lieb verloren hon! Waffen, iemer waffen!* (Ah God, what will become of me, since I have lost my love! Oh woe, woe evermore!)[94].

Just how much the tables have turned is shown by the activity of the woman. She undertakes a counteroffensive (probably modeled on CC 4,9). The title lines report that, in order to savor him fully, she shoots at Christ with the arrow of love. The miniature shows a nun, whose arrow has just hit her beloved[95]. She wants to make the most of the favorable moment and take him up completely in her heart. It is true that the limits of Christ's devotion are already apparent here. However, the argumentation he uses to check the bride in her desire rewards closer investigation. He pacifies the covetous soul with the example of the apostle Paul, whose intensive pleading remained unheard[96]. This is more than a psychological distraction technique. The context shows how significant Paul is here: he makes an appearance here inconspicuously, but he is undeniably a star witness to ecstatic visions[97] since the accusation originates in Paul's account of his ecstatic experience[98]. Directly in accordance with the cited authority for mystical experience, Christ promises the soul that she

---

[94] *Christus und die minnende Seele*, 1228-1230. Cf. also 1231 ff., 1310 ff., 1380 ff. (Cf. CC 5,6).

[95] See chapter 5 below, in which different variants of this type of love-aggression are compared.

[96] *Christus und die minnende Seele*, 1354-1361. Within the logic of the text, the reference to Paul serves to present the soul with a greater person who was refused the fulfillment of his wishes, more as an example for the exclusivity of experience than for the preaching vocation.

[97] Cf. Alois Haas 1989, 109-126, here 116.

[98] *Christus und die minnende Seele*, 1356-1359. Cf. 2 Cor 12:8-9. What in the epistle to the Corinthians is portrayed from the perspective of Paul is here transformed into the first-person speech of Christ and provided with the explanatory addition: *Do wolt ich ims nit anders fügen* (then I did not want to ordain otherwise for him), 1358.

will share in his secret, that is, in a special knowledge – "special" because of its source. This source is not any kind of book, as many a one who *ain gantzes iar gat süchen hinnan und vornen in den büchen* (searches backwards and forwards in books for a whole year) pursues it without success. She, on the other hand, would find *haimlichs (…) in dem gaist geschwind* (mysteries […] in the spirit quickly[99]. The designation *haimlichs*, a term of mystery which is applied to the female partner in the dialogue here for the first time[100], echoes the expression *arcana verba* in the Pauline account[101]. "Mysterious, ineffable" applies here not to something which can be achieved through intellectual effort, but a mystery

[99] *Christus und die minnende Seele*, 1363-1369.

[100] In 211 Christ mentions to the angel that the soul very definitely notices his *haimlichen influß* (secret influence). It is not clear what *haimlichs und güts* (secret and good things), 353, refers to in a formulation which is almost identical to 1366 f. Christ speaks in the third person of a female figure who could be either the virgin Mary (who is discussed from 297) or the *werde magt* (worthy virgin), 325, which could refer to either Mary or the soul. In any case the reaction of the soul (from 361) shows that she obviously does not feel that she is meant explicitly.

[101] *et audivit arcana verba* (2 Cor 12:4).

which is "found in the (divine) spirit". In this, *haimlichs* proves to be a verbal sign for a form of communication which transcends human boundaries. If in Christian prophecy it is mainly linked to a vocation to preach, here it appears to be indebted only to a rather vague social didactic mission. For to a large extent the protagonist closets herself in a space of amorous intimacy with her divine partner.

The woman, the soul, wishes to "bind" her beloved to her even more, even to "constrain him" and force him to her[102]. If one is to believe his confession, she succeeds[103]. Her triumphal gain in power is impressive: *Nieman mag wesen min gelich, In minen henden stand alle rich: Ich han in, der es alles geschaffen hat.* (no one can be my equal, all kingdoms are in my hands: I have him, who created all)[104]. But again Christ dismisses her claims to power. Gradually the relationship balances itself out; having reached a position of independence, the soul now becomes conciliatory[105]. Christ tempts the soul with worldliness one last time when he tips out a sack of gold pieces before the figure of the woman to "buy himself free". She is no longer open to bribery[106]. The soul professes her allegiance to her divine husband again. Of her own free will she looks back, so to speak, on many a secular wife who, despite her own virtue, leads a sorrowful life because she is attached to "an unbearable husband". Having learned from the "misfortunes of others", especially of women, she says decidedly to Christ: *Ich wil lieber dir haften an Ich wil dich, lieber herr, nun allain* (I would rather be attached to you [...] Now, dear Lord, I want you alone)[107]. Belatedly, but explicitly, the bride of Christ thus gives her consent for the spiritual marriage[108].

The next scene seems to celebrate this[109]. Christ strikes up on his fiddle like a *varend man* (wandering minstrel). The listener links the musical allegory with her career change from a secular wife to a religious one. As a wandering musician can extract any gift from a lord through his playing, Christ has bewitched her so much with his (dance-)music that she has given herself to the minstrel step by step. Captivated by the music, she becomes enslaved and allows her "worldly clothing to be stripped from her by force". Of course this makes her a common laughing-stock: "she looks as though she wants to bite God's toes

---

[102] *Christus und die minnende Seele*, section 14, from 1424.

[103] *Christus und die minnende Seele*, 1426-1427.

[104] *Christus und die minnende Seele*, 1434-1435.

[105] *Christus und die minnende Seele*, 1446-1449.

[106] *Christus und die minnende Seele*, section 15, from 1488.

[107] Cf. *Christus und die minnende Seele*, 1530-1539 and 1602.

[108] The voluntary nature of the soul's commitment to Christ, which she stresses frequently in the second part of the work, accords with the increasingly didactic attitude of the soul (cf. 1420 ff., 1698 ff. etc.)

[109] *Christus und die minnende Seele*, section 16, from 1607 ff.

off"[110]. She overhears this without difficulty, and she is spurred on to dance to his tune[111]. The bewitched soul knows exactly what the allegory of the violin signifies: *die gig ist götliche süßekait* (the fiddle is divine sweetness)[112].

[110] *Christus und die minnende Seele*, 1647-1648. An expression of mockery at the excessive affection of the bride of Christ which is idiomatically and contextually similar is "biting the heads off the statues (of Christ or the saints)". This is found in Anna Vetter's vision accounts. A neighbor who is suspected of harmful magic is supposed to have mocked Anna's frequent visits to church (her love of her bridegroom Christ) with this expression (the story of Anna Vetter. In G. Arnold's "Unpartheyischer Kirchen- und Ketzergeschichte, part III, chapter 27; here as reprinted in Marianne Beyer-Fröhlich (ed.), 74). Cf. also Lutz Röhrich, fressen, in: Lexikon der sprichwörtlichen Redensarten, which quotes several examples of expressions using "(fr)essen" with connotations of strong affection.

[111] *Christus und die minnende Seele*, 1651 and 1658-1659.

[112] *Christus und die minnende Seele*, 1672.

From the next scene onwards, both text and illustration open up new dimensions of erotic pitch[113]. Both the gesture of embrace and the appropriate setting of the *locus amoenus* signal a situation of courtly love. On the left, a little hare hops on the grass; another is hiding on the right. The basic condition for this absolute seclusion together is provided by the bride, who is separated from

[113] In section 17 the motifs of the kiss and the secret are combined (in Mz = 16 and 17); in section 18 the motif of whispering is picked up again. Banz identifies the animal in the tree on the left as a squirrel and the one on the right as a blue and yellow kingfisher (233). The fencing of the garden is reminiscent of the *hortus conclusus*.

everything: *Min lieb wil han ain raines hertz allain Und mit nieman han gemain.* (my love wants to have only a pure heart and to share it with nobody)[114].

The two kiss each other on the mouth, which signifies the communication of the secret mentioned above. Christ wants to let her know his secret, *sin haimlichait lon wissen*[115]. Kissing and whispering both refer to the mystery of incarnation, the mystical birth of Christ within the individual. This is presented as the epitome of human fulfillment[116]. Thus the intimate talk of the lovers – *allegorically* the presence of God's word in the individual – is heightened through Christ "whispering a secret word" to the soul, "sinking" himself into her soul, and thereby "flowing through" her[117]. Then the beloved becomes a space in which the *sacrum* and the *secretum*, the sacred and the secret, become one. It is appropriate that delimitation against the outside[118] gains in importance since the erotic art is secretive. The secrecy value of the love talk is apparent in several ways: it is there in principle already in Christ's hidden and mysterious *togenlicher minne*, then also the terms *runen*, and *toges wort*[119]. According to the tradition of bridal mysticism[120], however, central importance attaches to the terms *haimlich, haimlichait* and *haimlich züpflicht* (secret union), which belong to the same semantic field[121]. The couple being together

---

[114] *Christus und die minnende Seele*, 1698-1699.

[115] As stated in the title-lines of section 17 (1682-1683). The Latin heading for the equivalent scene in the Mainz picture-cycle reads here: "Hic reuelat *anime* secreta" – here he reveals secrets to the soul – (16, Williams-Krapp, 357). Christ promised the soul this *haimlichait* in 1368 ff.

[116] *Christus und die minnende Seele*, 1700-1704.

[117] *Christus und die minnende Seele*, 1754-1761.

[118] Cf. next section.

[119] *sin minn ist togenlich* (his love is secret), 1728; *runen* denotes quiet, intimate, and also secretive talking and whispering (Lexer II, 538-540). *Ich runen dir ain toges wort* (1756) refers to the whispering of God's word. This is the only instance of this word, which has negative connotations in the context of courtly communication (cf. Horst Wenzel 1995, 151-154). Other terms for intimate conversation (such as *kosen*) are not used. Rüdiger Brandt 1999 throws light on human speech in the religious context, particularly from the point of view of its articulatory quality.

[120] *Heimelich* and nominal derivations from *heimelich* play an important role in the writing of Mechthild von Magdeburg, particularly in the multiple combination of *wissen* and *haimelich(eit)* under discussion here (cf. IV,12 and VI,20). The term is also closely connected with Mechthild's understanding of herself as an author. Cf. Alois M. Haas 1989b, 206-233; Nigel F. Palmer 1992, 217-235; Marianne Heimbach-Steins 1995, 71-86, considers only the nouns against the theological background of prophecy.

[121] Adjectives and nouns deriving from *heimlich* are numerous throughout the work, particularly in sections 17 and 18. There they denote the secret of the lovers: *haimlichait* (1683, 1704), *haimliche* (2100) *haimlichs* (*adj* 353, 1368), *haimlich* (*adv*, 1690 (possibly also *n f*), 1895), *haimlich* (*adj*: 211, 1417, 1769). The expression *haimlich züpflicht* occurs twice (1417 and 1769). These instances of *haimlich* make it clear that semantically it can apply both to the historical incarnation of God and to the subsequent imprinting of God's word in the individual which this makes possible. To this is added – particularly in sections 17 and 18 – the emotional aspect of

Cristus sprach
Tú von dir remen vnd betten
Du muist mit mir den cappe trett

thus means experiencing an isolated and enclosed space, which is guarded just as protectively in this context as in that of the courtly *tougen minne*, secret love[122]. The intimacy of the lovers is (also) defined in spatial terms: Christ goes

closeness, eroticism, and intimacy which *haimlich* connotes. Mystical communication is (also) the intimate talk of love, and thus *haimlich* provides a link between the two contexts of this conversation. Another word in the same semantic field - *tougen* (secret, hidden) – is used less often here and (apart from in the expression *togenlich minne*, with its echoes of courtly love) then seldom to refer to emotion, closeness or erotic intimacy. Once the noun *betogni* is applied to the mystery of the incarnation and is synonymous with *haimlichait*. *Tougen* (or a derivative) is found in the following instances: *togen* (*adj*: 1756), *togenlich* (*adj*: 1728), *betogni* probably related to *tougenîe* 1713). Cf. Lexer II, 1483.

[122] Expressions such as *sin minn ist togenlich* (his love is secretive), 1728, with their echoes of *tougen minne*, are reminiscent of the courtly conception of *Minne*.

"in and out" in the soul[123]. Comparison with the motifs of the bride presented in chapter three reveals a crucial difference: for this *unio mystica*[124], the central point is not a reference to Salvation history, nor to the history of the motif, nor to the collective dimension of the church, as in the earlier tradition of bridal mysticism[125].

This suggests that the work is a private devotional book for a secular or religious reader. Few of the pieces of religious didactic advice go beyond the personal sphere, the perspective of the depiction concentrates on the individual's striving for happiness[126]. Nor does the nineteenth scene, which sets the actors in dancing motion, do anything to alter this[127]. The soul is glad to let herself be drummed into dancing, for she has enough sorrow all year long[128]. The drumming bridegroom becomes the leader of the dance. But the soul is confused by the fact that she is required to leave her exercises in piety: *Aber herr, du bist wol ain seltzen man, Das du mich nit wilt venien lan [...].* (but Lord, you are a strange man, that you do not wish me to leave me on my knees)[129]. This retort causes the bridegroom to assert the hierarchy between them one last time: she must continue to be subject to him if she wishes to remain with him[130].

The soul already begins to see a shimmer of nuptial and erotic happiness lighting up the horizon when she thinks of the "court" of the "rich and generous emperor", where there is nothing but contentment. She longs for the everlasting presence of the bridegroom: *So wölt ich mich an dich smuken Und dich an min hertz früntlich truken Und fügen in die sele min. Da müstist eweclich inne sin.* (I would want to nestle close to you and to press you affectionately to my heart and draw you into my soul. You would have to be inside it forever)[131]. He counters with sober logic that this would be impossible on earth. If she wants

---

[123] Cf. *Christus und die minnende Seele*, 1768-1771.

[124] It is true that the *unio mystica* is announced in the last section (2045 ff.), but sections 17 and 18, with the talk of love, also contain motifs of union. Precisely the imprinting of the word of God is taken up (from a different perspective) in the soul's speech in section 21.

[125] As tried to show in chapter 3, the monastic *St. Trudperter Hohelied* and the pastoral *Die Hochzeit*, but also Mechthild's *Das fließende Licht der Gottheit* interweave the collective and the individual dimension of Salvation history very closely; in *Christus und die minnende Seele*, at any rate, it is almost impossible to determine any sign of monastic or ecclesial community interest. From this "individualistic" point of view, *Christus und die minnende Seele* is more comparable to Hartmann von Aue's *Der arme Heinrich*.

[126] See, for example, *Christus und die minnende Seele*, 1710 ff. and 1758 f.

[127] *Christus und die minnende Seele*, from 1800.

[128] Cf. *Christus und die minnende Seele*, 1814-1823.

[129] *Christus und die minnende Seele*, 1806-1807.

[130] *Christus und die minnende Seele*, 1812-1813.

[131] *Christus und die minnende Seele*, 1840-1844.

her heaven here and now, she will have to go without it later[132]. On this, she promises him patient loyalty.

At the crowning of the bride, the soul remains self-assured but humble[133]: self-assured, because she does not want the crown, but rather the highest reward, the beloved; humble, because she will always live in fear of the world. For this reason – and this argument will interest us further – any public honor is treacherous. Not only would she draw everyone's attention to herself, making any lapse particularly sensational, but she would also call the devil onto the scene[134]. Accordingly, she would rather go without the honor and its associated trials. The linear development of the soul ends with a long didactic speech from the mouth of the soul about the imitation of Christ. The last section offers the union of the lovers, which again sounds all the notes in the scale of love[135], where only two lines come from the mouth of the man: *Lieb, ich und du sind all ain, Alsus wirt ains us uns zwain* (my love, you and I are all one, thus from

---

[132] *Christus und die minnende Seele*, 1844-1847.

[133] *Christus und die minnende Seele*, from 1868.

[134] *Christus und die minnende Seele*, 1872-1905; from 1906 there follows the allegorization of the crown (see below).

[135] *Christus und die minnende Seele*, from 2043.

the two there comes forth one). Fulfilled, she answers: *Ich han begriffen alles das, Deß min hertz ie begeren was. O herr, du bist min, so bin ich din; Die trúw sol iemer stät sin* (I have grasped everything that my heart ever desired. O Lord, you are mine, thus I am thine; this loyalty will be constant for ever)[136]. Then she praises her beloved and the beauty of them both, not forgetting to mention that she is now receiving her reward, which has been calculated exactly. This consisted not only in eternal life but also in God's surrender of himself. They said that this was the greatest. But, the soul reflects, she would give the title *maister* to one who could tell how *got und mensch sich schlúst in ain* (God and Man mingle as one)[137]. There then follows the confession of a first-person voice which must be identified not with the female protagonist but with the female or male author. Unfortunately, she or he has not lived such a saintly life that God would confide his secret in her or him[138]. The concluding prayer, in which the figure of the author prays for her or his own salvation, also accords with this gesture of humility[139].

The Couple and the Others

How does a couple which establishes itself in a privacy won through privation relate to the outside world? With the change from marital asceticism to erotic attraction, the polarity of internal and external reference is reversed. The woman becomes active and involves herself in the relationship: the *Minne*-dialogue suddenly shows a friendly face. What is more fascinating from a literary point of view, however, is the question of how an act of union can be exposed to the eyes of the reading public and simultaneously continue to exclude the outside world. The couple shut themselves off more and more from the outside world. There is an indicator for this: the relevance of public opinion[140], which is revealed in the attitude of outsiders to the couple. Certainly the topos of protecting an amorous secret is known in both secular and religious love poetry, as is that of the danger of pernicious gossip in the tradition of bridal mysticism, which is understandable in view of the monastic bonds of community. The

---

[136] *Christus und die minnende Seele*, 2045-2050.

[137] *Christus und die minnende Seele*, 2080-2092.

[138] Such confessions that one has not been blessed with mystical experience are found several times, for example, in Lamprecht von Regenburg's *Tochter Syon*.

[139] *Christus und die minnende Seele*, 2109-2113.

[140] I use the term here in the late medieval sense of a view which is shared by many and thereby becomes a supra-personal opinion. For the term itself, which is introduced into German in the course of the French Revolution as a loan-translation of "opinion publique", see the article Öffentlichkeit, in: Geschichtliche Grundbegriffe, 414-467, here 448-456, Peter von Moos 1998, and also Rüdiger Schnell 1998c.

main cause of pernicious gossip is retreating into the private sphere. This sort of antinomy between the sphere of individual and collective claims to control has already been identified in late medieval monastic culture and has been discussed with regard to monastic texts from the twelfth century[141]. But here it appears that the warnings about an outside world which is participating through observation also reflect the socially compact cultural life of the late medieval town.

Who is this outside world? Right from the beginning the *welt* is portrayed in a negative light because of its religious alienation. Though it is true that until the end of the work it is never completely out of sight in this basically didactic guise, increasingly it appears as a group of people with eyes and ears although there are no indications which would enable one to characterize this group more closely either qualitatively or quantitatively. This vague, hypostatized public can only be denoted through paired formulae: *iung und alt, frowen und man, wib und man* (young and old, ladies and men, women and men). If in the first part of the work this *welt* is related primarily to Christ, later increasing tensions arise between it and the intimacy of the couple, particularly the female half of the couple. The social danger which attaches to it in the second part of the work does not stop with the literary topos of, for example, the inherently secret character of the experience of grace or the secrecy traditional to the sphere of courtly love[142]. A circle of trespassers threatens to break into the space of the love dyad. Clearly the personal space of the "woman", of which her *fama* is an essential part, is more vulnerable[143]. It is she who imposes on herself this compulsory

---

[141] Urban Küsters 1985, chapter V. Gottesminne, Individualität, monastische Lebensform. "Öffentlich", public, is then a relative term which refers to the community within the monastery which encroaches on the individual nun or monk. Cf. also the interesting study by Peter von Moos about the so-called secrets of the heart, a guarded and precious personal area of the ego, and the associated repertoire of manners of encoding and dissimulating as well as revelatory techniques (von Moos 1995/1996 and 1997a).

[142] Cf. Rüdiger Brandt 1993a, 230 ff. and passim, in a different literary context also the book by Anthony C. Spearing. Brandt's suggestion that an idea of privacy may be possible within topical motifs is extremely interesting (Brandt 1993b, 105-111). It is a warning that one should be not be too quick to categorize amorous secrecy: the "dichotomy of society / public on the one hand and individuals on the other hand" is not necessarily at the forefront; secrecy could also be the partners' own attempt at a solution. Using the example of Reinmar der Alte, he demonstrates that in Minnesang the classical motifs of secrecy can easily incorporate possibilities which allow for it to be a private gesture of the couple to seal themselves off from within.

[143] Here one should point out the importance of her public *fama* for the woman. If it is possible to destroy the existence of a woman through her "rénommée", or her *fama publica*, then this can also reveal methods of disciplining her. Cf. Doris Ruhe, 72-90, here particularly 84-85, who demonstrates in the case of the *Ménagier de Paris* that the protection of the woman and her reputation can be a motivation for the cooperation of two marriage partners. Nicole Gonthier proves that sexual violence towards a (single, married, widowed) woman began with attacks on her respectability. For the importance of *fama*, or *infamia* in late medieval penal law

silence and discretion, who protects the inner borders of the couple against invading eyes and ears, and who has to hold this barely defined outside world at bay. How exactly does this woodcut-like public opinion endanger the couple?

A subtle rivalry with the "others" begins to develop already in the soul's hopes for private happiness on her own with Christ, which he immediately dashes[144]. The opposition to *frowen und man* becomes clearer when the bride praises Christ's generosity to her. She is aware that it would become uncomfortable for her if other people knew. For this reason she would never be so bold as to dare reveal her experience to anybody. If her special status became obvious, she would have to fear a general public which would react with hatred to the singling out of the chosen one: *Es ward uff mich schrygen frowen und man Und sprachent: wes nimmstu dich für ander lüt an?* (Women and men would begin to shout at me and say: why do you think yourself better than other people?)[145] Perhaps here again there are echoes of the account of Paul's visionary experience. He withholds his experience from the prying access of others by emphasizing the inherent unknowableness of what has happened and the possibility of appearing presumptuous in the eyes of others. In Paul at least the first traces of an awareness of public opinion are apparent when he states that he does not want to boast. The people standing around should form their opinion of him from what they observe in him (2 Cor 12,5-6).

Even louder mocking breaks out when the wife of the fiddle-playing bridegroom has allowed herself to be captivated and her secular clothing to be removed. Young and old mock her, shouting that she looks as though she wants to bite God's toes off[146]. The protagonist remains composed in the face of this public hostility by throwing herself into his love with all her strength[147]. But, on the whole, this composure with regard to her social reputation gives the impression of being more a small island of immunity. Or is it more a didactic *exemplum* of *contemptus mundi*? In any case the bride of Christ has not yet secured herself a stable position in her relationship to the world; for social and psychological reasons this is probably impossible during her lifetime. For no sooner has Christ, the leader of the dance, given her "great joy", than she must conceal this contentment from the others: *Das ich es vor den lüten nit getar ögen* (that I do not dare to reveal it before the people)[148]. This is the only way she

---

see Porteau-Bitker / Talazac-Laurent, La Rénommée, in: *Médiévales* 24 (1993), 67-80; for the allegorical representation of *fama*, see the study by Christiane Raynaud, *ibid.*, 57-67. For *fama* in the courtly context, see Horst Wenzel 1995, 154-156.

[144] Cf. *Christus und die minnende Seele*, 1324 ff.

[145] *Christus und die minnende Seele*, 1374-1375.

[146] *Christus und die minnende Seele*, 1645-1648.

[147] Cf. *Christus und die minnende Seele*, 1649 ff.

[148] *Christus und die minnende Seele*, 1832.

can forestall public condemnation as a fool, *tor*[149], since people would shout: *'si wil uns erdöben, Sy hat recht die sinne verlorn'* (she is trying to infuriate us, she has completely lost her mind). Their statement – that the woman is infuriating them on purpose and has taken leave of her senses[150] – seems elliptical. It remains unclear what exactly provokes this anger: is it envy or the sensational behavior of the soul? Or are the people indignant that Christ is hidden in his beloved's heart: *Da kunnent sy nit gesehen in* (which they cannot see into)[151], thus making the mysterious reason invisible?

After all, this reaction reveals an interhuman conflict which is reflected in mystical literature. About two hundred years before *Christus und die minnende Seele*, Lamprecht von Regensburg recommends those blessed with Grace to be discreet; in this he is thinking less of protecting the secret or the carrier of the secret than – with psychological sensitivity – of sparing those who are excluded from the secret, amongst whom he counts himself[152]. But here the greatest possible degree of concealment seems to be designed to ensure the best self-protection. Such actions to protect the intimacy of the couple and their secret, which include appropriate vocabulary, have already been pointed out. Terms of mystery fence off the inner space of the couple. Even when the sovereign and incommunicable nature of mystical experience is addressed[153], the text relates this to the personal reputation of the bride of Christ. This is central, because God's bringing forth his son within an individual is an extremely mysterious event. Even an experienced person would not tell anyone about this since, for lack of personal experience, the other would not believe it, even if He who is full of Grace were visible before him[154]. Consequently, her unusual experience places the bride of Christ in an unusual position in society. Remarkably, the tendency of the individual to self-isolation is intensified in mystical intimacy because, whatever its form, the concept of a social, ecclesiastical-prophetical, or literary mission is not applicable. A way out is provided by the intimacy of love, in which self-sanctification and the experience of God take a very private place: erotic happiness is privatized.

I will draw a short conclusion about the public which is present in woodcut form in the work. Public awareness begins with the bride letting slip something about her experience – which she does verbally and non-verbally, since the

---

[149] *Christus und die minnende Seele*, 1835. St Paul, too, describes himself as *insipiens* (2 Cor 13).

[150] Lexer I, 683 does not give *ertoben* as a transitive verb with the meaning 'to provoke rage in somebody', but only in the transitive or reflexive sense of 'to become enraged, to take leave of one's senses'. Here, however, the use of the pronoun 'uns' is evidence of transitive use. In his glossary, Banz notes that Swiss German has preserved the word *Täubi*, meaning 'anger'.

[151] *Christus und die minnende Seele*, 1837.

[152] Cf. Lamprecht von Regensburg, *Tochter Syon*, 2979-3040.

[153] E.g. *Christus und die minnende Seele*, 1741-1753.

[154] Cf. *Christus und die minnende Seele*, 1700-1721 and 1689 ff.

secret reaches out into the world through the senses[155]. What becomes public (*öffentlich*) is that which is *offen* (open), *offenbaere* (obvious), *offenlîche* (public): whatever can be seen or heard by a wider circle of people. The signals from the sender are completed by the receiver. What the eyes of the "people" see and what their ears hear is broadcast repeatedly and loudly by their mouths. It is very clear that the dreaded "shouting" of the people shows this aspect of perception, which is fixed in the etymology of the word *öffentlich*. Accordingly, what is wrenched from the private sphere of the individual only attains social range through the interplay of the senses.

The coronation scene at the end of the work shows the conflict between the couple and their social environment – and consequently also the endangering of the female half – from another perspective. The disparagement of the people is a threat, but their admiration is an even greater one. This holds a hidden trap which is equally capable of making one a laughing-stock in both divine and human eyes[156]. One is wise to arm oneself against attacks from him, who always sets about his work perfidiously, the devil. The crown which is decisively rejected by the soul signifies "worldly glory", the reputation of saintliness. It becomes visible and audible in renown and public *fama*: whoever is crowned "is noticed by many" and "praised above all religious people"[157] – public opinion as favorable as it is dangerous. The people are led astray into idolatrous devotion. The bride of Christ knows that the devil sees this as his opportunity: *[...] Und würde man mich han für ain abgot. Wäre das nit des tüfels spot?* ([...] they were to take me for an idol. Would not this be the mockery of the devil?)[158]. The very one who thinks *er hett es wol geschaffet* (that he has it made) is quickly *geaffet* (made a fool of) by the devil[159]. He "assails" the spiritual celebrity with temptations, as the female protagonist masterfully presents it[160]. Public honor therefore appears in an ambivalent light: on the one hand, it is a divine trial; on the other, a divine signal for "good people". But this too seems to be more of a disaster: God *verhengt*, imposes, honor on somebody. Soon afterwards the person in question will have to be prepared for the worst attacks of the devil and to defend his or her "crown"[161]. With such temptations through the granting or denying of *fama*, God tests people according to their individual dispositions.

---

[155] Cf. also 1645 and 1884. For the communicative function of the senses, cf. the original book by Horst Wenzel 1995, here primarily chapters 2 and 4.

[156] Cf. *Christus und die minnende Seele*, 1881-1882.

[157] *Christus und die minnende Seele*, 1903, 1913-1915.

[158] *Christus und die minnende Seele*, 1904-1905.

[159] *Christus und die minnende Seele*, 1561-1562 (cf. *Des Teufels Netz*, 1408-1409, which has the same rhyme *got:spott* in the same place).

[160] *Christus und die minnende Seele*, 1932-1933, or 1934-2010.

[161] *Christus und die minnende Seele*, 1909 ff., 1921 ff. and 2012 ff.

Besides this aspect of the psychology of salvation, regard in society also contains an important dynamic of social psychology. The person who is regarded is looked up to. But he or she may also be looked at. The double sense of the word is thus as ambivalent as the phenomenon itself. In a positive sense, "regard" means to look up to somebody. But in a negative sense it also comprises the idea of scandal, which seems to conform to a universal law: the higher the pedestal of sanctity, the more sensational the person's fall. Now the mocking shouts of *wib und man* are valid as a legitimate penalty for the lapse[162]. In shouting, the people give vent to their anger; after all, the false saint has taken them all in: who would ever have thought that somebody who, *haimlich und offenbar* in private and in secret as well as in public and within view had always behaved in such a saintly way and who had always seemed be the very foundation of the whole world, would have "cooked up" something like this?[163] The social damage is intensified in the bitter reproach: in whom *can* one then believe? The danger that the power of religious exemplary figures could be undermined also puts into question any thought of a private secret. In any case, in view of the danger that the devil might drag everything into public view, a total renunciation of social esteem is advisable. The bride of Christ renounces the crown.

[162] *Christus und die minnende Seele*, 1881-1886.
[163] *Christus und die minnende Seele*, 1886-1900.

Conclusion: Marriage between Heaven and Earth

In the concept of the bride of Christ as formulated by *Christus und die minnende Seele*, symbolical and real gender draw close in an extremely direct way. Accordingly, historical relations between the sexes intrude unchecked into mystical thought-patterns. The result is astounding: spiritual and secular marriage become variants of one and the same hierarchy of the sexes and become constellations of power. From then on, they determine female perspectives on life: either spiritual marriage as a bride of Christ and virgin in a convent or secular marriage as the bride of a man and mother. This type of application is only possible if images are brought into use which are drawn from a sphere which is partly made available for public access and partly strategically withheld: the amorous union of man and woman, the intimate life of a couple.

The text investigated here makes a considerable distinction between marital and erotic images, which manifests itself in the different character of the two halves of the work. Marriage as a motif is used with an original technique of encapsulation. Twice it reveals itself to be a hard school of disciplining and of the breaking of one sex by the other. This occurs first in the harsh scenes of marriage at the beginning of the work. Christ does not present the soul with an idyll of family life but with a depiction in minute detail of a domestic hell as a hypothetical reality. Almost lovingly, he paints a disastrous life for a woman; the stylized secular husband becomes a demon whom he, as the divine bridegroom Christ, wishes to banish. The second time marriage shows itself in the first half of the work, it is as an excessive allegory of passion mysticism. It becomes the epitome of ascetic privation. The distinction between the husbands, stressed so strongly by the divine bridegroom, rapidly becomes blurred as the violence of the secular husband is reflected in the actions of the divine husband. All these are to be interpreted in part literally and in part allegorically. In the heavenly marriage as in the earthly one, one sees a husband who domesticizes and privatizes his wife with shocking thoroughness. Thus the struggle for ascetic liberation from earthliness is fought out in earthly categories: gender, in all its historical and social mutability.

If the negative ritual of marriage continues to be exercised meticulously *in spiritualibus*, at least there is an erotic light on the horizon. The second half of the work with its sparkling lights of musicality, eroticism and intimate communication shows both protagonists – we could call them a couple – in a particularly intimate light. They come together, but not without first securing themselves against claims of others and their prying eyes and listening ears. Gestures which could betray them have to be hidden. This fascinating secrecy, and not in the first instance the eroticism, makes voyeuristic approaches all the more attractive. For this reason it is not surprising that the inevitable shadow falls in the form of the outside world, with its eyes and ears, which challenges the loving couple, but above all the female protagonist, in many ways.

I would like to conclude by throwing open some questions. The first area of interest concerns the value of the images of marriage and love respectively. *Christus und die minnende Seele* has recourse to images of familial, marital, and erotic proximity which are charged with both positive and negative values. One question, which no other text discussed thus far has featured to such an extent, is: why is marriage a suitable dispenser of negative images? Is there a suprapersonal and public consensus which sees marriage more as a hierarchical ordering system between husband and wife than as the sign of an emotional bond? Is it because of its subordination of the woman that marriage presents itself as an ideal allegory of the ascetic ritual which deprives the female partner of all self-determination? Is it the fact that mutual marital "debts" can be calculated so precisely that determines the discourse of marriage to be the rational conduit of asceticism? Two things are certain. First, the seclusion of the secular married couple delivers the wife into the hands of her husband, and this is presented as the true basis of marriage. Second, this asymmetry does not allow closeness or intimacy to develop between man and wife. Both facets are appropriate to the purpose of the author of the work because there could be no more striking way of illustrating mystical catharsis.

That the text must use other images to tell the affirmative side of the coming together of the lovers is clear. But why does it draw for this on the erotic discourse? Is this simply the result of the emotional vacuum which characterizes the discourse of marriage in *Christus und die minnende Seele*? Or is it the very fact that they are so removed from everyday practice that fits these literary love-configurations, topoi from the secular and religious field, to portray intimacy of any kind? Is it these that first provide the couple with that fascinatingly exclusive space – exclusive now in the positive sense of the word? For it is indeed hardly a coincidence that the work, in its second cycle, thematizes the problem of third-party knowledge by some kind of public, characterized by pernicious gossip. This involves the social integrity of the bride, who is protected by her unblemished reputation. Does the erotic discourse, above all the Song of Songs, offer the woman other modes of behavior? One aspect of this is certainly the role of the female love-aggressor, viewed as unfeminine according to the medieval understanding of gender. This will be the subject of the final chapter.

The second area of interest for my questions is the interaction of the secular and spiritual discourses of marriage, on the one hand, and the discourses of marriage and love, on the other. At first glance the work appears to be built around a dichotomy. It tells the story of a love relationship in terms which are sometimes borrowed from marriage in the real world, and sometimes modeled on conceptions of love which are formed predominantly by literature. From the perspective of these literary concepts in a manuscript, itself destined for both monastic and secular women, first owned by the patrician Margarete Ehinger, there arises the question: do these findings in the case of spiritual marriage reflect what late medieval concepts of marriage reveal about marriage in general? Does this mean that – at least in this kind of devotional text for a female public – all gestures of partnership, eroticism, and affection must be incorporated into the ordering discourse of marriage? Certainly the threads which bind the two halves of the work together in the token of marriage are thin ones. But precisely the gradual establishing of positive intimacy shows how much the love action is occupied by the model of marriage[164]. Considered from this standpoint, the Christ figure will have to admit that his claim of a difference between the husbands is on decidedly shaky ground. This conclusion is very relevant for my view on the whole idea of the bride of Christ: the fact that secular marriage can be constructed, but no longer maintained, as an antimodel to spiritual marriage can be seen as an infallible indication that the motif has reached riper years; the fact that Christ as husband is forced to distance himself so explicitly from a secular husband and simultaneously to establish a marital power structure which is so similar to it, undermines the credibility of love and husband as alternatives.

---

[164] Late medieval representations of marriage appear to propagate this. Cf. the views of Rüdiger Schnell (Schnell 1994a, 106-107) and also Heide Wunder's research on gender hierarchies in early modern period.

Chapter 5
Setting One's Sights on God: Attacks of Love

> *Sie [die Frauenzimmer] werden in der Geschichte*
> *sich nicht den Kopf mit Schlachten [...] anfüllen;*
> *denn es schicket sich vor sie eben so wenig, daß sie*
> *nach Schießpulver als vor die Mannspersonen, daß*
> *sie nach Bisam riechen sollen. – In history they*
> *[women] will not fill their heads with battles [...], for*
> *it becomes them just as little to reek of gunpowder as*
> *it does the males to reek of musk*[1].

Vrouwe Minne: Love as Aggressive Personification

In the first chapter, my aim was to show the results of the sexualization of the motif of the bride of God. It brings secular and spiritual relations between the sexes closer together and explains why gender-specific stereotypes are rehearsed in religious discourse. One of these stereotypes concerns the central issue of which party should be active, initiating, and aggressive in a love relationship and which should be passive, patient, and expectant. The third chapter suggests that, on the whole, the *sponsa Christi* is to be seen more as the one biding her time and re-acting than the party taking the initiative and acting. The fourth chapter begins with a comparable, even more radicalized, asymmetry between the lovers but ends with a balanced dynamic of partners under the aspect of the erotic *unio mystica*. This last chapter now presents the opposite extreme by focusing on the aggressive female lover as she springs into action in text and image. As active as she is aggressive, she fires her arrows at people to turn them into lovers – she even targets her beloved. Where the dash separates the two clauses, she changes her identity. In the sources investigated, including some previously mentioned, she undergoes a gradual metamorphosis from an artificial to a real woman. At the beginning, there stands the female personification of love, who attacks lovers of both sexes with bow and arrow in a

---

[1] Immanuel Kant, *Beobachtungen über das Gefühl des Schönen und Erhabenen*, 48-49, trans. Goldthwaith, 79.

suitably "masculine" way; at the end, she becomes a vehement lover who takes aim at her own beloved, Christ. The first consequence of this is that in the figure of the female archer – hence also in the bride of Christ – contradictory gender identities are united. Here, incidentally, is a reflection of our previously established requirement: religious women should harmonize both male and female role patterns within themselves. Second, in the love-archeress a gradual transition takes place from abstract allegorical being to real woman. Thus, she is a suitable emblem for reconsidering several of my central questions from a new perspective.

There is another reason to make obeisance to Lady Love in her own chapter. *Amor* and *dolor* are words which are not only close in sound. As terms for different sorts of passion[2], together they constitute the cornerstones of an archive of cultural history[3], which has filled literature, both religious and secular, in Latin and in the vernacular, to bursting point. In medieval love literature specifically, a lone protagonist practices her dangerous craft with bow and arrow. From her predecessors in antiquity she assumes her weapon and, in so doing, strengthens the age-old interchangeability of *eros* and *agon*: "Language (vocabulary) has long highlighted the equivalence of love and war: in both cases it is a matter of conquering, plundering, taking captive, etc"[4]. In inflicting life-threatening wounds on lovers, Love turns literature into a sort of casualty ward[5]. There, wounded minnesingers languish beside lovesick brides of Christ. A powerful maelstrom encompassing love, death, injury, aggression and illness thus comes together in the work of Lady Love, which explains[6], in a miraculously figurative way, many a *causa amoris* as well as

---

[2] For the double meaning of *passio*, see below Jeffrey F. Hamburger 1990, 74 ff.

[3] An overview is provided by Nancy Huston/Sam Kinser. – *Militat omnis amans* (in love, all are militant), maintained Ovid (Amores I,9), and in this he had a strong influence on the European Middle Ages. See, for example, Eugène Vance, 544-71. For the transmission of the motif to medieval German lyric and epic poetry (only secular literature), see Erika Kohler, 13-37; for Mechthild von Magdeburg's use of this imagery, see Paul Michel 1986, 508-526. Further examples of love-wounds in bridal mysticism are given by Réginald Grégoire, 713 ff.

[4] Rapture, in: Roland Barthes, 128.

[5] It goes without saying that in medieval literature there are also references to people wounded by arrows who are not the victims of personified Love. In the religious domain, for instance, God shoots at people with punitive arrows, and people crucify Christ anew with the arrows of their sins (probably inspired by Hebr. 6:6): *mit tötlicher sunden stral* (with the shafts of deadly sins), for example, in Tilo von Kulm, *Siben Ingesigel*, 4293). For God's arrows, see Peter Dinzelbacher 1986, 5-138, who assembles the relevant Bible passages (13 f., 20 etc.).

[6] Evidence of this is found in the idea of lovesickness as a medical concept and a literary motif (*amor hereos*, cf. Frances Mary Wack), the exegesis of verses from the Song of Songs (2:5, 4:9, also 5:8 and 8:6 f.) and other verses from the O.T. (Ps 44:6 and 63:8) which mention arrows, wounds or illnesses (and love), but also high medieval treatises on the power of love (Richard of St. Victor, see below).

many a *passio amoris*[7]. For this reason, this éminence grise can claim her rightful place in a book about the culture of bridal mysticism because she unites not only person and person, Man and Woman, and person and God but also segments of the medieval culture of love which have been carelessly separated.

An Archeress

So who is this potentate? A huntswoman is the first thing one notes with amazement. Her hermeneutic roots show that she is an allegorical woman because she personifies an abstract noun which is feminine in German. The initiated know the linguistic game of her aggressive gestures: the wounding glance of the beloved's eyes is part of the aggressive imagery of the language of love, in which the other is attacked, occupied, and even annexed. This calls for self-defense, and the defendant proceeds against Lady Love in a quasi-judicial way. With playful earnestness, Walther von der Vogelweide demands justice from Love. She has shot him while his beloved lady has remained untouched:

ir habet mich geschozzen,
und si gât genozzen;
ir ist sanfte und ich bin aber ungesunt.

You have shot me, and she has remained unharmed; she is fine and well, whereas I am wounded[8].

In the interests of fair distribution of the pain, Walther requests the cause of the suffering, *frowe minne*, to shoot arrows into the heart of the woman he adores:

Ich bin iuwer, frowe Minne;
schiezent dar dâ man iu widerstê.

I am [already] yours, Lady Love; shoot there, where you are resisted[9].

This clear distinction between the two women is dissolved skillfully by certain representatives of the courtly love lyric. They identify the beloved *vrouwe*

---

[7] For medieval ideas about how love comes into being, see the comprehensive work by Rüdiger Schnell, 1985, here esp. part III; for courtly literature in the German-speaking area and beyond, see Alois Wolf.

[8] Walther von der Vogelweide, *Ich hân ir sô wol gesprochen* (2,6-8), quoted in *Deutsche Lyrik des frühen und hohen Mittelalters*, 398-399.

[9] Walther von der Vogelweide, *Ich hân ir sô wol gesprochen* (4,1-2), quoted in *Deutsche Lyrik des frühen und hohen Mittelalters*, 400-401.

and *vrouwe Minne* (lady Love) with each other in text and image[10], as the human beloved learns from her fellow, the female love-allegory, the trick of wounding. In this way, the secular love lyric shows that amorous archery can be adopted – and adapted – from one woman by another: to be precise, from allegorical women by real, biologically female brides of Christ.

Vrouwe Minne, Lady Love, is a female allegorical personification[11]. As a synthetic woman, she is an artificial being, i.e., a woman created in accordance with the intentions of art[12]. This makes her a remarkable figure, both as a human being and as a woman: on the one hand, she corresponds to human women (she is similar or different and wounds them); on the other, she communicates with men by attacking them and adopting their aggressive behavior[13]. In this way, she becomes one of the few women who are active in matters of love[14]. This affects bridal mysticism because, as a result of a particular combining of functions, she finds her way into the scenery of spiritual love. Two figurative levels are linked in the aggressive female lover: one is the personification of love which is mythographically characterized as aggressive; the other is the allegorical bride of the Judaeo-Christian exegesis of the Song of Songs, whom her beloved refers to as 'ravishing him' (CC 4,9). I would like to start by focusing on two aspects from the path of development of this woman: first, the question of her gender; second, the question of her power and violence.

Her Sex

Is she a woman? Or is she masculine? Lady Love appears to be both. Like every biological being, the medieval personification of love had both male and female ancestors. They prepare the way for the shifting gender of this allegory, which takes shape in figures of the pre-Christian imagination – in the Greek Eros, as

---

[10] Rüdiger Schnell 1985, 452ff., analyzes various relations between the beloved lady and Lady Love (also with regard to the male speaker).

[11] In the context of the religious literature of the thirteenth to fifteenth century, the concepts of allegory so sharply differentiated from one another by Friedrich Ohly (the poetical and the hermeneutic concepts of allegory; cf. Friedrich Ohly 1977, 12-13) may overlap, as in the case of the aggressive female lover. For the terminology in connection with love, see Rüdiger Schnell 1985, 351ff.; for the rhetorical function of allegory, see Schnell 1985, 391ff.

[12] See Aleida Assmann 1994. She derives the synthetic status of allegory from an anecdote of the Greek artist Zeuxis, who extracts female ideality from five actually existing beauties and fuses this essence into an image.

[13] Cf. Sigrid Weigel 1994a, 7-26.

[14] For the dichotomy between activity and passivity, see chapters 1 and 2.

well as in the Roman Amor and Cupid or in their mother Venus[15]. The shifting sex of the representation of love – as well as the martial attributes with their
male connotations – are therefore true to its forebears. However, it is language-
immanent factors such as the grammatical gender of the abstract noun which
determine the gender of its personifications.

Grammatical gender is a sort of costume that an abstract concept must don if
it wants to take flesh – or at least the artificial flesh of an allegory. Grammatical
gender explains the sexual uniformity of nearly all Latin virtues and vices – all
these concepts are grammatically feminine and are thus imagined as allegorical
women. But grammatical gender also determines the variations in the sex of a
personification. This is the case for the medieval Latin terms for love, of which
some are masculine and others feminine. Grammatically masculine *amor*, on the
one hand, and feminine *caritas* or *dilectio*, on the other, can be represented sometimes as a man and sometimes as a woman. The gender problem is intensified
when the concept in question is grammatically masculine in one language but
feminine in another. Thus in Old French, the Latin term *amor* (m.) becomes
either the male *dieu d'amors* or the female *amour* (Provençale *amors*), who had her
special place in the lyric of the troubadours and the trouvères[16]. In addition, with
the transfer of one of the Latin terms for love into the German language, Love –
minne/Liebe (f.) – changes sex, a fate shared by other personifications[17]. Love then
takes flesh in the lordly figure of Lady Love. Despite this grammatically neater
situation in German, medieval German literature is also unable to avoid ambigu-
ities.

The problem of grammatical gender and sex arises as soon as the texts have
recourse to sources in a foreign language. Sometimes interesting solutions are
developed. One solution is for the personifications of love to accumulate, and
another is for two personifications of different sexes to overlap each other. The
former is chosen by Wolfram von Eschenbach in his *Parzival*, when he gets

---

[15] For the tradition of classical gods of love and their symbolic significance with regard to different types of love in the Middle Ages, above all for the 'Venuses' and 'Cupids' of English literature, see Theresa Tinkle; for a more general survey, Werner von Koppenfels. For the co-existence
of Amor, Cupid, Venus and Lady Love in the courtly world, see Erika Kohler, 5ff. and passim,
Erwin Panofsky, 155ff., Barbara Newman 1995, 153ff.; for the reception of the (love) mythology
of Antiquity and the relevant research literature, see Rüdiger Schnell 1985, 359ff. and passim.
On the subject of classical love-deities in the plastic arts in the Middle Ages and the Renaissance,
see Anna Frey Sallmann, Reinhard Lullies, Jean Seznec, Fritz Saxl et al., John B. Friedman, 51ff.,
Erwin Panofsky, chapter IV: Blind Amor.

[16] Barbara Newman 1995, 153-154.

[17] An illustrative example of this is the personification of the world, a male figure from Latin
mundus, but a female figure when derived from MHG *werlte* (cf. Wolfgang Stammler and, with
numerous illustrations, Eckart C. Lutz, 278ff.).

"Amor, Cupid and their mother Venus" to cooperate successfully[18]. The latter solution implies that *Her Amor* and *diu minne* appear simultaneously as the same authority. In Heinrich von Veldeke's *Eneit*, for example, the allegory of love constantly alternates between feminine and masculine forms, depending on whether the mother is thinking of the "one depicted" – Lord Amor, influenced by the Latin representation of Amor – or of *minne*, a Middle High German feminine[19]. Here one has an inkling of how problematic and fascinating such technical questions of translation and gender may become as soon as pictorial sources are in play[20]. Here too the paralleling of two figures of opposite sexes produces a confusingly simple solution: simultaneously a masculine representation in the picture and a feminine one in the text. It is also possible to let the image-determined sex of the personification dominate the one in the text[21].

One last observation on the question of the gender of the various Latin terms for love which are personified in the medieval German *vrouwe minne*. The Latin term *caritas* (f.) is the most positive term in the religious context, as it is originally restricted to God's love for humanity (1 Joh 4,16), and thus constitutes a contrast to the expressions *cupiditas* (f.) and *amor* (m.), which relate to human, sensual aspects. Not only *caritas*, but also *dilectio*, *cupiditas*, and *amor* become *vrouwe minne* in Middle High German or, as in Lamprecht von Regensburg's *Tochter Syon*, *frou Karitas* or *diu Minne*[22]. As a Franciscan author, he is obviously trying to integrate the noble Latin *caritas* of his source into his personification. For this reason, in his works arrows are launched not only by "Love" but also by "Lady Caritas"[23]. Thus, in the texts of bridal mysticism, at least, the multifaceted personification *minne* envelops herself in the sacred aura of *caritas*, making "sacred and secular" coincide[24]. Erwin Panofsky sees things in an equally conciliatory way from an iconographic standpoint: "On this basis the 13th century was in a position to achieve a temporary reconciliation between *cupiditas* and *caritas* (...)"[25].

All these sexual shifts, which are determined by grammatical gender and thus basically arbitrary, serve as a warning that one should be careful not to jump to

[18] Cf. 532,1ff.

[19] Heinrich von Veldeke, *Eneasroman*, 9818 ff. and 9910-9951.

[20] An example of the translation according to text and image of the masculine personification *peccato* into the German *sünde* is mentioned by Meinolf Schumacher 1996, 53, note 206.

[21] For extensive treatment of this, see Markus Müller, 172-194.

[22] Sometimes he uses both terms at once (Lamprecht von Regensburg, *Tochter Syon*, 3050).

[23] Lamprecht von Regensburg, *Tochter Syon*, 2943 ff. Lamprecht also leaves many other terms (other allegorical figures) in Latin.

[24] Barbara Newman 1995, 154. She discusses the personification with regard to the distinction between "bridal mysticism" and "mystique courtoise" (143 ff.).

[25] Erwin Panofsky, 155-156.

hasty conclusions about their significance[26]. However, notwithstanding all necessary relativization, it should be remembered that, from the point of view of medieval language awareness, two attitudes are possible. First, one may posit an optimistic belief that the relation of signs is reliable (the grammatical gender of a sign is an indication of the signified). Even Abraham a Sancta Clara still argues vehemently in this direction when he comments on *superbia*. In an excursus on the subject of the ambitions of Eve, he points to the grammatical gender of two Latin expressions: *Suberbia ist recht generis foeminini uel Ambitio* (it is right that *superbia* and *ambitio* are of the feminine gender)[27]. He later refers even more explicitly to the grammatical gender of both German and Latin terms: *superbia ist Generis feminini. der erste fall der Eua war die hoffart, dan sie wolt wie ein gettin sein* (*superbia* is of the feminine gender. Eve's first fall was pride, because she wanted to be like a goddess)[28].

Depending on one's point of view, the second attitude bears witness either to greater distrust of the surface of the word or greater trust in the spiritual dimensions of meaning in language. Here the decisive factor is productive suspicion: does the outer aspect of the linguistic sign perhaps conceal an essential inner aspect?[29] Isidore of Seville gives positive confirmation to this suspicion, by, for example, attaching an androgynous essence to the linguistic term for a virgin. He attempts to find the key to what is signified in language by his construction of the etymology of the term *virgo*. Since the virgin's being biologically female corresponds to the signifier's being grammatically feminine, this appears to be a reliable, if not exhaustive, expression of the essence of the signified itself. Isidore looks further, searches in the *nomen* for the latent *omen*, and reveals in the body of the word the deeper, in this case masculine, essence of the virgin. After all, the word *virgo* (virgin) incorporates the terms *vir* (man) and *virtus* (virtue, strength)[30]. Much later Gottfried von Strassburg, in his *Tristan*, would also conceive a double gender. When he establishes that certain women have male

---

[26] Meinolf Schumacher 1996, 53. Women are elevated to being men, and men relegated to being women. For gender-change and its significance for men and women, respectively, see Vern L. Bullough, in Jacqueline Murray / Konrad Eisenbichler (Eds.) 1996, 13-15.

[27] *Werke von Abraham a Sancta Clara*, ed. Karl Bertsche, 2, 213.

[28] *Werke von Abraham a Sancta Clara*, ed. Karl Bertsche, 2, 136. This sort of argumentation on grammatical grounds is found frequently in Abraham's misogynistic passages (see also Abraham a Sancta Clara, ed. Franz Eybl, 187).– It is interesting that he mentions the masculine gender of the word *Deus*, established by the *Gramatici*, precisely to highlight the contradiction of a *Theologus*, that *Deus est communis*: God turns to all humanity (247).

[29] For the concept of stratification of meaning in the understanding of words in the Middle Ages, see Friedrich Ohly 1977, 1-31; for attempts to decipher the signified from the signifier on the basis of etymology, see Paul Michel 1988, 207-260.

[30] Isidore of Seville, *Etymologiae*, XI, 2, 20 ff.

hearts, the linguistic term is no longer felt to be a meaningful sign: like the name *wîp* (woman) it is merely superficial; inwardly, she is *ein man mit muote* (a man in spirit)[31].

There is a widespread early Christian linguistic tradition of androgyny which holds that biological gender can become the empty frame for an Other, who can also be of a different sex. In this it supports Isidore's etymology. This is the tradition of the *mulier virilis*, of which Lady Love is one part. The idea that a qualitatively different, militant, and thus masculine being can fill a female body develops into a programmatic concept for religious life for women, which is repeated frequently from patristic times into the Middle Ages and beyond[32], thereby becoming an element of female hagiography[33]. Since martial ambitions with masculine connotations are an intrinsic part of the ascetic attainment of Salvation, *mulier virilis* becomes an honorary title for female Christian ascetics. In the works of Mechthild von Magdeburg personified Knowledge praises the soul with masculine terms full of honor when it is a question of her bravery in spiritual battle. But she resorts to feminine formulae if she wants to praise her aesthetic or erotic abilities. Linguistically she could not combine Agon and Eros, masculinity and femininity more closely in one entity: *Du bist ein menlich man an dinem strite, du bist ein wolgezieret*

---

[31] Gottfried von Strassburg, *Tristan*, 17975; see Rüdiger Schnell 1984, 16-21.

[32] The ideal of the *mulier virilis*, which is usually understood as a masculine virgin (a so-called *virago*), is formulated neatly and concisely in Pseudo-Chrysostom: *femina autem si virilitatem sanctam habuerit, etsi corpore femina est, animo est vir, et numeratur cum sanctis* (for if the woman has saintly virility, but is physically a woman, mentally she is a man and is numbered with the saints), *Opus imperfectum in Matthaeum* 25, PG 56,765. That in particular cases even the distinction between body and mind is not upheld is demonstrated by the *Passio Perpetuae* (BKV I/14, 336; see following note). For this early Christian ideal type of the militant woman, see Kerstin Aspegren; Claudia Opitz, 87ff. and 182ff.; Susann Elms 101ff. and Christine Haag; for a summarizing overview of the motif in patristic times, see Gillian Cloke, 214ff.; Peter Brown, chapters 7, 12 and 13. For the Middle Ages, see Barbara Newman 1995, passim, and Hildegard Elisabeth Keller 1998b; from a different perspective, Ivan Illich ²1995, 209, note 106. Peter Dinzelbacher makes an important reference to the tradition of *militia Christi*, which was appropriated mainly by men, but sometimes also by women (see Peter Dinzelbacher 1992, 51ff.). – Abraham of Sancta Clara sketches a late example of a *femina virilis* in St. Clare, who could not have been a *schwache, subdille undt haikliche Creatur* (a weak, subtle, and delicate creature) thus a woman, because she had *ein härtern wandl gfiert als Ein man* (revelled in taking the hard path like a man), *Werke von Abraham a Sancta Clara*, ed. Karl Bertsche, 2, 82. Réginald Grégoire provides further examples of the motif of the *mulier virilis* in the context of bridal mysticism. For the related topos of the strong woman in literature and the visual arts in the fourteenth and fifteenth centuries, see Susan L. Smith, 137ff. and Claudia Brinker-von der Heyde in: *Manlîchiu wîp, wîplich man.*

[33] As Peter von Moos (1972, 233-239) points out, this finds clear expression in female saints' lives. For biographies of women from late Antiquity, particularly those of the "virile" Melanie and Perpetua, see Walter Berschin 8, 156 ff. and 1, 49.

juncfröwe in dem palast vor dinem herren, du bist ein lustlichú brut in dinem minnebette gottes! ("You are a virile vassal in battle. You are a finely attired maiden in your Lord's presence in the palace. You are an eager bride in your bed of love with God")[34]. Joan Cadden shows, with relation to medieval teachings on conception, that the expression *mulier virilis* as a counterpart for *vir feminus* also finds support in ideas from the history of medicine[35]. Anatomical or physiological concepts of masculinity therefore also leave their mark on technical terminology. Thus expressions such as *virago, hommace*, and even *hommenine* occur as medical terms in Old French[36].

Against the background of this normative model of sanctity, in the religious context, masculine terms are not simply descriptive, but serve as exhortative signals. In this way, pastoral texts (mainly by monks) direct women with what are virtually calls to arms: fight like a warrior (*tegen*, in Middle High German)[37], or *stande manly agaynes al temptacions*, as it says in Middle English[38]. The Cistercian Bernard of Clairvaux seeks to counsel the newly widowed Melisende, queen of Jerusalem, with an exhortation to manliness. Her husband is dead, and their son is as yet too young to rule, so she must "be a man about it", so to speak: *Opus est ut manum tuam mittas ad fortia et in muliere exhibeas virum [...].* (it is your task to apply your hand to strong deeds and to reveal the man within the woman [...])[39]. Her entourage should recognize in her more a king than a queen (*regem te potius quam reginam*), despite all her objections – which he anticipates, placing the words in her mouth – that she is merely a weak woman (*ego autem mulier sum, corpore debilis, mobilis corde* [for I am a woman, weak in body, inconstant in heart]). The Dominican Heinrich Seuse, too, tries to encourage spiritual strength in a particularly weak woman using an image of masculinity. He describes to her in detail what is said to an inexperienced knight before battle: *"eia, werder held, tü hüt als ein frumer man und gebar kechlich und wer dich frischlich! Lass dir din herz nit enpfallen als ein zage; es ist besser erlich sterben, denn unerlich leben. So der erste just übertruket wirt, so wirt es lihter".* (There now, worthy hero, act today like a virtuous man and carry yourself bravely and defend yourself with daring! Do not allow your

---

[34] Mechthild von Magdeburg, *Das fließende Licht der Gottheit*, II,19,6-9; trans. Tobin, 81. – In VII,19,34 (trans. Tobin, 291) she calls Mary *ein menlich helferin der verzwifelten* ("the mighty [literally: 'virile'] helper of all those in despair").

[35] Joan Cadden, 201 ff. and 224.

[36] Cf. Chris E. Paschold, 35 f.

[37] Thus Christ to the soul, depicted as a female figure, in the poem *Die Kreuztragende Minne*, in *Christus und die minnende Seele*, 254.

[38] In a letter known by its incipit *Ego dormio* and ascribed to Richard Rolle, which is directed to a woman (quoted from *English Mystics*, ed. Barry Windeatt 1994, 31).

[39] Bernhard of Clairvaux, *Epistola* 354, ed. Winkler 3, 620-23, here 622,10-11.

heart to sink: it is better to die honorably than to live dishonored. Once the first joust is won, it will be easier)[40]. As in Seuse's own *Vita*[41], this courtly image of the tournament is applied to spiritual matters and is presented to his spiritual daughter as an encouragement: *Viriliter etc., daz sprichet: gebarend kůnlich und manlich ir alle, die got getrúwent! Des bedarfst du wol, tohter minú, daz du vast standest und den bŏsen reten des tiefels nit volgest* (*Viriliter*, etc., that means: behave in a brave and manly way, all of you, who put your trust in God! That is what you need to do, my daughter, so that you stand firm and do not follow the wicked suggestions of the devil)[42]. At the moment she had to withstand the worst, but brave endurance would pay off. He would gladly take all the blows aimed at her on himself, but this would be of little use to her, since *Als menig pfil dir wirt geschossen, als mengen rubin wirst du in der krone tragende.* (As many arrows as are shot at you, that many rubies will you wear in your crown [in the next world])[43]. What Seuse, that mystic knight of God *par excellence*, still holds back in addressing this woman is expressed by the spiritual guide in the late-medieval treatise *Der Schürebrand*. There two eighteen-year-old brides of Christ are called *liebe junge Gottes ritterin* (dear young "knightess" of God) and are spurred on *zuo ritterlicher vestekeit in allen uwern anestürmen und striten der manigvaltigen bekorungen* (to knightly stead-fastness in all your attacks and battles against manifold temptations)[44].

What this hagiographical and pastoral model of masculinity for women gives us to consider, is the coexistence and interweaving of two sexual identities, precisely within women in the convent. Thus, it makes sense that the series of texts and images which follows will trace the transition from the symbolic to the real human love-aggressor in just this human *sponsa Christi*.

Her Power and Violence

Lady Love operates with the characteristic attribute used already by Eros and Amor: the bow and arrow. In contrast to the graphic audacity of the image, wounding someone with an arrow is perceived as particularly cunning because the wound is inflicted invisibly and from a distance[45]. Both the simple possession

---

[40] Heinrich Seuse, *Briefbüchlein*, Letter IV, 370,22-27.
[41] Heinrich Seuse, *Vita*, chapter 44, 149 ff.
[42] Heinrich Seuse, *Briefbüchlein*, Letter IV, 370,30-33.
[43] Heinrich Seuse, *Briefbüchlein*, Letter IV, 371,7-8.
[44] *Der Schürebrand*, ed. Philipp Strauch, 47, 32-35.
[45] Even as early as Xenophon, the fact that gods of love "wound from a distance" is used to explain why they are called "archers" (*Memories of Socrates*, 52-53). The devil too attacks with such deceitful weapons, as Gregory the Great explains (*Moralia in Iob*, XXXI,41,81, CCL 143 B, 1606).

of a weapon and, even more, the bold manner in which it is used give masculine overtones to Lady Love's gender character, as Lamprecht von Regensburg emphasizes. As the mistress of passion she uses many instruments, as is shown by a drastic, but humorous, woodcut by Master Casper of Regensberg (fig. 13). But one thing is clear: Lady Love acquires her authority and power in a violent way[46].

The Middle High German term *gewalte* and New High German term *Gewalt*, like their Latin equivalent *violentia*, have a double semantic field which causes difficulties for the translator: *gewalte* means not only power and authority but also violence and aggression[47]. Only the context can decide which meaning is intended[48]. When Gottfried von Strassburg calls love a *gewaltaerinne*, he is undoubtedly referring to the two faces of the personification of love[49]. Love takes people – here first Riwalin and then Blanschefliure – violently into her power.

If one wished to find an explanation for the first semantic aspect, the universal power of love, it would be difficult to achieve one's aim, even though it is indisputably found in medieval German literature. It is easier to trace the origins of the second aspect, the violence of love. It is revealed in theological treatises in the religious context of the twelfth century. For subsequent vernacular mysticism, Richard of St. Victor pointed the way in his treatise *De quattuor gradibus violentiae caritatis*[50]. As one would expect from the title, Richard portrays violence, *violentia*, as the most sensitive sign of love. In four stages, it intensifies through the steps of weakening, wounding, and binding; it finally culminates in the annihilating strength whereby the human soul "dies in God"[51]. It can sound dramatic and acute even at the first stage. That fiery arrow of love – *igneus ille amoris aculeus* – shoots through the whole person to the core, pierces to the quick, and kindles a burning glow of longing[52]. The image of the arrow remains in the forefront since the intensification to the second stage (binding) gives occasion to compare the violence of love suffered thus far with close combat among men. It is better to escape one's enemy with

---

[46] See Gerhard Wolf, 136-137.

[47] Cf. Matthias Lexer 1, 972 ff. Several MHG nouns, adjectives and verbs in the semantic field of *gewalte* show this double meaning even more clearly, e.g. *gewaltec*, *gewalten* or *gewaltsam*. For the double meaning of feminine *Gewalt*, see also the rich and methodologically convincing study by Susan L. Smith.

[48] Cf. Margot Schmidt for the Latin polysemic words *violentus* and *violentia* (in her introduction to Richard von St. Viktor, *Über die Gewalt der Liebe*, 16).

[49] Gottfried von Strassburg, *Tristan*, 964.

[50] For the reception of this work, see Margot Schmidt's introduction in: Richard von St. Viktor, *Über die Gewalt der Liebe*, ed. Schmidt, 14 ff. Richard of St. Victor died in 1173.

[51] Cf. the third stage *quoddammodo mortificatur in Deum, in quarto quasi resuscitatur in Christum* (Ed. Margot Schmidt, 68-69).

[52] Ed. Margot Schmidt, 22-23.

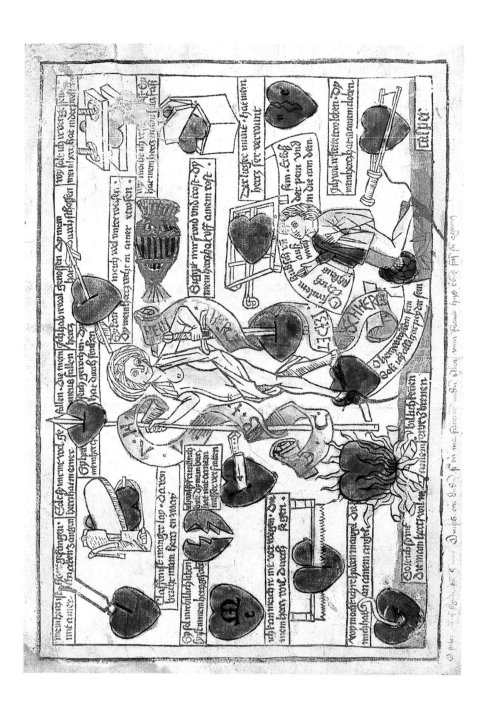

wounds than to become his captive with wounds[53]. Physical violence between men can function directly as an illustration of symptoms of love which are depicted no less physically. Love itself (*caritas, dilectio, amor*) is not personified. Borderlines – between masculine and feminine and between literal and allegorical meanings – become blurred in the attempt to give an adequate depiction of the overpowering force. Gender distinctions can be relinquished concerning the love which both derives from God and leads back to him, according to Gal. 3:28.

Richard of St. Victor's exposition of the *violentiae caritatis* reveals something decisive: his painstaking phenomenology of the violence of love derives from *human* experience. He shows what happens when love takes aim at a human being and overwhelms a person who, from his or her ontologically weaker position, must expect this or rather can expect this; for in Richard's eyes this violence is a blessing. Thus, the same religious context allows an intensification of the power and violence of love because Lady Love can fix the Almighty in her sights. Then, both in terms of power and authority and in terms of exercising violence, she is treading on dangerous ground. Lamprecht von Regensburg presents just such a bold constellation of female assailant and male victim[54].

The Main Points of Interest in Her Attacks

Lady Love – combining functions with the *sponsa* of the Song of Songs – presents an unusually aggressive action, in both text and image, which can then be imitated by the women addressed. The love aggressor gradually transforms herself in the process. I will investigate this metamorphosis by using sources which are related in their content: on the one hand, works of bridal mysticism centering on the theme of the Daughter of Zion[55]; on the other, works from the tradition of *Christus und die minnende Seele*[56], amongst which I include the scene

[53] Ed. Margot Schmidt, 24-25.

[54] Franz Reitinger (101-118) investigates in part both the tradition of *Christus und die minnende Seele* and the *Tochter Syon* texts; his main focus is on the pictorial evidence. He examines the idea of shooting at God in the broad context of the "assassination attempt on God" (a term which Reitinger himself coins and which he applies in the rest of his study with rather more felicity than with relation to mysticism). Reitinger recognizes the "spiritualization of the assassination attempt on God" as well as the concomitant re-evaluation of the motif, as the specific result of mysticism (80ff.); however, he disregards what I would see as important gender-specific aspects of the role of the female aggressor and those who take on this role. This leads him to overlook the subtle shift in the evaluation of the nun as a female aggressor – indeed he also seems to overlook several recent studies on these traditions (Werner Williams-Krapp, Bernd Konrad, Hildegard E. Keller).

[55] For the *Tochter Syon* of Lamprecht von Regensburg, see chapter 3 above.

[56] For the tradition of *Christus und die minnende Seele*, see chapter 4.

from the *Rothschild Canticles* illustrating the relationship between Christ and the soul. The target audience for these sources was primarily, if not exclusively, female[57].

My analysis is shaped by three main points of interest. First, I wish to highlight the changes undergone by the shooting woman on both pictorial and textual levels. This occurs in a *productive* way, tracing the onward development of the motif, because the traditions of text and image work together to form this motif of religious love[58]. Verbal and pictorial impulses acting together are the vehicle for the process of 'semiosis', of quotation and simultaneous variation[59]. The figure of love's archer seems to me to be a prime example of such an historical semiotics.

Second, the relationship between a role and the figure who enacts it can be re-examined more closely. The action of shooting seems to be an elaborate costume which can be put on by various parties: Lady Love, the bride of the Song of Songs, the soul, or a nun. Depending on who wears which costume, the roles of assailant and victim may shift as may the ways the action is viewed.

Third, one can observe how an allegorical figure shakes off its 'rigor mortis' and comes to life. By rigor mortis, I mean the static, statue-like visualization of an abstract concept (e.g., love). By contrast, if the allegorical woman starts to move, she acquires dramatic value within a given work. As soon as she begins to interact, she leaves her anonymity behind and becomes a protagonist[60]. Perhaps these same synthesized allegorical women could form the starting point for the strategy with which Aleida Assmann hopes to combat the use of the Feminine in the service of abstraction: "the consistent individualization and self-determina-

---

[57] For the Alemannic *Tochter Syon*, Christine Ebner and Adelheid Langmann can be attested as early readers (Ingeborg Glier, 102 and Schmidtke, 959f.); for the reception of other versions of *Tochter Sion*, see Schmidtke, 957 (on the prayer-book for Frau Elisabeth Ebran I and the Unterlinden version). In the case of *Christus und die minnende Seele*, not only the records of early owners and the manuscript transmission but also the structure of the text suggest that it is aimed at women (see chapter 4). For the *Rothschild Canticles*, which were intended for a nun, and for literature written for the spiritual guidance of women in the late Middle Ages (with particular attention to the visual arts), see Jeffrey F. Hamburger 1990, 3ff. and 157ff.

[58] The excellent book by Jeffrey F. Hamburger 1990 documents this in depth and detail.

[59] For important and stimulating methodological ideas, I am much indebted to a lecture given by Michael Curschmann on 20 June 1996 in the German department of the University of Zürich, with the title: 'Markolf oder Äsop: Zur Frage der Identität im Freiraum zwischen Text und Bild'.

[60] Cf. Walter Blank, 64-65.

[61] Cf. Aleida Assmann, 24-25. In the face of the abundance of female allegories, Aleida Assmann asks: "Why is there such a predilection for tailoring abstract concepts to fit women's bodies? What is it that makes the female body the preferred matrix of the invisible?". She attributes this to the idealization, differentiation, and lack of markedness of female figures; and she demands self-determination for actually existing women. Cf. Sigrid Weigel, Exkurs über die weibliche Form der Allegorie, in: Sigrid Weigel 1990, 167 ff. and Sigrid Weigel 1994a.

tion of women"[61]. In any case the love-archers can claim to counterbalance the far more powerful reverse situation of male aggressor and female victim. Examples of this which are typical for bridal mysticism include the bride crucified with, or even by, her bridegroom Christ or pierced by the arrow of her divine lover. Gian Lorenzo Bernini's statue of the ecstasies of Theresa of Avila (circa 1650) represents this in marble[62].

The Attacks of Lady Love

Case 1

One constellation of assailants and victims, which is also familiar from the courtly epic and lyric, portrays two lovers as the victims of a third, mysterious power. Love forces two people together with arrows. In this she acts randomly on her own initiative. This model is encountered in an identical form, transposed onto the spiritual, when Lady love binds the female figure of the soul to God, who is imagined as male. This new constellation is particularly striking because Lady Love is no longer faced with a human male. Wounding God with the arrows of love should not be such an easy task for her.

In the Alemannic *Tochter Syon*, Lady Love appears at the crucial moment as a mediator. She does this at the request of the lovesick soul, who is called "Daughter of Zion". With her and her servant girl Oratio, Lady Love undertakes a journey to the heavenly king. When he smiles at the soul, she is overwhelmed with love and loses consciousness. In the meantime, with great presence of mind Lady Love takes aim at God with her "love bow". The shot is doubly fatal since the arrow pierces both lovers simultaneously. Mutual vows of love[63] form a fulminating finale of love-mediation which is as efficient as it is all-powerful:

> *di Minne vergaz ir selber nit;*
> *sie tet nach irem alten sit,*
> *si nam iren minnen pogen*
> *piz an di oren eingezogen,*
> *si schoz den chunik auf seine [sic] trôn,*
> *daz er der tochter von Syon*
> *viel minnecleich an den arm.*
> *durch peide chom der viel gevarn;*

---

[62] Cf. for example Mechthild von Magdeburg, *Das fließende Licht der Gottheit*, II,3,1; trans. Tobin, 70.

[63] Lamprecht von Regensburg, *Tochter Syon*, 536-577.

er twanck sie in ein alsô
daz furpaz chainer sweren drô,
mangel, durst, noch hungers nôt,
daz swert, noch der bitter tôt
si schaiden mocht in chain wîs.

Love did not forget herself. She acted according to her age-old custom, she took her love-bow, drew it back to her ear and shot at the king on his throne, so he fell lovingly into the arms of the daughter of Zion. The arrow pierced through them both. It forced them together so that from then on no oppressive threats, neither privation, thirst or starvation, neither the sword nor bitter death could separate them in any way[64].

Case 2

The ideal situation of simultaneous wounding does not always occur; if only one of the parties involved is struck by love, it is all the more painful since the other has remained unaffected. Enactments of non-simultaneous or unreciprocated love belong to the standard repertoire of secular love; these are the sources of texts and images of the Minnesang. The situation in which only one of the parties is enflamed by love may also be the result of the other having been hit by the so-called lead arrow, which strikes one with imperviousness to love. However, this Ovidian doubling up of the arrows, which stems from the story of Apollo and the nymph Daphne who flees from him, is almost completely forgotten in the Middle Ages[65].

In the context of religious love relationships this disastrous case is fundamentally unthinkable because of its theological implications (1 Jn. 4:16). That each and every love initiative is divine was shown in chapter 3. However, one cannot exclude the possibility of delays in the process of coming together. Thus, in Lamprecht von Regensburg's unconventional *Tochter Syon*[66], delaying factors are built into the body of the work to increase the suspense[67]. One of Lamprecht's

---

[64] Alemannic *Tochter Syon*, 523-535.

[65] Ovid, *Metamorphosen* I, 416-567. One witness of this tradition is Heinrich von Veldeke's *Eneit*, 264,36 ff. For the motif of the twofold arrows of love, see the contribution by Lea Ritter-Santini.

[66] Lamprecht follows a different Latin version (W), which is reproduced in Karl Weinhold's book (285-291).

[67] Among these factors I include the motif, absent from the Alemannic *Tochter Syon*, of the healing of the lovesick soul with the "four drops" which Lady Love gains as "medicine" (= gifts of grace) from the wounds of the bridegroom she has shot at (from 3956), the interpretation of the kiss, and the wedding, which constitutes a separate social occasion (from 4033).

favorite techniques of illustration and narration is to depict the allegorical
women more vividly than in the Latin source and to interpolate didactic or
autobiographical digressions[68]. In this way, Lamprecht – at least in part – amal-
gamates the mystical text with the level of the experience of the author or, to put
it another way, the world of the allegorical beings (mostly women) with that of
the real world of the sexes. In Lamprecht's work Lady Love has also plunged the
soul into the sorrows of love, which is why she stands by her when she implores
her help. The action of mediating between the soul and God is, however, more
complicated and more violent than in the Alemannic *Tochter Syon*. Without the
soul, Lady Love journeys directly before the divine throne in heaven. "Virile",
"brave", and "fearless", as Lamprecht comments with admiration, she shoots the
divine bridegroom twice.

> *si trat dem künige vaste zuo,*
> *küenlîch und âne vorhte,*
> *menlichiu werch si worhte.*
> *den phîl si von dem bogen lie,*
> *daz er ze râme fluges gie,*
> *slehtes gegen dem künige hin,*
> *und traf in zuo dem herzen in.*

She stepped firmly towards the king, boldly and without fear; she carried out
a manly task. She so loosed the arrow from the bow that it flew swiftly to its
mark, directly towards the king, and struck him in the heart[69].

Unlike in the Alemannic version, the arrow does not unite the lovers. A second shot from Love's bow also does not fulfill this purpose but merely wounds
the bridegroom more deeply[70]. With *zwai verhwunden*, God is life-threaten-
ingly wounded – a result which provides some satisfaction for Lady Love. As
the conscientious confidante who takes care of the soul, however, she knows
that her mission is not yet accomplished. Later, as a "medicine", she dribbles the
drops from the bridegroom's arrow wounds directly into the soul's heart. This
initiates a union followed by wedding celebrations. Although in both *Tochter
Syon* texts Lady Love is at the service of the soul, she reveals herself to be a sovereign authority. In the course of the work, an alliance develops between Love
and the soul. This teaming up of the two "women" is not without its comic and
ironic aspects because it is presented as a secret strategy with regard to the
divine bridegroom. Lady Love undertakes the first journey to heaven as a secret

---

[68] Joachim Heinzle emphasizes their documentary value, as self-statements, with regard to the
conception of medieval individuality (²VL 5 [1985] 523).

[69] Lamprecht von Regensburg, *Tochter Syon*, 3608-14.

[70] Cf. Lamprecht von Regensburg, *Tochter Syon*, 3629-3633.

scout who is supposed to survey the state of affairs in the divine palace. Although in secret God and Love are essentially one[71], the alliance between the two women already paves the way for their merging in the figure of love's archer.

Brides Wound Too

Under these conditions the two female figures, Lady Love and the spouse of the Song of Songs, interpreted as the soul, can now move closer together. Before any alliance with Lady Love took place, we saw only the wounding bride. The latter recedes into the background. The bride of the Song of Songs acts in her own name in her original environment. What her aggression can signify in the Christian context, is shown very neatly and clearly in the following example.

Case 3

The bride of the Song of Songs wounds with the blink of an eye, complains her lover: *Vulnerasti cor meum soror mea sponsa, Vulnerasti cor meum in uno oculorum tuorum, et in uno crine colli tui.* (Thou hast ravished my heart, my sister, my spouse; thou hast ravished my heart with one of thine eyes, with one chain from thy neck)[72]. In a Christian interpretation, this verse points to the incarnation and passion of Christ[73]. An extraordinary illumination in the *Rothschild Canticles*[74] shows the wounded bridegroom Christ with his female attacker (fig. 14)[75]. The double picture shows, on the left hand, a woman with a lance taking aim directly at the open wound in the side of the naked lover on the oppo-

---

[71] Cf. Lamprecht von Regensburg, *Tochter Syon*, 3180 ff.

[72] Cant. 4:9. Abundant material on the wounding and wounded eye in Gudrun Schleusener-Eichholz, here particularly I, 924-929.

[73] Already in the *St. Trudperter Hohenlied* (at Cant. 4:9), God confesses that he has been wounded by Mary's virtuousness and that this will mean the sacrifice of his only son on the Cross (54,7-55,2).

[74] This manuscript, the date and location of which are difficult to determine, is associated by Hamburger on the one hand with the Rhineland mystics, on the other hand with the Franco-Flemish school of illumination, and is placed around 1300 in the area of Thérouanne (Jeffrey F. Hamburger 1990, 14; codicological information, 8 ff.). The motifs and allegorization of the Song of Songs is a considerable, though not the exclusive, source of the work (70 ff.).

[75] Fundamental ideas in this passage – the reference to Longinus, the martyring virtues and the meaning of *passio* here – are indebted to the interpretation of Jeffrey F. Hamburger 1990 (72-80).

[76] For further references on the subject of the representation of the naked Christ, see Jeffrey F. Hamburger 1990, 73-74.

site side[76]. The latter can be recognized by his halo as Christ. His right index finger guides the eye of the spectator to the wound. He illustrates the words from the Song of Songs by looking over at his attacker. She returns the look in mid-movement.

As if in a *tableau vivant,* the picture captures the action between them, which Jeffrey Hamburger, from the composition of the picture, characterizes as follows: "the subject is the wounding rather than the wound itself"[77]. In this an unusual role model is proffered to the observer, probably a female religious, whom one must imagine in pious contemplation before the book: that of the lover driving her lance into Christ's wounded side[78]. Hamburger points boldly to the sexual role reversal: "the Sponsa penetrating Christ with her phallic spear"[79]. The lance-bearing bride exhorts the religious woman to imitate her and the personified Caritas in the attitude of love emphasized in the first part of the illumination (fol. 18v). Hamburger finds support for this interpretation in the text given on fol. 17v, a paraphrase of Revelations 3,20. The wound in Christ's side could be viewed as a gateway at which the bride seeks entrance with the lance; the real goal is the heart of Jesus (*cor salvationis*), to which the bride must gain access[80]. In the footsteps of the allegorical wounding women, the female reader should also strive for an attitude of piercing love. This amorous aggression is a religious exhortation to the female observers. Thus, once again, symbolic and real gender flow into one another, if the female figure of the soul is supposed to take flesh in the female reading public.

In this similarity, which is quite literally crucial, a new love-aggressor is revealed. In terms of the passion of the Cross, she acts out a dictum of her beloved. The devotional picture projects the wound of the Song of Songs and the wound in Christ's side, in which the Crucifixion culminates, onto one another. Hamburger sees two possible sources for the stab of the lance: either the allegory of Caritas, who embraces Christ on the Cross and sticks a dagger in his back (as shown on the stained glass window in Wienhausen, fig. 15) or the action of the Roman soldier Longinus in piercing Christ.

His legend tells that he was blind and was healed when the blood of Christ touched him. For this reason, representations from the eighth century show

---

[77] Jeffrey F. Hamburger 1990, 72.

[78] For the devotional function of text and image in mysticism, see Jeffrey F. Hamburger 1990, chapter 1 (Art and Mysticism) and 157 ff., especially on the illumination of Cant. 4:9 under discussion here, which he interprets as an early reflection of the adoration of the Sacred Heart (Jeffrey F. Hamburger 1990, 75 f.).

[79] Jeffrey F. Hamburger 1990, 76 f.

[80] In this way Jeffrey F. Hamburger 1990, 74, points to the background of the beginnings of the adoration of the Sacred Heart of Jesus and of a passage from Bonaventure's text for the spiritual guidance of women (*De perfectione vitae ad sorores,* VI,2).

him kneeling or standing while he holds the lance in one hand and points to his healed eye with the other[81]. There are also Longinus legends which record his ability to heal the blind[82]. Thus, there is a line which stretches from Amor and Love to Longinus and the bride of the Song of Songs, connecting the eye, blindness, healing and love[83]. This shows again that the female love-aggressor unites masculine (soldier-like) and feminine (allegorical) traits within herself

---

[81] According to Jeffrey F. Hamburger 1990, 75, the legend is first written down in the *Historia Scholastica* of Peter Comestor.

[82] For the Longinus tradition, see, in detail, Konrad Burdach, 209-312 and, especially in medieval drama, Carla Dauven-van Knippenberg 1990.

[83] See Jeffrey F. Hamburger 1990, 75-77 and figs 141-143. For the (late) motif of blindness in personifications of love, see Erwin Panofsky, chapter 4: Blind Amor, with numerous illustrations.

and that her image is meant to have a hortatory effect on the female spectator. She sees the double meaning of the word Passion (*passio crucis* and *passio amoris*) depicted on opposite sides of the page: "The wound in Christ's side is an emblem of his love for mankind, enacted through the sacraments; the act of wounding, an expression of the soul's reciprocal love for Christ. There is a paradox in such a violent expression of love. The two meanings of *passion* – suffering and ecstatic love – fuse"[84]. It is this message which renders the icon of love suitable for adoption by secular art. In the thirteenth and fourteenth centuries, sacred representations, e.g., of the Crucifixion, mold secular representations of love, particularly those in which a woman shoots at a man[85].

Case 4

The text for religious instruction known as the *Buch der geistlichen Armuth*[86], the book of spiritual poverty, also gives shooting an exhortatory function. This refers back to Lady Love (cases 1 and 2), but also forward to the next example, case 5, because now the wounding bride of the Song of Songs and the shooting personification of love are interwoven in the interpretation. This occurs in the discussion of the mystical union with God, which is said to take place through piercing "staring" at the *blossen gotheit*, the naked Godhead. The process designated by the term "staring" is imagined as a timeless going into and being enveloped by God; thus, the individual "swims in him like a fish in the sea". The two expressions mentioned – staring and embracing – are reminiscent of verse 4:9 of the Song of Songs, which the text is alluding to. The soul which is enveloped in God is said to shoot at God and to reach her mark exactly as it states "in the book of the loving soul": *(...) und unser herre sprichet zuo siner brut: "mine fründin, du hast mich verwundet mit dem blick diner ougen"* ([...] and our Lord says to his bride: "my friend, you have wounded me with the glance of your eye")[87]. The interpretation of this utterance follows immediately. It is explained that the wounding eye means piercing love:

> *[...] mit der minne betwinget sie got, daz got můs tůn waz sie wil, und daz heisset ein verwunden, daz sie gottes gewaltig wurt, und sie spannet iren bogen und schůsset got in sin hertze. Der boge den sie spannet daz ist ir hertze; daz spannet sie und schůsset mit einer hitzigen begirde in got und triffet daz rechte zil. Und*

[84] Jeffrey F. Hamburger 1990, 75.
[85] Markus Müller highlights these sorts of genetic links (with numerous illustrations, 195).
[86] See on this text ²VL 1 (1978)1082-1085.
[87] *Das Buch der geistlichen Armuth*, 64,11-12.

also begriffet sie den höhsten puncten der vollekommenheit.

With this love the soul forces God to do what she wishes. This is called wounding because the soul acquires power over God, she draws her bow and shoots him in the heart. The bow which she draws is her heart. She draws it and shoots in heated desire for God and hits the true mark. In this way she attains the highest point of perfection[88].

To review, I would like here to look again at the metamorphosis of the aggressive lover. A female figure shoots at a male opposite with a bow and arrow. In contrast to the first two cases, it is now a shot in the interest of the bride, an independent attack with the weapon of Lady Love. The shooting bride of the Song of Songs and her counterpart, the shooting allegory of the soul, have now been created. Without this prerequisite, the constellation of assailant and victim in the next example would be unthinkable. Only a small step remains in the development: for a human bride of God to step into the costume of love's archer, which has been tailored to fit secular or religious women in their devotions since the *Rothschild Canticles*.

Case 5

The latest of the textual and pictorial witnesses presented here bring the metamorphosis to its conclusion. They are individual variants of late-medieval dialogues between Christ and a loving soul, which occurred originally in the form of picture-cycles with 20 or 21 scenes. "Picture-cycle mysticism" arose in the context of the women's mysticism which blossomed in the Southwest German-speaking area in the fourteenth century. Thus, one can assume that women were the primary audience. Although the form of a series of pictures with short commentary passages was probably the original one, all the surviving picture-sequences date only from the age of printing, the fifteenth or early sixteenth century. One picture, which is included here in reproductions from two early printed versions (cf. figs. 16 and 17), illustrates chapter 4 verse 9 of the Song of Songs: *HIC TANGIT 'WULNERASTI COR MEUM' (Cant. 4,9): Mich hat der mynnen smerczzin / gestoczin in myn hercze. RESPONSIO: Ich wolte daz ich genuosse, / daz ich dich gar durch schuosze.* (THIS RELATES TO 'YOU HAVE WOUNDED MY HEART' [Song of Songs 4:9]: The pain of love has stricken

---

[88] *Das Buch der geistlichen Armuth*, 64,13-19; trans. Niklaus Largier, 82.

[89] This is the comment only of the editor of the Mainz version (Williams-Krapp, 356-7). Neither the two woodcuts, nor the manuscript version edited by Banz, refer explicitly to the Song of Songs, but do allude to it indirectly (Banz, 86).

me in my heart. ANSWER: I wish that I could succeed in piercing right through you)[89].

    [90] Cod. Donaueschingen 106 (now in the Badische Landesbibliothek in Karlsruhe); Cod. Einsiedeln 710 (322), see Banz, 4 ff. and Hellmut Rosenfeld 1978. For the pictures in the Einsiedeln codex, see Banz, 223-249, for those in the Donaueschingen codex, see Bernd Konrad 1989, 57-92, esp. 69-70, Bernd Konrad 1992, and Bernd Konrad 1997.

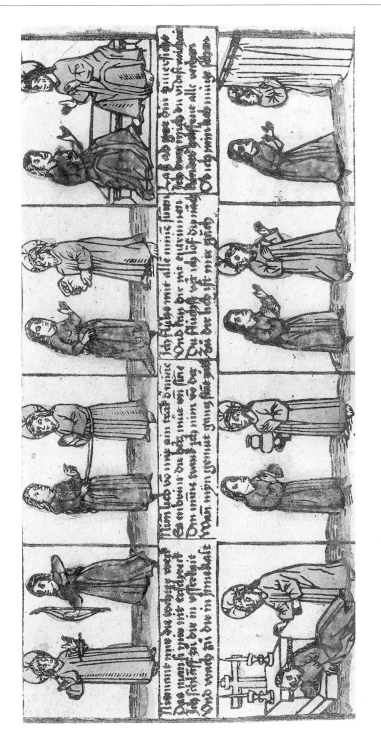

Even the two little printed pictures make clear the sex to which the figure of the soul belongs: here the soul is a long-haired woman dressed in flowing secular clothes. This can be confirmed even more clearly from two manuscripts[90] of the textually most extensive version of this material, *Christus und die minnende*

Seele. The Donaueschingen codex, splendidly illustrated by Rudolf Stahel, a professional painter from Constance, shows the soul as an attractive secular woman (fig. 18).

She has just loosed the arrow from the bowstring. Its goal is the heart of the bearded Christ, who can be recognized by his halo. The stylization of the shot of love is revealed in the schematized heart as well as the way the whole arrow is depicted in full flight. The prints, on the other hand, show an arrow which has already gone into Christ's body; the heart is not depicted, perhaps because the pictures are so small, and Christ's arms are not fully extended. The bearing of the protagonist, however, is represented in essentially the same way; but her spatial position varies. Thus, Rudolf Stahel's way of painting and his composi-

---

[91] Banz describes the pictures in the codex, Einsiedeln 710 (322) and tries to identify the painter, though without success (cf. Banz, 223-249).

tion of the motif emphasize the pictorial nature of the process, seeking – perhaps even counter to what is stated in the text – to recreate it.

In contrast, the equivalent picture in the anonymous Einsiedeln codex strengthens the link with reality (fig. 19). The unidentified illuminator[91] makes the inherently extreme nature of the scene all too obvious, which is in accor-

dance with the style of at least certain passages of the text (e.g., line 22ff.). The arrow is just piercing Christ; blood sprays all around from the wound in the sketched heart onto the skirt of the lover. The drops of blood are reminiscent of the realism of late-medieval representations of the Passion[92].

The iconic 'realization' of the shooting brings the female figure definitively

[92] Cf. the catalogue of the exhibition *Le jardin clos de l'âme*, Brussels, 1994.

out of the realm of allegory. In the woman portrayed, who points to the con-
templative reader in front of the codex, love's archer takes on flesh and blood;
she wears the habit of a religious order and shoots at Christ as a nun. In this
context it is also understandable that the text not only makes the aggressive lover
semiotically unambiguous but also evaluates her differently. The exhortation to
the addressee, which until now has been a positive one – imitate love's archer in
your love – is bent into a gentle warning: the bride should not selfishly claim
the bridegroom Christ for herself, as is intimated even by the title-lines:

Mit der minne stral schüßet si in,
Das wil sy han für gewin.

She shoots him with the arrow of love, that is what she seeks to gain[93].

The bride's enthusiasm for shooting is caused by her desire to "enjoy" her
bridegroom.

ich wil in schießen,
Ob ich sin iena mug genießen

I wish to shoot him so that I may enjoy him ever after[94].

Dutifully, he answers with the abbreviated verse from the Song of Songs:

Verwundet ist das hertze min,
Da hastu, lieb, geschossen in,
Das ich müß tun den willen din,
Das mag wol werden din gewin.

My heart is wounded, because you, my love, have so shot it that I will do
your will, that will be your reward[95].

She demands that he should open her heart and be united with her in it to
her full satisfaction[96]. It cannot be because of the mystical marker *fliezen*[97] that

---

[93] *Christus und die minnende Seele*, 1316-17.

[94] *Christus und die minnende Seele*, 1318-9. Both the manuscript version and the printed variants M and Mz rhyme *schiessen* with *geniessen* (finite or infinite form) here.

[95] *Christus und die minnende Seele*, 1320-4. For the reversal of the dynamic within the couple, see chapter 4.

[96] *Christus und die minnende Seele*, 1324-6.

[97] *Fliezen* (along with the semantic group of words centring on *influentia, inflûz,* etc.) belongs
to the 'classical' terminology of mysticism. In the context of love mysticism, the verb *fliezen* means
a deep dissolving in one another which, as *liquefactio animae,* is linked as with the interpretation
of a verse of the Song of Songs (5:6) which is important already for early vernacular mysticism (see
Hildegard Elisabeth Keller 1993, 372-394; for examples of *vliezen* in the context of tradition, see
Romuald Banz, 120; Grete Lüers, 278 ff; Kurt Berger, passim; K. Heisig, 338-342).

[98] *Christus und die minnende Seele*, 1329.

Christ distances himself from this wish. A rhyme reveals what it is that the bridegroom cannot tolerate about his bride's attitude: it would be *unfüg* (foolishness) to wish to have *gnüg* (enough) of Christ. "What would remain for the others?" asks Christ. This does not disconcert the bride in the slightest: *Da welt ich in den mangel lan.* (I would wish to leave them lacking)[98]. Christ sees now that clarification is necessary. Since he gives himself to all "servants of God", not only is what the bride is demanding wrong, but it is also more than she would be capable of taking in. She could not even absorb a thirtieth of what would be communicated to her.

> *Und woltest mich allain han,*
> *So wär ich wol ain doracht man.*
> *Ich tün dir doch so vil kunt,*
> *Das nicht kan reden din munt*
> *Noch din mund nit kan gesprechen,*
> *Und sölt ioch din hertz darumb zerbrechen.*
> *Du macht doch das drisgost nit behaben,*
> *Du hörest es denn andrest sagen.*

And if you wanted to have me to yourself, then I would be a foolish man [to give myself to you]. I will communicate so much to you that your mouth will not be able to say it, your mouth will not be able to speak; your heart would burst, but you could not absorb a thirtieth of it unless you heard it said again[99].

The harsh rebuke of the selfish love archer, who wants to bring in her bridegroom for herself, shows that the motif has suddenly become very ambivalent. *Christus und die minnende Seele* is aware of the interpretation of shooting known to us from the *Buch der geistlichen Armut* and the *Rothschild Canticles* – aiming one's love at God – and combines it at the end of the section with an exhortation to shoot in a positive sense[100]. However, this positive evaluation of the archer is preceded by a critical reflection on this idea of shooting, which highlights the problematic aspects of spiritual selfishness and exclusive claims of love. It also highlights the paradox of the Bride-Bridegroom allegory itself, i.e., the contradictory union between a bride who is absolutely faithful and a polygamous bridegroom – a paradox which is even more striking when the allegorical positions are sexualized.

What have this last example and its variations demonstrated? The group of texts and pictures about *Christus und die minnende Seele* further develop the aggressive lover further on two levels. First, the two female figures (Lady Love

---

[99] *Christus und die minnende Seele*, 1340-7.
[100] *Christus und die minnende Seele*, 1380 ff. and 1420 ff. respectively.

as a poetic abstract concept and the spouse of the Song of Songs as an important hermeneutic figure) blend into one. As a combined force they attack and
wound the man they love with bow and arrow. The amorous archery is reminiscent of the attribute of Lady Love, but all positive (masculine) qualifications
of the archeress are lacking. We are no longer dealing with a sacred aggressor.

This is certainly connected with the second line of development. The bride of
the Song of Songs – in fact an allegory for the soul which transcends gender –
becomes a woman who is dressed in either secular or monastic clothing. The
allegorical femininity materializes and 'realizes' itself. The pictures, above all, as
well as the textually most extensive version of the dialogue are decisive here since
they move the archers completely into the world in which women live, as was
shown in the last chapter. In the illustrations in the Donaueschingen codex,
these women appear to be not yet specified. The Einsiedeln codex however, not
professionally illuminated, once again makes matters less ambiguous by portray-
ing the female in the second half of the work as a monastic woman. These moves
to restrict it correlate with the intentions of the work. The units of text and
image serve as objects of fervent contemplation with an exhortatory function for
a female audience. Against this background one can understand the pedagogical
re-evaluation of the figure of love's archer and the exposing of the motives of her
action, which are human, all too human. Female love-aggression seems ambivalent if the bride wishes to have her beloved exclusively for herself, a beloved who,
one notes, wishes to give himself to all. The motif of love's archeress, concretized
and brought down to earth, takes bridal mysticism to its very limits – those of
grasping eroticism. Moreover, the concentration on women leaves open the
question of whether, because of the femininity which is expressed so clearly both
textually and iconographically, male readers could no longer identify with the
figure of the soul. They used the text – if indeed they read it at all for their personal devotions and not merely for pastoral motives – without pictures[101].

Conclusion: Female Metamorphosis

The textual and pictorial sources from this segment of the late-medieval literature of love make evident the evolution of the female aggressive lover. Although
shooting with a bow and arrow does not belong to the repertoire of classically
feminine pursuits, all the sources considered show the Love-archer as a woman.
Various reasons contribute to this. Grammatical gender paves the way for the

---

[101] It is remarkable that the Mainz print demonstrably belonged to the Carthusian Friedrich
von Eselweck and served as a book for personal devotions, but it contained only text and no pictures (edition in Williams-Krapp, 355-358) Cf. on this question Niklaus Largier.

sex of the allegory, two mythical-allegorical wounders (Lady Love and the bride of the Song of Songs) team up as sisters and offer their role for adoption by the female recipients of the texts and pictures. What then gradually changes is the hermeneutic status of the archer. With each new figure that takes on the role, the allegorical aspect diminishes in favor of a concreteness that intentionally moves the text closer to its addressees. As a figure for identification, love's archer should urge them into action. But once the archer is indeed incarnate in human form, either as a nun or a secular woman, the interpretation of her attack changes – it can then be interpreted as an unjustified and selfish claim.

Obviously an action which is labeled as masculine cannot be transferred from an artificial to a real woman without tensions. In the costume of an imagined being a woman may become an aggressive lover, but she may only appear to do so on the surface, as the last case demonstrates clearly. No sooner is the enthusiasm for the hunt kindled in the bride than it is checked. Here two central contradictions come into play, which the bride of Christ has to wrestle with within herself: first, the claim of a faithful individual towards a bridegroom who gives himself to all (brides); second, the paradoxical demand that she should take on the role of the bride of Christ, which is defined as feminine, but should do so ideally as a *mulier virilis*. This conflict is formulated very convincingly by Barbara Newman: "(…) we can now discern the lived paradox of innumerable religious women who, from the time of Heloise onward, wrestled in spirit with the conflicting gender ideals their masters set before them. On the one hand, the virile woman – fearless, outspoken, always ready for death – unmoved alike by family ties and tyrannical force. On the other, the bride of Christ – intimate, impassioned, always ready for love – and moved by every suffering creature's pain"[102]

The series of motifs thus shows how intricately grammatical, symbolical, and biological gender can interlock in one work, how productively text and picture can work together, and how effectively the audience of readers is drawn in. Reduction of a motif can mean narrowing and concretizing, pro-duction can mean extending the role into new situations with new figures. Both developments balance one another. Thus, the aggressive lover enters by the back door from the imaginary world of personified abstract concepts into a real world. She takes on flesh and blood. In this "incarnatory" sense in *Christus und die minnende Seele* the aggressive lover may have reached the end of her metamorphosis in text and image. At the beginning, Lady Love shoots at the King of Heaven in the service of the soul; in the middle, the spouse of the Song of Songs wounds her beloved Christ with a lance, and a soul shoots arrows at the Godhead; at the end, a nun takes aim at Christ and shoots arrows into the heart of her divine bridegroom.

---

[102] Barbara Newman 1995, 247.

Here a didactic limit reveals itself. The amorous offensive and the unusual boldness of the allegorical women cannot be entrusted to actual women without limitations. The human bride of Christ may lay a hand on her divine beloved, but she may not lay an exclusive claim to him as her victim.

Epilogue

> *Seyn Sie doch nicht traurig, Sie haben ja*
> *so lange gelebt, daß Sie wohl wissen, daß das Leben*
> *hier auf der Welt wenig auf sich hat. – Vicktorine ist*
> *jetzt glückselig, und eine Braut Christi, was wär es*
> *denn gewesen, wenn sie statt dessen einen schlechten*
> *Mann bekommen hätte? – Do not be sad; you have*
> *lived long enough to know that life here in the world*
> *has little to recommend it. – Viktorine is now happy,*
> *and a bride of Christ; what if she had had a bad*
> *husband instead?*[1]

Images of a Hermeneutic Tightrope Act

The Christian amalgamation of eros and religion develops a phenomenology which is perhaps signaled at its two extremes by the mottos heading the Introduction and Epilogue. I began with Meister Eckhart's suprasexual image of the marriage between God and the soul as the ultimate aim of human existence; I end with the letter, written more than 500 years later, in which Annette von Droste-Hülshoff glances at a woman's life as a religious and obviously thinks automatically of marriage in the world. In Droste-Hülshoff's time, this sexualized concept had long been familiar: being a bride of God was known as the exclusive domain of religious women.

The Christian variety of erotic spirituality therefore does not incorporate any discourse which is entirely free of all that is human, historically concrete, and gender-related – which is, in a word, abstract. Precisely the history of the motif of the bride of God itself, both its gender-specific fixing of the role of the bride of God and its attempts to force open such narrowings make clear that the human world of the sexes and its historically-determined mechanisms push their way into spiritual eroticism by the back door. This world molds both the human, mainly female bride as well as the masculine transcendent beloved. In the last instance, then, the motif of the erotic relationship with God serves for

---

[1] Annette von Droste-Hülshoff in her letter of 23 August 1840 to Jenny von Lassberg, Historisch-Kritische Ausgabe IX,1, 117, quoted in Meinolf Schumacher 1998.

the stylization of both sexes: female stereotypes settle in the figure of the bride of God; male ones, in turn, settle in the part of the divine bridegroom. In this way, the protagonists of an erotic spirituality take on the burden of the worldly hierarchy of the sexes. The more closely the role of the bride of God is coupled to the female sex, the more unrestrainedly this inheritance comes into force.

Sexualization affects the female role in a way that is incomparably more drastic. Gender stereotypes make their way into defamatory religious terms such as *prostituta* or *adultera Christi*, or bride of the Devil. Long before it turns up in the handbooks of the witch hunters, this terminology is used in spiritual guidance by male and female religious for disciplining and educating women to become faultless brides of God. But the gender stereotypes also influence positive concepts such as that of the bride of God, which served for many years to characterize religious women. The fact that the bride of God is erotically centered on a divine love-partner held promise of a delicate purity. She may be made the satirical butt of the late medieval *maere* (comic tale), which turned her into a seducible subject; in eighteenth-century pornographic novels she, together with priests and monks, becomes the personification of lasciviousness[2], exaggerated for anticlerical aims; but these are just further signs of the basic tendency which is the motif's constant companion. Once erotic, sexual, or marital spirituality no longer amounts to anything but its – perhaps inevitable – social and biological references to the human world, these sorts of religious concepts turn into an *idée fixe* with earthbound gravity: distortions of copulation. Then, what is probably the most precious element of religious eroticism – the integrity of the experiencing and reflecting subject – falls away, and one remains caught in that polarizing category which, from a Christian perspective, is ultimately irrelevant since it is bound to temporality: the category of gender.

Images of the Ineffable

Despite this tight-rope act spiritual bridal mysticism attained a fundamental significance not only for the pedagogical and pastoral literature of the Middle Ages but also for much that is altogether beyond language and cognitive understanding. Erotic formulas, sexual images, or patterns of order within marriage make it possible to articulate things which could scarcely be spoken about except in

---

[2] Here I am thinking of the novels in: Denkende Wollust, Jean-Claude Gervaise de Latouche: *Histoire de Dom B… Portier des Chartreux, écrite par lui-même* (1740 or 1741) and Jean-Baptiste d'Argens: *Thérèse philosophe, ou Mémoires pour servir à l'histoire du Père Dirrag & de Mademoiselle Éradice* (1748). On the (anticlerical) inspirational potential of this sort of literature, see the essay, "Denkende Wollust oder die sexuelle Aufklärung der Aufklärung" by Robert Darnton (English: "Sex for Thought", printed in the *New York Review of Books* in 1994).

metaphors, for example, ways of imagining God, images of death, and individual experiences of God. In this way, the representation of God as a man – as lover, bridegroom and husband (wealthy, powerful, faithful, cuckolded, avenging, jealous) – is part of the rich history of personal metaphors for God, which blossomed time and again under the protective mantel of Christian delight in images and had to be dismantled each time by the iconoclasts. Human death can be transformed by the idea of an erotically-charged homecoming and festive wedding celebration. Earthly life before death becomes the time of betrothal and preparation so that salvation occurs in accordance with the dramaturgy of marital law on earth. Latin and vernacular texts from the mystical literature of the Middle Ages draw on erotic models to depict the individual development of a human being as the special path of someone gifted by God. The advantages and the perils of this particular personal guise of spirituality have been shown up by the analysis of the primary sources and the cross-links between the chapters.

The synoptic analysis of the literary versions of the bride gave rise to a typology of brides who may exercise very different functions. This complements all recent research on the functional connections between text-categories, concepts of gender and the discourses of marriage and love[3]. It extends from the self-willed, even eccentric, bride who tells of her own experiences to the wax dummy in the display window who is commented on by a presenter, like a demonstration model. The fact that the brides of God have many faces is determined by their literary representation and their function. The vast majority of the texts no longer show the erotic relationship as the universally valid offer it originally was, but as an option reserved for women. Thus, already in early Christianity, it comes to the institutionally-ensured, exclusive rights of nuns to the divine bridegroom. As consecrated virgins, they are the truest brides of Christ, and this influences their daily life in the convent and the texts for their spiritual guidance. So the faces given to the individual brides and bridegrooms and the exhortations placed in their mouths are dependent on the text in question. The intended function of the text decides what dresses they wear when they step onto the inner stage of the readers or listeners.

One of the very few brides of God in the texts presented who is (still) related to all Christians, and therefore to both sexes, is presented to a non-specific audience in the didactic poem *Die Hochzeit*. By means of the simple allegory of a marriage contracted under Germanic law and its multiple interpretations, the believer should be able to recognize himself or herself as part of the bride, the Church. A didactic model tailored for religious women refers to the Song of Songs in order to present a professional bride of God. A commentator takes on the task of mediation and creates all the links between the bride and

---

[3] Cf. Rüdiger Schnell 1997, 1998a, and 1998b.

the monastic identity of the women listening. This means that the *St. Trud-perter Hohelied* acquires all the characteristics of a spiritual didactic dialogue between the text and its audience, effectively between the person giving away the brides and the brides in his charge.

For a woman author it is possible to have a bride of God narrating in the position of an 'I', quasi-autobiographically, while the author simultaneously has her act, commenting on her actions in the third person. Mechthild von Magdeburg has mastered this technique with great virtuosity in *Das fließende Licht der Gottheit*, with a poetic directness which makes her text stand out in Middle High German literature and shows the motif itself and its own poetics to its best advantage. Then there are the more or less fictionalized narrations of factual brides of God. As the protagonist in a mystical love-novel – this, in any case, is how the Franciscan Lamprecht von Regensburg recounts the development of a soul into a joyous bride of Christ in his *Tochter Syon* –, a bride of God becomes a both instructive and amusing figure against an allegorical backdrop. The theologically educated Priester Wernher acts as the biographer of the mother of God, Mary. On the one hand, he writes the chronicle of her love of, and marriage with, God; on the other, in line with his apocryphal source, he integrates her into God's family history. This unique retelling of the story aims to instruct its readers and to honor the loving couple and their son. Here authorial comments rather than explicit requests to the addressees send out a hidden exhortation to the *imitatio sponsae*. Precisely in this exceptionally dialogical text – as in certain passages in Mechthild's work, in *Christus und die minnende Seele* or in Seuse's *Exemplar* (as has been investigated by Jeffrey F. Hamburger) – dialogue can be shown to be a corner-stone of mystical didactic practice as well as of authorship and authority. Hartmann von Aue turns the young bride of God into one of the figures which move his plot forward. It is only apparently paradoxical that she does this precisely by wanting to be put to death or by refusing marriage and suffering hardship on this account. Essentially, in Hartmann's farmer's daughter the archaic idea of sacrifice as I presented it in Ambrose's prototypical concept is born again and is exaggerated in a super-realistic plot. She is allowed to wish to be a bride of God until – like other female protagonists in Hartmann's works – it becomes necessary for her to be led into the other married life for a woman. Accordingly, being a bride of God is only a temporary identity, which seems, without irony, to serve as a preparatory training for a married woman in the world.

Images of Perpetual Motion

The texts investigated here show a very narrowly delineated section of the Christian history of the erotic relationship with God. Even this closely delimited segment bears witness to the unease which a sexually defined model introduces into the relationship between a soul thought of as asexual and a God imagined as asexual (in a few rare cases, transsexual). This unease is primarily hermeneutically-determined, which is why it is a driving factor in the constitution of meaning through text and image. This process can never be concluded, partly precisely because the women addressed are drawn into the text as actual or potential brides of God. This pull results, for example, in the metamorphosis of the personification of Love as archer into the bride of God as archeress.

Secondly, certain structural features, which are also characteristic for the texts I have chosen, encourage endless variation. For the one part, the concrete examples of erotic relationships with God represent mainly an exegetical collage of the Song of Songs and marriage allegory, as well as of a dynamic passional code and a rather more sober legal code. For the other part, the intricate intertwining of patterns of marriage – collective and individual, eschatalogical and timeless, worldly and spiritual – gives certain passages the appearance of a palimpsest. Reading this palimpsest can be as complex as the following graphic presentation of the many layers of the palimpsest of bridal mysticism: through the eyes of a human bride (by virtue of an infinite system of erotic encapsulation), there gazes the bridal soul; at the creation of the first bride, Eve, the divine bridegroom already calls the (more faithful) bride, Mary, but also all the human brides who have yet to be born, into his bed-chamber. In each case, the historical hierarchy of the sexes on earth shows through in the timeless marriage with God; the hope of marital security overlays an abyss of passion in which losing and finding one another alternate unceasingly; and behind each divine husband there is always the possible alternative, i.e., the human husband through whom this God, imagined as masculine, seems to define himself in the texts, according to their structural and functional possibilities.

In the light of the literary documents recording the experiences of individuals, what God brings about in people seems like madness. This thought is in no way new. In his *Phaidros*, Plato distinguishes four types of transformations which are brought about in people by divine intervention and are consequently called 'divine madness'[4]. Among these is the madness caused by Eros, which wreaks havoc in humans alongside prophetic, ritual, and poetic madness. This daemon, who rages frenetically in both the sexual and the non-sexual domain, is the unique connecting force which reconciles the divine ego and the chained animal within each human being. He thus also mediates between human beings, as well as between the human and the divine sphere, as Plato emphasizes in his *Symposion*[5]. Accordingly, only eros seems to possess that transcendent

---

[4] Plato, *Phaidros*, 244A-245A and 265A, quoted in Erec R. Dodds, 43ff.
[5] Plato, *Symposion*, 202 E; cf. Erec R. Dodds, Chapter III and VII.

power which makes the loveplay between God and human being into a univer-sal *perpetuum mobile*.

In all the love stories told by the medieval texts, a cosmic dimension shines through; and it is with this that I wish to conclude. I emphasize the following facts: that the Christian cosmogony is imagined as a love duet in a puzzlingly polygamous structure; that the order of Creation represents a sort of divine embrace of all that is made; that humanity as a whole as well as every individ-ual is created as a bride; that this bride is repudiated, rehabilitated and, in the end, carried home; and that God bears witness and acts timelessly in partner-ship with his human bride. All these erotic variations, formulated in Christian art through the centuries, may be among the most forgotten Christian myths of all, although the imagery itself continues to be used as a formula for success. One and all, they are powerful evocations of a universal and archaic unity of all that has being. They are songs which hymn this precarious unity and thus are also the daily mystery proclaimed by the motto of this book[6].

---

[6] I owe it – along with many other ideas – to Bernard McGinn (*Iggeret ha-Kodesh*, after Cohen: Holy Letter, 50, quoted in Bernard McGinn 1992, 227).

Bibliography and Illustrations

The publication details for all primary and secondary sources are given in the language in which they are published.

Primary Sources

Abaelard. Letters 2-8. Letters 2-5, and 6-7. Ed. J. T. Muckle, Mediaeval Studies 15 (1953), 47-94 and 17 (1955), 240-81. Letter 8. Ed. T. McLaughlin, Mediaeval Studies 18 (1956), 241-92.

Abelard and Heloise. Trans. Betty Radice. London 1974.

Abaelard. Die Leidensgeschichte und der Briefwechsel mit Heloisa. Hg. Eberhard Brost. Mit einem Nachwort von Walter Berschin. München [4]1979.

Abraham a Sancta Clara. Werke. Hg. von der Akademie der Wissenschaften. Bearbeitet von Karl Bertsche, 3 Bde. Wien 1943-45.

Abraham a Sancta Clara. Ladschreiben eines gewissen Herrn an seinen guten Freund, seinem Hochzeitlichen Ehren-Tag. In: Ein Karren voller Narren und andere kleine Werke. Hg. Franz Eybl, Salzburg / Wien 1993.

Alemannische Tochter Syon. Hg. Th. Merzdorf. In: Ferdinand Vetter (Hg.). Lehrhafte Litteratur des 14. und 15. Jahrhunderts. Zweiter Teil. Geistliches. Berlin / Stuttgart 1889 (Deutsche Nationallitteratur 12/2) 21-37.

Ambrosius. De virginibus / De vidvis. Tutte le opere di Sant'Ambrogio. Opere morali II/I. Introduzione, traduzione, note e indici di Franco Gori. Milano / Roma 1989 (Vol. 14/1).

Ambrose. De Virginibus. St Ambrose. The Nun's Ideals. Trans. James Shiel. Dublin 1963.

Ambrosius. De virginitate / De institutione virginis / Exhortatio virginitatis. Tutte le opere di Sant'Ambrogio. Opere morali II/II. Introduzione, traduzione, note e indici di Franco Gori. Milano/Roma 1989 (Vol. 14/2).

Banz, Romuald. Christus und die minnende Seele. Untersuchungen und Texte. Breslau 1908 (Germanische Abhandlungen 29).

Bernhard von Clairvaux. Sämtliche Werke lateinisch / deutsch. Hg. Gerhard B. Winkler / Alberich Altermatt / Denis Farkasfalvy / Polykarp Zakar. 9 Bde. Innsbruck 1992-1998.

Bernard of Clairvaux. The Works of Bernard of Clairvaux. 7 vols. Kalamazoo 1970-1977.

The Book of Margery Kempe. Ed. Barry Windeatt. London et.al. 2000 (Longman Annotated Texts).

Book of Margery Kempe. Trans. Barry Windeatt. Harmondsworth 1985.

Caesarius von Heisterbach: Wundergeschichten. Hg. A. Hilka. Bd. 1. Bonn 1933.

Das Buch von geistlicher Armuth, bisher bekannt als Johann Taulers Nachfolgung des armen Lebens Christi. Hg. Heinrich Seuse Denifle. München 1877.

Das Buch von der geistigen Armut. Eine mittelalterliche Unterweisung zum vollkommenen Leben. Ins Neuhochdeutsche übersetzt und kommentiert von Niklaus Largier. München / Zürich 1989.

Deutsche Lyrik des frühen und hohen Mittelalters. Edition der Texte und Kommentare von Ingrid Kasten. Übersetzungen von Margherita Kuhn. Frankfurt a.M. 1995 (Bibliothek des Mittelalters 3)

Deutsche Mystiker des vierzehnten Jahrhunderts. Hg. Franz Pfeiffer. 2 Bde. Leipzig 1857 / Reprint Aalen 1962.

Die Hochzeit. In: Frühe deutsche Literatur und lateinische Literatur in Deutschland 800-1150, 784-849. *(Walter Haug's German translation is the basis for our English translation).*

English Mystics of the Middle Ages. Ed. Barry Windeatt. Cambridge 1994.

Friedrich Sunder. Gnadenleben. In: Siegfried Ringler. Viten- und Offenbarungsliteratur in Frauenklöstern des Mittelalters. Quellen und Studien. Zürich / München 1980 (Münchner Texte und Untersuchungen 72) 391-444.

Frühe deutsche Literatur und lateinische Literatur in Deutschland 800-1150. Hg. Walter Haug / Benedikt Vollmann. Frankfurt a. M. 1991 (Bibliothek des Mittelalters 1).

Gottfried von Strassburg: Tristan. Nach dem Text von Friedrich Ranke. Hg. Rüdiger Krohn. Stuttgart [5]1990.

Gregor von Nyssa: In Canticum Canticorum Homiliae. Homilien zum Hohenlied. 3 Bde. Übers. und eingel. von Franz Dünzl. Freiburg u.a. 1994 (Fontes Christiani 16/1-3).

Gregor von Nyssa. Der versiegelte Quell. Auslegung des Hohen Liedes. Hg. Hans Urs von Balthasar. Einsiedeln 1984.

Guillaume de Saint-Thierry. De la nature du corps et de l' âme. Éd. Michel Lemoine. Paris 1988 (Collection Auteurs Latins du Moyen Age).

Hadewijch. Das Buch der Visionen. Teil I Einleitung, Text und Übersetzung von Gerald Hofmann. Teil II Kommentar. 2 Bde. Stuttgart 1998 (Mystik in Geschichte und Gegenwart 12 / 13).

Hartmann von Aue. Iwein. Hg. Thomas Cramer. Berlin / New York 1974.

Hartmann von Aue. Der arme Heinrich. Hg. Hermann Paul. Neu bearbeitet von Kurt Gärtner. Tübingen [16]1996.

Hartmann von Aue. Der arme Heinrich. Übersetzt von Siegfried Grosse. Hg. Ursula Rautenberg. Stuttgart 1993.

Hartmann von Aue. Gregorius. Hg. Paul Haupt. 13., neu bearbeitete Auflage besorgt von Burghart Wachinger. Tübingen 1984 (Altdeutsche Textbibliothek 2).

Hartmann von Aue. Gregorius der gute Sünder. Mittelhochdeutscher Text nach der Ausgabe von Friedrich Neumann. Übertragung von Burkhard Kippenberg. Nachwort von Hugo Kuhn. Stuttgart 1963.

Heine, Heinrich. Sämtliche Schriften in zwölf Bänden. Hg. Klaus Briegleb. München / Wien 1976.

Heinrich Seuse. Deutsche Schriften. Hg. Karl Bihlmeyer. Stuttgart 1907. Reprint Frankfurt a.M. 1961.

Henry Suso. The Exemplar, with two German Sermons. Trans. and ed. Frank Tobin. New York 1989.

Henry Suso. Wisdom's Watch upon the Hours. Trans. Edmund Colledge. Washington 1994.

Heinrich von Veldeke. Eneasroman. Nach dem Text von Ludwig Ettmüller ins Neuhochdeutsche übersetzt. Mit einem Stellenkommentar und einem Nachwort von Dieter Kartschoke. Stuttgart 1986.

Hildegard von Bingen. Epistolarium. Hg. Lieven van Acker, Turnhout 1991-1993 (CCCM 91-91A). *English translation: Saint Hildegard. The Letters of Hildegard von Bingen. Trans. Joseph L. Baird and Radd K. Ehrman. Vol I. Oxford 1994 / Vol. II. Oxford 1998.*

Hildegard von Bingen. Briefwechsel. Hg. Adelgundis Führkötter. Zweite, verbesserte Auflage. Salzburg 1990.

Hildegard von Bingen. Im Feuer der Taube. Die Briefe. Hg. Walburga Storch OSB. Augsburg 1997 *(follows the critical edition of all the letters)*.

The Historia Occidentalis of Jacques de Vitry. A Critical Edition by John Frederick Hinnebusch O.P. Fribourg / Switzerland 1972.

Holy Maidenhood / Hali Meidenhad. A Letter on Virginity. In: *Medieval English Prose for Women.* Selections from the Katherine Group and Ancrene Wisse. Ed. Bella Millett / Jocelyn Wogan-Browne. Oxford 1990.

Isidor von Sevilla. Etymologiarum sive originum libri XX. Ed. W. M. Lindsey. Oxford 1911.

Kant, Immanuel. Beobachtungen über das Gefühl des Schönen und Erhabenen. In: Von den Träumen der Vernunft. Kleine Schriften zur Kunst, Philosophie, Geschichte und Politik. Hg. Steffen and Birgit Dietzsch. Leipzig / Weimar 1979. – *English translation: Kant, Immanuel. Observations on the Feeling of the Beautiful and Sublime. Trans. John T. Goldthwait. Berkeley 1960.*

Lamprecht von Regensburg. Sanct Francisken Leben und Tochter Syon. Hg. Karl Weinhold. Paderborn 1880.

Lenz, Jakob Michael Reinhold. Philosophische Vorlesungen für empfindsame Seelen. Faksimiledruck der Ausgabe Frankfurt und Leipzig 1780. Hg. Christoph Weiss. St.Ingbert 1994.

Lettre sur la sainteté. Le secret de la relation entre l'homme et la femme dans la cabale. Étude préliminaire, traduction de l'hébreu et commentaires par Charles Mopsik. Paris 1986.

Marienlegenden aus dem Alten Passional. Hg. Hans-Georg Richert. Tübingen 1965.

Mechthild von Hackeborn. Das Buch vom strömenden Lob. Auswahl, Übersetzung und Einführung von Hans Urs von Balthasar. Einsiedeln 1955.

Mechthild von Magdeburg. Das fließende Licht der Gottheit. Nach der Einsiedler Handschrift in kritischem Vergleich mit der gesamten Überlieferung hg. von Hans Neumann. Band 1 Text. Besorgt von Gisela Vollmann-Profe, München / Zürich 1990. Band 2 Untersuchungen. Ergänzt und zum Druck eingerichtet von Gisela Vollmann-Profe. München 1993 (Münchner Texte und Untersuchungen 100).

Mechthild of Magdeburg: Flowing Light of the Divinity. Trans. Christiane Mesch Galvani. New York 1991

Mechthild of Magdeburg. The Flowing Light of the Godhead. Trans. and intr. Frank
    Tobin. Preface by Margot Schmidt. New York 1997 *(all quotations from this translation)*.

Mechthild von Magdeburg. Das fließende Licht der Gottheit. Herausgegeben, über-
    setzt, eingeleitet und erläutert von Margot Schmidt. Stuttgart-Bad Cannstatt 1995
    (Mystik in Geschichte und Gegenwart 11).

Meister Eckhart. Werke in zwei Bänden. Hg. Niklaus Largier. Frankfurt a.M. 1993
    (Bibliothek deutscher Klassiker 20 / 21).

Meister Eckhart. Deutsche Mystiker des vierzehnten Jahrhunderts. Hg. Franz Pfeiffer.
    Band 2. Leipzig 1857 / Reprint Aalen 1962.

Meister Eckhart. German Sermons and Treatises. Translated with introduction and
    notes by M. O'C. Walshe. London / Dulverton 1979 / 1981 / 1987.

Origène. Homélies sur Ezéchiel. Éd. Marcel Borret. Paris 1989 (Sources chrétiennes 352).

Origenes und Gregor der Grosse. Das Hohelied. Hg. Karl Suso Frank. Einsiedeln 1987.

Priester Wernher. Maria. Bruchstücke und Umarbeitungen. Hg. Carl Wesle. Zweite
    Auflage besorgt durch Hans Fromm. Tübingen 1969.

Richard von St. Viktor. Über die Gewalt der Liebe. Ihre vier Stufen. Hg. Margot
    Schmidt. München et.al. 1969.

Der Schürebrand. Ein Traktat aus dem Kreise der Straßburger Gottesfreunde. Hg.
    Philipp Strauch. In: Studien zur deutschen Philologie. Festgabe der germanistischen
    Abteilung der 47. Versammlung deutscher Philologen und Schulmänner in Halle zur
    Begrüssung dargebracht von Philipp Strauch, Arnold E. Berger und Franz Saran.
    Halle 1903.

Das St. Trudperter Hohelied. Eine Lehre der liebenden Gotteserkenntnis. Hg. Friedrich
    Ohly unter Mitarbeit von Nicola Kleine. Frankfurt a.M. 1998 (Bibliothek des Mit-
    telalters 2).

Des Teufels Netz. Satirisch-didaktisches Gedicht. Hg. Karl A. Barack. Stuttgart 1863 /
    Reprint Amsterdam 1968.

Theophrast von Hohenheim. Ethische, soziale und politische Schriften. Schriften über
    Ehe, Taufe, Buße und Beichte. Bearbeitet von Kurt Goldammer, 2. Abt. II. Wies-
    baden 1965.

Tilo von Kulm. Siben Ingesigel. Hg. Karl Kochendörffer. Berlin 1907.

Wolfram von Eschenbach. Parzival. Text nach der Ausgabe von Karl Lachmann. Hg.
    Wolfgang Spiewok. 2 Bände. Stuttgart 1981.

Xenophon. Erinnerungen an Sokrates. Hg. Peter Jaerisch, München / Zürich [4]1987.

Secondary Sources

Acklin Zimmermann, Béatrice. Neue Perspektiven für die theologische Erschließung
    sogenannter frauenmystischer Literatur. In: Freiburger Zeitschrift für Philosophie
    und Theologie 39 (1991) 175-191.

Acklin Zimmermann, Béatrice (Hg.). Denkmodelle von Frauen im Mittelalter. Freiburg
    / Schweiz 1994 (Dokimion 15).

Aers, David / Staley, Lynn (Eds.). The Powers of the Holy. Religion, Politics, and Gen-
    der in Late Medieval English Culture. Pennsylvania 1995.

Allen, Prudence. The Concept of Woman. The Aristotelian Revolution, 750 B.C.–A.D. 1250. Grand Rapids ²1996.

Alverdes, Paul. Der mystische Eros in der geistlichen Lyrik des Pietismus. Diss. masch. München 1921.

Angenendt, Arnold. Geschichte der Religiosität im Mittelalter. Darmstadt 1997.

Ariès, Philippe / Duby, Georges (Eds.). A History of Private Life. Vol I. From Pagan Rome to Byzantium. Ed. Paul Veyne. Cambridge, Mass. / London 1988.

Ariès, Philippe / Duby, Georges (Eds.). A History of Private Life. Vol II. Revelations of the Medieval World. Ed. Georges Duby. Cambridge, Mass. / London 1988.

Aspegren, Kerstin. The Male Woman. A Feminine Ideal in the Early Church. Uppsala 1990.

Assmann, Aleida. Der Wissende und die Weisheit. In: Sigrid Schade / Monika Wagner / Sigrid Weigel (Hgg.) 11-25.

Assmann, Aleida und Jan (Hgg.). Schleier und Schwelle. Archäologie der literarischen Kommunikation V,1. Geheimnis und Öffentlichkeit. München 1997.

Assmann, Aleida und Jan (Hgg.). Schleier und Schwelle. Archäologie der literarischen Kommunikation V,2. Geheimnis und Offenbarung. München 1998.

Astell, Ann W. The Song of Songs in the Middle Ages. Ithaca / London 1990.

Atkinson, Clarissa. 'Precious Balsam in a Fragile Glass'. The Ideology of Virginity in the Later Middle Ages. In: Journal of Family History 8 (1983) 131-143.

Baldwin, John W. The Language of Sex. Five Voices from Northern France around 1200. Chicago 1994.

Barth, Susanne. Jungfrauenzucht. Literaturwissenschaftliche und pädagogische Studien zur Mädchenerziehungsliteratur zwischen 1200 und 1600. Stuttgart 1994.

Barthes, Roland. A Lover's Discourse. Fragments. London 1979.

Bauer, Gerhard. Claustrum animae. Untersuchungen zur Geschichte der Metapher vom Herzen als Kloster. Bd. 1 Entstehungsgeschichte. München 1973.

Beer, Frances. Women and Mystical Experience in the Middle Ages. Woodbridge/ Rochester 1992.

Bejick, Urte. Die Katharerinnen. Häresieverdächtige Frauen im mittelalterlichen Süd-Frankreich. Freiburg i.Br. et.al. 1993.

Bellinger, Gerhard J. Im Himmel wie auf Erden. Sexualität in den Religionen der Welt. München 1993.

Bennewitz, Ingrid. Mediävistische Neuerscheinungen aus dem Bereich der Frauen- und Geschlechtergeschichte. In: Zeitschrift für deutsche Philologie 113 (1994) 416-426.

Berger, Kurt. Die Ausdrücke der unio mystica im Mittelhochdeutschen. Berlin 1935 (Germanische Studien 168).

Bériou, Nicole / d'Avray, David L. The Image of the Ideal Husband in Thirteenth Century French Sermons. In: Revue Mabillon. Nouvelle Série I, 62 (1990) 111-141.

Berkenbusch, Irene. Speculum Virginum. Mittelniederländischer Text. Edition. Untersuchungen zum Prolog und einleitende Interpretation. Frankfurt a. M. et.al. 1995.

Berschin, Walter. Biographie und Epochenstil im lateinischen Mittelalter. Stuttgart 1986 (Quellen und Untersuchungen zur lateinischen Philologie des Mittelalters 1-8).

Beyer-Fröhlich, Marianne. Selbstzeugnisse aus dem dreißigjährigen Krieg und dem Barock. Darmstadt 1970 (Reihe deutsche Selbstzeugnisse 6).

Biale, David. Eros and the Jews. From Biblical Israel to Contemporary America. New York 1992.

Bishop, Clifford. Sex and Spirit. London 1996.

Blamires, Alcuin. The Case for Women in Medieval Culture. Oxford 1997.

Blank, Walter. Die deutsche Minneallegorie. Gestaltung und Funktion einer spätmittel-alterlichen Dichtungsform. Stuttgart 1970 (Germanistische Abhandlungen 34).

Bloch, Horward R. Medieval Misogyny and the Invention of Western Romantic Love. Chicago 1991.

Blumenfeld-Kosinski, Renate / Szell, Timea (Eds.). Images of Sainthood in Medieval Europe. Ithaca / London 1991.

Børresen, Kari Elisabeth. L'usage patristique de métaphores féminines dans le discours sur Dieu. In: Revue théologique de Louvain 13 (1982) 205-220.

Borret, Marcel (Éd.). Origène. Homélies sur Ezéchiel. Paris 1989 (Sources chréti-ennes 352).

Boyle, Marjorie O'Rourke. Divine domesticity. Augustine to Thagaste to Theresa of Avila. Leiden et.al. 1997 (Studies in the History of Christian Thought, Vol. 74).

Brall, Helmut / Haupt, Barbara / Küsters, Urban (Hgg.). Personenbeziehungen in der mittelalterlichen Literatur. Düsseldorf 1994 (Studia humaniora 25).

Brall, Helmut. Reflections of Homosexuality in Medieval Poetry and Chronicles. In: Queering the Canon. Defying Sights in German Literature and Culture. Ed. Christoph Lorey / John L. Plews. Rochester / Woodbridge 1998, 98-105.

Brandt, Rüdiger. Enklaven – Exklaven. Zur literarischen Darstellung von Öffentlichkeit und Nichtöffentlichkeit im Mittelalter. München 1993 (Forschungen zur Geschichte der älteren deutschen Literatur 15)[=1993a].

Brandt, Rüdiger. 'Liebe auf Zeit'. Ansätze von Privatheitsvorstellungen in Reimar d.A. XV,6? In: Zeitschrift für deutsche Philologie 112 (1993) 105-111 [= 1993b].

Brandt, Rüdiger. *Fama volante – publica inspectio – populo moribus acceptus.* Vorstellun-gen von Öffentlichkeit und Nichtöffentlichkeit in den *Casus Sancti Galli.* In: Melville, Gert / von Moos, Peer (Hgg.) 609-628 [= 1998].

Brandt, Rüdiger. *murmeln.* Zu einer Schnittstelle frühneuzeitlicher Diskurse über Reli-gion, Sprechen, Sprachhandeln und Artikulation. In: Osnabrücker Beiträge zur Sprachtheorie 58 (1999). Sprache in religiösen Kontexten, 92-116.

Brinker, Claudia / Herzog, Urs / Largier, Niklaus / Michel, Paul (Hgg.). *Contemplata aliis tradere.* Studien zum Verhältnis von Literatur und Spiritualität. Bern et.al. 1995.

Brooke, Christopher. The Medieval Idea of Marriage. Oxford 1989.

Brown, Peter. The Body and Society. Men, Women, and Sexual Renunciation in Early Christianity. New York 1988.

Brown, Catherine. *Muliebriter.* Doing Gender in the Letters of Heloise. In: Jane Chance (ed.) 25-51.

Brümmer, Vincent. The Model of Love. A Study in Philosophical Theology. Cambridge 1993.

Brundage, James A. Concubinage and Marriage in Medieval Canon Law. In: Journal of Medieval History 1 (1975) 1-17.

Brundage, James A. Law, Sex, and Christian Society in Medieval Europe. Chicago / London 1987.

Brundage, James A. Medieval Canon Law. London 1994.

Brundage, James A./ Bullough, Vern L. (Eds.). Handbook of Medieval Sexuality. London / New York 1996.

Bugge, John. Virginitas. An Essay in the History of a Medieval Ideal. Den Haag 1975 (International Archives of the History of Ideas. Series Minor, Vol. 17).

Bullough, Vern L. Sex in History. A Redux. In: Jacqueline Murray / Konrad Eisenbichler (Eds.) 1996, 3-22.

Bumke, Joachim. Geschichte der deutschen Literatur im hohen Mittelalter. München 1990.

Burdach, Konrad. Der Gral. Forschungen über seine Ursprung und seinen Zusammenhang mit der Longinuslegende. Stuttgart 1938 / Darmstadt 1974.

Bürkle, Susanne. Weibliche Spiritualität und imaginierte Weiblichkeit. Deutungsmuster und -perspektiven frauenmystischer Literatur im Blick auf die Thesen Caroline Walker Bynums. In: Zeitschrift für deutsche Philologie 113 (1994) Sonderheft Mystik, 116-143.

Burns, Jane. The Man Behind the Lady in Troubadour Lyric. In: Romance Notes 25 (1985) 254-270.

Bußmann, Hadumod / Hof, Renate (Hgg.). Genus. Zur Geschlechterdifferenz in den Kulturwissenschaften. Stuttgart 1995.

Bynum Walker Caroline. Jesus Mother. Studies in the Spirituality of the High Middle Ages. Berkeley et.al. 1982.

Bynum Walker Caroline / Harrell St. / Richman P. Gender and Religion. On the Complexity of Symbols. Boston 1986.

Bynum Walker Caroline. Holy Feast and Holy Fast. The Religious Significance of Food to Medieval Women. Berkeley et.al. 1987.

Bynum Walker Caroline. Fragmentation and Redemption. Essays on Gender and the Human Body in Medieval Religion. New York 1991.

Bynum Walker Caroline. The Resurrection of the Body in Western Christianity, 200-1336. New York 1995.

Cadden, Joan. Meanings of Sex Difference in the Middle Ages. Medicine, Science, and Culture. New York 1993 (Cambridge History of Medicine).

Camby, Philippe. L'érotisme et le sacré. Paris 1989.

Camille, Michael. Image on the Edge. The Margins of Medieval Art. Cambridge 1992.

Camille, Michael. The Book of Signs. Writing and Visual Difference in Gothic Manuscript Illumination. In: A History of Book Illustration. 29 Points of View. Ed. Bill Katz. Meteuchen 1994, 160-201.

Carne, Eva Maria. Die Frauengestalten bei Hartmann von Aue. Ihre Bedeutung im Aufbau und Gehalt der Epen. Marburg 1970.

Carruthers, Mary. The Book of Memory. A Study of Memory in Medieval Culture. Cambridge 1990.

Chance, Jane (Ed.). Gender and Text in the Later Middle Ages. Gainesville et.al 1996.

Chavasse, C. The Bride of Christ. An Inquiry into the Nuptial Element in Early Christianity. London 1940.

Chenu, Marie-Dominique. L'éveil de la conscience dans la civilisation médiévale. Montréal / Paris 1969.

Chydenius, Johan. Love and the Medieval Tradition. Helsingfors / Helsinki 1977 (Commentationes Humanarum Litterarum 58).

Chydenius, Johan. The Symbolism of Love in Medieval Thought. Helsingfors / Helsinki 1970 (Commentationes Humanarum Litterarum 44/1).

Clanchy, Michael T. Abelard – A Medieval Life. London 1997. *German Translation: Abaelard. Ein mittelalterliches Leben. Darmstadt 2000.*

Clark Elizabeth A. Asceticism, Piety and Women's Faith. Essays on Late Ancient Christianity. Lewiston / Queenston 1986 (Studies in Women and Religion 20).

Clark, Susan L. Hartmann von Aue. Landscapes of Mind. Houston 1989.

Cloke, Gillian. 'This female man of God'. Women and spiritual power in the patristic age. AD 350-450. London / New York 1995.

Coakley, Sarah (Hg.). Religion and the body. Cambridge 1997 (Cambridge Studies in Religious Traditions 8).

Consolino, Franca Ela. Il monachesimo femminile nella tarde antichità. In: Segundo seminario sobre el Monacado. Monacado y sociedad, Codex Aquilarensis 2 (1989) 33-57.

Consolino, Franca Ela. Veni huc a Libano. La sponsa del Cantico dei Cantici come modello per le vergini negli scritti esortatori di Ambrogio. In: Athenaeum 62 (1984) 399-415.

Cooper, Kate. The Virgin and the Bride. Idealized Womanhood in Late Antiquity. Cambridge / London 1996.

Cormeau, Christoph / Kuhn, Hugo. Hartmann von Aue. Darmstadt 1973 (Wege der Forschung 359).

Cormeau, Christoph / Störmer, Wilhelm. Hartmann von Aue. Epoche – Werk – Wirkung. 2. überarb. Auflage. München 1993.

Curschmann, Michael. Imagined Exegesis. Text and Picture in the exegetical Works of Rupert of Deutz, Honorius Augustodunensis, and Gerhoch of Reichersberg. In: Traditio 44 (1990) 145-169.

Dauven-van Knippenberg, Carla. Einer von den Soldaten öffnete seine Seite…: Eine Untersuchung der Longinuslegende im deutschsprachigen geistlichen Spiel, Amsterdam et.al. 1990 (= Amsterdamer Publikationen zur Sprache und Literatur 87).

Dauven-van Knippenberg, Carla. *Es ist aber nit frummer frawn recht.* Über Gender-Forschung und geistliches Schauspiel des Mittelalters. In: *Manlîchiu wîp, wîplich man,* 34-46 [=1999].

D'Avray, David L. The Gospel of Marriage Feast of Cana and Marriage Preaching in France, in: The Bible in the Medieval World. Essays in memory of B.Smalley, ed. K. Walsh / D. Wood, Oxford 1985 (Studies in Church History, Subsidia 4), 207-224.

Daxelmüller, Christoph. Zauberpraktiken. Eine Ideengeschichte der Magie. Zürich et.al. 1993.

Day, Lucille. In the Hidden Garden. Two Translations of the Song of Songs. In: The Hudson Review. Summer 1995, 259-269.

de Boor, Helmut. Die höfische Literatur. Vorbereitung, Blüte, Ausklang. 1170-1250. Elfte Auflage. Bearbeitet von Ursula Hennig. München 1991 (Geschichte der deutschen Literatur II).

Dean-Jones, Lesley Ann. Women's Bodies in Classical Greek Science. Oxford 1994.

Dellagiacoma, Vittorio. Israele Sposa di Dio. La metafora nuziale del Vecchio Testamento. Exc. Diss. PUL. Verona 1961.

Denkende Wollust. Robert Darnton. Denkende Wollust oder Die sexuelle Aufklärung. Jean-Charles Gervaise de Latouche. Die Geschichte des Dom Bougre, Pförtner der Kartäuser. Jean-Baptiste D'Argens. Thérèse philosophe oder Memoiren zu Ehren der Geschichte von Pater Dirrag und Mademoiselle Éradice. Die andere Bibliothek. Hg. Hans Magnus Enzensberger. Frankfurt a.M. 1996.

Deutsche Mystik im abendländischen Zusammenhang. Neu erschlossene Texte, neue methodische Ansätze, neue theoretische Konzepte. Kolloquium Kloster Fischingen. Hg. Walter Haug / Wolfram Schneider-Lastin. Tübingen 2000.

Dictionnaire de spiritualité ascétique et mystique doctrine et histoire. Fondé par Marcel Viller et.al. Paris 1937-1994.

Die deutsche Literatur des Mittelalters. Verfasserlexikon. Begründet von Wolfgang Stammler. Fortgeführt von Karl Langosch. 5 Bde. Berlin / New York 1933-1955 [= VL].

Die deutsche Literatur des Mittelalters. Verfasserlexikon. Hg. Kurt Ruh zusammen mit G. Keil, W. Schröder, B. Wachinger und F.J. Worstbrock. Zweite, völlig neu bearbeitete Auflage. Berlin / New York 1977ff [= ²VL].

Dinzelbacher, Peter. Vision und Visionsliteratur im Mittelalter. Stuttgart 1981.

Dinzelbacher, Peter. Die tötende Gottheit. Pestbild und Todesikonographie als Ausdruck der Mentalität des Spätmittelalters und der Renaissance. In: Analecta Cartusiana 117/2 (1986) 5-138.

Dinzelbacher, Peter. Miles Symbolicus. Mittelalterliche Beispiele geharnischter Personifikationen. In: Symbole des Alltags. Alltag der Symbole. FS für Harry Kühnel zum 65. Geburtstag. Graz 1992, 49-85.

Dinzelbacher, Peter (Hg.). Europäische Mentalitätsgeschichte. Stuttgart 1993.

Dinzelbacher, Peter. Die Gottesbeziehung als Geschlechterbeziehung. In: Brall, Helmut / Haupt, Barbara / Küsters, Urban (Hgg.) 3-36.

Dinzelbacher, Peter. Die Gottesgeburt in der Seele und im Körper. Von der somatischen Konsequenz einer theologischen Metapher. In: Th. Kornbichler/W. Maaz. Variationen der Liebe. Historische Psychologie der Geschlechterbeziehung. Tübingen 1995, 94-128 [= 1995a].

Dinzelbacher, Peter. Heilige oder Hexen? Schicksale auffälliger Frauen in Mittelalter und Frühneuzeit. Zürich 1995 [= 1995b].

Dodds, Erec Robertson. The Greeks and the Irrational. Berkeley / Los Angeles 1966.

Dorlcy, Hohn P. Love, Celibacy and the Inner Marriage. Toronto 1987.

Duby, Georges / Perrot, Michelle (Eds.). A History of Women in the West. Vol. I. From Ancient Goddesses to Christian Saints. Ed. Pauline Smitt Pantel. Cambridge, Mass. / London 1992 (quoted as Duby/Perrot 1).

Duby, Georges / Perrot, Michelle (Eds.). A History of Women in the West, Vol. II. Silences of the Middle Ages. Ed. Christiane Klapisch-Zuber. Cambridge, Mass. / London 1992 (quoted as Duby/Perrot 2).

Duby, Georges. The Knight, the Lady and the Priest. Trans. Barbara Bray. London 1984.

Duby, Georges. Medieval Marriage. Trans. E. Forster. Baltimore 1978.

Duby, Georges. Die Frau ohne Stimme. Liebe und Ehe im Mittelalter. Frankfurt a.M. 1993.

Duby, Georges. Love and Marriage in the Middle Ages. Transl. Jane Dunnett. Cambridge 1994.

Duckworth, David. The Leper and the Maiden in Hartmann's Der Arme Heinrich. Göppingen 1996 (Göppinger Arbeiten zur Germanistik 627).

Dünzl, Franz. Braut und Bräutigam. Die Auslegung des Canticum durch Gregor von Nyssa. Tübingen 1993 (Beiträge zur Geschichte der biblischen Exegese 32).

Egerding, Michael. Die Metaphorik der spätmittelalterlichen Mystik. 2 Bände. Paderborn et.al. 1997.

Eggers, Hans. Die Entdeckung der Liebe im Spiegel der deutschen Dichtung der Stauferzeit. In: Herrenalber Texte 1978/2, 10-25.

Ehlert, Trude. Die Funktionen des Hochzeitsfestes in deutscher erzählender Dichtung vornehmlich des 12. und 13. Jahrhunderts. In: Feste und Feiern im Mittelalter. Paderborner Symposion des Mediävistenverbandes. Hg. Detlev Altenburg / Jörg Jarnut / Hans-Hugo Steinhoff. Sigmaringen 1991, 393-400.

Eicheldinger, Martina. Friedrich Spee – Seelsorger und *poeta doctus*. Die Tradition des Hohenliedes und Einflüsse der ignatianischen Andacht in seinem Werk. Tübingen 1991.

Eisenmann, Hartmut. Konstanzer Institutionen des Familien- und Erbrechts von 1370 bis 1521. Konstanz 1964. (Konstanzer Geschichts- und Rechtsquellen 14).

Éliade, Mircea. Le sacré et le profane. Paris 1965. *German translation: Mircea Éliade. Das Heilige und das Profane. Vom Wesen des Religiösen. Frankfurt a.M. 1985.*

Éliade, Mircea. Sur l'érotique mystique indienne. Paris 1997 (Collection Confidences).

Elliott, Dyan. Spiritual Marriage. Sexual Abstinence in Medieval Wedlock. Princeton 1993.

Elm Susannah. The Virgins of God. The Making of Asceticism in Late Antiquity. Oxford 1993.

Faber, Birgitta Maria. Eheschließung in mittelalterlicher Dichtung vom Ende des 12. bis 15. Jahrhundert. Diss. Bonn 1974.

Feistner, Edith. Historische Typologie der deutschen Heiligenlegende des Mittelalters von der Mitte des 12. Jahrhunderts bis zur Reformation. Wiesbaden 1995 (Wissensliteratur im Mittelalter 20).

Fietze Katharina. Spiegel der Vernunft. Theorien zum Menschsein der Frau in der Anthropologie des 15. Jahrhunderts. Paderborn et.al. 1991.

Fisher Sheila/Halley Janet E.(eds.). Seeking the Woman in Late Medieval and Renaissance Writings. Essays in Feminist Contextual Criticism. Knoxville 1989.

Forbes Christopher. Prophecy and Inspired Speech in Early Christianity and its Hellenistic Environment. Tübingen 1995 (Wissenschaftliche Untersuchungen zum Neuen Testament. 2.Reihe 75).

Fradenburg, Louise/Freccero, Carla (eds.). Premodern Sexualities. London/New York 1996.

Frenzel, Elisabeth. Stoffe der Weltliteratur. Ein Lexikon dichtungsgeschichtlicher Längsschnitte. Stuttgart [8]1992.

Frey Sallmann, Alma. Aus dem Nachleben antiker Göttergestalten. Die antiken Gottheiten in der Bildbeschreibung des Mittelalters und der italienischen Frührenaissance. Leipzig 1931.

Freytag, Hartmut. Die Theorie der allegorischen Schriftdeutung und die Allegorie in deutschen Texten besonders des 11. und 12. Jahrhunderts. Bern / München 1982 (Bibliotheca Germanica 24).

Friedman Lionel J. "Occulta Cordis". In: Romance Philology 9 (1957-1958) 103-119.

Friedman, John B. L'iconographie de Vénus et de son miroir à la fin du Moyen Âge. In: L'Érotisme au Moyen Âge. Éd. Bruno Roy. Montréal 1977.

Fromm, Hans. Untersuchungen zum Marienleben des Priesters Wernher. Turku 1955 (Annales Universitatis Turkuensis Ser. B. Tom. 52).

Fuchs, Gotthard (Hg.). Die dunkle Nacht der Sinne. Leiderfahrung und christliche Mystik. Düsseldorf 1989.

Ganz, Peter. "Die Hochzeit". *fabula* und *significatio*. In: Studien zur frühmittelhochdeutschen Literatur. Cambridger Colloquium 1971. Hg. Leslie P. Johnson / Hans-Hugo Steinhoff / Roy A. Wisbey. Berlin 1974, 58-73.

Gärtner Kurt. Neues zur Priester-Wernher-Kritik. Mit einem Abdruck der kleineren Bruchstücke von Priester Wernhers 'Maria'. In: Studien zur frühmittelhochdeutschen Literatur. Cambridger Colloquium 1971. Hg. Leslie P. Johnson / Hans-Hugo Steinhoff / Roy A. Wisbey. Berlin 1974, 103-135.

Gärtner, Kurt. Ein bisher unbekanntes Fragment von Priester Wernhers 'Maria'. In: Zeitschrift für deutsches Altertum 101 (1972) 208-213.

Geißmar-Brandi, Christoph/Louis Eleonora (Hgg.). Glaube Liebe Hoffnung Tod. Ausstellungskatalog. Wien 1995.

Genette, Gérard. Paratexts. Thresholds of interpretation. Trans. Jane E. Lewin. Cambridge 1997.

Gijsel, Jan. Die Quelle von Priester Wernhers *Driu liet von der maget*. In: Archiv für das Studium der neueren Sprachen und Literaturen 215 (1978) 250-255.

Glier, Ingeborg (Hg.). Die deutsche Literatur im späten Mittelalter 1250-1370. Zweiter Teil. Reimpaargedichte, Drama, Prosa. Geschichte der deutschen Literatur von den Anfängen bis zur Gegenwart. München 1987 (Geschichte der deutschen Literatur III/2).

Gonthier, Nicole. Cris de haine et rites d'unité. La violence dans les villes, XIIIème - XVIème siècle. Turnhout 1992.

Gössmann, Elisabeth (Hg.). Ob die Weiber Menschen seyn, oder nicht? München 1988 (Archiv für philosophie- und theologieschichtliche Frauenforschung 4).

Gössmann, Elisabeth. Das Konstrukt der Geschlechterdifferenz in der christlichen theologischen Tradition. In: Concilium 27 (1991) 483-488.

Gössmann, Elisabeth. Die Makro-Mikrokosmik als umfassendes Denkmodell Hildegards von Bingen. In: Béatrice Acklin Zimmermann (Hg.). Denkmodelle von Frauen im Mittelalter. Freiburg / Schweiz 1994, 19-41.

Gössmann, Elisabeth. Hildegard von Bingen. Versuche einer Annäherung. München 1995 (Archiv für philosophie- und theologiegeschichtliche Frauenforschung. Sonderband).

Grégoire, Réginald. Il matrimonio mistico. In: Il matrimonio nella società altomedievale, 701-815.

Haag, Christine. Das Ideal der männlichen Frau in der Literatur des Mittelalters und
seine theoretischen Grundlagen. In: *Manlîchiu wîp, wîplich man*, 228-248.

Haas Alois Maria. Schreibweisen der Frauenmystik. In: Deutsche Literatur. Eine
Sozialgeschichte. Hg. Horst A. Glaser. Bd. 1. Aus der Mündlichkeit in die
Schriftlichkeit. Höfische und andere Literatur. 750-1320. Hg. Ursula Liebertz-Grün.
Reinbek bei Hamburg 1988, 359-366.

Haas, Alois Maria. Sermo mysticus. Studien zu Theologie und Sprache der deutschen
Mystik. Freiburg / Schweiz 1979 (Dokimion 4).

Haas, Alois Maria. Geistliches Mittelalter. Freiburg / Schweiz 1984 (Dokimion 8).

Haas, Alois Maria. Gottlieben – Gottleiden. Zur volkssprachlichen Mystik im Mittelalter. Frankfurt a.M. 1989 [= 1989a].

Haas, Alois Maria. Mechthilds von Magdeburg dichterische heimlichkeit. In: Rüdiger
Schnell (Hg.). *Gotes und der werlde hulde*. Literatur in Mittelalter und Neuzeit. Bern
/ Stuttgart 1989, 206-233 [= 1989b].

Haas, Alois Maria. Todesbilder im Mittelalter. Fakten und Hinweise in der deutschen
Literatur. Darmstadt 1989 [= 1989c].

Haas, Alois Maria. Die Kunst rechter Gelassenheit. Themen und Schwerpunkte von
Heinrich Seuses Mystik. Bern et.al. 1995.

Haas, Alois Maria. Mystik als Aussage. Erfahrungs-, Denk- und Redeformen
christlicher Mystik. Frankfurt a.M. 1996.

Haas, Alois Maria. Das Subjekt im „sermo mysticus" am Beispiel der spanischen Mystik des 16. Jahrhunderts. In: Fetz, Reto Luzius et.al. (Hgg.). Geschichte und
Vorgeschichte der modernen Subjektivität. Berlin / New York 1998, 612-640.

Hamburger, Jeffrey F. The Rothschild Canticles. Art and Mysticism in Flanders and the
Rhineland circa 1300. New Haven / London 1990.

Hamburger, Jeffrey F. Nuns as Artists. The Visual Culture of a Medieval Convent.
Berkeley / Los Angeles 1997.

Hamburger, Jeffrey F. Medieval Self-Fashioning: Authorship, Authority, and Autobiog-
raphy in Seuse's *Exemplar*. In: Christ among the Medieval Dominicans. Representations of Christ in the Texts and Images of the Order of Preachers. Ed. Kent Emery,
Jr. / Joseph Wawrykow. Notre Dame 1998, 430-461 (and figures).

Handwörterbuch zur deutschen Rechtsgeschichte. Hg. Adalbert Erler / Ekkehard Kauf-
mann. 5 Bände. Berlin 1971-1998.

Haug, Walter. Wandlungen des Fiktionalitätsbewußtseins vom hohen zum späten Mittelalter. In: Walter Haug. Brechungen auf dem Weg zur Individualität. Kleine
Schriften zur Literatur des Mittelalters. Tübingen 1995, 251-264.

Haug, Walter. Das Geständnis. Liebe und Risiko in Rede und Schrift. In: Horst Wenzel (Hg.) 1997, 23-41.

Haug, Walter. Kulturgeschichte und Literaturgeschichte. Einige grundsätzliche Überlegungen aus mediävistischer Sicht. In: Kultureller Austausch und Literaturgeschichte im Mittelalter. Transfert culturels et histoire littéraire au moyen âge.
Éd. Ingrid Kasten / Werner Paravicini / René Pérennec. Sigmaringen 1998 (Beihefte
der Francia 43) 23-33 [=1998a]

Haug, Walter. Geheimnis und dunkler Stil. In: Aleida und Jan Assmann (Hgg.) 1998, 205-217 [=1998b]

Haverkamp, Alfred. Tenxwind von Andernach und Hildegard von Bingen. Zwei 'Weltanschauungen' in der Mitte des 12. Jahrhunderts. In: Lutz Fenske / Werner Rösener / Thomas Zotz (Hgg.). Institutionen, Kultur und Gesellschaft im Mittelalter. Sigmaringen 1984, 515-548.

Haverkamp, Anselm (Hg.). Haus und Familie in der spätmittelalterlichen Stadt. Köln et.al. 1984.

Heidemann, Kyra. "Zu leyden in dem stand der eh...". Die Griseldis-Novelle als Ehelehre. In: Maria E. Müller (Hg.) 47-78.

Heimbach, Marianne. "Der ungelehrte Mund" als Autorität. Mystische Erfahrung als Quelle kirchlich-prophetischer Rede im Werk Mechthilds von Magdeburg. Stuttgart-Bad Cannstatt 1989 (Mystik in Geschichte und Gegenwart 6).

Heimbach, Marianne. Trinität – Minne – Prophetie. Grundstrukturen theologischen Denkens im Werk Mechthilds von Magdeburg. In: Béatrice Acklin Zimmermann (Hg.) 83-106.

Heimbach-Steins, Marianne. Gottes und des Menschen "heimlichkeit". Zu einem Zentralbegriff der mystischen Theologie Mechthilds von Magdeburg. In: Brinker, Claudia / Herzog, Urs / Largier, Niklaus / Michel, Paul (Hgg.) 71-86.

Heinzle, Joachim (Hg.). Literarische Interessenbildung im Mittelalter. Stuttgart / Weimar 1994.

Heinzle, Joachim. Wandlungen und Neuansätze im 13. Jahrhundert. Königstein/Ts. 1984 (Geschichte der deutschen Literatur von den Anfängen bis zum Beginn der Neuzeit 2/2).

Heisig, Karl. Deutscher Einfluß. In: PBB 86 (1964) 338-342.

Hellgardt, Ernst. Zur Poetik frühmittelhochdeutscher Dichtung. In: Klaus Grubmüller et.al. (Hgg.). Geistliche Denkformen in der Literatur des Mittelalters. München 1984 (Münstersche Mittelalter-Schriften 51).

Henkel, Nikolaus. Religiöses Erzählen um 1200 im Kontext höfischer Literatur. Priester Wernher, Konrad von Fussesbrunnen, Konrad von Heimesfurt. In: Jackson, Timothy R. et.al. (Hgg.) 1-21.

Herz, Martin. *Sacrum Commercium*. Eine begriffsgeschichtliche Studie zur Theologie der römischen Liturgiesprache. München 1958 (Münchner theologische Studien 15).

Hexen und Hexenverfolgung im deutschen Südwesten. Hg. Sönke Lorenz im Auftrag des Badischen Landesmuseums Karlsruhe und in Zusammenarbeit mit dem Institut für Geschichtliche Landeskunde und Historische Hilfswissenschaften der Universität Tübingen. Karlsruhe 1994 (Volkskundliche Veröffentlichungen des Badischen Landesmuseums Karlsruhe Bd. 2/1 und 2/2).

Holenstein, Pia. Der Ehediskurs in der Renaissance in Fischarts Geschichtklitterung. Kritische Lektüre des fünften Kapitels. Bern et.al. 1991 (Deutsche Literatur von den Anfängen bis 1700 10).

Hollywood, Amy. The Soul as Virgin Wife. Mechthild of Magdeburg, Marguerite Porete, and Meister Eckhart. Notre Dame 1995 (Studies in Spirituality and Theology Series Vol. 1).

Holmer, Shari. The Maiden, The Virgin, and Christ. In: Yearbook. Pedagogical Seminar for Germanic Philology 6 (1983) 5-13.

Hörberg, Norbert. *Libri sanctae Afrae*. Göttingen 1983 (Veröffentlichungen des Max Planck-Instituts für Geschichte 74. Studien zur Germania Sacra 15) 245-247.

Huston, Nancy / Kinser, Sam. À l'amour comme à la guerre. Paris 1984.

Ibarra Benlloch, Martín. Mulier fortis. La mujer en las fuentes cristianas (280-313). Zaragoza 1990 (Monografías de Historia Antigua 6).

Il matrimonio nella società altomedievale. 22-28 aprile 1976. 2 vols. Spoleto 1977 (Settimane di studio del Centro Italiano di Studi sull' alto medioevo 24).

Illich, Ivan. Genus. Zu einer historischen Kritik der Gleichheit. München ²1995.

Imkamp Wilhelm. Das Kirchenbild Innocenz' III. (1198-1216). Stuttgart 1983 (Päpste und Papsttum 22).

Irigaray, Luce. Speculum – Spiegel des anderen Geschlechts. Frankfurt a.M. 1980.

Jackson, Timothy R. Erotische Metaphorik und geistliche Dichtung. Bemerkungen zu Frauenlobs 'Marienleich'. In: Werner Schröder (Hg.): Wolfram-Studien 10. Cambridger 'Frauenlob'-Kolloquium 1986. Berlin 1988, 80-86.

Jackson, Timothy R. / Palmer, Nigel F. / Suerbaum Almut (Hgg.). Die Vermittlung geistlicher Inhalte im deutschen Mittelalter. Internationales Symposium Roscrea 1994. Tübingen 1996.

Jackson, Timothy R. Erotic imagery in medieval spiritual poetry and the hermeneutics of metaphor. In: Bernhard Debatin, Timothy R. Jackson and Daniel Steuer (Eds.): Metaphor and Rational Discourse. Tübingen 1997.

Jones, Martin H. Changing Perspectives in the Maiden in *Der arme Heinrich*. In: Timothy Mc Farland / Silvia Ranawake (Ed.). Hartmann von Aue. Changing Perspectives. Lodon Hartmann Syposium 1985. Göppingen 1988 (Göppinger Arbeiten zur Germanistik 486) 211-231.

Kälin, Beatrice. *Maria, muter der barmherzekeit*. Die Sünden und die Frommen in den Marienlegenden des Alten Passionals. Bern et.al. 1993 (Deutsche Literatur von den Anfängen bis 1700. Bd. 17).

Kartschoke, Dieter. Geschichte der deutschen Literatur im frühen Mittelalter. München 1990.

Kasten, Ingrid. Ehekonsens und Liebesheirat in Mai und Beaflor. In: Oxford German Studies 1993, 1-20.

Kasten, Ingrid. Formen des Narrativen in Mechthilds Fließendem Licht der Gottheit. In: Brinker, Claudia / Herzog, Urs / Largier, Niklaus / Michel, Paul (Hgg.) 1-18.

Kay, Sarah / Rubin, Miri (Eds.). Framing Medieval Bodies. Manchester / New York 1994.

Keller, Hildegard Elisabeth. Wort und Fleisch. Körperallegorien, mystische Spiritualität und Dichtung des St.Trudperter Hoheliedes im Horizont der Inkarnation. Bern et.al. 1993 (Deutsche Literatur von den Anfängen bis 1700 15).

Keller, Hildegard Elisabeth. Von handfestem Geist und durchsichtigem Fleisch. Impressionen aus der deutschsprachigen Hoheliedauslegung des 12. Jahrhunderts. Hg. Paul Michel. Bern 1995 (Schriften der Schweizerischen Gesellschaft für Symbolforschung 10) 121-137 [= 1995a].

Keller, Hildegard Elisabeth. *wan got geschuof inen nie schemeliche lide*. Zur Geschichte der Sexualität und Scham im Spiegel des "Fließenden Lichts der Gottheit" der Mechthild von Magdeburg. In: Brinker, Claudia / Herzog, Urs / Largier, Niklaus / Michel, Paul (Hgg.) 19-46 [= 1995b].

Keller, Hildegard Elisabeth. *Von dem toben und wüten, das wib und man mit ain ander hond*. Szenen weltlicher und spiritueller Ehen in "Christus und die minnende Seele". In: Jahrbuch der Oswald von Wolkenstein-Gesellschaft 9. Oswald und die Wende zur Neuzeit. 3.-6. Juni 1995 in Brixen/Südtirol (1996/1997) 341-359 [= 1997a].

Keller, Hildegard Elisabeth. Die *minnende Seele* in des *Teufels Netz*. Geschlechter-polemik kontrafaziert. In: Text im Kontext. Anleitung zur Lektüre deutscher Texte der frühen Neuzeit. Hg. Alexander Schwarz / Laure Abplanalp. Bern et.al. 1997 (Tausch 9) 109-126 [= 1997b].

Keller, Hildegard Elisabeth. *înluogen*. Blicke in den heimlichen Raum. Beispiele aus der deutschsprachigen Literatur des 12. bis 15. Jahrhunderts. Hg. Paul Michel, Bern 1997 (Schriften der Schweizerischen Gesellschaft für Symbolforschung 11) 353-376 [=1997c].

Keller, Hildegard Elisabeth. Von ehelicher Privation zu erotischer Privatheit? Allegorese der Geschlechterbeziehung. Ein Beitrag zu *Christus und die minnende Seele*. In: Melville, Gert / von Moos, Peter (Hgg.) 461-498 [= 1998a].

Keller, Hildegard Elisabeth. *Diu gewaltaerinne minne*. Von einer weiblichen Großmacht und der Semantik von Gewalt. In: Zeitschrift für deutsche Philologie 117 (1998) 17-37 [= 1998b].

Keller, Hildegard Elisabeth. Absonderungen. Mystische Texte als literarische Insze-nierung von Geheimnis. In: Deutsche Mystik im abendländischen Zusammenhang [= 2000].

Kellner, Beate. Gewalt und Minne. Zu Wahrnehmung, Körperkonzept und Ich-Rolle im Liedcorpus Heinrichs von Morungen. In: PBB (Beiträge zur Geschichte der Sprache und Literatur) 119 (1997) 33-66.

Kersting, Martin. Text und Bild im Werk Heinrich Seuses. Untersuchung zu den illus-trierten Handschriften des Exemplars. Diss. masch. Mainz 1987.

Kiening, Christian. Anthropologische Zugänge zur mittelalterlichen Literatur. Konzepte, Ansätze, Perspektiven. In: Hans-Jochen Schiewer (Hg.). Forschungs-berichte zur Germanistischen Mediävistik. Bd. C 5.1. Bern 1996.

Klinger, Cornelia. Beredtes Schweigen und verschwiegenes Sprechen. Genus im Diskurs der Philosophie. In: Bußmann, Hadumod / Hof, Renate (Hgg.) 34-59.

Köbele, Susanne. Bilder der unbegriffenen Wahrheit. Zur Struktur mystischer Rede im Spannungsfeld von Latein und Volkssprache. Tübingen / Basel 1993 (Bibliotheca Germanica 30).

Kohler, Erika. Liebeskrieg. Zur Bildersprache der höfischen Dichtung des Mittelalters. Stuttgart / Berlin 1935 (Tübinger germanistische Arbeiten 21).

Konrad, Bernd. Rudolf Stahel und seine Werkstatt. In: Jahrbuch der Staatlichen Kunst-sammlungen in Baden-Württemberg 26 (1989). München / Berlin 1989, 57-92.

Konrad, Bernd. Die Konstanzer Malerwerkstätten von 1500 bis zum Beginn der Refor-mation (1527). Diss. Freiburg i. Br. 1992.

Konrad, Bernd: Die Buchmalerei in Konstanz, am westlichen und am nördlichen Bodensee von 1400 bis zum Ende des 16. Jahrhunderts. In: Buchmalerei im Bodenseeraum. 13. bis 16. Jahrhundert. Hg. im Auftrag des Bodenseekreises von Eva Moser. Friedrichshafen 1997, 109-154.

Köpf Ulrich. Bernhard von Clairvaux in der Frauenmystik. In: Peter Dinzelbacher / Dieter R. Bauer (Hg.). Frauenmystik im Mittelalter. Stuttgart-Bad Cannstatt 1985, 48-77.

Köpf, Ulrich. Hoheliedauslegung als Quelle einer Theologie der Mystik. In: Margot Schmidt (Hg.) 1987, 50-72.

Krausch, Christiane. Art. Gewalt gegen Frauen. In: Europäische Enzyklopädie zu Philosophie und Wissenschaften. Hg. Hans Jörg Sandkühler. Bd. 2. Hamburg 1990, Sp. 447-454.

Kristeva, Julia. Tales of Love. New York 1989.

Kruse, Britta-Juliane. Verborgene Heilkünste. Geschichte der Frauenmedizin im Spät-mittelalter. Berlin/New York 1996 (Quellen und Forschungen zur Literatur- und Kulturgeschichte 5 [239]).

Küsters, Urban. Der verschlossene Garten. Volkssprachliche Hoheliedauslegung und monastische Lebensform im 12. Jahrhundert. Düsseldorf 1985 (Studia humaniora 2).

Lagorio, Valerie Marie. The Fourteenth-Century English Mystics. A Comprehensive Bibliography. New York 1981.

Laiou, Angeliki E. (ed.). Consent and Coercion to Sex and Marriage in Ancient and Medieval Societies. Washington D.C. 1993.

Largier, Niklaus. Der Körper der Schrift. In: Mittelalter. Neue Wege durch einen alten Kontinent. Hg. Jan-Dirk Müller / Horst Wenzel. Stuttgart 1999.

Lautenschläger Gabriele. Hildegard von Bingen. Die theologische Grundlegung ihrer Ethik und Spiritualität. Stuttgart-Bad Cannstatt 1993.

Le Jardin clos de l'âme. L'imaginaire des religieuses dans les Pays-Bas du Sud, depuis le 13e siècle. Paul Vandenbroeck avec des contributions de Luce Irigaray, Julia Kristeva, Birgit Pelzer et d'autres. Société des Expositions. Palais des Beaux-Arts de Bruxelles. 25 février – 22 mai 1994. Brüssel 1994.

Le Moyen Age. Ouvrage préparé par Robert Bossuat, Louis Pichard et Guy Raynaud de Lage. Édition entièrement revue et mise à jour sous la direction de Geneviève Hasenohr et Michel Zink. Paris 1964.

Lechner, Gregor Martin. Maria Gravida. Zum Schwangerschaftsmotiv in der bildenden Kunst. München / Zürich 1981.

Leclercq, Jean. The Love of Learning and the Desire for God. A Study of Monastic Culture. 2nd edn. London 1978.

Leclercq, Jean. Monks on Marriage, a Twelfth-Century View. New York 1982.

Leisegang Hans. Pneuma Hagion. Der Ursprung des Geistbegriffs der synoptischen Evangelien aus der griechischen Mystik. Leipzig 1922.

Lentes, Thomas. Vita Perfecta zwischen Vita Communis und Vita Privata. Eine Skizze zur klösterlichen Einzelzelle. In: Melville, Gert / von Moos Peter (Hgg.) 125-164.

Lerchner, Karin. Lectulus floridus. Zur Bedeutung des Bettes in Literatur und Hand-schriftenillustration des Mittelalters. Köln et.al. 1993 (Pictura et Poesis 6).

Lewis, Gertrud Jaron (Hg.). Bibliographie der deutschen Frauenmystik des Mittelalters.

Mit einem Anhang zu Beatrijs von Nazareth und Hadewijch von F. Willaert und M.J. Govers. Berlin 1989 (Bibliographien zur deutschen Literatur des Mittelalters 10).

Lexer, Matthias. Mittelhochdeutsches Handwörterbuch. Nachdruck der Ausgabe Leipzig 1872-1878 mit einer Einleitung von Kurt Gärtner. 3 Bde. Stuttgart 1992.

Lexikon der christlichen Ikonographie. 8 vols. Ed. Engelbert Kirschbaum et.al. Rom 1968-1976.

Lexikon des Mittelalters. Hg. Robert Auty et.al. München / Zürich 1980-98.

Lexikon für Theologie und Kirche. Hg. Josef Höfer / Karl Rahner. 2., völlig neu bearb. Aufl. 10 Bde. und Register-Bd. Freiburg 1957-1967.

Liebesfreuden im Mittelalter. Kulturgeschichte der Erotik und Sexualität im Mittelalter. Hg. Gabriele Bartz / Alfred Karnein und Claudio Lange, Stuttgart / Zürich 1994.

Link, Luther. The Devil: a Mask without a Face. London 1994.

Lochrie, Karma. Margery Kempe and the Translation of the Flesh. Philadelphia 1991.

Lüers, Grete. Die Sprache der deutschen Mystik des Mittelalters im Werke der Mechthild von Magdeburg. München 1926.

Lullies, Reinhard. Die Kauernde Aphrodite. München 1954.

Lundt, Bea. Der Inhalt ist recht wundersam. Alltagserfahrung und Geschlechtsidentität in den 'Miracula' des Caesarius von Heisterbach. In: Das Wunderbare in der mittel-alterlichen Literatur. Hg. Dietrich Schmidtke. Göppingen 1994 (Göppinger Arbeiten zur Germanistik 606) 137-171.

Lutz, Eckart Conrad. Spiritualis fornicatio. Heinrich Wittenwiler, seine Welt und sein 'Ring'. Sigmaringen 1990 (Konstanzer Geschichts- und Rechtsquellen 32).

MacDonald, Margaret Y.. Early Christian Women and Pagan Opinion. The Power of Hysterical Woman. Cambridge 1996.

Manlichiu wîp, wîplich man. Zur Konstruktion der Kategorien 'Körper' und 'Geschlecht' in der deutschen Literatur des Mittelalters. Hg. Ingrid Bennewitz und Helmut Tervooren (Beihefte zur Zeitschrift für deutsche Philologie 9 [1999]).

Marenbon, John. The Philosophy of Peter Abelard. Cambridge 1997.

Masser, Achim. Bibel, Apokryphen und Legenden. Geburt und Kindheit Jesu in der religiösen Epik des deutschen Mittelalters. Berlin 1969.

Masser, Achim. Bibel- und Legendenepik des deutschen Mittelalters. Berlin 1976 (Grundlagen der Germanistik 19).

Matter, Ann E. The Voice of My Beloved. The Song of Songs in Western Medieval Chris-tianity. Philadelphia 1990.

Matter, Ann E. Il matrimonio mistico. In: Donne e fede. Santità e vita religiosa in Italia, a cura di Lucetta Scaraffia e Gabriella Zarri. Roma 1994, 43-60.

Mazzucco, Clementina. "E fui fatta maschio". La donna nel Christianesimo primitivo (secolo I-III). Firenze 1989 (Fondo di Studi Parini-Chirio, Letterature 1).

McGinn, Bernard. The Foundations of Mysticism. Origins to the Fifth Century. New York 1991.

McGinn, Bernard. "With the Kisses of the Mouth". Recent Work in the Song of Songs. In: Journal of Religion 72 (1992) 269-275 [= 1992a]

McGinn, Bernard. The Language of Love in Jewish and Christian Mysticism. In: Mys-ticism and Language. Ed. by Steven Katz, New York 1992, S. 202-35 [=1992b].

McGinn, Bernard. Mysticism and Sexuality. In: The Way. Supplement 77 (1993) 46-53.

McGinn, Bernard (Ed.). Meister Eckhart and the Beguine Mystics. Hadewijch of Bra-
bant, Mechthild of Magdeburg and Marguerite Porete. New York 1994 [= 1994a].

McGinn, Bernard. The Growth of Mysticism. Gregory the Great to the Twelfth Century. New York 1994 [= 1994b].

McGinn, Bernard. God as Eros. Metaphysical Foundations of Christian Mysticism. In:
New Perspectives on Historical Theology. Essays in Memory of John Meyendorff.
Ed. Bradley Nassif. Grand Rapids 1996, 189-209.

McGinn, Bernard. Tropics of Desire. Mystical Interpretation of the Song of Songs. In:
That Others May Know and Love. Essays in Honor of Zachary Hayes OFM. Ed.
Michael F. Cusato / Edward Coughlin. St. Bonaventure 1997, 133-158.

McGinn, Bernard. The Flowering of Mysticism. Men and Women in the New Mysticism (1200-1350). New York 1998 [=1998a].

McGinn, Bernard. Visions and Critiques of Visions in Thirteenth-Century Mysticism.
In: Rending the Veil. Ed. Elliot R. Wolfson. Spring Hill 1998, 117-142 [=1998b].

Meier, Christel. Wendepunkte der Allegorie im Mittelalter: Von der Schrifthermeneu-
tik zur Lebenspraktik, in: Robert E. Lerner unter Mitarbeit von Elisabeth Müller-
Luckner (Hg.). Neue Richtungen in der hoch-und spätmittelalterlichen Bibelex-
egese. München 1996 (Schriften des Historischen Kollegs 32), 39-64.

Meier, Christel / Ruberg, Uwe (Hgg.). Text und Bild. Aspekte des Zusammenwirkens
zweier Künste in Mittelalter und Neuzeit. Wiesbaden 1980.

Meier, Christel. Überlegungen zum gegenwärtigen Stand der Allegorieforschung. In:
Frühmittelalterliche Studien 10 (1976) 1-69.

Meier, Christel. Von der Privatoffenbarung zur öffentlichen Lehrbefugnis. Legitima-
tionsstufen des Prophetentums bei Rupert von Deutz, Hildegard von Bingen und
Elisabeth von Schönau. In: Melville, Gert / von Moos Peter (Hgg.) 97-124 [= 1998].

Melville, Gert/von Moos, Peter (Hgg.). Das Öffentliche und Private in der Vormod-
erne. Köln et.al. 1998 (Norm und Struktur. Studien zum sozialen Wandel in Mittelalter und Früher Neuzeit 10).

Mertens, Volker. Gregorius Eremita. Eine Lebensform des Adels bei Hartmann von Aue
in ihrer Problematik und ihrer Wandlung in der Rezeption. München / Zürich 1978
(Münchner Texte und Untersuchungen 78).

Messerer, Wilhelm. Illustrationen zu Wernhers 'Drei Liedern von der Magd'. In: Deutsche
Literatur im Mittelalter. Hugo Kuhn zum Gedenken. Stuttgart 1979, 447-472.

Messikommer, Hans. Die Auferstehungssekte und ihr Goldschatz. Ein Beitrag zur Sek-
tiererei im zürcherischen Oberlande. Zürich 1908.

Metz, René. La consécration des vierges dans l'église romaine. Etude d'histoire de la
liturgie romaine. Paris 1954.

Michel, Paul. 'Durch die bilde über die bilde'. Zur Bildgestaltung bei Mechthild von
Magdeburg. In: Abendländische Mystik. Hg. Kurt Ruh. Stuttgart 1986, 508-526.

Michel, Paul. Alieniloquium. Elemente einer Grammatik der Bildrede. Bern et.al. 1987
(Zürcher Germanistische Studien 3).

Michel, Paul. Etymologie als mittelalterliche Linguistik. In: Alexander Schwarz / Linke,
Angelika / Michel, Paul / Scholz Williams, Gerhild (Hgg.). Alte Texte lesen. Bern
et.al. 1988, 207-260.

Michel, Paul. *Quomodo amor excitet animam pigram.* Ein Dialog im Fließenden Licht Mechthilds von Magdeburg. In: Brinker, Claudia / Herzog, Urs / Largier, Niklaus / Michel, Paul (Hgg.), 47-70.

Mommaers, Paul. Was ist Mystik? Frankfurt a.M. 1979.

Morris, Colin. The Discovery of the Individual 1050-1200. New York et.al. 1972 / Toronto et.al. ²1987.

Müller, Maria E. (Hg.). Eheglück und Liebesjoch. Bilder von Liebe, Ehe und Familie in der Literatur des 15. und 16. Jahrhunderts. Weinheim/Basel 1988.

Müller, Maria E. Jungfräulichkeit in Versepen des 12. und 13. Jahrhunderts. München 1995 (Forschungen zur Geschichte der älteren deutschen Literatur 17).

Müller, Markus. Französische Minnedarstellungen des 13. und 14. Jahrhunderts. Köln et.al. 1996.

Müller, Ulrich (Hg.). Hartmann von Aue. Der arme Heinrich. Materialien und Abbildungen zur gesamten handschriftlichen Überlieferung. Stuttgart 1971 (Litterae 3).

Müller, Ulrich. Mechthild von Magdeburg und Dantes 'Vita Nova' oder Erotische Religiosität und religiöse Erotik. In: Liebe als Literatur. Aufsätze zur erotischen Dichtung in Deutschland. Hg. Rüdiger Krohn. München 1983, 163-176.

Murk-Jansen / Saskia M. The Use of Gender and Gender-Related Imagery in Hadewijch. In: Chance, Jane (Ed.). Gender and Text in the Later Middle Ages. Gainesville et.al. 1996, 52-68.

Murray, Jacqueline / Eisenbichler, Konrad (Eds.). Desire and Discipline. Sex and Sexuality in the Premodern West. Toronto/Buffalo/London 1996.

Newman, Barbara. From Virile Woman to Woman Christ. Studies in Medieval Religion and Literature. Philadelphia 1995.

Ohly, Friedrich. Der Prolog des 'St.Trudperter Hohenliedes'. Zeitschrift für deutsches Altertum 84 (1953) 198-232.

Ohly, Friedrich. Hohelied-Studien. Grundzüge einer Geschichte der Hohelied-Auslegung des Abendlandes bis um ca. 1200. Wiesbaden 1958.

Ohly, Friedrich. Schriften zur mittelalterlichen Bedeutungsforschung. Darmstadt 1977.

Ohly, Friedrich. Gebärden der Liebe zwischen Gott und Mensch im St.Trudperter Hohenlied. In: Literaturwissenschaftliches Jahrbuch 34/1993, 9-31 (also in: Friedrich Ohly 1995) [=1993].

Ohly, Friedrich: Die Trinität berät über die Erschaffung des Menschen und über seine Erlösung. In: PBB 116 (1994) 242-284.

Ohly, Friedrich. Ausgewählte und neue Schriften zur Literaturgeschichte und zur Bedeutungsforschung. Stuttgart / Leipzig 1995.

Opitz, Claudia. Evatöchter und Bräute Christi. Weiblicher Lebenszusammenhang und Frauenkultur. Weinheim 1990.

Palmer, Nigel F. Das Buch als Bedeutungsträger bei Mechthild von Magdeburg. In: Wolfgang Harms / Klaus Speckenbach (Hgg.). Bildhafte Rede in Mittelalter und früher Neuzeit. Probleme ihrer Legitimation und ihrer Funktion. Tübingen 1992, 217-235.

Panofsky, Erwin. Studien zur Ikonologie. Humanistische Themen in der Kunst der Renaissance. Köln 1980.

Partner, Nancy F. Did Mystics Have Sex? in: Jacqueline Murray / Konrad Eisenbichler (Eds.), 296-311.

Paschold, Chris E. Die Frau und ihr Körper im medizinischen und didaktischen Schrifttum des französischen Mittelalters. Pattensen 1989 (Würzburger medizinhistorische Forschungen 47).

Pellegrini, Giovan Battista. Terminologia matrimoniale. In: Il matrimonio nella società altomedievale, 43-91.

Persson, Inga. Ehe und Zeichen. Studien zu Eheschließung und Ehepraxis anhand der frühmittelhochdeutschen religiösen Lehrdichtungen "Vom Rechte", "Hochzeit", und "Schopf von dem lône". Göppingen 1995 (Göppinger Arbeiten zur Germanistik 617).

Peters, Ursula. Religiöse Erfahrung als literarisches Faktum. Zur Vorgeschichte und Genese frauenmystischer Texte des 13. und 14. Jahrhunderts. Tübingen 1988 (Hermaea NF 56).

Pichler, Gerd / Reichert, Hermann. Neue Fragmente von Priester Wernhers 'Maria'. In: Zeitschrift für deutsches Altertum 2 (1996) 202-8.

Raurell Frederic. El càntic dels càntics en els segles XII-XIII. Lectura de Clara d'Assís. Facultat de Teologia de Catalunya. Associació bíblica de Catalunya. Barcelona 1990.

Reallexikon für Antike und Christentum. Sachwörterbuch zur Auseinandersetzung des Christentums mit der antiken Welt. Hg. Theodor Klauser. Stuttgart 1950ff.

Regensburger Buchmalerei. Von frühkarolingischer Zeit bis zum Ausgang des Mittelalters. Ausstellung der Bayerischen Staatsbibliothek München und der Museen der Stadt Regensburg. Katalogredaktion F. Mütherich / K. Dachs. München 1987.

Reicke, Siegfried. Geschichtliche Grundlagen des deutschen Eheschließungsrechts. In: Weltliche und kirchliche Eheschließung. Beiträge zur Frage des Eheschließungsrechtes. Hg. Adolf Dombois / Friedrich Karl Schumann. Gladbeck 1953 (Glaube und Forschung 6) 27-62.

Reitinger, Franz. Schüsse, die ihn nicht erreichten. Eine Motivgeschichte des Gottesattentats. Paderborn et.al. 1997.

Religion and the Body. Ed. Sarah Coakley. Cambridge 1997 (Cambridge Studies in Religious Traditions, Vol. 8).

Ricœur, Paul. La métaphore nuptiale. In: André Lacocque / Paul Ricœur (éds.). Penser la Bible. Paris 1998, 411-457.

Rinaldi, Mavi. "… und la mich fúrbas sinken dur din ere". Das Bild des Sinkens im Fließenden Licht der Gottheit der Mechthild von Magdeburg. Diss. Zürich 1986.

Ringler, Siegfried. Viten- und Offenbarungsliteratur in Frauenklöstern des Mittelalters. Quellen und Studien. Zürich / München 1980 (Münchner Texte und Untersuchungen 72).

Ritter-Santini, Lea. Der goldene und der bleierne Pfeil. Die Wunde der Nymphe Daphne. In: Jahrbuch der deutschen Schiller-Gesellschaft 16 (1972) 659-688.

Roper Lyndal. Oedipus and the Devil. Witchcraft, sexuality and religion in early modern Europe. London 1994.

Rosenfeld, Hans-Friedrich / Rosenfeld, Hellmut. Deutsche Kultur im Spätmittelalter. Wiesbaden 1978.

Rosenfeld, Hellmut. Der mittelalterliche Bilderbogen. In: Zeitschrift für deutsches Altertum 85 (1953) 66-75.

Ruh, Kurt. Hartmanns "Armer Heinrich". Erzählmodell und theologische Implikation. In: *Mediaevalia litteraria*. Festschrift für Helmut de Boor. München 1971, 315-329.

Ruh, Kurt. Geschichte der abendländischen Mystik. Zweiter Band. Frauenmystik und Franziskanische Mystik der Frühzeit. München 1993.

Ruhe, Doris. Etappen der Domestizierung. Geschlechterrollen im französischen Exemplum des Spätmittelalters. In: Archiv für das Studium der neueren Sprachen und Literaturen 231 (1994) 72-90.

Ruhrberg, Christine. Der literarische Körper der Heiligen. Leben und Viten der Christina von Stommeln (1242-1312). Tübingen / Basel 1995 (Bibliotheca Germanica 35).

Rupprich, Hans. Die deutsche Literatur vom späten Mittelalter bis zum Barock. Zweiter Teil. Das Zeitalter der Reformation 1520-1570. München 1973 (Geschichte der deutschen Literatur IV/2).

Rush, Alfred C.. Death as a Spiritual Marriage. Individual and Ecclesial Eschatology. In: Vigiliae Christianae 26 (1972) 81-101.

Salzer, Anselm. Die Sinnbilder und Beiworte Mariens in der deutschen Literatur und lateinischen Hymnenprosa. Mit Berücksichtigung der patristischen Literatur. Eine literarhistorische Studie. Darmstadt 1967.

Sauer-Geppert, Waldtraut-Ingeborg. Wörterbuch zum St.Trudperter Hohen Lied. Ein Beitrag zur Sprache der mittelalterlichen Mystik. Berlin / New York 1972 (Quellen und Forschungen zur Sprach- und Kulturgeschichte der germanischen Völker 50 [174]).

Saxl, Fritz et.al. (Ed.). Catalogue of Astrological and Mythological Illuminated Manuscripts of the Latin Middle Ages. 2 vols. London 1953.

Schabert, Ina. Gender als Kategorie einer neuen Literaturgeschichtsschreibung. In: Hadumod Bußmann/Renate Hof (Hgg.) 162-204.

Schade, Sigrid / Wagner, Monika / Weigel, Sigrid (Hgg.). Allegorien und Geschlechterdifferenz. Köln et.al. 1994 (Literatur – Kultur – Geschlecht 3).

Scheper George L. The Spiritual Marriage. The Exegetic History and Literary Impact of the Song of Songs in the Middle Ages. Diss. Princeton Unversity. Ann Arbor 1971.

Scheper George L. Reformation Attitudes toward Allegory and the Song of Songs. In: PMLA 89 (1974) 551-562.

Schiess Emil. Die Hexenprozesse und das Gerichtswesen im Lande Appenzell im 15.-17. Jahrhundert. Trogen / Schweiz 1920.

Schiewer, Hans-Jochen. Auditionen und Visionen einer Begine. Die 'Selige Schererin', Johannes Mulberg und der Basler Beginenstreit. Mit einem Textabdruck. In: Timothy R. Jackson et.al. (Hgg.) 1996, 289-317.

Schimmel, Annemarie. Wie universal ist die Mystik? Die Seelenreise in den großen Religionen der Welt. Freiburg i. Br. 1996.

Schleusener-Eichholz, Gudrun. Biblische Namen und ihre Etymologie. In: *Verbum et Signum*, 267-293.

Schleusener-Eichholz, Gudrun. Das Auge im Mittelalter. München 1985 (Münstersche Mittelalter-Schriften 35/I und II).

Schmidt, Margot/Bauer, Dieter (Hg.). "Eine Höhe, über die nichts geht". Spezielle Glaubenserfahrung in der Frauenmystik? Stuttgart-Bad Cannstatt 1986 (Mystik in Geschichte und Gegenwart 4).

Schmidt, Margot / Bauer, Dieter (Hg.). Grundfragen christlicher Mystik. Wissenschaftliche Studientagung Theologica mystica in Weingarten vom 7.-10. November 1985. Stuttgart-Bad Cannstatt 1987 (Mystik in Geschichte und Gegenwart 5).

Schmidt, Margot. "Die spilende minnevlût". Der Eros als Sein und Wirkkraft in der Trinität bei Mechthild von Magdeburg. In: Margot Schmidt / Dieter Bauer (Hg.) 1986, 71-133.

Schmidt, Margot. "Frau Pein, ihr seid mein nächstes Kleid". Zur Leidensmystik im 'Fließenden Licht der Gottheit' der Mechthild von Magdeburg. In: Gotthard Fuchs (Hg.), 63-107.

Schmidt, Margot. "minne dú gewaltige kellerin". On the nature of minne in Mechthild of Magdeburg's *fliessendes lieht der gotheit*. In: Vox Benedictina 4 (1987) 100-125.

Schmidt, Margot. Versinnlichte Transzendenz bei Mechthild von Magdeburg. In: Dietrich Schmidtke (Hg.) 61-88.

Schmidtke, Dietrich (Hg.). "Minnichlichiu gotes erkennnusse". Studien zur frühen abendländischen Mystiktradition. Stuttgart-Bad Cannstatt 1990 (Mystik in Geschichte und Gegenwart 7).

Schmökel, Luis Alonso. I nomi dell' amore. Simboli matrimoniali nella Bibbia. Casale Monferrato 1997.

Schnell, Rüdiger. Andreas Capellanus. Zur Rezeption des römischen und kanonischen Rechts in *De Amore*. München 1982 (Münstersche Mittelalter-Schriften 46).

Schnell, Rüdiger. Der Frauenexkurs in Gottfrieds Tristan (V. 17858-18114). In: Zeitschrift für deutsche Philologie 113 (1984) 1-26 [= 1984a].

Schnell, Rüdiger. Literatur als Korrektiv sozialer Realität. Zur Eheschließung in mittelalterlichen Dichtungen. In: *Non nova, sed nove*. Mélanges de civilisation médiévale dédiés à Willem Noomen. Hg. Martin Gosman / Jaap van Os. Groningen 1984 (Mediaevalia Groningana 5) 225-238 [=1984b].

Schnell, Rüdiger. *Causa Amoris*. Liebeskonzeption und Liebesdarstellung in der mittelalterlichen Literatur. Bern/München 1985 (Bibliotheca Germanica 27).

Schnell, Rüdiger (Hg.). *Gotes und der werlde hulde*. Literatur in Mittelalter und Neuzeit. Bern / Stuttgart 1989.

Schnell, Rüdiger. Liebesdiskurs und Ehediskurs im 15. und 16. Jahrhundert. In: The Graph of Sex and the German Text. Gendered Culture in Early Modern Germany 1500-1700. Ed. Lynne Tatlock. Amsterdam 1994 (Chloe. Beihefte zum Daphnis. 19) 77-120 [= 1994a].

Schnell, Rüdiger. Unterwerfung und Herrschaft. Zum Liebesdiskurs im Hochmittelalter. In: Joachim Heinzle (Hg.). Modernes Mittelalter. Bilder einer populären Epoche. Frankfurt a.M. / Leipzig 1994, 103-133 [= 1994b].

Schnell, Rüdiger (Hg.). Text und Geschlecht. Mann und Frau in Eheschriften der frühen Neuzeit. Frankfurt a.M. 1997.

Schnell, Rüdiger (Hg.). Geschlechterbeziehungen und Textfunktionen. Studien zu Eheschriften der Frühen Neuzeit. Tübingen 1998 [= 1998a].

Schnell, Rüdiger. Frauendiskurs, Männerdiskurs, Ehediskurs. Frankfurt a.M. / New York 1998 [=1998b].

Schnell, Rüdiger. Die 'Offenbarmachung' der Geheimnisse Gottes und die 'Verheimlichung' der Geheimnisse der Menschen. Zum prozeßhaften Charakter des Öffentlichen und Privaten. In: Melville, Gert / von Moos, Peter (Hgg.) 359-410. [=1998c].

Scholem, Gershom. Die jüdische Mystik in ihren Hauptströmungen. Zürich 1957.

Scholem, Gershom. Zur Kabbala und ihrer Symbolik. Zürich 1960.

Scholz Williams, Gerhild. Defining Dominion. The Discourses of Magic and Witchcraft in Early Modern France and Germany. Ann Arbor 1995. *German translation: Hexen und Herrschaft. Die Diskurse der Magie und Hexerei im frühneuzeitlichen Frankreich und Deutschland. Aus dem Amerikanischen übersetzt von Christiane Bohnert. Überarb. Neuausgabe. München 1998.*

Schreiner, Klaus. "Er küsse mich mit dem Kuß seines Mundes" (*Osculetur me osculo oris sui*, Cant 1,1). Metaphorik, kommunikative und herrschaftliche Funktionen einer symbolischen Handlung. In: Hedda Ragotzky / Horst Wenzel (Hgg.). Höfische Repräsentation. Das Zeremoniell und die Zeichen. Tübingen 1990, 89-132.

Schreiner, Klaus / Schnitzler, Norbert (Hgg.). Gepeinigt, begehrt, vergessen. Symbolik und Sozialbezug des Körpers im späten Mittelalter und in der frühen Neuzeit. München 1991.

Schreiner, Klaus. Maria. Jungfrau Mutter Herrscherin. München et.al. 1994.

Schreiner, Klaus. "Deine Brüste sind süßer als Wein". Ikonographie, religiöse Bedeutung und soziale Funktion eines Mariensymbols. In: *Pictura quasi fictura*. Die Rolle eines Bildes in der Erforschung von Alltag und Sachkultur des Mittelalters und der frühen Neuzeit. Wien 1996 (Forschungen des Instituts für Realienkunde des Mittelalters und der frühen Neuzeit. Diskussionen und Materialien 1) 87-127.

Schröter, Michael. "Wo zwei zusammenkommen in rechter Ehe...". Sozio- und psychogenetische Studien über Eheschließungsvorgänge vom 12. bis 15. Jahrhundert. Frankfurt a.M. 1990.

Schubart, Walter. Religion und Eros. Hg. Friedrich Seifert. München 1941 / ²1966.

Schumacher, Marlis. Die Auffassung der Ehe in den Dichtungen Wolframs von Eschenbach. Heidelberg 1967.

Schumacher, Meinolf. Sündenschmutz und Herzensreinheit. Studien zur Metaphorik der Sünde in lateinischer und deutscher Literatur des Mittelalters. München 1996 (Münstersche Mittelalter-Schriften 73).

Schumacher, Meinolf. Annette von Droste-Hülshoff und die Tradition. Das 'Geistliche Jahr' in literarhistorischer Sicht. In: Dialoge mit der Droste. Hg. Ernst Ribbat. Paderborn et.al. 1998, 113-145.

Schumacher, Meinolf. Ein Wüstenherold für die Noth. Zu Pragmatik und Aktualität von Annette von Droste-Hülshoffs 'Geistlichem Jahr' In: Droste-Jahrbuch 5 (in press).

Schweizer-Vüllers, Regine: Die Heilige am Kreuz. Studien zum weiblichen Gottesbild im späten Mittelalter und in der Barockzeit. Bern et.al. 1997 (Deutsche Literatur von den Anfängen bis 1700, 26).

Schwert in Frauenhand – Weibliche Bewaffnung. Hg. Gabriele Frohnhaus / Barbara Grotkamp-Schepers / Renate Philipp. Ausstellungskatalog Deutsches Klingenmuseum. Essen 1998.

Scribner, Robert. Vom Sakralbild zur sinnlichen Schau. Sinnliche Wahrnehmung und das Visuelle bei der Objektivierung des Frauenkörpers in Deutschland im 16. Jahrhundert. In: Schreiner/Schnitzler (Hgg.) 1991, 309-336.

Seiffert, Leslie. The maiden's heart. Legend and fairy-tale in Hartmanns *Der arme Heinrich*. Deutsche Vierteljahresschrift 37 (1963) 384-405.

Seznec, Jean. The survival of the pagan god. New York 1953 (Studies of the Warburg Institute XI. Bollingen Series XXXVIII).

Singer, Irving. The Nature of Love. Vol. 1-3. Chicago 1984-1987.

Smith, Susan L. The Power of Women. A *Topos* in Medieval Art and Literature. Philadelphia 1995.

Smits, Kathryn. Enite als christliche Ehefrau. In: Interpretation und Edition deutscher Texte des Mittelalters. Festschrift John Asher zum 60. Geburtstag. Berlin 1981, 13-25.

Smits, Kathryn. Bemerkungen zu den Motiven der Diesseitsflucht und Eheflucht im "Armen Heinrich" Hartmanns von Aue. In: Festschrift Siegfried Grosse. Göppingen 1984.

Spearing, Anthony Colin. The Medieval Poet as Voyeur. Looking and Listening in Medieval Love-Narratives. Cambridge 1993.

Speculum 68 (1993). Studying Medieval Women. Sex, Gender, Feminism.

Spitz, Hans-Jörg. Zur Lokalisierung des St.Trudperter Hohenliedes im Frauenkloster Admont. In: Zeitschrift für deutsches Altertum 121 (1992) 174-177.

Spitz, Hans-Jörg. *ez ist sanc aller sange*. Das >St.Trudperter Hohelied< zwischen Kommentar und Dichtung. In: Honemann, Volker / Tomasek, Tomas (Hgg.). Germanistische Mediävistik. Münster 1999, 61-88.

Spreitzer, Brigitte. Störfälle. Zur Konstruktion, Destruktion und Rekonstruktion von Geschlechterdifferenz(en) im Mittelalter. In: *Manlîchiu wîp, wîplich man*, 249-263.

Stackmann, Karl. Magd und Königin. Deutsche Mariendichtung des Mittelalters. Göttingen 1988 (Bursfelder Universitätsreden 7).

Stahlmann, Ines. Jenseits der Weiblichkeit. Geschlechtergeschichtliche Aspekte des frühchristlichen Askeseideals. In: Was sind Frauen? Was sind Männer? Geschlechterkonstruktionen im historischen Wandel. Hg. Christiane Eifert et.al. Frankfurt a.M. 1996, 51-75.

Stammler, Wolfgang. Frau Welt. Eine mittelalterliche Allegorie. Freiburg /Schweiz 1959 (Freiburger Universitätsreden, NF 23).

Stargardt, Ute. Male Clerical Authority in the Spiritual (Auto)biographies of Medieval Holy Women. In: Women as Protagonists, 209-233.

Strauch, Gabriele L. Mechthild of Magdeburg and the Category of Frauenmystik. In: Women as Protagonists, 171-186.

Szarmach, Paul E. (Ed.). An Introduction to the Medieval Mystics of Europe. Fourteen Original Essays. Albany 1984.

Teuber, Bernhard. *Allegoria apophatica*. Über negative Theologie und erotischen Exzess bei Dionysius Areopagita, San Juan de la Cruz und José Lezama Lima. In: Studies in Spirituality 3 (1993) 213-247.

Thomas, Cramer. Geschichte der deutschen Literatur im späten Mittelalter. München 1990.

Tinkle, Theresa. Medieval Venuses and Cupids. Sexuality, Hermeneutics, and English Poetry. Stanford 1996.

Tobin, Frank. Mechthild von Magdeburg. A Medieval Mystic in Modern Eyes. Columbia 1995.

Tobler, Eva. *daz er sî sîn gemahel hiez*. Zum Armen Heinrich Hartmanns von Aue. In: Euphorion 81 (1987) 315-329.

Tomalin, Margaret. The Fortunes of the Warrior Heroine in Italian Literature. An Index of Emancipation. Ravenna 1982.

Turner, Denys. Eros and Allegory. Medieval Exegesis of the Song of Songs. Kalamazoo 1995.

Uitz, Erika. Die Frau in der mittelalterlichen Stadt. Stuttgart 1988.

Vance, Eugène. Le combat érotique chez Chrétien de Troyes. De la figure à la forme. In: Poétique 12 (1972) 544-71.

Verbum et Signum. Erster Band. Beiträge zur mediävistischen Bedeutungsforschung. Hg. Hans Fromm, Wolfgang Harms und Uwe Ruberg. München 1995.

Vogt, Kari. "Männlichwerden" – Aspekte einer urchristlichen Anthropologie. In: Concilium. Internationale Zeitschrift für Theologie 21 (1985).

Vollmann-Profe, Gisela. Mechthild – auch "in Werktagskleidern". Zu berühmten und weniger berühmten Abschnitten des "Fließenden Lichts der Gottheit". In: Zeitschrift für deutsche Philologie 113 (1994) Sonderheft Mystik, 144-158.

Vollmann-Profe, Gisela. Wiederbeginn im hohen Mittelalter. Königstein/Ts. 1986 (Geschichte der deutschen Literatur von den Anfängen bis zum Beginn der Neuzeit, 1/2).

von Arb, Giorgio / Lehmann, Norbert / Vogler, Werner (Hgg.). Klosterleben. Klausur-Frauenklöster der Ostschweiz. Zürich 1993.

von Flemming, Victoria. Arma Amoris. Sprachbild und Bildsprache der Liebe. Kardinal Scipione Borghese und die Gemäldezyklen Francesco Albanis. Mainz 1997 (Berliner Schriften zur Kunst 6).

von Koppenfels, Werner. Esca et hamus. Beitrag zu einer historischen Liebesmetaphorik. München 1973.

von Moos, Peter. Consolatio. Studien zur mittellateinischen Trostliteratur über den Tod und zum Problem der christlichen Trauer. München 1972 (Münstersche Mittelalter-Schriften 3/I-III).

von Moos, Peter. Occulta cordis. Contrôle de soi et confession au Moyen Age. In: Médiévales 29 (1995) 131-140 / 30 (1996) 117-137.

von Moos, Peter. 'Herzensgeheimnisse' (occulta cordis). Selbstbewahrung und Selbstentblößung im Mittelalter. In: Aleida und Jan Assmann (Hgg.) 1997, 89-109 [=1997a].

von Moos, Peter. Heloise und Abaelard. Eine Liebesgeschichte vom 13. zum 20. Jahrhundert. In: Mittelalter und Moderne. Entdeckung und Rekonstruktion der mittelalterlichen Welt. Hg. Peter Segl. Sigmaringen 1997, 77-90 [=1997b].

von Moos, Peter. Das Öffentliche und das Private im Mittelalter. Für einen kontrollierten Anachronismus. In: Melville, Gert / von Moos, Peter (Hgg.) 3-83 [=1998].

Wack, Mary Frances. Lovesickness in the Middle Ages. The 'Viaticum' and its Commentaries. Philadelphia 1990.

Wallmann, Johannes. Bernhard von Clairvaux und der deutsche Pietismus. In: Bernhard von Clairvaux. Rezeption und Wirkung im Mittelalter und in der Neuzeit. Hg. Kaspar Elm. Wiesbaden 1994, 345-374.

Walter, Gödden. Tag für Tag im Leben der Annette von Droste-Hülshoff. Paderborn 1996.

Watt, Diane. Secretaries of God. Rochester 1999.

Weber, Hermann J. Die Lehre von der Auferstehung der Toten in den Haupttraktaten der scholastischen Theologie. Freiburg et.al. 1973 (Freiburger theologische Studien 91).

Wehrli, Max. Geschichte der deutschen Literatur. Vom frühen Mittelalter bis zum Ende des 16. Jahrhunderts. Stuttgart ²1984.

Weigel, Sigrid / Stephan, Inge. Die verborgene Frau. Sechs Beiträge zu einer feministischen Literaturwissenschaft. Hamburg 1988 (Literatur im historischen Prozess N.F.6=Argument-Sonderband 96].

Weigel, Sigrid. Die Stimme der Medusa. Schreibweisen in der Gegenwartsliteratur von Frauen. Reinbek bei Hamburg 1989.

Weigel, Sigrid. Topographie der Geschlechter. Kulturgeschichtliche Studien zur Literatur. Reinbek bei Hamburg 1990.

Weigel, Sigrid. Geschlechterdifferenz und Literaturwissenschaft. In: The Graph of Sex and the German Text. Gendered Culture in Early Modern Germany 1500-1700. Amsterdam 1994 (Chloe. Beihefte zum Daphnis 19) 7-26 [= 1994a].

Weigel, Sigrid. Von der ‚anderen Rede' zur Rede des Anderen. In: Schade, Sigrid / Wagner, Monika / Weigel, Sigrid (Hgg.) 159-170 [= 1994b].

Wemple, Suzanne F. Consent and Dissent to Sexual Intercourse in Germanic Societies from the Fifth to the Tenth Century. In: Angeliki E. Laiou (ed.) 227-244.

Wenzel, Horst. Hören und Sehen. Zur Lesbarkeit von Körperzeichen in der höfischen Literatur. In: Brall, Helmut / Haupt, Barbara / Küsters, Urban (Hgg.) 191-218.

Wenzel, Horst. Hören und Sehen. Schrift und Bild. Kultur und Gedächtnis im Mittelalter. München 1995.

Wenzel, Horst (Hg.). Gespräche – Boten – Briefe. Körpergedächtnis und Schriftgedächtnis im Mittelalter. Berlin 1997 (Philologische Studien und Quellen 143) [=1997a].

Wenzel, Horst. Die Beweglichkeit der Bilder. Zur Relation von Text und Bild in den illuminierten Handschriften des "Welschen Gastes". In: Zeitschrift für deutsche Philologie 116 (1997) 224-257 [= 1997b].

Wettlaufer, Jörg. Das Herrenrecht der ersten Nacht. Hochzeit, Herrschaft und Heiratszins im Mittelalter und in der frühen Neuzeit. Frankfurt / New York 1999 (Campus Historische Studien Bd. 27).

Wiegand, Herbert Ernst. Studien zur Minne und Ehe in Wolframs Parzival und Hartmanns Artusepik. Berlin / New York 1972 (Quellen und Forschungen zur Sprach- und Kulturgeschichte der germanischen Völker 49 [173]).

Williams-Krapp, Werner. "Dise ding sint dennoch nit ware zeichen der heiligkeit". Zur Bewertung mystischer Erfahrungen im 15. Jahrhundert. Zeitschrift für Literaturwissenschaft und Linguistik 20 (1990) 61-71.

Williams-Krapp, Werner. Bilderbogen-Mystik. Zu 'Christus und die minnende Seele'. Mit Edition der Mainzer Überlieferung. In: Überlieferungsgeschichtliche Editionen und Studien zur deutschen Literatur des Mittelalters. Kurt Ruh zum 75. Geburtstag. Hg. Konrad Kunze / Johannes G. Mayer / Bernhard Schnell. Tübingen 1989, 350-364.

Williams-Krapp, Werner. Frauenmystik und Ordensreform im 15. Jahrhundert. In: Joachim Heinzle (Hg.). Literarische Interessenbildung im Mittelalter. Stuttgart / Weimar 1994, 301-313.

Williams-Krapp, Werner. Observanzbewegung, monastische Spiritualität und geistliche Literatur im 15. Jahrhundert. Internationales Archiv für Sprache und Literatur 20 (1995) 1-15.

Windeatt, Barry (Ed.). English Mystics of the Middle Ages. Cambridge 1994.

Windisch, Hans. Der zweite Korintherbrief. Hg. Georg Strecker. Göttingen [10]1970.

Wolf, Alois. Das Faszinosum der mittelalterlichen Minne. Freiburg / Schweiz 1996 (Wolfgang Stammler Gastprofessur, Heft 5).

Wolf, Gerhard. Das Herz in der Mausefalle. In: Glaube Hoffnung Liebe Tod. Hg. Christoph Geißmar-Brandi / Eleonora Louis. Wien 1995, 136-137.

Wolff, Christian. Der zweite Brief des Paulus an die Korinther. Theologischer Handkommentar zum Neuen Testament VIII. Berlin 1989.

Women as Protagonists and Poets in the German Middle Ages. An Anthology of Feminist Approaches to Middle High German Literature. Ed. Albrecht Classen. Göppingen 1991.

Wunder, Heide. He Is the Sun, She Is the Moon. Women in Early Modern Germany. Trans. Thomas Dunlap. Cambridge, Mass. 1998.

Wynn, Marianne. Heroine without a Name. The Unnamed Girl in Hartmann's Story. In: German Narrative Literature of the Twelfth and Thirteenth Centuries. Festschrift Roy Wisbey. Ed. Volker Honemann. Tübingen 1994, 245-259.

Zeimentz, Hans. Ehe nach der Lehre der Frühscholastik. Eine moralgeschichtliche Untersuchung zur Anthropologie und Theologie der Ehe in der Schule Anselms von Laon und Wilhelms von Champeaux, bei Hugo von St. Viktor, Walter von Mortagne und Petrus Lombardus. Düsseldorf 1973.

Ziegeler, Hans-Joachim. Der literarhistorische Ort der Mariendichtungen im Heidelberger Cpg 341 und in verwandten Sammelhandschriften. In: Timothy R. Jackson et.al. (Hgg.) 1996, 55-78.

Zika, Charles. Fears of Flying. Representation of witchcraft and sexuality in early sixteenth-century Germany. In: Australian Journal of Art 8 (1989-1990) 19-48.

Zollà, Elémire. L'amante invisibile. L'erotica schiamanica nelle religioni, nella letteratura e nella legitimazione politica. Venezia 1986.

Zumthor, Paul. La Mesure du monde. Paris 1992.

List of Illustrations

Figure 1, p. 29 (Chapter 1) Illumination in the so-called *Exemplar* of Heinrich Seuse, from the Vita ("Das Buech, das da heisste der Süse", around 1490, Stiftsbibliothek Einsiedeln, Cod. 710 (322), fol. 28[v]. – *The illustration shows the union between Christ and the soul, each in the form of a homunculus. The soul is portrayed naked in accordance with the tradition. The two, both to a certain extent 'inner' figures, are seated on the lap of a monk, who is being crowned by two angels from above as a sign of grace. What is striking is that the portayal of the 'unio mystica' is sexualized in two such very different ways in one and the same codex (see below): in Seuse's case the whole scene of the union seems childlike, not at all eroticized, and the monk himself adopts a maternal or paternal stance; in the case of the soul portrayed as a nun, on the other hand, the visualization of the intimacy between Christ and the soul is unambiguously erotic. The fact that there is a couple (rather than a group of three) might also make the nun a more attractive figure for the (female) reader of the codex to identify with.*

Figure 2, p. 30 (Chapter 1) Seuse Incunable. Stiftsbibliothek Einsiedeln, Jnc 447 (518) Augsburg, Anton Sorg, "Das Büchlin, das da heisset der Seüsse", 1482, fol. 14ᵛ. – *This late-medieval representation of the 'unio mystica' again shows two 'inner figures' on the monk's lap, this time a fatherly Christ providing refuge for the even more childlike soul. The motif has the appearance of a male variation on the female group of three found in representations of St. Anne with the Virgin and child. The incunable is older than the illumination in Cod. 710 (322).*

Figure 3, p. 31 (Chapter 1) *Christus und minnende Seele.* Stiftsbibliothek Einsiedeln, Cod. 710 (322), fol. 17ʳ, unknown artist. – *The illustration shows a scene of erotic union, with the heading: Hier wil er sich laßen kússen und sy sin haimlichait lon wissen (Here he desires to be kissed and to allow her to experience his intimacy).*

Figure 4, p. 195 (Chapter 4) *Christus und minnende Seele.* Badische Landes-Bibliothek Karlsruhe, Cod. Donaueschingen 106, fol. 4ᵛ, artist: Rudolf Stahel of Constance. Photograph Bernd Konrad, Berlin. – *Hie haist er sy uffston hin zu der metti gon (Here he bids her arise and go to Matins).*

Figure 5, p. 205 (Chapter 4) *Christus und minnende Seele.* Stiftsbibliothek Einsiedeln, Cod. 710 (322), fol. 6ʳ, unknown artist. – *Hie wil er kestgen iren lib Das sy dest minder in der welt belib (Here he desires to chastize her body So that she stays in this world even less).*

Figure 6, p. 209 (Chapter 4) *Christus und minnende Seele.* Badische Landes-Bibliothek Karlsruhe, Cod. Donaueschingen 106, fol. 19ᵛ, artist: Rudolf Stahel of Constance. Photograph Bernd Konrad, Berlin. – *Hie wil er sy hencken Das sy von im nit mug wenken (Here he wishes to hang her so that she cannot stray from him).*

Figure 7, p. 213 (Chapter 4) *Christus und minnende Seele.* Badische Landes-Bibliothek Karlsruhe, Cod. Donaueschingen 106, fol. 29ᵛ, artist: Rudolf Stahel of Constance. Photograph Bernd Konrad, Berlin. – *Hie wil sy in binden und zwingen Das sy in nach ir mag bringen (Here she wishes to bind and constrain him so that she may draw him to herself).*

Figure 8, p. 215 (Chapter 4) *Christus und minnende Seele.* Stiftsbibliothek Einsiedeln, Cod. 710 (322), fol. 16ʳ, unknown artist. – *Hie machet er ir daz saiten spil Das er ir ab gewinne vil (Here he plays the strings for her, So that he may have great gains from her).*

Figure 9, p. 216 (Chapter 4) *Christus und minnende Seele.* Stiftsbibliothek Einsiedeln, Cod. 710 (322), fol. 17ᵛ, unknown artist. – *Hie wil er ir zü runen ain wort Das ist ir nútzer denn aller zitlicher hord (Here he wishes to whisper her a word, it is much worthier than all temporal things).*

Figure 10, p. 218 (Chapter 4) *Christus und minnende Seele*. Stiftsbibliothek Einsiedeln, Cod. 710 (322), fol. 18ʳ, unknown artist. – *Hie wil er ir vor drummen und springen Das sy belib by iren sinnen (Here he wishes to drum and dance for her, so that she may remain conscious)*.

Figure 11, p. 220 (Chapter 4) *Christus und minnende Seele*. Stiftsbibliothek Einsiedeln, Cod. 710 (322), fol. 18ᵛ, unknown artist. – *Hie wil er ir uff setzen ain kron, Mit der sy besitzen mag den ewigen lon (Here he wishes to place a crown on her head; with it she will possess the eternal reward)*.

Figure 12, p. 226 (Chapter 4) *Christus und minnende Seele*. Badische Landes-Bibliothek Karlsruhe, Cod. Donaueschingen 106, fol. 34v, artist: Rudolf Stahel of Constance. Photograph Bernd Konrad, Berlin. – *Hie sind sy komen über ain und wend nu alle ding hab gemein (Here they have come together and now wish to share all things)*.

Figure 13, p. 242 (Chapter 5) *Master Casper of Regensberg, Lady Venus and the Lover*. Staatliche Museen zu Berlin, Preussischer Kulturbesitz. – Coloured single folio woodcut from the late 15ᵗʰ century, showing a young man begging for deliverance and embrace. He laments to Lady Venus about his many and various pains of love, which are depicted graphically and in banderoles. The personification he implores stands with her feet buried deep in one heart, and holds up a second, pierced with a sword.

Figure 14, p. 249 (Chapter 5) *The Rothschild Canticles*. The Beinecke Rare Book and Manuscript Library, Yale University, New Haven, fol. 18ᵛ-19ʳ.

Figure 15, p. 251 (Chapter 5) *Christ wounded by Charity*. Cistercian Convent, Wienhausen.

Figure 16, p. 254 (Chapter 5) *Christus und die minnende Seele*. Bayerische Staatsbibliothek München, Photograph Bayerische Staatsbibliothek München, single folio print M, III, 52ᶠ, probably from the (early) sixteenth century.

Figure 17, p. 255 (Chapter 5) *Christus und die minnende Seele*. Staatliche Museen zu Berlin, Preussischer Kulturbesitz, Kupferstichkabinett Schreiber 1837a. – Block-print Bn, Swabian, circa 1470, 16 lines.

Figure 18, p. 256 (Chapter 5) *Christus und die minnende Seele*. Badische Landes-Bibliothek Karlsruhe, Cod. Donaueschingen 106, fol. 26ʳ, artist: Rudolf Stahel of Constance. Photograph Bernd Konrad, Berlin. – *Mit der minne stral schüsset sy in das wil sy han für einen gwin (She shoots him with the rays of love, that is what she seeks to gain)*.

Figure 19, p. 257 (Chapter 5) *Christus und minnende Seele*, Stiftsbibliothek Einsiedeln, Cod. 710 (322), fol. 13ᵛ, unknown artist. – *Mit der minne stral schüßet si in, Das wil sy han für gewin. (She shoots him with the rays of love, that is what she seeks to gain)*.

PRINTED ON PERMANENT PAPER • IMPRIME SUR PAPIER PERMANENT • GEDRUKT OP DUURZAAM PAPIER - ISO 9706

ORIENTALISTE, KLEIN DALENSTRAAT 42, B-3020 HERENT